Toward
Old
Testament
Ethics

Toward
Old
Testament
Ethics

Walter C. Kaiser, Jr.

Academie
Books
Grand Rapids,
Michigan
Zondervan Publishing House

ACADEMIE BOOKS are published by Zondervan Publishing House,
1415 Lake Drive, S.E., Grand Rapids, Michigan 49506

TOWARD OLD TESTAMENT ETHICS
Copyright © 1983 by The Zondervan Corporation
Grand Rapids, Michigan

Library of Congress Cataloging in Publication Data
Kaiser, Walter C.
   Toward Old Testament ethics.

   Bibliography: p.
   Includes index.
   1. Ethics in the Bible.   2. Bible. O.T.—Criticism,
interpretation, etc.   I. Title.
BS1199.E8K34   1983   241   83-17095
ISBN 0-310-37110-4

Edited by Mark Hunt
Designed by Mark Hunt

ACADAMIE BOOKS is an imprint of Zondervan Publishing House

Printed in the United States of America

90 91 92 93 94 / BB / 9 8 7 6 5

To
Kenneth and Ruth Kantzer,
extraordinary servants of Christ's church
and
patient mentors, colleagues, and
kindest of friends.
1 Cor. 2:9

Contents

Contents

Part III   CONTENT OF OLD TESTAMENT ETHICS

Contents

Part IV MORAL DIFFICULTIES IN THE OLD TESTAMENT

Contents

Part V CONCLUSION: OLD TESTAMENT ETHICS AND NEW TESTAMENT APPLICATIONS

Introduction

Brevard S. Childs's 1970 assessment fairly well describes the situation today: "In spite of the great interest in ethics, to our knowledge, there is no outstanding modern work written in English that even attempts to deal adequately with the Biblical material as it relates to ethics . . . [even though] there has come a host of ethical treatises that usually make some use of the Bible."[1]

The time is long overdue for a separate treatment of biblical ethics, but especially in the area totally neglected in this century: a monograph in English on Old Testament ethics. Gerhard von Rad was of the opinion that: "We to-day are far from possessing . . . a generally accepted view of what 'law' in the Old Testament means. . . . We must re-learn from the Old Testament what Israel meant by 'law'."[2] To make matters worse, David Flusser concluded, "It is doubtful . . . that a serious exposition on Jewish law exists in contemporary Christian theology."[3]

This work must suggest and probe rather than stand as a *fait accompli*; therefore, I have again, for the third time, used the word "toward" in the title of one of my monographs. This is more than a protective device against adventurous reviewers; it is an honest statement of my respect for the magnitude of the field, the complexity of the issues, and my frustration at finding all too few guides who have blazed the trail before me. If some are prone to judge this book harshly, I honestly accept every legitimate

---

[1]Brevard S. Childs, *Biblical Theology in Crisis* (Philadelphia: Westminster, 1970), 124.

[2]Gerhard von Rad, *Old Testament Theology*, 2 vols., trans. D. M. G. Stalker (New York: Harper and Row, 1956), 2:389.

[3]David Flusser, "Forward: Reflections of a Jew on a Christian Theology of Judaism" in *A Christian Theology of Judaism*, ed. Clemens Thomas, trans. Helga Croner (New York: Paulist Press, 1980), 6.

and factually founded critique, but I will urge those same respondents to both walk softly and to carry a *small* stick until they too have taken pen in hand and delivered their own tome to the world of scholars and the church.

This work embraces five major sections: I. Definition and Method, II. Summarizing Moral Texts in Old Testament Ethics (including the Decalogue, the Book of the Covenant, the Law of Holiness, and the Law of Deuteronomy), III. Content of Old Testament Ethics, IV. Moral Difficulties in the Old Testament, and V. Old Testament Ethics and New Testament Applications.

It is a special joy to present this pioneering book for the inspection, reflection, growth, and encouragement of all who study and read the Old Testament, whether they be in scholarly fields or the church.

My only remaining task is to thank the Board of Directors of Trinity Evangelical Divinity School in Deerfield, Illinois, who graciously provided me with a generous sabbatical from my teaching and administrative duties, which allowed me to complete this project. I must also acknowledge my debt to my colleague, Dr. Warren Benson, Vice President of Academic Administration, who assumed most of my administrative duties in addition to his own tasks while I was on sabbatical; to Mrs. Lois Armstrong, Executive Secretary to the Academic Dean; and to several other faculty secretaries who typed major portions of the manuscript, including Mrs. Renae Grahms and Ms. Sherri Kull. My wife also dedicated large portions of her vacation to typing the remaining portions of the manuscript. A special word of thanks is also due to Dr. Stan Gundry of The Zondervan Corporation for his encouragement and special assistance in seeing this project come to fruition and to Mr. Mark Hunt who guided this work through its editorial steps. It is a pleasure to acknowledge the helpful comments and criticisms that I received from my friend Dr. Elmer Martens and two of my former students, Mr. Tim Addington and Mr. Richard Schultz. Most of the indices were prepared by my graduate assistant, Mr. Ray Lubeck. They, of course, are in no way responsible for the views adopted here, even though they did their best to remove a number of the obvious infelicities. For this help I am deeply grateful.

May this work be the first of a number of monographs on Old Testament ethics. But in the meantime, may this book enable its readers to enjoy the OT with a sympathetic reading of the text and with more discernment about how that text may be used today by the believer and the church to guide behavior and make ethical decisions.

Soli Deo Gloria

Walter C. Kaiser, Jr.

PART I
DEFINITION AND METHOD

Chapter 1

The Importance of
Definition and Methodology

Few aspects of Old Testament study have proven to be so difficult as Old Testament ethics. In the last century, only six men have attempted to write a monograph on this subject: W. A. Jarrel in 1883,[1] W. S. Bruce[2] in 1895 (with a second and enlarged edition in 1909), Hinckley G. Mitchell[3] in 1912, J. M. Powis Smith in 1923,[3] Johannes Hempel[4] in 1938 (with extensive supplementation in a new edition in 1964), and H. van Oyen[5] in 1967. Should we restrict ourselves to works in English that deal technically with the whole field of ethics, only the first two books by Jarrel and Bruce remain, and both of these appeared in the last century!

This evidence should be enough warning to those considering entry into the field. Indeed, R. E. Clements concluded that "the subject of Old

---

[1]W. A. Jarrel, *Old Testament Ethics Vindicated* (Greenville, Tex.: privately published, 1883. Available through McCormick Theological Seminary Library, Chicago).

[2]W. S. Bruce, *The Ethics of the Old Testament*, 2d rev. ed. (Edinburgh: T. & T. Clark, 1909).

[3]Hinckley G. Mitchell, *The Ethics of the Old Testament* (Chicago: University of Chicago Press, 1912). Very similar is the work by J. M. Powis Smith, *The Moral Life of the Hebrews* (Chicago: University of Chicago Press, 1923).

[4]Johannes Hempel, *Das Ethos des alten Testaments* (Berlin: Verlag Alfred Töpelmann, 1964).

[5]H. van Oyen, *Die Ethik des alten Testaments* (Gütersloh: Gütersloher Verlagshaus Gerd Mohn, 1967).

Testament ethics has proved to be a most difficult one to deal with. . . .
The literature devoted to it has been surprisingly sparse. . . . It has been
difficult to avoid the merely superficial."[6] Nevertheless, while being fully
aware of the high risks, the immense difficulty, and many of the hidden
pits along the way, there still is an enormous need in Old Testament
scholarship and in the church at large for an Old Testament ethics that will
treat the subject as systematically and irenically as possible. All too frequently modern readers of the Old Testament have had the unpleasant
experience of meeting head-on what certainly appeared to be insuperable
obstacles to their enjoyment, much less any contemporary application, of
the ethos and ethics of that canon. If no other reason existed than this one,
a new Old Testament ethics would be needed. But the vision and need for
a text goes beyond any such minimal apologetics; it must also include some
program for approaching the ethical content of the testament, an evalua-
tion of its substance, and a consideration of the normativeness of this
ethical material. All of this is a huge order—especially when one considers
that the Old Testament contains about 77 percent of the total biblical
corpus! What, then, is entailed in the study of Old Testament ethics?

DEFINITION OF OLD TESTAMENT ETHICS

The word "ethics" is derived from the Greek ἔθος or ἦθος (*ethos* or
ēthos). The former term occurs twelve times[7] in the New Testament while
the latter one appears only once, in the plural form in 1 Corinthians 15:33:
"evil associations corrupt good *manners.*" Thus our English term may
mean "manner of life," "conduct," "custom," or "practice" as prescribed
by some competent authority.

Of course there is no abstract, comprehensive concept in the Old
Testament that parallels our modern term "ethics." In fact, the older
testament usually avoided abstract terms such as "ethics," "virtue,"
"ideals," and the like. The closest that it came to "ethics" was the use of
מוּסָר ("discipline" or "teaching") in later Hebrew or דֶּרֶךְ ("way" or "path")
in the canonical wisdom literature.[8]

---

[6]R. E. Clements, *One Hundred Years of Old Testament Study* (Philadelphia: Westminster, 1976), 107.

[7]Cf. Luke 1:9; 2:42; 22:39; John 19:40; Acts 6:14; 15:1; 16:21; 21:21; 25:16; 26:3;
28:17; Hebrews 10:25.

[8]This reminds us of the New Testament term ἀναστροφή ("way of life, lifestyle").
John Murray, *Principles of Conduct* (Grand Rapids: Eerdmans, 1957), 11, n. 2, reminds us
that this term occurs thirteen times in the New Testament; nine times in the good sense.
The most significant usage is in 2 Peter 3:11.

Old Testament ethics is concerned with the manner of life that the older covenant prescribes and approves. Its ethical contents are not offered in isolation, but are viewed as demands, actions, and character that God expects from men and women. This close connection between ethics and theology constitutes one of the distinctive features of the Bible's own set of ethics. Accordingly, what God is in his character, and what he wills in his revelation, defines what is right; conversely it is right, good, acceptable, and satisfying to all because of his known character and will.

Some of the key questions for this study are: "What ought I to do?" "How should I act?" "What is meant by 'good'?" "Who is the good person?" But how comprehensive should this list be? Which questions, if any, have a priority over other questions? And even more frustrating than all of these questions, and similar to the one that is raised in an Old Testament theology,[9] is the question: Is there *an* "Ethics of the Old Testament" just as we ask, is there *a* "Theology of the Old Testament"? Is there an "integrating core" or "unifying principle" that gives cohesiveness, wholeness, and unity to a total picture of ethics in the Old Testament?

In Eichrodt's view there was basically a single ethic throughout the Old Testament even though at times this ethic was replaced or contaminated with more popular ideas. As he stated it, there was ". . . a struggle for the profounder comprehension of the ethical norms. It should therefore occasion no surprise that at points in the early Israelite tradition it becomes apparent that the struggle was denied full success, and that popular morality refused to accept the progressive influence of the divine revelation."[10]

This issue must be dealt with at length in chapter two, but I believe that it is possible to trace out a consistent and unified approach to Old Testament ethics, even though the types of biblical literature in which it is embedded are as varied as narratives, law codes, wisdom injunctions, or prophetic oracles. My reason for adopting this stance is not to be attributed to some prior doctrinal commitment about the special status of the Bible (though I am willing to face this question on other grounds), but rather because of *the claims* made by the collection of Old Testament books themselves. They conceive of their message to be a contribution to an ongoing and continuing story about the character and will of God as the basis for answering the questions "What kind of a person ought I to be?" and "What should a person do that is right, just, and good?" The internal claims of each of the writers, and their use of explicit citations and evident

---

[9]See my discussion on the question of a center or integrating core in Walter C. Kaiser, Jr., *Toward an Old Testament Theology* (Grand Rapids: Zondervan, 1978), 20–40.

[10]Walther Eichrodt, *Theology of the Old Testament*, trans. J. A. Baker (Philadelphia: Westminster, 1967), 2:322–23.

3

allusions to those writers and books that chronologically preceded their writings, must be treated seriously on their own terms *before* we make any critical judgments about the accuracy, legitimacy, or validity of those claims. If we could raise one cry in our day directed at all studies in the humanities, much less biblical scholarship, it would be that a book must always be *taken on its own terms first* if we wish to be objective, fair, and sensitive exegetes. Of course those claims must then be tested and measured for accuracy by all the empirical, logical, historical, and experiential data that we can bring to test these claims. But all too frequently the Bible has been judged in the post-enlightenment era to be guilty until proved innocent! We plead for the application of the American system of jurisprudence to the biblical text: it is innocent until proven guilty. Surely this would cure much of the skepticism and minimal results occuring in contemporary Old Testament theology and Old Testament ethics.

BASIC CHARACTERISTICS OF OLD TESTAMENT ETHICS

In contrast to philosophical ethics, which tend to be more abstract and anthropocentric, Old Testament morality was never considered apart from the religion or theology with which it was connected.[11] Without using the words "duty," "supreme good," "virtue," "motive," or "end," the Old Testament presents each of these topics, and more, in concrete terms and examples. The Old Testament cannot discuss religion apart from morality or faith that does not issue in right character and life. Hence, as Greene observed, ". . . the irreligious men are the immoral men and the immoral men are the irreligious men. Thus Psalms xiv.1, 'The fool hath said in his heart, There is no God. They are corrupt, they have done abominable works, there is none that doeth good.'"[12] Nowhere does the Old Testament pause to demonstrate that man has a moral nature; instead, it everywhere assumes this case as much as it assumes the reality of theism. What is theistic is ethical, and vice versa. The two are everywhere bound together.

Now while the Old Testament lacks most of the abstract philosophical ethical terms, it has a distinctive set of characteristics of its own.

---

[11]This section draws heavily on William Brenton Greene, Jr., "The Ethics of the Old Testament," *Princeton Theological Review* 27 (1929): 155–70; also in *Classical Evangelical Essays in Old Testament Interpretation*, ed. Walter C. Kaiser, Jr. (Grand Rapids: Baker, 1972), 207–35.

[12]Greene, "Ethics," 156.

Old Testament Ethics Are Personal

Old Testament ethics are *personal* both in its ground and its subject. "The ground of the ethical in the Old Testament is the express commands of the absolutely holy person, God, made known by historical acts of revelation."[13] The reason why this must be so is that for Jewish history *the* distinctive event with world-wide significance was the fall of man and woman in the Garden of Eden. Since Adam and Eve, and thus the entire race, had fallen, they could never ferret out for themselves what was the good, the right, and the ethical; rather, they must appeal "to the law and to the testimony" (Isa. 8:20) and to the revealed will and character of the one who enjoined: "Be holy because I, the LORD your God, am holy" (Lev. 19:2). "Hence, the Old Testament conceives of duty as what God *tells* man to do; it conceives of virtue as obedience to God's expressed commands; it conceives of the supreme good as perfect likeness to God and so perfect sonship with reference to Him and so perfect bliss in Him. . . . It regards idolatry as the sin of all sins: for this, since it is apostacy from God, cuts the roots of all obedience to Him. Thus, the Old Testament grounds its ethics on the definitely expressed will of the divine Person."[14]

Nor is the subject of Old Testament ethics any less personal than its ground. People are both free and responsible to obey. The conditional "If you follow my decrees and are careful to obey my commands . . . " (Lev. 26:3; cf. 26:14, 18, 21, 23, 27) captures the spirit of the Old Testament ethic. People can and must decide. They are addressed both as individuals and as members of a corporate group,[15] but always as those whose participation in the blessings and joys of the promised benefits of the covenant are decided by their personal response to the living God and his law.

Old Testament Ethics Are Theistic

Old Testament ethics are decidedly *theistic*. It is Israel's depiction of God that sets it off from most other ethical systems. To know the God of Israel was to know and practice righteousness and justice. Jeremiah 22:15–16 puts it this way:

> "He did what was right and just,
> so all went well with him [you].

---

[13]Greene, "Ethics," 157.

[14]Greene, "Ethics," 157–58.

[15]See chapter 4 for a more detailed discussion of the currently debated role of individualism and collectivism in the Old Testament.

He defended the cause of the poor and the needy
    and so all went well.
Is that not what it means to know me?"
    declares the LORD.

Consequently, the Old Testament knows nothing about an autonomo
ethic; it is intimately joined to a personal knowledge of God. It is
Proverbs 3:5–7 assesses it:

Trust in the Lord with all your heart
    and lean not on your own understanding;
in all your ways acknowledge him,
    and he will make your paths straight.
Do not be wise in your own eyes:
    fear the LORD and shun evil.

The Old Testament celebrates God for his personality, his infinite
feelings of compassion, his graciousness, his presence, and his acts of
wisdom and power; but it is his holiness that is most decisive for Old
Testament ethics. Holiness at once expresses the otherness of God and his
moral character. An ontological and a moral gap exists between God and
humanity. God is creator and humankind are creatures; therefore, this gap
in "being" will remain forever. Since the Fall humanity is also morally
distinct from God: God remains pure, righteous, and just; but people are
deficient and practice less than their capabilities in each of these
categories.

The biblical call to holiness is often repeated in the Old Testament,
but nowhere is it given more frequently than in the "Law of Holiness" of
Leviticus 18–20. The standard for the good, the right, the just, and the
acceptable is nothing less than the person of the living God: "Be holy
because I the Lord your God am holy" (italics added, Lev. 19:2, 9, 14; cf.
Matt. 5:48). Deities of other nations indulge in many, if not all, of the vices
of their worshipers, but Yahweh's character is revealed in Habakkuk's
prayer, "Your eyes are too pure to look on evil; you cannot tolerate wrong"
(Hab. 1:13).

The Hebrew word קָדוֹשׁ ("holy") and its family of related roots are
used over six hundred times in the Old Testament to indicate moral perfection. It signifies "holy, sacred, pure, free from defilement or vice" and
is the opposite of חָנֵף ("impure, profane"). Since God is *pure* from defilement of evil, he is *separated* from any partnership with it. No wonder then
that Isaiah 59:2 exclaims, "Your iniquities have separated you from your
God; your sins have hidden his face from you, so that he will not hear."
Thus we are led to the conclusion that God, as the God of holiness, is the
model for Old Testament men and women. He is incomparably pure and

spotless beyond all human calculation; the standard for all individuals, races, and nations.

Old Testament Ethics Are Internal

Old Testament ethics are as much concerned with the *internal* response to Old Testament morality as to the outward acts. Repeatedly in assaying the acts of ritual or deeds of kindness in the Old Testament, the text focuses on the intention and heart attitude of the individual rather than the sheer act itself. David had to learn the hard way that what God wanted, even before he would accept any of his sacrifices in contrition for his sin with Bathsheba, was "a broken spirit; a broken and contrite heart" (Ps. 51:17; cf. vv. 16 and 18). In fact, people, then as now, tended to "look on the outward appearance" while "The LORD looks at the heart" (1 Sam. 16:7). Repeatedly the prophets lament the fact that Israel tried to substitute outward acts of piety for the necessary inward prerequisite for offering these gifts (Isa. 1:11–18; Jer. 7:21–23; Hos. 6:6; Mic. 6:6–8).

But all of this was challenged by B. D. Eerdmans[16] in 1903 when he advocated that the tenth commandment with its proscription against coveting did not involve the intentions of the heart. For Eerdmans the Old Testament did not meddle with the inner thoughts of a person, but only with the bare deed itself. Two examples, he felt, demonstrated this thesis conclusively: (1) The foreign ruler was liable to punishment merely for his *deed* of taking what he believed to be the patriarch's sister (Gen. 12:10–20; 20:1–18; 26:1–16), and (2) Jonathan was guilty for the *deed* of eating a little honey even when he knew nothing of his father's ban on any food until the king had been avenged of his enemies (1 Sam. 14:24–45).

B. Gemser contested Eerdmans's thesis that "Old Testament ethics do not meddle with the inner thoughts of men"[17] by pointing out among other things that the second passage in the first example contains this telling verse:

> Yes, I know that you did this with a clear conscience, and so I have kept you from sinning against me. That is why I did not let you touch her (Gen. 20:6).

---

[16]B. D. Eerdmans, "Oorsprong en betekenis van de 'Tien Woorden'," *Theologisch Tijdschrift* 37 (1903): 19–35 as reported in B. Gemser, "The Object of Moral Judgment in the Old Testament," in *Adhuc loquitur: Collected Essays by Dr. B. Gemser*, ed. A. van Selms and A. S. van der Woude: Pretoria Oriental Series 7 (Leiden: Brill, 1968), 78–95. It originally appeared in *Homiletica en Biblica* 20 (1961): 2–9, 35–39.

[17]As cited by Gemser, *Adhuc loquitur* 81; See Eerdmans, "Oorsprong en betekenis," 25.

Gemser also pointed to 1 Samuel 16:7 where "The LORD looks on the heart," but Eerdmans had already disqualified this evidence by complaining that the choice of a successor to Saul was not a matter of sin; furthermore, he claimed, the LXX reading of this text said, "The Lord looks *with* his heart [εἰς καρδίαν]" (i.e., more penetratingly)! Yet, even this reading showed that God's estimate of man went more than skin deep.

Eerdmans's curious claim about the tenth commandment was that it did not forbid the desire for other's possessions but only the actual possession of them![18] More than twenty-five Old Testament texts have played a role in the discussion of the meaning of חָמַד ("desire"). These may be conveniently surveyed under our discussion of the tenth commandment in chapter 15, but the point of inner motives of the heart as being part of Old Testament ethics is extremely important for a proper estimate of the subject, as well as properly evaluating the relation between New Testament ethics and those of the old covenant.

Many tended to side with Eerdmans's limited view. One such scholar was W. A. L. Elmslie. In his view ". . . the whole conception of righteousness was forensic: what counted was the overt act, and a man was reckoned, and reckoned himself, in the right or the wrong (just or unjust), according as he should stand acquitted or condemned on trial. It follows that the fundamental moral importance of the motives of the heart was almost unrealized."[19] Even Th. C. Vriezen concludes, "We must therefore agree with Eerdmans when he says that the Israelite *did not know of sins in thought*, but we must emphatically oppose the thesis that 'Old Testament morality does not penetrate as far as man's heart.'"[20] Gemser appropriately complains that Vriezen's distinctions are too subtle to be understood: how can he rightly agree that there is an ethic of intention in the Old Testament while adamantly denying that Israel had any idea what it meant to sin by thoughts? Is a simple thought not to be linked up with a whole mental disposition?

Gemser responds by finding thirty-six places where the Hebrew words for "thought," "plan," "counsel," "intent," or "deliberation" are

---

[18]As Gemser explains (*Adhuc loquitur*, p. 79), Eerdmans's motivation was to preserve the genuineness of the tradition that Moses was the author of the Decalogue; therefore it was necessary, he felt, to give up the deeper ethical sense of the commandment.

[19]W. A. L. Elmslie, "Ethics," in *Record and Revelation: Essays on the Old Testament by Members of the Society For Old Testament Study*, ed. H. Wheeler Robinson (Oxford: Oxford University Press, 1938), 279.

[20]Th. C. Vriezen, *An Outline of Old Testament Theology*, 2d ed., rev. and enl. (Newton, Mass.: Branford, 1970), 393. Vriezen explains his italicized words in note 4: "In the sense that 'the Israelite did not separate the *thought* from the *act*.'" *Theologisch Tijdschrift*, 39 (1905) 308ff.

linked with ethical judgments. Some of these texts are:

Genesis 6:5

The LORD saw how great man's wickedness on the earth had become, and that every inclination of the thoughts of his heart (יֵצֶר מַחְשְׁבֹת לִבּוֹ) was only evil all the time.

1 Chronicles 28:9

. . . serve him [God] with wholehearted devotion (בְּלֵב שָׁלֵם) and with a willing mind (וּבְנֶפֶשׁ חֲפֵצָה), for the LORD searches every heart and understands every motive behind the thoughts (מַחְשָׁבוֹת יֵצֶר).

Proverbs 6:16–18

There are six things the LORD hates . . . a heart that devises wicked schemes (לֵב חֹרֵשׁ מַחְשְׁבוֹת אָוֶן).

Proverbs 15:26

The LORD detects the thoughts (מַחְשְׁבוֹת) of the wicked.

Isaiah 59:7

Their thoughts (מַחְשְׁבֹתֵיהֶם) are evil thoughts (מַחְשְׁבוֹת אָוֶן).

Jeremiah 4:14

How long will you (בְּקִרְבֵּךְ) harbor wicked thoughts (אוֹנֵךְ מַחְשְׁבוֹת)?

Ezekiel 38:10

On that day thoughts (דְבָרִים) will come into your mind (עַל־לְבָבְךָ) and you will devise an evil scheme (מַחֲשֶׁבֶת רָעָה).

Psalm 94:11

The Lord knows the thoughts (מַחְשְׁבוֹת) of man, he knows that they are futile.

Proverbs 21:27

The sacrifice of the wicked is detestable—; how much more when brought with evil intent (בְזִמָּה)!

In order to understand the question, "what is morally judged in the Old Testament, the single act or the disposition and the act of the person?" Gemser advises us to study the following six questions:

(1) "The place and significance allotted to the heart" in the Old Testament;

(2) "Whether the single act or the person and type of person" are also evaluated;

(3) "Whether abstract notions like righteousness, modesty, laziness, pride and the like are used in texts of a paraenetic character";

(4) "Whether thoughts, counsels and intentions are qualified as being good or bad";

(5) "Whether . . . the intent of the sacrificer [counts as much as the sacrifice itself]"; and

(6) Whether a distinction is made "between intentional and unintentional tresspasses" in juridical texts, e.g. between murder and manslaughter by accident.[21]

It should be clear enough from what has been said thus far that a person's inner disposition and motives were judged as culpable before God during the Old Testament. Without attempting to select our material from special epochs of Old Testament history, we have discovered texts from the Pentateuch, Wisdom Books, and Prophets that clearly focus on a person's interior state of mind and heart as well as on his or her actions.

Old Testament Ethics Are Future Oriented

Old Testament ethics are oriented toward the *future* as well as the present. It is a morality of hope even though the vision of the future is by no means as clear as the developed message of the New Testament. What is clear is that the entire testament looks forward to its fulfillment and completion in Christ. The Messiah, his person, office, rule, and reign, are the keys to the testament. The promise of the coming of the Seed of the woman (Gen. 3:15), the Seed of Abraham as the means of blessing all the families of the earth (Gen. 12:3), and the establishment of the throne of David as an everlasting kingdom of righteousness (2 Sam. 7:11,16; 23:3,5; Ps. 89) tended to put all of the past and the present against the perspective of the future.

Indeed, the writer of Hebrews 11 argued that the Old Testament saints' faith was definitely oriented toward the future. A few intimations of a hope for the future (as well as an expectation of judgment for some) and the fact that the dead will be resurrected can be found in such incidents as: Moses at the bush calling the living Lord "the God of Abraham, the God of Isaac and the God of Jacob" (Exod. 3:6; cf. Luke 20:37), the translation of Enoch (Gen. 5:21–24) and Elijah (2 Kings 2:11), David's hope of going to be with his dead child (2 Sam. 12:18–23), and such plain teaching as is

---

[21]Gemser, "Object of Moral Judgment," 87.

found in Job 14:14; 19:26–27; Genesis 25:8; Deuteronomy 31:16; 32:50; Proverbs 14:32; Psalms 9:17; 16:10; 37:37–38; 49:13–15; Isaiah 26:19; Ezekiel 33:8–9; 37:1–14 (of the nation as a collection of individuals); Daniel 12:2–3; and Malachi 4:1. The promise of future reward or the threat of future punishment was not given to encourage otherworldliness or despondency, but to stimulate purity of life since the present was not the last or final measuring stick for what was good or evil.

The belief in immortality was not in itself so novel, for already whole cultures such as that of Egypt were centuries, even millennia, along in organizing all of present life around the goal of getting ready for the afterlife. So-called primitive people thought more about this phenomena than modern people in our plastic age, who carefully isolate themselves from scenes of death, much less the philosophical and religious aspects of the subject. Nevertheless, the use of eternal rewards and punishments as a clear motivation for morality in the Old Testament is minimal when compared to the New Testament. Greene[22] suggests that the reason for this absence in the Old Testament was deliberately effected to avoid a crass materialism and a selfish narrowness that would strive for personal well-being before the fully enlightened spiritual man had seen the resurrected Christ. Perhaps that is partially true, though a better explanation may rest simply in the nature of progressive revelation.

Old Testament Ethics Are Universal

Old Testament ethics are *universal*, embracing the same standard of righteousness for all the nations of the earth as it does for Israel. Never did the biblical writers conceive of justice, righteousness, or the good as the special corner of the truth reserved for Israel alone; on the contrary, for Abraham the question was "Will not the Judge of all the earth do right?" (Gen. 18:25). But the "outcry" (זְעָקָה) against Sodom and Gomorrah (Gen. 18:20) was intense because their sin was "so grievous." The moral standing of the inhabitants of these five cities of the plain is stated in Genesis 13:13: they "were wicked and were sinning greatly against the LORD." Therefore, when the inevitable disaster came upon them, it was because "the outcry to the LORD against its people is so great that he has sent us to destroy it" (Gen. 19:13).

The Hebrew root צָעַק / זָעַק is hardly well represented by the mild English translation of "outcry" or "outrage." It indicates the anguished cry of the oppressed and the agonized plea of the victim(s) for relief from the great injustices and indignities suffered. In some ways, it represents the

---

[22]Greene, *Classical Essays*, 222–24.

very antithesis of "righteousness," for in Isaiah 5:7 God looked for "justice" in Israel and received "bloodshed" instead; He looked "for righteousness" (לִצְדָקָה) and found an "outcry" (זְעָקָה) instead. In fact, Israel had become so wicked in Isaiah's day that it had earned the title "rulers of Sodom" and "people of Gomorrah" (Isa. 1:10).[23] Nahum Sarna makes this excellent point:

> As with the Flood, the Sodom and Gomorrah narrative is predicated upon the existence of a moral law of universal application for the infraction of which God holds all men answerable. *The idea that there is an intimate, in fact, inextricable, connection between the socio-moral condition of a people and its ultimate fate is one of the main pillars upon which stands the entire biblical interpretation of history.*[24]

Indeed, long sections and even books of the Old Testament are specifically addressed to the nations at large such as Isaiah 13–23, Jeremiah 45–51, Ezekiel 25–32, Daniel 2 and 7, Amos 1–2, Obadiah, Jonah, and Nahum. At the heart of those messages, often sent by messengers and ambassadors to the foreign nations (e.g., Jer. 27:3; 51:61), was God's standard of righteousness. Accordingly, any narrow, chauvinistic, or parochial interpretation of Old Testament ethics that limits its application to a single people in a particular socio-economic setting stands in opposition to the claims of the text.

In one of the most celebrated chapters in the history of international relations among nations, Isaiah 19, the prophet bewails Egypt's impending disaster because of her refusal to come to terms with Yahweh, his righteousness, and his plan for history. Even though the chapter concludes (Isa. 19:18–25) with one of the most marvelous predictions of full partnership and equality between Egypt, Israel, and Iraq (the contemporary equivalent of ancient Assyria), few readers will miss the fact that the standard of right and wrong expected of Israel was the same one held up for Egypt to follow.

Even the unrighteous act of one pagan king perpetrated against another pagan king was grounds for the rebuke and judgment of God. When Moab burned to lime the bones of the king of Edom, that was the last straw, as it were (interpreting "For three . . . even for four" as a final nail in the coffin of wickedness in Amos 2:1–3). There was no monopoly

---

[23]I am indebted to Nahum M. Sarna, *Understanding Genesis* (New York: McGraw, 1966), 144–46 for this discussion. He also refers us to 2 Kings 8:3,5; Jer. 20:8; Hab. 1:2; and Ezek. 16:49–50 for more uses of the term "outrage."

[24]Sarna, *Understanding Genesis*, 145–46.

held by any people, race, or religion on righteousness; justice, goodness, and truth were the standards for all mortals on planet earth or they would have to explain any deviations to Yahweh himself!

METHODS OF APPROACHING OLD TESTAMENT ETHICS

How shall we approach this large, and somewhat intractable subject of Old Testament ethics? Is it true that there is no such thing as a morality of the Old Testament?[25] And if so, are we thereby reduced to choosing between the relativism of history or a smorgasbord of a variety of insights and ideals collected from various parts of the canon?

Perhaps part of our difficulty is as John Barton[26] observes. We must distinguish between three types of affirmations about Old Testament ethics: (1) most, or all, Israelites held a morality; (2) certain groups of Old Testament writings such as the Prophets, Wisdom Books, etc., support the view that a morality exists within these texts; and (3) the Old Testament taken as a whole supports the view that the Old Testament affirms a morality. It is indeed all too easy to slide from Old Testament "attitudes" over into what may be regarded as "normative morality."

But it is just as easy to presuppose that any search for harmony in the biblical texts has been based on some prior commitment to a dogmatic interest or some type of deficient scholarship. Oliver M. T. O'Donovan properly counters this accusation: "In fact the search for diversity is as much the result of prior methodological decision as is the search for harmony, and cannot be defended on purely empirical grounds. Empirical investigation reveals points of diversity and points of harmony too."[27] J. L. Houlden is much too pessimistic and overwhelmed by some compelling dogma in saying, "There is, strictly, no such thing as 'the X of the New Testament'. . . . It is only at the cost of ignoring the individuality of each, in thought and expression, that the unified account can emerge. . . . There can be no initial assumption of harmony."[28] The ethicist cannot

---

[25]I have adapted this question from J. L. Houlden, *Ethics and the New Testament* (Middlesex, England: Penguin, 1973), 2. The whole concept of *varieties* of morality or New Testament ethics has been stressed since at least 1947 in E. F. Scott, *Varieties of New Testament Religion* (N.Y.: Scribner, 1947); also in J. T. Sanders, *Ethics in the New Testament* (London: SCM, 1975); J. D. G. Dunn, *Unity and Diversity in the New Testament* (London: SCM, 1977); and R. E. O. White, *Biblical Ethics* (Atlanta: Knox, 1979), 9.

[26]John Barton, "Understanding Old Testament Ethics," *Journal for the Study of the Old Testament* 9 (1978): 45. I have modified his types to fit my argument.

[27]Oliver M. T. O'Donovan, "The Possibility of a Biblical Ethic," *Theological Students Fellowship Bulletin* 67 (1973): 19.

[28]Houlden, *Ethics and the New Testament*, 2.

obscure either the continuities or the discontinuities; nor can the ethicist decide in advance on the basis of some alleged scientific canon of historical scholarship that the search for individuality, variety, diversity, and multiplicity are more scholarly and acceptable than the search for signs of harmony, unity, and continuity. This question must be dealt with in greater detail, but for now let it be observed that the priority placed on diversity and the freezing out of harmony as a presupposition does not arise directly out of the biblical materials themselves, but comes from the ethicist's own interests and order imposed on the texts themselves.[29] All of this must be demonstrated from the texts themselves rather than delivered as a scientific precondition.

What, then, are some of the methodological approaches that have been made to Old Testament ethics? It must be remembered that the subject is most difficult and the contributions have been surprisingly sparse.[30] Moreover, there have been no sustained discussions of the various approaches to this subject, much less a technical prolegomena to the whole discipline of Old Testament ethics. The reader's careful scrutiny and sympathetic indulgence is requested as we go into these uncharted waters. In my view, about six different approaches can be discerned in the recent history of Old Testament ethics books, chapters, and articles.

Sociological Approach

Johannes Hempel[31] began his article in the *Interpreter's Dictionary of the Bible* this way:

> The ethics of the Old Testament is based, not on a philosophical or
> theoretical system, but on the traditions of both Israel and Canaan,
> on the sociological necessities of the people, and on the personal
> religious experiences of the leaders of the congregation.[32]

As Hempel viewed it, there were three different social groups with three different ethical traditions in the Old Testament: (1) The seminomadic cattle-breeders whose ethic included brotherhood and dependence on God who protected them and asked only for faithfulness to himself and among covenant members in return, (2) the peasants who were traditionalists tied to the land and to the ancestor's teaching which they transmitted to their sons, and (3) the city dwellers who represented an amalgamation of Canaanites and Israelites and whose financial superiority and abilities as

---

[29]A point made by O'Donovan, "Possibility of Ethic," 19.

[30]The point already made above by R. E. Clements, see n. 6.

[31]Johannes Hempel, "Ethics in the Old Testament," in *Interpreter's Bible Dictionary* (Nashville: Abingdon, 1962), 2:153–61.

[32]Hempel, "Ethics," 153. For greater detail, see Johannes Hempel, *Das Ethos des alten Testaments*, 2d ed. (Berlin: Verlag Alfred Töpelmann, 1964).

artisans allowed them to loan money at interest to the poor even though Israel's covenant spoke out against this process. Thus there was no uniform or homogeneous Old Testament ethical tradition.

In fact, the influence of the sociology of Israel could be seen in the movements from (1) the confederation of tribes to (2) the decline of collectivism and to (3) the decline of objectivism (i.e., the decline of a situation where sin might exist without a person knowing it or intending to willfully violate a commandment). The emphasis here is on the very deep changes that affected Israel's ethical traditions and the sociological forces that brought them about—both within the nation and from extra-Israelite sources. Hempel finds differing obligations laid on each social group (nomad, shepherd, farmer, and city-dweller) and that these social groups appear in roughly this historical sequence.

It would appear that Hempel's sociology contains a trace of a linear development of morality along the lines of older evolutionary reconstructions.[33] Barton criticizes Hempel for ignoring the possible contemporaneous existence of these different social groups and then for abstracting from that given group what is then made normative for the whole period when, in Barton's view, it may just as well be *atypical*.[34] Barton wants to argue that it is wrong to assume that extant evidence of our biblical sources is equal to typical or complete evidence.

Barton's position also has a shortcoming, since it fails to take into account the fact that the biblical writers are claiming a divine, prescriptive, and revelatory standpoint instead of a mere descriptive and sociologically derived message. A sociology of Old Testament religion, with its emphasis on descriptive categories rather than authorially derived estimates, evaluations, or assessments that reflect the divine viewpoint, will yield minimal results for Old Testament ethics and tend not to take the full claims of the authors in their present canonical shape seriously enough. Henry McKeating summarized this point best by saying:

> . . . The ethics of the Old Testament and the ethics of ancient Israelite society do not necessarily coincide, and the latter may not be represented altogether accurately by the former. Old Testament ethics is a theological construction, a set of rules, ideals and principles theologically motivated. Throughout and in large part religiously sanctioned. . . . There are grounds for separating the two projects.[35]

---

[33]Cf. Harry Emerson Fosdick, "The Idea of Right and Wrong," *Guide to Understanding the Bible* (1938; reprint, New York: Harper and Brothers, 1956), 98–151.

[34]Barton, "Understanding Old Testament Ethics," 48.

[35]Henry McKeating, "Sanctions Against Adultery in Ancient Israelite Society, With Some Reflections on Methodology in the Study of Old Testament Ethics," *Journal for the Study of the Old Testament* 11 (1979): 57–72, especially 70–71.

Moral Theology Approach

It was not uncommon in the past for writers on ethics of the Old Testament or New Testament to order their subject according to our western program of topics. Often there is a systematic treatment of moral theology, as for example in some Roman Catholic writers, along the lines of Aquinas's *Summa Theologica*. A New Testament example of this type is found in C. Spicq.[36] In his opening chapter he compares the morality of the new covenant with Judaism, and Judaism emerges in an unfavorable light. He also lists the three key characteristics of New Testament morality and some of the supplementary themes. He takes up basic themes of the Christian moral life with conversion, baptism, and their consequences, followed by chapters on faith, hope, charity, pastoral instructions, liberty, and the image of God.

An example of a modified use of this approach to Old Testament ethics can be seen in Leonard Hodgson.[37] The four main points in "pre-Christian Judaism" (as he labelled it) were:

(1) The will of God as the source of obligation;
(2) The use of man's moral insight as his guide to distinguishing between right and wrong;
(3) The law as the content of God's will; and
(4) The sinful character of wrongdoing and man's inability to cure himself.[38]

Hodgson is mainly concerned with the opposing trends of utilitarianism (acts are good if they promote human welfare: thus consequences determines the good) and moral law (an act is right or good if it observes an eternal moral law). The focus of such discussions falls on whether Old Testament ethics is "deontological" (moral judgments are justified by their correspondence to duty) or "teleological" (proposed actions are weighted by what brings the greatest good to the greatest number). Does the Old Testament prescribe conduct on the basis of what is intrinsically right or on the basis of virtue and pragmatic effects? Hodgson's way of resolving this dilemma is to distinguish between the *formal* aspect and *material* content of Old Testament ethics:

> The recognition that the source of obligation is to be found in God's call to his people to do his will gave the true account of

---

[36]Celas Spicq, *Theólogie Morale du nouveau testament*, 2 vols. (Paris: Gabalda, 1964).

[37]Leonárd Hodgson, "Ethics in the Old Testament," *The Church Quarterly Review* 134 (1942): 153–69.

[38]Hodgson, "Ethics in the Old Testament," 167.

ethics on its *formal* side, but this needed to have its *material* content supplied by knowledge . . . that he is a God who cares for virtue for itself and not for what is to be gained by it. . . .[39]

Synchronic Approach

The synchronic method of Old Testament ethics uses a structured approach apart from chronological considerations as to development of each moral concept in all the respective eras. Thus it is as topical in its approach as is the moral theology approach, yet it derives its categories solely from the Old Testament and not from an external source such as Greek philosophy, natural law, conscience, or systematic theology.

Probably the best representative of this position is Th. C. Vriezen.[40] For him, it is the one Judge of the whole earth, and his will, that gives unity and uniqueness to Old Testament ethics. The will of God may be found in the cultic, ritual, and moral laws in the Old Testament. But the "central motive of moral life is the *sense of community* which "does not clash with another element that also takes a very prominent place in Israel, namely the idea of individual responsibility." These central motives have a proper "atmosphere: the 'humanitas'" (man's self-respect). The principal moral conception is the "communal sense" (חֶסֶד, "lovingkindness, faithful love") that results in maintenance of law (מִשְׁפָּט) and justice (צֶדֶק) with man's disposition (his heart attitude) playing an important part in Old Testament ethics. Surprisingly, however, Vriezen states ". . . in some places the heart, man's disposition is also mentioned emphatically (cf. Lev. xix. 17f). But the *judgment* on sin can of course only be given *on the ground of the act itself.*"[41] Vriezen locates several summarizing moral texts in:

(1) Ethical decalogues—Exodus 20 and Deuteronomy 5;
(2) Cultic texts like Psalms 15, 24, and Ezekiel 18;
(3) Civil texts like the one for judges in Exodus 23;
(4) Social and ethical texts like Leviticus 19:12ff;
(5) Ethical rules of life in wisdom books like Proverbs, Ecclesiastes, and Job; and
(6) Prophetic summaries such as Hosea 4:2 and Jeremiah 7:19.

---

[39]Hodgson, "Ethics in the Old Testament," 169. On the discussion of deontological and teleological ethics, see Elmer H. Martens, "The Problem of Old Testament Ethics," *Direction* 6 (1977): 25–26 and Ben C. Ollenburger's "Response" following Martens's article on pp. 35–37. Martens argues for deontological and Ollenburger claims both are present in the Old Testament.

[40]Vriezen, *Outline of Theology*, 377–404.

[41]Vriezen, *Outline of Theology*, 394.

Vriezen concludes his essay by noting five "limitations" to Old Testament ethics.[42]

The striking feature of this approach is that it does penetrate beyond the issue of variety and pluralism (which we would expect from a polytheistic ethic) to a unified approach that one might expect from monotheism. However no attempt has been made to validate from the summarizing moral texts, or anywhere else for that matter, that the central motives, the chosen atmosphere of man's self-respect and the principal moral conception of חֶסֶד ("faithful love"), is indeed the Old Testament's *own* center. Nor can we agree that the limitations are properly identified even as we have already argued on two of them (national and internal) under "characteristics of Old Testament ethics" earlier in this chapter.

Diachronic Approach

Old Testament ethics is organized along chronological lines by writers like Hinckley Mitchell[43] and Walther Eichrodt.[44] Mitchell's starting point is this:

> The discussion of the contents of the Old Testament in chronological order makes possible a connected historical survey of their ethical teachings. . . . The attempt will be made to discuss the teaching of the Hebrew Scriptures concerning man's duties to himself and to his fellows . . . found . . . in the express precepts and regulations for the conduct of life. . . . When the material thus gathered has been arranged in the order of its age, it should show whether, and to what extent, the Hebrews made progress, during the period covered by the Old Testament, in their ethical ideas and requirements.[45]

Immediately Mitchell plunges into his task and for the next 385 pages follows this general historical/chronological outline: the legendary period (Gen. 1–11); the patriarchal period; the period of the Exodus (the last four books of the Pentateuch); the heroic period (Joshua, Caleb, Barak, Ehud, Jael, Gideon, Samson, Saul, Jonathan); the period of David and Solomon; the first century of separate kingdoms (Elijah and Elisha, Micaiah ben

---

[42]Vriezen, *An Outline of Theology*, 398–404. These will be discussed in chapter 2.

[43]Hinckley G. Mitchell, *The Ethics of the Old Testament* (Chicago: University of Chicago Press, 1912).

[44]Walther Eichrodt, *Theology of the Old Testament*, trans. J. A. Baker (Philadelphia: Westminster, 1967), 316–79.

[45]Mitchell, *Ethics of the Old Testament*, 11, 18. A similar work is J. M. P. Smith, *The Moral Life of the Hebrews* (Chicago: University of Chicago Press, 1923). See Robert Davidson's critique of both volumes in "Some Aspects of the Old Testament Contribution to the Pattern of Christian Ethics," *Scottish Journal of Theology* 12 (1959): 374.

Imlah); Amos and his times; the Ephraimite source ("E" document from migration of Abraham to reign of David); Hosea and his times; Isaiah and Micah and their times; secondary elements ("J²" document) in Judean and Ephraimite narratives; Deuteronomic ethics (Book of Deuteronomy, the third decalogue of Exodus 34, secondary elements in Deuteronomy and earlier narratives); prophecies of Zephaniah, Habakkuk and Nahum, Jeremiah and his times; the Deuteronomic element in the books of Kings, Ezekiel and his times; the Book of Lamentations, Isaiah 40–55 and related prophecies (Haggai and Zechariah) and their times; the Priestly narrative ("P" document); Isaiah 56–66 and related prophecies, prophecies of Obadiah and Malachi, Book of Ruth, Book of Job, books of Joel and Jonah, Book of Proverbs, Song of Solomon, the books of Chronicles, Ezra and Nehemiah, Book of Ecclesiastes, the books of Daniel and Esther, and the Book of Psalms.

The outline is cumbersome and painfully detailed, with an obvious adherence to the documentary hypothesis and its earlier form of the developmental theory in which history moved by means of the Hegelian dialectic (e.g., the priests' cry for bloody sacrifices versus the prophets' plea for justice, mercy, and love) and sociological evolution (simpler and cruder forms of morality and narrative precede more advanced and less crass forms of both). The result is a *survey* of the Old Testament that emphasizes morality and ethical decisions of the key figures and events in the continuing narrative. This will hardly help us to answer the hermeneutical questions of these materials or the even weightier problem of their contemporary use.

A more sophisticated diachronic approach can be found in Eichrodt—perhaps because he groups his chronological eras in three epochs and blends this approach with three synchronic rubrics of key topics, namely, "The *norms* of moral conduct," "The *goods* of moral conduct," and "The *motives* of moral conduct."[46] Eichrodt pictures the struggle of popular morality in the Yahwist primal history and the Elohist patriarchal sagas against the progressive influence of the divine revelation with its totally new understanding of the will of Yahweh in the prophetic movement. Thus "the old popular ethic, in which national self-assertion was felt to have the force of a religious obligation . . . gave way on the prophetic side . . . to an *ethic of suffering* . . . in the figure of the ʿ*ebed yhwh* ['Servant of the Lord']."[47] But the validity of the ethical norms established by the prophets was threatened in the exilic and postexilic period when priestly elements narrowed this

---

[46]Eichrodt, *Theology of Old Testament*, 316–79, italics added.
[47]Eichrodt, *Theology of Old Testament*, 331.

view into a "particularist sense" and made the law "the condition to be established by men with the help of the legal system."[48]

Will this approach prove to be comprehensive enough to embrace most, if not all, of the ethical materials of the Old Testament? While we admire the selection of the topics of norms, goods, and motives, these can hardly substitute for a full treatment of the issues in the Old Testament. This contribution affects the formal side more than the material side of Old Testament ethics. Both are needed!

Central Theme Approach

While denying that the Old Testament contains a system of ethics or a body of ethical principles, James Muilenburg selects obedience as the key to Old Testament ethics. Even though its ethic is derived from many literary forms and types that possess no "uniformity or homogeneity in its formulations," "Biblical ethics is inextricably related to religion. What God wills is right and it is right because it is God who wills it. Ethics is conformity . . . to the will of God. To the question, 'What ought I to do?' the answer is 'Obey God!' "[49] It is clear that Muilenburg is not ready to reduce everything to obedience; nevertheless, the concept is central for him.

Similar to the theme of obedience is the view of Walter Kornfeld: ". . . Old Testament ethics . . . is . . . inseparably connected with Old Testament religion and [is] fundamentally aimed at making human behavior conform to the will of Yahweh. The more clearly God's personal will is recognized in its authoritative claim upon all spheres of life the more exalted does the ethical message become. . . . God's will is the highest ethical norm (Gen. 6:9; 7:1)."[50] Kornfeld then traces Yahweh's will through a chronological axis including: (1) traditions in Genesis, (2) legislation, (3) prophets, and (4) Psalms and Wisdom Literature.

Another possible "mainspring" of Old Testament ethics is the holiness of God. His holiness, as Ellen Flesseman[51] explains it, has two dis-

---

[48]Eichrodt, *Theology of Old Testament*, 342–43. Similar to Eichrodt's outline is that of W. A. L. Elmslie, "Ethics [of Old Testament]," *Record and Revelation*, ed. H. Wheeler Robinson (Oxford: Oxford University Press, 1938), 275–302. Elmslie divides his discussion into three periods: (1) pre-prophetic, (2) prophetic, and (3) post-prophetic period (last four centuries B.C.), pp. 276, 285, 292.

[49]James Muilenburg, "Old Testament Ethics," *Dictionary of Christian Ethics*, ed. H. MacQuarrie (Philadelphia: Westminster, 1967), 236.

[50]Walter Kornfeld, "Old Testament Ethics," *Sacramentum Mundi*, ed. Karl Rahner (New York: Herder and Herder, 1969), 280.

[51]Ellen Flesseman, "Old Testament 'Ethics'", *Student World* 57 (1964): 218–27.

tinctive sides: (1) it expresses the otherness, the numinous character of God and (2) it also expresses the righteousness and goodness of God. It is here that the תּוֹרָה (*torah*) comes to play the central role in the ethos of Israel, for the ritual and cultic laws correspond with the first aspect while the moral laws answer to the second. תּוֹרָה or "law" must not be understood as an obligation or in a casuistic and legalistic sense; instead, "it is an expression . . . of God's covenant love. It shows what it means to live as God's people, to be holy."[52]

All three of these examples are interesting and tend to express approximately the same idea. They appeal to obedience to the will of a holy God and therefore all are deontological (from the Greek word δεον, "ought" or "binding"; the view that the rightness or wrongness of an action or rule is not contingent on its results, but are directly related to specific commands that have been issued from God). To these three writers could be added a fourth, Dennis Kinlaw.[53] "The doctrine of creation provides a universalistic base and potential for the ethic of the Old Testament."[54] But it is Yahweh's moral nature, summed up in his holiness, that determines the character of ethical demands, and the election and calling of Israel gives Old Testament ethics a particularistic, historical, and nationalistic character that signals the fact that it is preparatory and not final according to Kinlaw.

No one can deny that all four essayists have hit on a significant idea in Old Testament ethics; but if each were sustained in a full-length treatment, would each embrace the totality of the subject? Would the needs and questions of readers who turned to a volume on Old Testament ethics be met from a sustained discussion on any one of these central concepts, or should we look for greater scope, more extensive coverage, exposition of summarizing texts, and some discussion of moral difficulties associated with the Old Testament? I believe all of these topics and more fall within the domain of Old Testament ethics. Therefore, I propose a combination approach that includes elements of the synchronic, diachronic, central theme approach along with exegetical studies of summarizing texts and apologetical analysis of key moral difficulties in the canon. Since the focus will fall on all the Old Testament books as the sole source for constructing a new Old Testament ethics textbook, it is labeled the comprehensive approach.

---

[52]Flesseman, "Ethics," 222.
[53]Dennis F. Kinlaw, "Old Testament Ethics," *Baker's Dictionary of Christian Ethics*, ed. Carl F. H. Henry (Grand Rapids: Baker, 1973), 469–72.
[54]Kinlaw, "Ethics," 471.

Comprehensive Approach

The volume that comes closest to fitting the ideal of what should be involved in the scope and contents for an Old Testament ethics book is W. S. Bruce's *The Ethics of the Old Testament*. This volume is still being reprinted today by T. & T. Clark from the 1909 second enlarged edition that appeared fourteen years after it was first published. Bruce treats what we may call matters of prolegomena or introduction in his first five chapters. Included are the subjects: the nature of Old Testament ethics, the different aims of Old Testament theology and Old Testament ethics, developmental concepts, doctrine of evolution, the determinative principle of morality in the Old Testament, and the impact of election, individualism, righteousness and the giving of the law on Old Testament ethics. Next he devotes three chapters and almost one hundred pages to explaining the Decalogue followed by two chapters on the implications of Mosaic Law for nature, legislation, sanitation, the poor, women and children, worship, and sacrifice. Before concluding with two chapters and fifty pages on moral difficulties, he discusses, in three more chapters, the Old Testament view of a future life and eudaemonism, the advance and development of morality and the ethics of later Judaism.

Bruce's volume has, more often than not, raised the right questions and suggested a more comprehensive structure for an Old Testament ethics volume. The outline proposed here will cover these major areas:

Part I: Introduction
            (Definitional and methodological processes)
Part II: The Decalogue and Summarizing Old Testament Texts
            (Exegetical in nature)
Part III: Content of Old Testament Ethics
            (Synchronic ethical theology)
Part IV: Moral Difficulties
            (Apologetical studies in Old Testament hermeneutics)
Part V: Conclusion
            (Old Testament ethics and New Testament applications)

Old Testament ethics, then, has a special contribution to make to biblical studies and to ethics. It can be defined, its distinctive set of characteristics listed, and a methodological approach defended that sets forth a distinctive program of study comprehensive enough to meet the wide scope of issues and needs engendered by the older covenant.

Chapter 2

The Nature and Task
of Old Testament Ethics

A decided "Marcionite tendency may be fairly traced in much modern discussion of Christian ethics," opines Robert Davidson, "nor is this tendency confined to scholarly discussion."[1] Many of the Christian laity would confess that they too find little or no ethical value in the Old Testament. And this in the face of the huge amount of material that the older testament presents, much less the testimony of their Lord who declared that he had come to fulfill the law and not to abrogate it!

The tragedy is this:

> There is almost an embarrassment of riches for the student of Old Testament ethics, yet it is many years since the last handbook on the ethics of the Old Testament appeared *in English. The Ethics of the Old Testament* by H. G. Mitchell was published in 1913 [sic; 1912]; *The Moral Life of the Hebrews* by J. M. P. Smith in 1923. Neither of these volumes attempted more than the writing of the history of Hebrew morals, based on the rearrangement of the books of the Old Testament in the chronological sequence demanded by the scholarship of the day. In neither is there any inquiry as to whether it is possible to speak distinctively of the

---

[1]Robert Davidson, "Some Aspects of the Old Testament Contribution to the Pattern of Christian Ethics," *Scottish Journal of Theology* 12 (1959): 374.

ethics of the Old Testament, or wherein the unifying principle, or principles, of such an ethic may lie.[2]

The same point is made by Brevard S. Childs:

> In spite of the great interest in ethics, to our knowledge, there is no outstanding modern work written in English that even attempts to deal adequately with the Biblical material as it relates to ethics . . . [even though] there has come a host of ethical treatises that usually make some use of the Bible.[3]

Childs goes on to point out that one group may use the Bible—usually the New Testament—as "a sort of atmosphere of ethical concern," another as "a backdrop" (contrasting all the while their "tough-minded realistic ethics" with the "simple directives" of the biblical world), and still others working with a "vague appeal to the Bible" and a set of ethical principles related to the Bible, but requiring "a system of casuistry" to apply them to our day. The result, as Childs sees it, is that ". . . no clear-cut answer in respect to the use of the Bible has emerged."[4]

Clearly, the time is long overdue for a holistic approach to the subject. And even before we can begin to discuss the material content or even the problem of Old Testament ethics, it is necessary that the formal side of this topic be considered first.

THE POSSIBILITY OF OLD TESTAMENT ETHICS

M. T. O'Donovan[5] succinctly argues that there are three main assumptions that an ethicist makes when using an ethical text from the past for moral decisions, actions, and character in the present. The three assumptions are that the moral statements are: (1) universalizable, (2) consistent, and (3) prescriptive. Exactly so! On these three questions hang the whole possibility of an ethics of the Old Testament. Each of these need to be examined in turn.

Universalizability

O'Donovan contests Karl Barth's judgment that the Bible contains no "universal" ethical commands. Barth complained that such a claim is an

---

2Davidson, "Aspects of Christian Ethics," 375. We might add, nor has a textbook in English appeared since he wrote in 1959 until the present.

3Brevard S. Childs, *Biblical Theology in Crisis* (Philadelphia: Westminster, 1970), 124.

4Childs, *Biblical Theology*, 124–25.

5M. T. O'Donovan, "The Possibility of a Biblical Ethic," *Theological Students Fellowship Bulletin* 67 (1973): 15–23.

"untenable assumption," for "the command of God . . . is always an individual command for the conduct of this man, at this moment and in this situation. . . ."[6]

O'Donovan's response is that Barth has falsely equated "universality" with "generality," that is, a command must be indefinite, imprecise, or vague in order to be universal, "Yet moral philosophy since Kant has used 'universal' as the opposite of 'particular', not of 'special' or 'specific'. A universal rule is one which applies to every case of a certain class, however minutely specified that class may be." Furthermore, ". . . a command or precept is 'universal' whenever its content and the persons it addresses are indicated entirely by classification; where either the content of the command or its addressee is indicated by a demonstrative, a 'this' or a 'that', a time reference, a proper name, etc. etc., it is particular."[7]

Every biblical command, whether it appeared in a biblical law code, a narrative, Wisdom text, or was part of a prophetic message, was originally addressed to someone, some place, some situation in some particular historical context. Are these commands only "particular," not universalizable? Perhaps these, O'Donovan teases, are only paradigms for our moral reflection instead of universalizable commands. But O'Donovan responds: ". . . if a particular and specific command is to be a paradigm for the application of a highly generalized universal principle, there must be a middle term, a specific universal which will derive from the general principle and justify the particular." Consequently, the addressees, date lines, or addresses on biblical commands were not meant to prejudice their usage in other times, places, or persons. "No command or principle . . . could be justified ethically except by a reference to a universal; an ethic without universals would be no ethic, a series of disconnected, arbitrary imperatives." O'Donovan does acknowledge that there are some particularistic commands such as Paul's request, "Bring the cloak that I left with Carpus at Troas" (2 Tim. 4:13), which makes no appeals to universals and thus to ethics. However, "I entreat Euodia and Syntyche to agree in the Lord" (Phil. 4:2) has "lurking in the near background the implied assertion that agreeing together is something two Christian women ought to do."[8]

Old Testament ethics, are possible, then, since at least some of its commands and precepts contain "specific universals" that provide the very

---

[6]Karl Barth, *Church Dogmatics*, trans. A. T. Mackay (Edinburgh: T. & T. Clark, 1961) 3/4:11.

[7]O'Donovan, "Possibility of Ethic," 17.

[8]O'Donovan, "Possibility of Ethic," 18.

grounds for commanding the "particular" that is derived from a general principle.

Consistency

But this raises the celebrated problem of contextualization, for even while universals are granted to the biblical ethicist, perhaps those universals have no relevance or application to modern ethical problems. In short, some may grant that the biblical precepts and commands are universalizable, but they may also claim that the type of pressures, social institutions, societal patterns, or ethical situations that give rise to these universals are so different from our own ethical situations, societal patterns, social institutions, and moral pressures that there exists "a class of situations now without members."[9]

All that is required for our argument here that Old Testament ethics are possible, is to contend, as O'Donovan does so effectively, that the biblical author has given us more than just a list of, "bare, uninterpreted imperative[s]." That same biblical writer has also supplied elsewhere a whole pattern of ethical thought that has led up to the contextualized and particularistic injunction. O'Donovan argues, "Such extrapolation assumes no more than a certain consistency in the author's thought. If at one point he gives a specific injunction that suggests, in connection with something he says elsewhere, a more general principle accounting for both, the reader assumes that the author will stand by that principle, that he does not change his mind from one moment to the next."[10]

At this point, some biblical scholars will balk. For many it is too much to assume that there is consistency within one book or even a series of books alleged to have been written by the same author, for many contend that various forms of literary criticism have suggested composite documents often traditionally posing under one single author. This argument, more than any other argument in the last two hundred years, has been responsible for cutting the main nerve of the case for the unity and authority of the biblical message. It would take us beyond the limits of our study to counter this mammoth structure in a paragraph or two.[11] Perhaps the most effective argument at this point is the canonical argument. Cer-

---

[9]O'Donovan, "Possibility of Ethic," 18.

[10]O'Donovan, "Possibility of Ethic," 19.

[11]Readers are referred to the sound cases for the unity and authority of the claims of Scripture in Gleason L. Archer, Jr., *A Survey of Old Testament Introduction*, rev. ed. (Chicago: Moody Press, 1974); R. K. Harrison, *Introduction to the Old Testament* (Grand Rapids: Eerdmans, 1969); Kenneth Kitchen, *Ancient Orient and the Old Testament* (Downers Grove: InterVarsity, 1964); and Meredith Kline, *Treaty of the Great King* (Grand Rapids: Eerdmans, 1962).

tainly in its final form (as many would argue), the present text represents the only shape of the text that can be demonstrably fixed. All other revisions, deletions, arguments for extraneous sources that were subsequently added are purely hypothetical reconstructions—none of which have gained any *uniform* acceptance among the scholars themselves. Failing to find that agreement, let us proceed with what we have—until such a time as there arises objective evidence for a fabricated and piecemeal text. In other words, we are pleading for the American system of evidential argument and jurisprudence to be applied to biblical studies, that is, the text is innocent and its claims are to be trusted as being true *until* the evidence forces us to deny this status of innocence to the text. Since 1753 literary criticism has been carrying out its investigations—and we would defend the right and necessity for higher critical studies (i.e., the need to discuss date, authorship, addressees, etc.). But in fairness it must be reported that the results thus far have produced no convincing objective criteria for parcelling up the various books and documents of the Old Testament, nor have they gained anything approaching the uniform consent of all responsible scholars in the field. Therefore, the extrapolation of more general principles in an author's work for understanding specific commands is reasonable enough.

The argument must be carried one step further, however. Even if we finally grant consistency within the paragraph, pericope, or even the whole book of the biblical author being exegeted, what evidence is there for consistency within the Old Testament, or within the New Testament or even between the testaments? The approved scholarly assumption, these days, is diversity and not harmony or consistency within sections, testaments or the whole of the biblical corpus.

We have already dealt with this issue in chapter 1.[12] The search for diversity is as much "the result of [a] prior methodological decision as is the search for harmony, and cannot be defended on purely empirical grounds."[13] It would be as wrong for the ethicist to conceal evidences of harmony as to cover-up evidences for diversity. However, we would take exception to O'Donovan and others who would contend ". . . that the continuity of ethical content is discernible only from the point of view of a certain strand of New Testament theology. The biblical ethicist has become a Christian ethicist, discerning a unity and coherence in the course of Old Testament development which appears to him as he looks back on it from a New Testament viewpoint."[14]

---

[12]See chapter 1, nn. 26–27.

[13]O'Donovan, "Possibility of Ethic," 19.

[14]O'Donovan, "Possibility of Ethic," 20. See also his quote of Otto Pipen, *Christian Ethics* (London: Nelson, 1970), 123: "New revelations are connected with earlier ones and reinterpreted in the light of the later ones."

Nothing could be more damaging to the cause of harmony and consistency, for it tends to use what the diversity scholars had feared would be utilized, namely, "some overwhelmingly compelling dogma."[15] Instead of imposing the New Testament grid of doctrine and ethics over an Old Testament text in order to gain consistency or harmony, we would urge the use of an "informing theology"[16] or "informing ethic" where the Old Testament text under examination contains within it some facet of ethics that already was part and parcel of the received inspired teaching in the community of faith and formed the backdrop against which this new word was heard and received. In other words, instead of using the method of "the analogy of faith" (which has its proper location when used judiciously in the discipline of systematic theology), our contention is that what is needed here is "the analogy of [antecedent] Scripture."[17] Old Testament ethics, then, will build its case for harmony from the *accumulating* moral explanations, injunctions in the progress of revelation[18] using the same diachronic procedures as does Old Testament biblical theology. The question that ethicists need to ask at this point is this: Does the Old Testament as a whole and in its individual parts give explicit and implicit evidence that it is conscious of some guiding determinative principle or organizing tenet? This issue must be taken up as a separate section in this chapter, but for now let us turn to the third and last assumption that needs to be defended if Old Testament ethics are to be considered possible.

Prescriptivity

Old Testament ethical claims and demands purport to guide behavior and to direct action. The point is not the authority status of Old Testament ethical prescriptions; rather it is their claim to command mortals made in the image of God. Whether the ethical injunctions are in the imperative or the indicative mood makes very little difference to our argument here; the fact remains that the writers of Scripture are "doing more than offering information": they are "attempting to direct behavior."[19] This is not to decide for the moment whether or not that command or action may legitimately lay its claim over *my* life; it is simply to fairly report that the Old Testament purports to prescribe certain actions. Beyond this

---

[15]J. L. Houlden, *Ethics and the New Testament* (Middlesex: Penguin, 1973), 2.

[16]The term comes from John Bright, *The Authority of the Old Testament* (Grand Rapids: Baker, 1975), 143, 170.

[17]See my arguments for this methodology in W. C. Kaiser, Jr., *Toward an Old Testament Theology* (Grand Rapids: Zondervan, 1978), 14–19; W. C. Kaiser, Jr., *Toward an Exegetical Theology* (Grand Rapids: Baker, 1981), 134–40.

[18]See chapter 3 for a discussion of Progressive Revelation.

[19]O'Donovan, "Possibility of Ethic," 21.

minimal claim lie other questions that take up the issue of the *context* in which the proffered guidance can and is to be received. Some of these questions will appear in chapter 3 on the use of the Bible in deriving ethical norms and later discussions on law and grace. But the fact that the Old Testament *prescribes*—and what it prescribes has an internal *consistency* with the whole Old Testament canon, which has often been derived from what are specific injunctions in which can be discerned general or *universalizable* principles—forms the heart of the case for the possibility of Old Testament ethics.

THE CENTRAL ORGANIZING TENET
OF OLD TESTAMENT ETHICS

What gives wholeness, harmony, and consistency to the morality enjoined in the Old Testament? Is the Old Testament ethic, in some sense, an ordered whole? And if there is such a thing as a center to the Old Testament in the ethical realm, how can such a claim be substantiated without giving a detailed examination of every particular ethical directive given in the Old Testament?

The Character of God

Biblical ethics has a distinctive source and content, and it commands a distinctive response from all mortals. The first context in which the ethicist can define his total enterprise is found in the Old Testament ethical depiction of God. The Old Testament writers carefully avoided resting their case for ethics on any conception of man's moral nature or capacities; rather, their foundation was laid ". . . *in the ethical conception of God, whose character and will had been made known to them both in words and deeds of grace. [This] they found [to be] the one grand and positive principle of all moral life.*"[20] The ethical directions and morality of the Old Testament were grounded, first of all, in the nature of God directly. Thus, what God required was what he himself was and is. At the heart of every moral command was the theme "I am the Lord" or "Be holy as I the Lord your God am holy" (Lev. 18:5, 6, 30; 19:2, 3, 4, 10, 12, 14, 18, 25, 31, 32, 33, 36, 37, etc.).

"Any variation in [the laws founded on the nature and character of God] would imply a change in the nature of God," argued William Brenton Greene, Jr. "Any representation of God, therefore, as countenancing a lie, as approving pride or envy, as calling on men to act from a malicious or

---

[20]W. S. Bruce, *The Ethics of the Old Testament*, 2d ed. enl. (Edinburgh: T. & T. Clark, 1909), 42.

cruel spirit are not only immoral, but absurd. They represent God as doing what He cannot do just because He is *God.*[21] That is the point made in Psalm 25:8–10.

> Good and upright is the LORD;
> therefore he instructs sinners in his ways.
> He guides the humble in what is right
> and teaches them his way.
> All the ways of the LORD are loving and faithful
> for those who keep the demands of his covenant.

In this definition lies one of the great sources of unity and harmony within the Old Testament, for everywhere the biblical writers depict their situations as being under the character and will of this God whose very nature sets forth the "way" men and women ought to go. His demands and teachings, which the writers claim came by way of a divine revelation to them, constitute what is normative, ethical, and moral. Goodness, righteousness, truthfulness, faithfulness, and all other ethical concerns throughout the Old Testament are what he, the living God, is! Therein lies the strongest and first presumption for the unity, consistency, and harmony of the Old Testament ethics. Laws based on the character and nature of God we call "moral laws." Their permanence is set by the immutability or unchangeableness of the character of God.

Positive Law

But clearly aligned to this standard are two other determining principles and central organizing concepts for morality in the Old Testament. The first is related to the *will* and word of God (sometimes exhibiting moral law when it is anchored in the character of God and at other times "positive or statute law") while the second is related to the *work* of God—especially his work of creation.

The divine injunctions may be an expression of his character and therefore express his moral law,[22] but they may also be "positive laws" or "statute laws" which bind only because of the authority status of the one who gave these laws. The power of positive laws to bind men and women and claim their allegiance exists only for *as long* and over *as many* in *as different situations* as that authority determines. Thus when God commanded Adam in the Garden of Eden, ". . . you must not eat from the

---

[21]William Brenton Greene, Jr., "The Ethics of the Old Testament," *Princeton Theological Review* 27 (1929), 179–80.

[22]See this distinction worked out in William Brenton Greene, Jr., "War Neither Absolutely Right nor Absolutely Wrong in Itself," *Princeton Theological Review* 16 (1928): 642–45.

tree of the knowledge of good and evil . . . " (Gen. 2:17), or the Lord told his disciples, "Bring [the five loaves and two fish] here to me" (Matt. 14:17–18), and "Untie [the colt]" (Luke 19:30), the basis for the action commanded rested with the status of his authority and was true only to the person or persons addressed and for as long as he intended it. As we have already argued above, even these specific commands reflect general principles and are universalizable. But the status for their immediate authority rests on the status of the one who spoke these words. Positive laws, then, are enacted by a competent authority and they cease to bind any time they are repealed by that same competent authority.

Creation Ordinances

One final basis for ethical decision comes from the work of God, the "creation ordinances." These ordinances reflect the work of God in creation and depict "the constitution of things" as they were intended to be from the Creator's hand. They cover and regulate the whole gamut of life: bearing children, superintending the earth as a responsible steward before and under God, responsibly ruling the creatures of all creation, finding fulfillment and satisfaction in work labor, resting on the Sabbath, and enjoying marriage as a gift from above.

The importance of creation theology for the Wisdom Books has been one of the great insights of contemporary biblical theology.[23] What needs to be done now is for someone to relate that creation emphasis in the Wisdom Books to its ethical and moral themes. Moreover, the link between creation ordinances and the matters of marriage, human sexuality, duties to parents, duties to superiors and underlings, property, work, life, the lower created forms, and the like must now be developed in future studies. To do this, however, one must assume that an "informing ethic" has continued in the progress of revelation and that the presumption in favor of the unity of Old Testament ethics is a better working hypothesis than a presumption for its diversity and disunity.

THE MOTIVATION FOR OLD TESTAMENT ETHICS

What possible reasons could be given for attempting to produce a new Old Testament ethics volume? If we have managed to get along without one in English almost since the turn of the century, is this not evidence enough that neither the field of Old Testament studies nor Christian ethics has been too much the poorer for the absence?

---

[23]Walther Zimmerli, "The Place and Limits of Wisdom in the Framework of Old Testament Theology," *Scottish Journal of Theology* 17 (1964): 146–58.

The Basis of Completeness

But that is the very question we wish to raise: have we not been sadly lacking both in Old Testament studies and in moral development just because of an incipient Marcionitism in ethics and a lapse in Old Testament studies? Is it not true that one of the greatest obstacles for most Christians' appreciation of the Old Testament lies in the numerous moral difficulties that the Old Testament seems to present? And is it not likewise true that most ethicists who give any attention to biblical or theological ethics begin with slightly more than a passing glance and a curtsy to the Old Testament and proceed to devote almost all of their energies on the New Testament contribution to the field?

The church has been shortchanged by this conspiracy of silence. The lecturn of the academy and the pulpit of the local congregation should have been aiding God's people to come to understand the wholeness of biblical revelation. How could the pulpit have preached grace without the preparatory work of law? Even then, those who have used the Old Testament in its preparatory work (as Luther urged us) often forgot to instruct God's people in the so-called third use of the law (teaching and exhorting us to do God's will). There is a positive base for morality and ethical action in the Old Testament, and we will abandon it at the peril of our own ability to walk and live as our God has directed us to go. Paul could say after a mere three-year ministry at Ephesus, "I have not hesitated to proclaim to you the whole will of God" (Acts 20:27). To do likewise provides us with our first motivation for presenting an Old Testament ethics.

The Personal Basis

Repeatedly the grounds of one moral injunction after another is found in just this simple, but profound concluding statement, "I am Yahweh, your God" (e.g., Lev. 19:2, 3, 4, 10, 12, 14, 16, 18, 25, 28, 31, 32, 34, 36, 37). The highest motivation of all is to be found in the personal relationship to the Lord God. In fact, the whole of human moral life can be summed up in these words of Edmond Jacob: "If the nature of man can be defined by the theme of the image of God, his function can be qualified as the imitation of God."[24] He sets the standard for truth, right, justice, mercy, goodness, etc. Nowhere has the entire biblical canon given a more detailed picture of what was involved in the holiness and character of Yahweh than in that portion of the Bible that occupies some 77 percent of the total corpus.

---

[24]Edmond Jacob, *Theology of the Old Testament* (New York: Harper and Row, 1958), 173.

The Historical Basis

Over 125 times Israel was reminded that "I am the LORD your God who brought you up out of the land of Egypt." Usually this reminder went along with a command or ethical injunction. Most dramatically, it appears as the prologue, and hence the grounds for the Decalogue, in Exodus 20:2 and Deuteronomy 5:6. In other words, the context or environment of law and obligation in the Old Testament was the redemption of Israel from Egypt. The Christian need not feel left out in this discussion, for the new covenant of Jeremiah 31:31–34 appeals to the same deliverance (v. 32) even though it is the same covenant that became the new word addressed not only "to the house of Israel and the house of Judah" (v. 31), but also to the church as the use of this passage in Hebrews 8:8–12 and 10:16–17 proves.

This historical reminder serves as the motivator for many of the individual laws as well as the great legislative sections like the Decalogue. For example, Exodus 22:21 warns, "Do not mistreat an alien or oppress him, for you were aliens in Egypt." Just as biblical theology is uniquely grounded in history, so too is biblical ethics. Consequently, the saving actions and deliverances of God in the past should be the occasion for more than just doctrinal statements about soteriology: they provide the grounds for urging us to a holiness of life, character, and action that responds to so great a salvation. The Old Testament commands and its injunctions cannot be jettisoned in a cavalier manner by contemporary Christians without denying or rewriting our history of salvation—a stance which most Christians are loathe (fortunately) to take.

Foundational Basis

The ethics of the Old Testament are an absolute necessity for formulating New Testament ethics or any kind of Christian ethics, for only in the Old Testament can the proper foundations be laid for all biblical, theological, or Christian ethical theory or action. Those interpreters of the biblical text who say that the New Testament alone provides us with an adequate basis for moral theory and action are certainly mistaken. First, they must revise the estimate of Jesus himself who declared the reverse: "Do not think that I have come to abolish the Law or the Prophets; I have not come to abolish them but to fulfill them" (Matt. 5:17). Second, there are scores of ethical instructions and injunctions given in the Old Testament that are not repeated in the New Testament, but are part of the "informing ethic," background, and given assumptions of the new community in Christ. Where, for example, will we find as full a statement as Leviticus gives on the holiness of God? Where will we find the image of God discussed with the implications it has for cases of premeditated murder as in Genesis 9:6? Where will we obtain authoritative materials on the abortion question if the Old Testament is not consulted? This type of question could be multiplied many times over, but the point is clear. Some of the greatest summarizing texts, which are classical teaching passages on the moral law of God, are encapsulated in the Old Testament. No longer can the Christian church regard Old Testament ethics as an *ab extra* or as an optional luxury to be dismissed in the interests of time or relevancy; it must be restored to its rightful foundation place in moral theology.

THE LIMITATIONS OF OLD TESTAMENT ETHICS

Old Testament morality does have its limitations, however. While contemporary ethicists must take the Old Testament seriously if they are going to properly represent the total canonical contribution to biblical or theological ethics, Old Testament ethics is not the final chapter in the canonical spectrum of concepts. This testament reaches out beyond itself for fulfillment in Jesus Christ and the New Testament. Therefore, it is necessary for us to acknowledge at least four limitations to our discipline along the lines discussed by Vriezen.[25]

National Limitations

Even though the Old Testament canon in the shape that it has been received by the Jewish and Christian community begins with a cosmopolitan and even a universal concern for "all the families [and nations] of the earth" in Genesis 1–11, it is also fair to say that most of the laws, commands, and ethical directions are primarily addressed to a small group of Semites who eventually became the nation Israel. We must quickly add that this does not ultimately limit its general or universal appeal (as we have already argued under the "possibility of Old Testament ethics"), but there is an obvious limitation on a *prima facie* reading of the text.

The best illustration of the national limitations of certain laws is seen in Deuteronomy: "No Ammonite or Moabite or any of his descendants may enter the assembly of the LORD, even down to the tenth generation" (Deut. 23:3). Yet, even in this law one must not read a vacillating estimate of the potential worth, dignity, or value of all men, races, and nations. The charge of chauvinism that assumes Yahweh had elevated Israel to a pedestal and reduced everyone else to some degraded status will

---

[25]Consult Th. C. Vriezen, *An Outline Of Old Testament Theology*, 2d ed., rev. and enl. (Newton, Mass.: Branford, 1970), 398–404 for an enlarged and slightly different perspective than the one given here. Also see John Goldingay, *Approaches to Old Testament Interpretation* (Downers Grove: InterVarsity, 1981), 61–65, "The 'Limitations' of Old Testament Standards."

be dealt with in detail later. The only point that must be made here is that the "assembly of the Lord" and becoming part of the "people of God" had theological overtones and these must not be used to count against either the same righteousness required of all men or the worth and value that all men and women had as a result of their being made in the image of God. Even Amos argued that God had conducted many exoduses of nations besides Israel's miraculous escape from Egypt: "Did not I bring Israel up from Egypt, the Philistines from Caphtor and the Arameans from Kir?" (Amos 9:7).

For both the "resident alien" (גֵּר) and the "foreigner" (נָכְרִי) were protected by the ethical injunctions laid on Israel. The "stranger" or "resident alien" (גֵּר) was to be treated as if he had been "native-born" (אֶזְרָח; Lev. 19:34) while the humane treatment demanded of a female prisoner-of-war (Deut. 21:10–14) illustrates this same value for the human person even if there is a level of slavery still present.

Israel's gracious gifts from her Lord were to be mediated to all nations. Through her seed "all the peoples on earth will be blessed" (Gen. 12:3). She was to be nothing less than a "light for the Gentiles" in her role as the "Servant of the Lord" (Isa. 42:6; 49:6). The tragedy is that Israel usually failed to carry out this missionary function; hence, the nationalistic limitation arises more from the limited religious and ethical experience of the people than from the norm to which they were called. Fortunately the biblical text never looses sight of this ultimate goal of including all nations, races, and peoples in the universal kingdom of God; for this eschatological hope remains strong, especially in the vision of the prophets (e.g., Isa. 19; Zech. 14:16–19; Mal. 1:5). Even in the stream of history these nations were not forgotten as the long prophetic sections of prophecies to the nations argue (e.g., Isa. 13–23; Jer. 46–51; Ezek. 25–32; Amos 1–2) or books like Jonah, Nahum, Obadiah, and Ruth argue.

There is a nationalistic limitation to Old Testament ethics, but it is less dramatic than most have imagined and relates more to the silence of Scripture on this topic and to Israel's experience than to approved attitudes of prejudice inculcated by divine revelation.

Historical Limitations

Many things were permitted during the Old Testament era—even after a higher moral standard had been announced and then rejected by the people. Slavery, polygamy, and low views of women are reported in the Old Testament as prime examples where God was pleased to work through history. As John Murray expressed it:

> How could God allow his people, in some cases the most eminent of Old Testament saints, to practice what was a violation of his

preceptive will? . . . Our lord . . . tells us explicitly that [it was] for the hardness of their hearts. . . . Sufferance there indeed was, but no legitimation or sanction of the practice. . . . In the earlier periods of revelation transgression of a law would not be as aggravated as that same transgression becomes in the fuller and brighter light of the revelation of its wrong and of the sanction with which it is attended. . . . It was the sufferance of forbearance, not the sufferance of approval or sanction."[26]

Therefore, when the light of revelation in the progress of that revelation[27] shines brighter, the degree of responsibility is increased even though the Old Testament nowhere excuses or rescinds the ordinances of creation that certainly continued to apply to many of these same matters. It is a matter of "degree of guilt or of punitive sanction"[28] and hence one of historical limitations that must be seriously discussed especially when the narrative sections of the Old Testament are appealed to for ethical direction.

Legalistic Limitations

"It is the nature of law, whether divine or human, when imposed as a bond of order or discipline, to work from without inwards—acting as an external pressure or constraint," opined Patrick Fairbairn.[29] What the law lacks is an inner source of motivation or something to compel me to achieve what it commands. While the whole essence of the law can be summarized in love, it cannot of itself produce that love.

Not that anything was deficient in the law itself, but there was a limitation because of the imperfection of men. Thus, the law had more the effect of being a parent for children in training while it used its magisterial form (the principle of fear and the threat of a curse) to deter men and women from sin.

Nevertheless, there was a "spiritual element" in the law that contained the "great moral truths" of that covenant.[30] This spiritual element comes out in the way the law of God appears in Psalms, Proverbs, and is reiterated in the preaching of the prophets. In fact, Jeremiah specifically locates the problem and limitation of the law in the *people* instead of in the law of God itself. Said Jeremiah: "I will make a new ['renewed' in Hebrew] covenant . . . because *they broke* my covenant . . . " (Jer. 31:31–32; ital-

---

[26]John Murray, *Principles of Conduct* (Grand Rapids: Eerdmans, 1957), 16–19.
[27]See our fuller discussion under "Progressive Revelation" in the next chapter.
[28]Murray, *Principles of Conduct*, 18.
[29]Patrick Fairbairn, *The Revelation of Law in Scripture* (1869; reprint, Grand Rapids: Zondervan, 1957), 182.
[30]Fairbairn, *Revelation of Law*, 185.

ics added). Therefore we must once again be acutely aware that most of the limitations that come from using the law in the Old Testament came because of the people's own failure and not because of any intrinsic weakness in the instrument itself.

Materialistic Limitation

For many, the tone of the Old Testament appears to be much too earthly and concerned with doing righteousness in order that one might prosper in his flocks, herds, fields, and number of children. All too frequently the motivation given for obedience, or compliance with the will and command of God is riches, honor, long life, and reputation. This presents us with the famous problem of eudaemonism[31] or utilitarianism.

There is admittedly much truth to the complaint. The Old Testament did purposely embrace a holistic view of life that refused to separate existence into the neat compartments of a spiritual and material realm. Yahweh was Lord of everything: "The earth is the LORD's and everything in it, the world, and all who live in it" (Ps. 24:1). No book labors harder to demonstrate this fact than does Ecclesiastes. That is the positive side to this question.

However, the spiritual side was not all that evident as yet. Consequently, the main barometer of blessing, obedience, and fellowship with God was material prosperity. Many of the commands of God, such as the Decalogue's injunction to honor one's parents, had the promise of long life attached to it. Yet even in this fact lies an undivided unity that modern men have all too frequently missed: there was a quality of life here and now, when lived in fellowship with God, that was sanctified by God and that contributed to continued eternal fellowship with God. So something must be said on both sides of this question. For the moment, it will be enough to acknowledge that material blessings were highly regarded in the Old Testament and this emphasis constitutes a stumbling block and limitation which must be placed in perspective when dealing with a total approach to Old Testament ethics.

SUMMARY

Old Testament ethics, we conclude, is not only possible, but demanded from the Christian church if we are to be faithful to the whole counsel of God and if we are to set forth the principles needed by the community and individual for ethical and moral living approved by God.

---

[31]See Part IV: Moral Difficulties in the Old Testament for more complete discussions.

The character, will, word, and work of God supply the determining principles and central organizing tenets of Old Testament ethics. Therefore, Old Testament ethics remain a foundational basis for any future direction in this whole discipline, even though there are several acknowledged limitations present that usually can be explained by the fact that the progress of revelation is set in the process of history and to that degree limited thereby in the good plan and pleasure of God.

Chapter 3

The Use of the Bible
in Establishing Ethical Norms

Should Christian ethics be linked and identified with biblical ethics? And even if they should be somehow joined, can a successful method of their linkage be described? If these questions are answered affirmatively, in what way would an Old Testament ethic also be normative and binding?

The traditional link between the Bible and Christian ethics has been seriously challenged and flatly repudiated in our century. Carl F. H. Henry[1] quotes from several prominent ethicists who illustrate this rupture. Reinhold Niebuhr declared in his Gifford Lectures that any use of the Bible as an authority in ethics was to make it "a vehicle of sinful sanctification of relative standards of knowledge."[2] Likewise, C. J. Barker would have nothing to do with such a linkage: "For Christianity, ethical conduct is . . . not adherence to a closed book of rules and regulations." He went on to say, "No supposed exegesis must ever be allowed to force upon man a doctrine repugnant to his moral and religious convictions." When Barker would appeal to the New Testament, it was ". . . to acknowledge the

---

[1]Carl F. H. Henry, *Christian Personal Ethics* (Grand Rapids: Eerdmans, 1957), 236–37.

[2]Reinhold Niebuhr, *The Nature and Destiny of Man* (New York: Scribner, 1943), 2:152.

source that inspired the idea set down [rather] than to produce corrobative evidence." His function as an ethicist was to capture ". . . the spirit breathing through the New Testament. . . ."[3]

It is an agreed state of the discipline of Christian ethics in this century that the nature and content of morality is not to be equated with any formulation of the divine will supposedly found in biblical command-ments, principles, precepts, or examples. Yet, even while "revealed mo-rality" was declared impotent for many Protestant ethicists, the search for some limited use of the Bible in ethics continued mainly under the stimu-lus of European "crisis theology"—most notably under Karl Barth. Whether it was Karl Barth, H. Richard Niebuhr, or post-Vatican II Roman Catholic ethicists, the situation now was as James Gustafson described it:

> . . . The Bible is more important for helping the Christian com-munity to interpret the God whom it knows in its existential faith than it is for giving a revealed morality that is to be translated and applied in the contemporary world. . . .
>
> The Christian moral life, then, is not a response to moral imperatives, but to a Person, the living God . . . .
>
> What the Bible makes known, then, is not a morality, but a *reality*, a living presence to whom man responds.[4]

Or put even more succinctly by Bruce Birch and Larry Rasmussen,

> The Bible's use by a number of ethicists, then, was as the source for discerning the organic shape of God's action in Christ. . . . In current terms, the use of the Bible in ethics was more as the primary "story" for the moral life and less the source of laws, principles, ideals, and other norms. Biblical ethics *per se* were of little direct interest and importance.[5]

The same was true for Catholic writers living in the new freedom of post Vatican II. They too picked up the cry for "response" or "relational ethics" and they began to use the Bible only as a "pointer to the supreme drama in the Christian moral life."[6]

It is this crucial linkage—the relation of biblical thought to ethical research—that has received so little attention in recent years. Once again,[7]

---

[3]C. J. Barker, *The Way of Life: A Study in Christian Ethics* (London: Lutterworth, 1946), 4, 14, and 12.

[4]James Gustafson, "Christian Ethics," *Religion*, ed. Paul Ramsey (Englewood Cliffs, N.J.: Prentice-Hall, 1965), 287.

[5]Bruce C. Birch and Larry L. Rasmussen, *Bible and Ethics in the Christian Life* (Minneapolis: Augsburg, 1976), 24.

[6]Birch and Rasmussen, *Bible and Ethics*, 27.

[7]In a previous volume, I referred to the crisis in Exegetical Theology, Biblical Theology, Systematic Theology, and plain Bible knowledge. See Walter C. Kaiser, Jr., *Toward An Exegetical Theology* (Grand Rapids: Baker, 1981), 17–40.

we have another of the infamous gaps that have continued to afflict biblical studies in our specialty conscious age. This chasm, in many ways generically related to the gulfs that exist between exegesis and homiletics or between biblical theology and systematic theology, must be addressed by biblical scholarship even at the risk of intruding into territories traditionally labelled off-limits to amateurs in ethical theory and parlance.

HERMENEUTICAL ISSUES

Before examining in more detail some of the positions recently posed for resolving the acknowledged gap between the Bible and ethical theory, it would be well to describe the total shape of the problem that meets us here.

Hermeneutical Models

For most Christian ethicists, the Bible is somehow normative, but the question remains: *in what way is it normative?* David Kelsey[8] offers three models of biblical usage in theologizing that we can also apply to the field of ethics. The first model uses the Bible in an *ideational* mode and sees the Bible as offering explicit teaching for doctrine (Warfield) or, at least, for supplying main ideas and concepts (Bartsch, Wright). The second use of the Bible stresses its role as witness (Barth) and is therefore the mode of *concrete actuality*. But when the Bible is viewed as consisting of images that point to "authentic existence" (Bultmann) or to a power that is mediated through Christ (Tillich), then Kelsey calls this third mode *ideal possibility*. The emphasis of each of the three modes would turn to the Bible for different reasons: the first for moral direction mostly set in prescriptive terms; the second stresses personal and existential modelling in Jesus Christ as the best atmosphere in which to make moral decisions, while the third mode tries to discover what it means to be fully "human" by means of biblical images, symbol, and myths. This clarifies the shape of the problem, but it seems to add nothing essentially new to the solution of the issue.

The Variety of Biblical Forms

Another hermeneutical dilemma arises from the fact that there are so many different types of moral materials in the Bible. There are codes of law (such as the Decalogue[s], the covenant code, ceremonial sections such as Leviticus 1–7); narrative portions with potential examples of what

---

[8]David H. Kelsey, *The Uses of Scripture in Recent Theology* (Philadelphia: Fortress, 1975), 161.

to do and what not to do described in actions and lives of groups and individuals; isolated laws; wisdom materials with proverbs, aphorisms, and riddles; parables; allegories; prophetic preaching; paraenetic instruction (e.g., Deuteronomy); and eschatological discourse with emphasis on ethical living in the present. How is one to go about drawing out any consistent type of approach, much less content, from the multiplicity of literary forms in which the material is embedded?

What we need is a lodestone or a stance from which we can view the whole testament. We believe that point can be identified. The heart of Old Testament ethics is to be placed squarely on the explicit commands found mainly in the Pentateuch, but also to a lesser degree in the Prophets and Wisdom Books. However, many of these explicit commands are no longer binding today. On what grounds, then, can we appeal to some if not to all? This raises another hermeneutical problem.

The Specificity of Old Testament Commands

What was a help and an aid to Israel's use and application of the ethical injunctions of the Bible often turns out to be our stumbling block. The precise specificness and particularity of the Bible was not meant to prejudice its universal usefulness, but to make the principles involved all the more concrete, real, and personal. The problem of particularity occurs in other aspects of biblical studies,[9] but even there one can witness the Bible's own direct application of earlier historical events. The use of first person "we" or "us," as if the people addressed several centuries after the event took place were still participating in that ancient event bears witness to the Bible's refusal to let the specific and particular block any appeal to universals or general applications. This principle is strikingly exhibited in Hosea's use (Hos. 12:3–6) of Genesis 25:26 and 32:24ff. Thus, while there are fewer general principles than there are specific commands, this should not affect the eventual usefulness of most, if not all, of the injunctions.[10]

Another difficulty appears in the fact that so frequently in the Pentateuch (e.g., the covenant code of Exod. 21–23) or the Wisdom Books (e.g., Proverbs), the laws and specific demands seem largely independent of each other, exhibiting very little pattern or clearly observable nexus.

---

[9]Walter C. Kaiser, Jr., *Toward an Exegetical Theology*, pp. 37–40; Patrick Fairbairn, "The Historical Element in God's Revelation," in *Classical Evangelical Essays in Old Testament Interpretation*, compiled and ed. by Walter C. Kaiser, Jr. (Grand Rapids: Baker, 1972), 67–86. (See also New Testament use of this phenomenon: Matt. 15:7; Mark 7:6; Acts 4:11; Rom. 4:23ff; 15:4; 1 Cor. 9:8–10; 10:11; Heb. 6:18; 10:15; 12:15–17.

[10]I am heavily indebted to John Goldingay, *Approaches to Old Testament Interpretation* (Downers Grove: InterVarsity, 1981), 51–53 for many observations in this section.

Often, not even an analysis of the immediate context will yield the connection between individual provisions of the law.

In these cases, it is necessary to appeal to the wider context of the whole book, other books from the same era of biblical revelation, and ultimately to the whole Old Testament canon in order to gather some sense of ordering, priorities, organization, and relationship between these laws and moral precepts. Repeatedly, the law turns up in the prophetical writings and often the Wisdom writers merely cast into an aphoristic or poetic form what had been part of the apodictic or case laws of the Pentateuch. The Decalogue has the whole of Exodus as its setting and the covenant code and subsequent laws in the Pentateuch seem to embody concretely what had been set forth in the general principles of the Decalogue. Thus, Calvin's commentaries on these books proceeded in the manner of a harmony, as if the rest of the materials after the Decalogue in Exodus 20 were only illustrations of the abstract and universal moral laws. Likewise the legal specifications of Deuteronomy 12–26 are placed in the context of the covenantal and paraenetic generalizations found in their preface from Deuteronomy 5 to 11.

A third consequence of the Bible's specificness is that it is addressed to a particular historical situation in a particular cultural situation that is almost certainly very different from those faced by persons making ethical decisions today. This is the problem of contextualization. The reverse side of this problem is that contemporary men and women live in particular cultural situations so utterly different from the Bible that there are hosts of ethical questions that we now face but are never directly addressed by the Bible.

We have encountered this problem already in the last chapter under the "possibility of Old Testament ethics," but we need to face it again as a hermeneutical issue. The interpretive task often will be as involved as it is straightforward at other times. Goldingay suggests these steps:

(1) Examine the statement in light of comparable ones where the principles may be more overt;

(2) Ask what, if any, is the theology that "undergirds" or "informs" the statement and thereby contributes to its abiding normativeness;

(3) Check for any illumination that may come from parallel extrabiblical materials; and

(4) Look for principles behind the specificity of the text which function somewhat like that which ethicists label "middle axioms," i.e., a principle somewhere between a general abstraction such as "justice" and a specific, concrete policy.[11]

---

[11]Goldingay, *Approaches to Interpretation*, 54–55.

At times, of course, we will not always be able to say just what the significance, contemporary value, and ethical principle behind a text may be. Three times the Pentateuch warns, "Do not cook a young goat in its mother's milk" (Exod. 23:19; 34:26; Deut. 14:21). If this law is paralleled, as some believe, by a Ugaritic text that prescribes for pagan fertility what the Bible proscribes, then indeed we may have hit upon the reason for this command. What is needed in each case is an understanding of the meaning of the words, an appreciation for the times in which that word was received, and a location of that particular injunction in its canonical (Old Testament) setting.

C. Freedman Sleeper explicitly warns us against each step we have outlined above:

> First, we should *not* try to find Biblical *strategies or solutions* to modern problems. . . . Attempts to find "the biblical answer" by an appeal to prooftexts is simply wrong because the Bible did not anticipate many contemporary issues, because there is development within the Bible itself, and because the Biblical solutions are historically conditioned. By itself, the Bible cannot tell us what to do. . . . Second, we should *not* try to find *parallels* between our own situation and that of the biblical writers in order that the Bible might "speak to us". . . . Third, we should *not* try to extrapolate from the Bible *only one ethical norm*—the polarity of law and gospel . . . ; love . . . ; the imitation of Christ; the kingdom of God; natural law. . . . [for] by reducing Christian ethics to a single norm, other important aspects . . . are neglected.[12]

But, it is all too easy to be against "proof-texting." Of course, it is wrong procedure. That, observes Goldingay, is "no more adventurous than [being] against sin."[13] What is needed, instead, is a responsible handling of the texts concerned. The fact of cultural continuity and the presence of implicit universals behind particularized commands is a real option to be tested by prior hermeneutical decision as is cultural change and disconnected and seemingly arbitrary imperatives.[14]

The Threefold Division of the Law

One of the most common ways of attempting to deal with this problem of particularism or specificity of Old Testament commands was to make a distinction between the civil, ceremonial, and moral law of God in the Old Testament. O'Donovan[15] believes that this distinction was first

---

[12]C. Freedman Sleeper, "Ethics as a Context for Biblical Interpretation," *Interpretation* 22 (1968): 451.

[13]Goldingay, *Approaches to Interpretation*, 53.

[14]Goldingay, *Approaches to Interpretation*, 53.

[15]O. M. T. O'Donovan, "Towards an Interpretation of Biblical Ethics," *Tyndale Bulletin* 27 (1976): 59.

adumbrated in the patristic period by Justin Martyr. However, C. G. Montefiore contended that:

> The Rabbis, we may say, were familiar with the distinction between ceremonial and moral commands, and *on the whole* they regarded the "moral" as more important and more fundamental than the "ceremonial". . . . Again, there was some tendency to distinguish "heavy" and "light" commands according to certain punishments or threats. . . . Nevertheless, on the whole the "heavy" commands are the moral commands. The "heaviest" (apart from circumcision) are commands such as the prohibition of unchastity, idolatry, or murder, the honoring of parents, the Sanctification of the Name. The distinction between "light" and "heavy" commands was well known, and is constantly mentioned and discussed.[16]

Gustaf Dalman agreed:

> The Rabbis did not differentiate between the smallest and the greatest commandments but rather between "light" (Hebrew *ḳallīn*) and "heavy" (Hebrew *ḥamārīn*). . . . "Light" and "heavy" commandments are not those which are in themselves easy or difficult to keep, but such that cause the keeping of other commandments to be either light (*ḳōl*) or "heavy" (*ḥōmer*). . . . The freeing of the mother bird (Deut. xxii.6) is considered to be the "lightest" of all; the "heaviest" of all—the honoring of father and mother (Exod. xx.12). . . . Our Lord's "least" is in the category of these "lightest" commandments of the Rabbis.[17]

There is a fifth-century A.D. work known as the *Speculum "Quis ignorat"* that appeals to the common knowledge of the Christian community by asking:

> Who does not know that within Holy Scripture . . . there are propositions to be understood and believed . . . and commands and prohibitions to be observed and acted upon? . . . Among the latter class some have a meaning hidden in sacramental ritual so that many commands given to be obeyed by the people of the Old Testament are not now performed by Christian people. . . . Others, however, are to be observed even now.[18]

---

[16]C. G. Montefiore, *Rabbinic Literature and Gospel Teaching* (New York: Ktav, 1970), 316–17.

[17]Gustaf Dalman, *Jesus-Jeshua: Studies in the Gospels*, trans. Paul P. Levertoff (London: SPCK, 1929), 64–65.

[18]As cited by O'Donovan, "Interpretation of Ethics," 59; *Speculum "Quis ignorat,"* *Patrologiae Latinae* 34, cols. 887–1040. Some credit this work to St. Augustine, but there is no real evidence for that.

He then copies out all the moral commands of the Old and New Testament that are still to be obeyed by the New Testament believer.

Our point is that the law of God was not regarded as such a monolithic unity as to have no distinctions between heavier and lighter aspects of that same law. If contemporary Christians are hesitant on this point, their Lord is *not;* he taught that there were "weightier matters" to the law (Matt. 23:23–24).[19] This did not mean that it was a matter of adiaphora which of the commands we, or Israel, observed so long as we chose one or another command that we conceived to be weightier! We may not arbitrarily jettison (when *we* think it necessary or when we are forced) the "lighter" and the "least" commands; it is only when the Lawgiver himself releases us from the specifics of the "lesser laws" (civil and ceremonial?) that we may no longer feel an obligation to them in all their particularity. Anything less than this leads to ethical latitudinarianism. We may not substitute our own hierarchy or priority of laws—even within the realm of moral law! The threefold distinction was an attempt to avoid this type of arbitrariness in deciding which commands were or were not to be observed by Christians.

Many will object that this threefold distinction within the one law of God is anachronistic (ancient Israel made no such distinctions) and atypical (all torah has its own *Sitz im Leben,* "setting in life," within its own social institutions and hence the transfer to new social institutions in our day must be labelled arbitrary). To the first complaint, we only reply, as O'Donovan does, that the threefold distinction is not intended to be an account of the way Israel had to regard her own laws, rather it is only a catalogue of its constituent elements and it functions much like our catalogue of literary genres in our detailed description of literary *Gattungen* which also were unknown to the Old Testament writers and readers.[20] Let the interpreter beware, however, for the distinction was not so odd that the ancient hearers missed the fact that the "Covenant Code" had a heading that referred to its laws as מִשְׁפָּטִים, "judgments" or "cases" for the *judges* to use as precedents (Exod. 21:1). Furthermore, they could see that the Decalogue carried no socially recognizable setting with its laws, and that the tabernacle material from Exodus 25 through Leviticus 7 (at least) had an expressed word of built-in obsolescence when it noted several times over that what was to be built was only a model ("pattern," תַּבְנִית, e.g., Exod. 25:9, 40)—the real had not yet emerged, but was, as Hebrews 10:1

---

[19]For further discussion of this point see: W. C. Kaiser, Jr., "The Weightier and Lighter Matters of the Law: Moses, Jesus and Paul," in *Current Issues in Biblical and Patristic Interpretation:* Studies in Honor of Merrill C. Tenney, ed. Gerald F. Hawthorne (Grand Rapids: Eerdmans, 1975), 176–92.

[20]O'Donovan, "Interpretation of Ethics," 60.

argues, "only a shadow of the good things that are coming—not the realities themselves." As for the contextually-bound social institutions of these laws, every statement or command is said to someone at sometime. Thus, this is not a feature limited to one special group of sayings or even limited to the Bible. "If the Mosaic saying is irrelevant because of its context-dependence, it would seem to follow that anything said by anybody in the past is irrelevant for the same reason."[21] This context-dependency only means that these laws, argues O'Donovan, have a special *task* to perform within the community and its institutions. These laws expressing a particular social task continue at that same time to contain, even if only hypothetically, a moral principle that claims the higher allegiance of the community and makes possible the obligation that is laid on its hearers.[22]

But this discussion must be taken one more step. When we ask: "Do the commands of the Old Testament apply to us today?" we are asking an ambiguous question as far as O'Donovan is concerned.[23] The *question of claim*, "Is that text ordering *me* to do something?" is separate from the *question of authority:* "Who is it that said that and ought I therefore to do it?"[24] Thus the command to Abraham in Genesis 12:1 ("Leave your country") has no *claim* over any of us. It is a special command to a special person at a special juncture of the history of an emerging people that demanded a special *task* to be performed. But, we cannot reason from this text, as the prevailing custom of scholarship goes today, to say that *all* Old Testament commands must be understood in this way. Nor can we say that it has no moral authority over us, for Abraham is an example ("By faith Abraham, when called to go . . . obeyed," Heb. 11:8); but he is an example of obedience, not of how we should "leave our country" or the like. On the other hand, the command to Abraham and to all his descendants in Genesis 17:10 ("Every male among you shall be circumcised") Paul felt free to contravene. For Galatian Christians to be circumcised would be a misunderstanding of the gospel. "There is, therefore, in Paul's treatment of circumcision an issue of *authority*, rather than of *claim*. He finds grounds within the Gospel for denying that some of the Old Testament commands, however much they may [appear to] claim us, have any right to be obeyed."[25]

The question of claim and the question of authority advance the interpretive criteria beyond the threefold distinction. The particularity of many (but not all) Old Testament commands can and must be acknowl-

---

[21]O'Donovan, "Interpretation of Ethics," 64.
[22]O'Donovan, "Interpretation of Ethics," 64–67.
[23]O'Donovan, "Interpretation of Ethics," 58.
[24]The terms and distinctions are O'Donovan's.
[25]O'Donovan, "Interpretation of Ethics," 68.

edged. Each particular injunction can be justified in terms of the task or goal it aims at in some special situation even while it still carries the right of authority over us because of the moral principle recognized in all its admitted particularism. On the other hand, universalizable commands may be justified by reference to a universal principle (often attached to the command) that may be either normative (such and such ought to be, or is, our duty) or descriptive (such and such is what Jesus, the prophets, or apostles said).[26] But what of the scholarly community? How have they responded to these same issues and can we sharpen our criteria any more by means of dialogue with them?

SIX CONTEMPORARY HERMENEUTICAL STANCES

Recently, a number of ethicists, and only one or two brave biblical scholars, have ventured into this enormously important, but difficult field. What follows is a survey of seven recent writers who have grappled with the problem of how and in just what way the Bible is normative for Christian ethics.[27]

The Bible Used a General Orientation to Ethical Issues

James M. Gustafson outlines four ways Scripture has been used in Christian ethics.[28]

(1) As moral law—a "most stringent use of Scripture," for those who violate revealed law would be judged in error;

(2) As embodying the moral ideals of the Bible—an ambiguous, if not Greek or futuristic ethic devoid of content and application;

(3) As analogy wherein actions similar to biblical actions come under the same praise or condemnation they received in the Bible; but as to which controls (the present or Scripture) and what constitutes a genuine analogy, we do not know; and

(4) As communal reflection, for given the plethora of moral values, norms, and principles found in the vast variety of biblical literature, Scripture can be only one source among many that the community uses to decide on what is morally right even though this method is very loose and is an easy prey to the subjectivity

---

26O'Donovan, "Interpretation of Ethics," 54, 62–63.

27The reader will observe that I am dependent on the fine discussions of Birch and Rasmussen, *Bible and Ethics*, 45–78.

28James M. Gustafson, "The Place of Scripture in Christian Ethics: A Methodological Study," *Interpretation* 24 (1970), especially pp. 439–47. Reprinted in James M. Gustafson, *Theology and Christian Ethics* (Philadelphia: Pilgrim, 1974), 309–16.

of feelings or prevailing cultural values. This model is Gustaf-son's own recommendation.

The accent here is on the community (especially the church) and the variety of the biblical data; Scripture alone is not enough. It can only supply a basic *orientation* towards particular decisions.[29] Gustafson has left untouched the issue of biblical authority and the criteria for using the various types of biblical materials. In his most explicit statement, he allows the Gospels to provide "paradigms of action, intention, and disposition,"[30] but we will answer this later in the chapter.

The Bible Used in Multiple Variations

Edward LeRoy Long, Jr., is not about to say precisely how the Bible may be used—except he is sure there is no one way.[31] There are three ways the Bible provides ethical insight:
   (1) In prescriptive terms in which the content of ethical action is derived from the Bible as a law book;
   (2) In supplying guiding ethical ideals and principles without binding us to the language and precise categories used by the Bible; and
   (3) In showing us a pattern of response for the moral life where the relational element, context situation, and community are valued rather than the principles or precepts of the Bible.

Pluralism is the favored approach. There is no one right way—that is one right conclusion! We cannot move directly to Christian ethics from the Bible (which would seem to rule out his first way), nor can we do Christian ethics without some understanding of what lies at the center of New Testament proclamation.[32] But what that understanding is and how it works he, too, is careful not to say.

The Bible Used as a Source of Images

C. Freedman Sleeper's essays emphasize three stages in the interpretive process.[33] These stages go from perspective (pre-understanding posed not so much in existentialist terms as from the data of social sci-

---

[29]Gustafson, "Place of Scriptures," 455.

[30]As cited by Birch and Rasmussen, *Bible and Ethics*, 53–54; James M. Gustafson, *Theology and Christian Ethics*, 159.

[31]Edward LeRoy Long, Jr., "The Use of the Bible in Christian Ethics," *Interpretation* 19 (1965): 149–62. See also his work, *A Survey of Christian Ethics* (New York: Oxford University Press, 1967).

[32]Long, "Bible in Ethics," 162.

[33]C. Freedman Sleeper, "Ethics as a Context for Biblical Interpretation," *Interpretation* 22 (1968): 443–60; also *idem*, "Language and Ethics in Biblical Interpretation," *Journal of Religion* 48 (1968), especially 304–10.

ences), to sources (a new appreciation for the concrete situation opened up by the symbolic character of biblical language), and to communication (the task of finding political and social symbols that convey to contemporary people the meaning of biblical and Christian faith). "We cannot expect to find biblical solutions to contemporary problems. . . . However, the exegesis [of the Bible] can clarify the way in which the biblical writers approached the problems of their own day."[34] In applying these steps to ethics, Sleeper has three levels to his third step of communication in which he proposes to:

(1) Explore the dynamic character of biblical language including "images" which may be defined as "the total impression of facts and values that we have in any area of our knowledge of our environment." (He would here note how ethical norms are inseparable from christological and anthropological concerns, how social and cultural forces shaped the New Testament and early Christianity and how the eschatology of the Bible impacted its ethics);

(2) Explore the relation between "images" of the Bible and "models" in the social sciences to see how "biblical images illumine the meaning of this structure";

(3) "Draw out the implications of biblical images for ethical theory"; yet, not in a reductionistic way to one norm, but one that preserves a variety of ethical insights.[35]

There are no policy or strategy decisions that can be obtained from the Bible. In fact, Sleeper warns, its normative quality lies in "its peculiar and important insights into the nature of human responsibility," not in the fact that "it proposes a distinctive ethical theory."[36]

The use of images, symbols, paradigms, signs, and the like occurs so frequently in these hermeneutical models for ethical decision and character that a word must be addressed to this analysis from our perspective. Will description of "the total *impression* of facts and values" deliver us from the questions of claim and authority that the Bible makes on us? Is this not an attempt to settle the place and role of the Bible in Christian ethics simply by relabelling the biblical ethical data? In O'Donovan's words: "The proposed programme for deriving a Christian ethic, starting afresh . . . and deriving our own norms . . . , is logically defective by the old formal canon that 'you can't derive an "ought" from an "is."'"[37] He goes on to say that we have either attached our own value-judgments

---

[34]Sleeper, "Language and Ethics," 305.
[35]Sleeper, "Language and Ethics," 305–9.
[36]Sleeper, "Language and Ethics," 310.
[37]O'Donovan, "Interpretation of Ethics," 72.

arbitrarily or we have correctly derived those which were already present. The assumption behind all appeals to the Bible—in whatever capacity—is that there is not a radical divorce between fact and value and that the Bible, even if it is judged to contain merely models, images, paradigms, or the like, must be an image or model of *some task*. Have the problems of time and particularity been overcome in these solutions? Or have they not just been obscured and removed by another step even granting the many insights provided in the meantime along the way?

The Bible Used as a Witness to God's Will

For Brevard S. Childs "the central problem for the study of Biblical ethics [comes from] within the Scriptures themselves. The issue turns on the question to what extent God's will has been made clear and unequivocal for his people."[38] In Childs's judgment, "the Biblical Theology movement failed in the end to provide an adequate theological approach to the Bible [in that it selected categories that] did not speak to the burning issues of the day. . . . The relation of the Bible to questions of social ethics remained a nebulous one. . . . In spite of the great interest in ethics, to our knowledge, there is no outstanding modern work written in English that even attempts to deal adequately with the Biblical material as it relates to ethics."[39]

There were a number of ethical treatises that attempted to fill the gap, but biblical scholars themselves provided very little material that the ethicists could use in their field. Usually these treatises, continued Childs, fell in one of three groups in their attempt to use the Bible. For one the Bible provided little more than the *atmosphere* of ethical concern; for others the Bible served as a *backdrop* consisting of simple directives vis-à-vis the tough complexities of the modern world, while on occasions some moral theologians did attempt to relate their ethical principles to the Bible but not without an awkward system of casuistry. More recently the activistic wing of the church, says Childs, has tended to drop all appeals to the Bible and have replaced it with an appeal to intuition, conscience, or the welfare of the community.[40]

How then does the Bible aid the Christian in making concrete ethical decisions? There is a tension between some biblical texts (e.g., Deut. 30:11,14; Mic. 6:6–8) that imply that God has indeed made his will clearly known to his people and other texts that seem to say that the will of God is not to be taken for granted or received as a cognitive given, but

---

[38]Brevard S. Childs, *Biblical Theology in Crisis* (Philadelphia: Westminster, 1970), 126.

[39]Childs, *Biblical Theology,* 124.

[40]Childs, *Biblical Theology,* 124–25.

learned by doing, testing, discerning, and understanding that will. Thus the will of God can be known through:

(1) "clear, straightforward imperatives";
(2) "seeking and inquiring after God" and a confrontation of God himself; and
(3) an "extreme amount of freedom in bearing witness to the eternal will of God" with "elements of extreme particularity" not to "be deduced from an ethical principle."[41]

Childs summarizes his point this way: "It is of fundamental importance to recognize that at no point within the Bible is there ever spelled out a system or a technique by which one could move from the general imperatives of the law of God, such as [are] found in the Decalogue, to the specific application within the concrete situation."[42]

There are two approaches, then, to the biblical tradition when Scripture is read *in* the community of believers—and, according to Childs, the Bible does not function as Scripture apart from that community! First, it may "sketch the *full range* of Biblical witnesses" in the canon on a particular ethical issue. Second, it may trace "the inner movement of the various witnesses along their characteristic axes" or "characteristic patterns" of thought on some of the Bible's favorite themes such as impartial justice for the poor in court. "It is obviously a mistake to approach every issue with only one Biblical model in mind." But the study of the scope and inner structure of the biblical witness will uncover a number of "warrants" on different subjects and situations, none of which are infallible rules of thumb or eternal principles, but only time-conditioned testimonies to God's will. These warrants may provide: (1) a clear unequivocal imperative for some situations, (2) a set of guidelines where the polarities are set forth in two conflicting responsibilities, or (3) a sequence of priorities. Thus the movement from the past to the present, from the text to the ethical agony of decision is creative and filled with mystery and surprise instead of being a road lined with infallible propositions. Sometimes there will be a transparently fresh imperative; at other times the biblical warrant will only delimit the area in which the decision is to be made, while in other situations the Bible will offer us a "variety of alternatives for moral decisions" and in still other instances we will not know what to do except to wait and pray.[43]

The suggestions offered by Childs are certainly the strongest and most helpful we have seen. His appreciation and insistence on the full

---

[41]Childs, *Biblical Theology*, 126–29.
[42]Childs, *Biblical Theology*, 129.
[43]Quoted material taken from Childs, *Biblical Theology*, 132–38.

canon of Scripture, rather than a selected canon within a canon, is another advance in the field. It is the cure that is needed for conservative proof-texting and nonconservative text expunging. But it is Childs's pluralism that catches our eye: the canon offers not only a great variety of approaches to an issue, but, apparently, also answers to the same problem. One is left with the impression that only rarely does one gain a clear, fresh imperative from the Bible; more frequently we are presented with a wide range of alternatives from the text. Furthermore, the particularity of the text has left us with nothing more than the experiences of fellow-believers who can only "witness" (apparently in Barthian terms) to what God did for them or they did in regards to him. The questions of claim and authority have not, as yet, been fully addressed here. What is the authority status of the Old Testament? In what sense(s) is it to be equated with the divine will? What guarantees the validity of that equation? If we must design a grid or some criteria for distinguishing between the human and divine parts of the canon, must not we, or our grids, contain the infallibility we deny the apostles and prophets because of their human condition? Since the text was addressed always to someone in some setting, does that not raise the problem of the text's particularity so that I may not be addressed at all in any of the text, not even in the "clear, straightforward imperatives"? The questions are so basic and methodological in nature that we cannot stop with this solution.

The Bible Used as One Source Among Many

Charles E. Curran[44] outlines six important contributions that the biblical renewal movement has had on moral or ethical theology. These include: (1) the emphasis on a religious ethic emphasizing the saving intervention of God[45] (versus a Pelagian mentality picturing man saving himself by his own effort and works), (2) the primacy of a dialogical understanding of man responding to the covenant (in place of the older deontological [duties, obligations, imperatives] or even Thomistic teleological [ends, goals, outcome setting the standard] models), (3) the realization that *all* Christians and not just the clergy were called to perfection, (4) the emphasis on growth, development, and creativity instead of mere passive conformity to minimalistic laws, (5) the application of historical tools to trace

---

[44]Charles E. Curran, "Dialogue With the Scriptures: The Role and Function of the Scriptures in Moral Theology," in *Catholic Moral Theology in Dialogue* (Notre Dame: University of Notre Dame Press, 1976), 24–64.

[45]Curran credits two men for this achievement mainly in post Vatican II Catholicism: Bernard Häring, *The Law of Christ*, 3 vols. (Westminster, Md.: Newman Press, 1961, 1963, 1966) and Rudolf Schnackenburg, *The Moral Teaching of the New Testament* (1954; American version, New York: Herder and Herder, 1965), 13–53.

salvation history and the cultural and temporal limitations of Scripture, and (6) the stress on inferiority and the total person.

But there were limitations to the use of Scripture. Said Curran, ". . . biblical ethics is not the same as Christian ethics. . . . The biblical renewal has emphasized the historical and cultural limitations of the Scriptures so that one cannot just apply the Scriptures in a somewhat timeless manner to problems existing in different historical circumstances. In addition the Scriptures were not really confronted with many of the moral problems we face today." "What might be a valid and true norm in biblical times might not be adequate today." Accordingly, ". . . the Scriptures are not the sole source of ethical wisdom for the Christian, but . . . Christian ethics also derives wisdom and knowledge from other human sources. This generic approach will rely on human wisdom and reason as well as the Scriptures. . . ."[46]

In general, the contribution of Scripture will be greater on questions of stance (the structure of Christian experience) and model (in Curran's case the choice of responsibility and relational ethics over deontological or teleological) than more specific ethical considerations in the decision-making process.[47]

To reply briefly, we can only ask why should Scripture be used with heavier weight in decisions of the *whole* of ethical structure, but with lesser on the *parts* of ethical decision? What or who is to vouch for the relevance and utility of the stance and general model, especially when what was valid and normative in that day may not be normative today? If it is only theological and ecclesiastical commitments that mandate this necessary framework, why should we attempt to mix this model by introducing an "authoritative" Scripture and even a canon from within that canon? all of which raises the question of authority and revelation all over again. Furthermore, if the Bible must be used within the confines of methodological safeguards, are not these methodological safeguards ultimately more authoritative than the Bible? In short, how can I be judge of the Bible and still have it be judge of me? That is a great feat if we can pull both of these tasks off at the same time in the same sense! No, reason and traditional wisdom are sovereign here and the Bible functions at best as an equal even if at times only a poorer second cousin.

The Bible Used as a Shaper of Moral Identity

The Bible's use in decision-making and action, argue Birch and Rasmussen, is not as significant or helpful as it is in character formation;

---

[46]Curran, "Dialogue with Scriptures," 37, 32, 53.
[47]Curran, "Dialogue with Scriptures," 55.

but it can and ought to be a major force in "molding perspectives, disposi-
tions, and intentions." This is not to say that the Bible has a singular,
normative meaning of Christian character in mind. It is only the *whole
Biblical panorama* rather than a specific type of biblical material that
effects this shaping process. The "gestalt nature of identity prohibits . . . every form of 'genre reductionism' [wherein] . . . only certain
kinds of biblical materials . . . are used."[48]

But when the Bible is used for decision-making issues, then specific
texts begin to come into play. The ways in which this can happen are that
the Bible may function as:

(1) The source of a norm such as "righteousness," "*shalom*,"
agape love, or be a norm in the sense of a theological category
(like covenant) which embraces many moral norms, or even
transforms a norm already used in the human enterprise;

(2) A source of setting "guidelines for locating the burden of proof
on a given moral issue";[49] and

(3) A source for establishing boundaries of moral behavior without
setting a single biblical norm ("Norm-reductionism").[50]

Thus Birch and Rasmussen conclude by stressing: (1) the diversity
of the Bible's ethical instruction, (2) the importance of the community as
the proper context for ethical decision, (3) the polarity and dialectical
nature of decision making, (4) the relational and response type model of
ethics, (5) the major role of creativity, freedom, and imagination in making
up our minds, and (6) the rich resources that exist for decision making in all
types of literary forms including apocalyptic, symbols, moral admonition,
accounts, images, and exemplary figures. One must be ready for the fact
that often there will be "no clear and straightforward moral point in this
textual presentation," but one can gain "insights," general illumination
and "a mind-expanding picture" stimulating us to creative vision.[51]

The accent of Birch and Rasmussen, as with the other five hermeneutical stances, is on diversity. Clearly, they are more comfortable
with a general and holistic use of the Bible in shaping character than they
are in the more difficult task of asking how specific texts affect specific
moral decisions. In this latter category the Bible offers more general
themes, provides overall boundaries and loosely guides the decision
maker. But we must ask again how can we appeal to the *whole* if we find
the *parts* too specific and temporally conditioned?

---

[48]Birch and Rasmussen, *Bible and Ethics*, 107, 109.
[49]Birch and Rasmussen, *Bible and Ethics*, 116.
[50]Birch and Rasmussen, *Bible and Ethics*, 115.
[51]Birch and Rasmussen, *Bible and Ethics*, 121.

SUMMARY

From even this brief and merely programatic chapter it is clear that most ethicists are moving away from a deontological and teleological type of moral theory in favor of a responsibility and response type. It is also increasingly clear that Scripture is not viewed as supplying the content (whether propositional or conceptual) for ethical character or decision making. More popularly it is viewed as presenting a set of witnesses (either to the mighty acts of God in history or to the person of Christ himself) or a set of images. However, both models are bedeviled by internal problems of the model's own making!

For example, how can the community or individual receive the biblical *claim* of a witness to the person or the events in Scripture while pretending to not notice a similar claim to propositional revelation in the same canon? Can such selectivity and reductionistic revelation be defended in all fairness to the Bible?

Likewise, will an appeal to images and symbols or to the total impression that a text makes deliver us from facing the questions of particularity and claim? The necessary association of fact and value, whole and its parts also calls for some justification when we attempt to utilize one without the other. Even if the image and symbolic value is granted, which may indeed apply in some contexts even if not in the whole, is there not implicit a universal or some normative stance behind the image? It must be an image or model of some type of moral character or of some ethical task.

Modern men and women are much too frightened by all attempts to raise the question of propositional truth or unity of thought within a discipline. Of course there are risks, but it is foolish to think that one has avoided all the risks and served the interests of truth best by favoring minimalistic, piecemeal, and relational solutions. Each of the solutions contains aspects of the truth, some much more than others, but most are trying to go from the "is" of the Bible to the "ought" of ethical theory—and it will not work. Somehow and in someway Christian ethicists are going to need to grapple with the ethical and moral materials of the Bible (in all their genre) seriously and exegetically in detail or finally give up altogether on the chimera that there is any connection between the Bible and ethics.

Chapter 4

Exegetical and Theological Principles in Old Testament Ethics

Christian ethics will continue to be possible only where ethics and the Bible go together. Setting one against the other could lead to disastrous consequences—especially in those Christian communities that confess *sola scriptura*. There just are no two ways about it; the church, if she is to continue to be Christ's church, must come to terms with the Scriptures to which he pointed and affirmed "these are the Scriptures that testify about me" (John 5:39), "Scripture cannot be broken" (John 10:35), and "not the smallest letter, not the least stroke of a pen, will by any means disappear from the Law until everything is accomplished" (Matt. 5:18). To reject them or the sense in which they were intended is ultimately to reject him as Lord of his church.

While there is no royal route in moving from the Bible to particular ethical decisions, there is more in the Scriptures on this subject than just a basic orientation, stance, or vision of goodness focused in Jesus Christ. But when we attempt to move beyond this minimalistic affirmation, we are constantly hounded by questions about the *diversity* Scripture exhibits and its *time-conditioned* perspective. Before turning to four topics that speak more directly to the time-conditioned aspect of Scripture, a look at the charge of diversity would be in order.

The change that has taken place in biblical scholarship on this question since the middle of this century can be dramatically illustrated in both the Roman Catholic tradition and in the Ecumenical Movement. As recently as 1893, Leo XIII condemned the critical study of Scripture in his Encyclical *Providentissimus Deus* resulting in the Anti-Modernist Oath of 1910. But with the Encyclical of Pius XII in 1943 entitled *Divino afflante Spiritu*, Catholic scholars began to enter into critical biblical studies, with full encouragement coming in the Second Vatican Council of 1962–65 and the decree of that council, *De Ecumenismo*. This opened up cooperation in ecumenical studies and led to a new exploration in biblical criticism.

The pace was accelerated when the Ecumenical Movement turned the attention of the World Council of Churches to the twin problems of interpretation and the authority of Scriptures. The result was a document entitled "Guiding Principles For the Interpretation of the Bible" that was produced in 1949 at Wadham College, Oxford, and two years later included in a collection of essays. The significant fact about this report for our purposes is that the Bible was considered as a unity and it was still possible in 1949 and 1951 to speak about *the* biblical message. The last sentence of the first section (of four) says: ". . . any teaching that clearly contradicts *the* [emphasis added] Biblical position cannot be accepted as Christian."[1] Precisely so! Our point in this volume is exactly where the ecumenical church bodies stood at the middle of this century.

This understanding seemed to come to an end however in the lecture given by E. Käsemann at the Faith and Order Movement of the World Council of Churches meeting in Montreal in 1963. He concluded that "No romantic postulate, dressed up as a salvation history, can relativize the sober fact that the historian simply cannot speak of an unbroken unity of New Testament ecclesiology."[2] "This lecture caused quite a commotion, . . . [for] it was felt that to emphasize the irreconcilable diversity of the canon could only have negative results. It [was] curious to see how theological thought [had] completely changed direction in only a few years."[3]

Four years later, at the Faith and Order Meeting at Bristol in 1967, we learn that "The awareness of the differences in the Bible will lead us towards a deeper understanding of our divisions and will help us to interpret them more readily as possible and legitimate interpretations of one and the same Gospel."[4] The accent of the Bristol report fell on the diver-

---

[1]The collection was entitled *Biblical Authority for Today*, ed. Alan Richardson and Wolfgang Schweitzer (London: SCM, 1951), 240–43, cf. also Ronald H. Preston, "From the Bible to the Modern World: A Problem for Ecumenical Ethics," *Bulletin of the John Rylands Library* 59 (1976–77): 164–87. The quotation is from p. 241.

[2]As cited by Ellen Flesseman-van Leer, "Biblical Interpretation in the World Council of Churches," *Study Encounter* 8, no. 2 (1972), 3.

[3]Flesseman-van Leer, "World Council," 3–4.

[4]Flesseman-van Leer, "World Council," 4.

sity of the Bible as seen in its various traditions and the layers of tradition there. But this only raised the crucial question of an appropriate set of criteria to decide between the traditions and layers. Once again, the questions of truth and authority reared their heads and begged for some fair analysis from biblical scholars.

The Louvain Report came in 1971, and the results only sealed what Käsemann had started. Flesseman-van Leer stressed these points:

1. The Bible does not possess authority as a matter of course . . . [Its] authority . . . depends on the fact that it is experienced as such.
2. Biblical testimonies do not all carry the same weight of authority for us, partly because they do not all speak to us with the same force, and partly because some testimonies focus on the Christ-event, while others point to it less directly.
3. What was included or excluded from the canon was defined by tradition . . . [so] the boundary between canonical and non-canonical writings "is not a hard and fast one . . . but more a matter of fluid boundary."
4. The Bible offers a number of varying interpretations of God's redeeming acts in Israel and in Jesus Christ . . . [so that] our contemporary interpretation process is in fact simply "the prolongation of the interpretative process" which begins in the Bible itself. . . .
5. We cannot say a priori that the Bible is inspired. Only if and in so far as the biblical testimonies have proved themselves to be authoritative can we confess . . . they are inspired. . . .[5]

Our response to this case for diversity in the Bible is the same as that of Ellen Flesseman-van Leer: "The Louvain Report attempts to create a measure of order in this diversity by indicating the mutual relationship, from the point of view of the contents, among the various witnesses. To say that every testimony is in some way related to the Christ-event as 'centre' (or, in the case of the Old Testament, one could say related to the covenant) is too general and obvious to mean anything."[6] Indeed, we shall be reduced to a few meaningless platitudes if we do not come to terms, not with a theologically imposed unity or even a material center, but with the biblical author's own claims to be in a continuing conversation with antecedent books,[7] themes, and history. Only after we have taken the text and its claims on its own terms and examined the evidence for those claims will

---

[5]Flesseman-van Leer, "World Council," p. 7. Cited in part from *Faith and Order, Louvain*, 1971, World Council of Churches, Geneva, 9–23.

[6]Flesseman-van Leers, "World Council," 7.

[7]See my case for a "canonical theological center" in Old Testament Theology, W. C. Kaiser, Jr., *Toward an Old Testament Theology* (Grand Rapids: Zondervan, 1978), 20–40.

we be ready to discuss the question of the unity of the Bible.

But how, we are asked, can we return to talk about "*the* biblical position" or a case for unity throughout the canon when we all agree that there was "progressive revelation." What is meant by "progressive revelation"?

PROGRESSIVE REVELATION

Both terms in this concept of "progressive revelation" are susceptible to a wide variety of meanings. Therefore, as James Barr declared, "Everything depends on what is meant by the term."[8] We hear less of the term today than in the past, James Packer opined, "because [recent theological fashions] are all, in their different ways, anti-evolutionary and anti-historicist. They view Scriptures functionally, as a means of revelation in the present, rather than as a revelatory record of a revelatory process in the past."[9]

There are four negative ways in which progressive revelation has been used:[10] (1) From a critical standpoint, the idea has been used to downgrade and label as unauthentic those elements scholars are skeptical about while it elevates what are regarded as the "higher" truths of Scripture. (2) From an apologetic standpoint, the term has been used as a rationale by which one could excuse and justify the more "primitive morality of the Bible by means of a later revelation that allegedly corrected it. (3) From a hermeneutical point of view, progressive revelation often became a slogan for the arbitrary and inconsistent process of selecting a few favorite teachings that would map out a path through the Bible highlighting what was worthwhile while regarding the rest of Scripture as "base" or "primitive." (4) Finally from a theological stance, progressive revelation was welcomed as a way of removing the focus of attention from divine disclosure and attaching it instead to human insight, discovery, and genius.

All of this is too convenient. Even C. H. Dodd, who devoted chapter thirteen of his book *The Authority of the Bible* to this theme, noted the dilemma in the four views adopted above (even though he paralleled their

---

[8]James Barr, *The Bible in the Modern World* (New York: Harper and Row, 1973), 144. On this subject one must carefully read H. S. Curr, "Progressive Revelation," *Journal of Transactions of the Victorian Institute* 83 (1951): 1–23; J. B. Mozley, "The End Test of a Progressive Revelation," in *Ruling Ideas in Early Ages and Their Relation to Old Testament Faith* (New York: Dutton, 1878), 222–53; and D. L. Baker, "Progressive Revelation," *Two Testaments, One Bible* (Downers Grove, Ill.: InterVarsity, 1976), 76–87.

[9]James I. Packer, "An Evangelical View of Progressive Revelation," in *Evangelical Roots: A Tribute to Wilbur Smith*, ed. Kenneth S. Kantzer (Nashville: Nelson, 1978), 143.

[10]This analysis is dependent on Barr, *Bible in Modern World*, 145; and Packer, "Progressive Revelation," 146–47.

views very closely). He said: "Thus there may be successive revelation, but can there be in the strict sense progressive revelation? If, on the other hand, the term 'progressive' is allowed its full ordinary meaning, is it not progressive *discovery* of which we are speaking, rather than revelation? In discovery men do advance from the erroneous to the true." Dodd felt it was only "a matter of verbal expression" to decide whether "men progressively discovered a revelation which in God's intention [was] eternally complete and unalterable, or that God himself proportioned the measure of his revelation to the stages of human progress."[11]

It is only Dodd's second alternative in this last sentence that I feel is worthy of the claims of Scripture.[12] Such an evolutionary and random selection of biblical materials, which lays such heavy emphasis on the human capacity to discover, is plainly inadequate. But there can be little doubt that the Old Testament is a series of successive divine revelations leading up to the grand disclosure in Jesus Christ. That was the point of the writer of Hebrews as he began his book: "In the past God spoke to our forefathers through the prophets at many times and in various ways, but in these last days he has spoken to us by his Son . . . " (Heb. 1:1–2). This phenomena can also be seen in our Lord's words to his disciples: "I have much more to say to you, more than you can now bear. But when he, the Spirit of truth, comes, he will guide you into all truth" (John 16:12–13).[13] Thus, we are not left to analogy or scientific models; we have an explicit statement of Scripture in the first citation, and our Lord's own promise of the New Testament canon to his disciples in the second.

It must be strictly observed, however, that while there is development and succession from the beginning to the end of revelation there is also perfection of revealed truth at all stages in the process, even though that perfection often may only be a perfection in seminal form with an incipient potentiality for increasing clearness and fullness in the progress of revelation and history. It is as Geerhardus Vos described it: "The organic nature of the progression of revelation . . . [includes the] absolute perfection at all stages. . . . The organic progress is from seed-form to the attainment of full growth; yet we do not say that in the qualitative sense the seed is less perfect than the [grown] tree. . . . In the seed-form the minimum of indispensable knowledge was already present. . . . Again, revela-

---

[11]C. H. Dodd, "Progressive Revelation," *The Authority of the Bible*, 2d ed. (1929; reprint, New York: Harper and Row, 1958), 269, 277.

[12]See the case built by Packer, "Progressive Revelation," 148–52.

[13]This verse is used by C. S. Gerhard, "The Progressive Nature of Revelation," *The Homiletical Review* 25 (1893): 3–10. While he grants that "the truth . . . was germinally grasped and uttered by the apostles" (p. 7), yet what the apostles received were "seed thoughts" that "set their minds to working" (p. 3).

tion . . . does not proceed with uniform motion, but rather is epochal'. . . . The discovery of so considerable an amount of variableness and differentiation in the Bible [is not] fatal to the belief in its absoluteness." Instead, this only shows that truth carries with it "a multiplicity of aspects . . . [that it] is inherently rich and complex, because God is so Himself. . . . The truth having inherently many sides, and God having access to and control of all intended organs of revelation shaped each one of these for the precise purpose to be served."[14]

Daniel Lys fails to catch this point. To his way of thinking there are only three possibilities: (1) "either revelation is total at one point in history" (and it isn't) or (2) "revelation is fragmentary and progressive"—but in this case would it still be God's? or (3) "revelation is in each instance total, but repeated again and again"—in this case why history?[15] He correctly sees that both the Ebionite and Docetic heresy must be avoided—sacrificing either one term or the other, history or eternity. Daniel Lys's warning to those who stress the historical side at the expense of the revelational side is well spoken:

> It must be emphasized that it is not a dogmatic a priori that necessitates this judgment. But it is simply a scientific interpretation which wants to know what the author . . . meant to say. . . . It is in the very name of liberalism that it is necessary to accuse liberalism of ebionism every time when, on the pretext of scientific objectivity, it glosses over the primary claim of a text to be the revelation of the eternal Word of God through the temporal words of man, and instead places in the foreground [other alternatives]"[16]

But there is a fourth option that Lys missed. Revelation can be true, eternal in its source and organically or seminally perfect without yet being (1) complete in its statements or history, (2) fully developed in its supporting doctrines, or (3) fully apprehended by its listeners.[17] The fact that the germ had the complete gene potentiality for the full truth that was to come must be stressed. Only when this is realized does the conflict between

---

[14]Geerhardus Vos, *Biblical Theology: Old and New Testaments* (Grand Rapids: Eerdmans, 1954), 15–16. See the same use made of Vos's point in ethics by William Brenton Greene, Jr., "The Ethics of The Old Testament," *Princeton Theological Review* 27 (1929): 184–91.

[15]Daniel Lys, *The Meaning of the Old Testament* (Nashville: Abingdon, 1967), 29. See his whole discussion, pp. 28–39.

[16]Lys, *Meaning*, 38.

[17]These three general laws basically follow Greene, "Ethics," 184–91; Packer, "Progressive Revelation," 157; and James Orr, "The Progressiveness of Revelation-Moral Difficulties," in *The Problem of the Old Testament* (London: Nisbet, 1909), 465–78, especially pp. 471–77.

progress and revelation begin to suggest ways of being resolved. The historical process was a necessity and one event had to follow another to lead up to the climax in Christ. Likewise, the process of revelation was pedagogically graded for our learning as the race grew, studied, and profited from the former revelations. Hence the law prepared the way for the prophets, and the earlier prophets prepared the way for the later prophets. Finally, it was necessary for the demands of obedience to be proportioned to the development of the person or of the age. This, again, did "not mean that the standard of right, and so the divine nature, changes. . . . It claims only that no one may be expected to realize that in the standard which he cannot, so far as his mentality, *capacity* or his *opportunity* is concerned, appreciate. . . ."[18] Louis Matthews Sweet agrees: "Man . . . must learn gradually. This fact conditions all revelation . . . [therefore revelation] must be progressive, and since it must be progressive it must necessarily involve, in its earlier stages, the principle of accommodation. In order to gain access to man's mind it must take him where he is and link itself with his natural aptitudes. . . ."[19]

In some ways, J. B. Mozley's observation needs to be heeded:

> It is evident, then, that a progressive revelation . . . must be judged by its end and not by its beginning. . . . According to any rule of judging in such cases, the morality of a progressive dispensation is not the morality with which it starts, but that with which it concludes. The test is not the commencement but the result.[20]

So long as this is not understood as giving the case to teleological ethics, and so long as the imperfections noted in the ages are *descriptions* of the age's ability (or lack thereof) to follow the ethical teaching and precepts of the living God, we agree. Thus, the divine revelation can set forth a truth, bring about a relationship, and establish a principle, but it cannot guarantee the recipient a total comprehension of all that is involved or even a faithful obedience to any of its precepts, principles, or new relationships. Understanding and obedience remain bound up in the freedom and responsibility of a person's response. Thus, we must constantly distinguish between the germinal perfection of every new revelation of God, and the consciousness, state of heart, and the moral sensitivities of the culture into which that revelation was introduced.

We conclude by emphasizing the organic perfection and truthfulness of God in each and every revelatory event and disclosure of his Word:

---

[18]William Greene, "Ethics," 189–91.

[19]Louis Matthews Sweet, "Accomodation," in *International Standard Bible Encyclopedia*, ed. James Orr (Grand Rapids: Eerdmans, 1939), 1:31.

[20]J. B. Mozley, *Ruling Ideas*, 236–37.

yet, we also want to stress the fact that it was successive and truly in the context of history with all the humanness, primitiveness, error, and unevenness of growth that that fact implies. Only by carefully regarding these twin truths will we be able to properly assess the element of progressive revelation in Old Testament morality.[21]

PRINCIPLES FOR MORAL INTERPRETATION OF THE OLD TESTAMENT

Without attempting to be exhaustive, a brief treatment of some guidelines for dealing with Old Testament passages containing moral instruction might be beneficial at this point. Since we have a book that was written in the Ancient East, even though it was given by divine revelation, it will be noticed that the Oriental manner of presenting moral topics in a highly figurative style with frequent use of figures of speech is quite different from the Greek and Latin writers with whom we are more accustomed.

In particular, precepts are given in a popular, rather than a scholarly or philosophical style. The following set of principles will aid us in approaching many of these popularly cushioned precepts in accordance with the truth intentions of the authors.[22]

(1) Universal moral statements are frequently found in Scripture, however the expressions by which they are conveyed must often be understood with certain limitations found in the nature of the thing or various other circumstances. Some of the limitations and their examples are:

(a) Some universal or indefinite moral prescriptions often stress only the tendency of a thing to produce a certain effect even though that effect may not always necessarily take place. Thus in Proverbs 15:1, Solomon observes that "a gentle answer turns away wrath" even though in an obstinate and wicked man it may actually at times produce the opposite result.

(b) Other universal or indefinite moral prescriptions intend only to tell what generally or often takes place without implying that there are no exceptions to the rule. Proverbs 22:6 urges, "Train a child in the [or 'his'] way he should go, and when he is old he will not turn from it." This is indeed

---

[21]See an older attempt to trace this growth in Frederic Gardiner, "The Progressive Character of Revelation," in *The Old and New Testaments in Their Mutual Relations* (New York: Pott, 1885), 28–61.

[22]I am indebted to Thomas Hartwell Horne for many of the insights in this section. It appears in *An Introduction to the Critical Study and Knowledge of The Holy Scriptures*, 8th ed., rev. and enl. (New York: Carter and Brothers, 1858), 1:395–99.

the frequent consequence of wise parental education, but
the text does not mean to hold that there are no exceptions
to this rule or that there are no other intrusive factors that
could frustrate the good training laid down. Included in
this rule would be all characterizations of the manners,
virtues, and vices of particular ages, people, or nations.
Thus when Paul says, "nothing good lives in me" (Rom.
7:18), he is not implying that there is nothing morally good
in people, but that no one is by nature spiritually good in
the eyes of God.

(c) Other universal prescriptions state what *ought* to be done,
not what actually takes place always. Accordingly, Malachi
2:7 says, "the lips of a priest ought to preserve knowledge"
and Proverbs 16:10 affirms, "the lips of a king speak as an
oracle, and his mouth should not betray justice."

(d) Often moral precepts are set forth generally and absolutely
when they are to be taken with certain limitations. For
example, when we are told "do not swear not at all" (Matt.
5:34; Lev. 19:12), this does not forbid us from taking any
legitimate oaths in court or the like, for Moses urged in
another text, "take your oaths by his name" (Deut. 6:13) as
does Jeremiah (Jer. 4:2) and our Lord when he was adjured
by the high priest, in the name of the living God, to declare
whether he was the Christ (Matt. 26:63, 64). Our Lord did
not refuse the question put to him in this judicial form, but
he answered.

(2) Universal moral truths often must be understood *comparatively*
even though they are not cast in that form. Thus God "desired
mercy, not sacrifice" (Hos. 6:6; Matt. 9:13; 12:7) yet the sacrificial system was part of his revelation as well. This, then, must
be understood in terms of priorities and by way of saying, "this
first and then that" (cf. 1 Sam. 15:22; Ps. 51:17, 19; Jer.
7:22–23).

(3) Negative moral principles include affirmatives and affirmatives
include negatives so that when any sin is forbidden, the opposite duty is urged upon us and when any duty is encouraged,
its opposite sin is forbidden. So, when Deuteronomy 6:13 commands us to serve God, we are thereby forbidden to serve any
other god—without the text explicitly forbidding it. Likewise,
when we are commanded to honor our parents (Exod. 20:12),
we are forbidden to curse them. Stealing is prohibited (Exod.
20:15), but diligence in our job and whole tenor of life is therefore also set forth.

(4) Negatives are binding at all times and we must never do anything forbidden even though good may ultimately come from it (Rom. 3:8).

(5) Some moral precepts in Scripture will allow for exceptions in some situations on account of other duties or moral precepts that ought to predominate according to biblical instruction. Frequently Solomon laid down rules for putting up security for others (Prov. 6:1–2; 11:15; 17:18; 20:16). While he does not condemn the practice, which love, justice, and prudence might demand in some cases, he does urge us to avoid doing so rashly and without considering the person and his or her ability to pay off the debt.

(6) Changes in circumstances change moral things, therefore contrary actions may be taken in the moral realm on account of differences of circumstances. Thus in Proverbs 26:4–5 we meet two such approaches to morality: "Do not answer a fool according to his folly, or you will be like him yourself"; and "Answer a fool according to his folly, or he will be wise in his own eyes." But notice, we must pay attention to the *biblically* sponsored reason in each case. It is not a matter of *adiaphora* which rule we adopt—so long as it meets our need or some imagined higher value. These are not two inconsistent or even contradictory rules, but two distinct rules of conduct that will be severely observed, depending on which set of circumstances *noted in the text* are operable at the time. In one case we are advised to pay fools back in their own coin, with the aim of showing them their foolishness. But in other instances the best policy would be to avoid answering altogether to avoid playing the fool ourselves.

(7) It is important to distinguish between what is being described and what is being prescribed in the character, actions, and judgments of men, nations, and events in the Old Testament. Are these positive commands merely counsels and opinions of the participants in the historical drama unfolded in the Bible? Likewise, it is important to separate out those precepts or items that are merely circumstantial and temporary from what is abiding, essential, and therefore obligatory and permanent for all ages. This is the problem of the time-conditioned nature of many of the precepts in the Old Testament that we have already addressed earlier and to which we shall need to return in the actual discussion of many of the passages that are to follow.

This is by no means a complete list, but it does suggest that the interpreter has more to do than to merely assemble a set of texts based on one's prima facie reading of those texts. The exegesis of texts involving moral statements or principles can be extremely hazardous if these types of principles are not kept clearly in mind and if a good dose of common sense is not used along with all the usual skills and tools of interpretation.

SPECIAL FEATURES IN OLD TESTAMENT ETHICS

From time to time one Old Testament concept, or another, has been proposed almost as an "open sesame" that would simultaneously unlock the secrets of the Hebrew mind and language. Among those that have vied for recognition in this spot, whether they were credited with being *the* definitive concept or institution that would open the door to the rest of the riches of the Old Testament or not, are: corporate solidarity, individualism, talion, חֵרֶם or the "ban/curse," volitionalism (also objectivism or culpability) and imprecation (or prayers of cursing). While there is no need to propose any of these concepts as a central organizing theme for understanding the Hebrew mind or culture, there is a case to be made for studying each of these special features if we are going to be able to handle Old Testament morality properly.

Corporate Solidarity

In 1911 H. Wheeler Robinson introduced the term "corporate personality" into Old Testament studies,[23] but the idea had already presented itself to him in his 1907 *Century Bible Commentary* on Deuteronomy and Joshua. The Achan incident in Joshua 7 illustrated the "non-individualistic or corporate idea of personality." In Robinson's usage, however, we find that not only was the term itself objectionable, but also the content of the term was ambiguous since it meant, in J. W. Rogerson's view, at least two things: corporate responsibility and corporate representation.[24]

The source of Robinson's ideas owes more to Sir Henry Maine[25] and the writings of L. Lévy-Bruhl than to the Old Testament itself.[26] Initially, he was also stirred by reading J. B. Mozley's (*Ruling Ideas in Early Ages*) discussion on Achan's sin and visiting the sins of the fathers

---

[23]H. Wheeler Robinson, *The Christian Doctrine of Man* (Edinburgh: T. & T. Clark, 1911), 8.

[24]J. W. Rogerson, *Anthropology and the Old Testament* (Atlanta: Knox, 1978), 55. See also Rogerson's article, "The Hebrew Conception of Corporate Personality: A Re-Examination," *Journal of Theological Studies* 21 (1970): 1–16.

[25]Sir Henry Maine, *Ancient Laws*, 12th ed. (London: n.p., 1888), Robinson acknowledged this debt in his *Deuteronomy and Joshua* (Edinburgh: T. and E. C. Jack, 1907), 18.

[26]L. Lévy-Bruhl, *Primitive Mentality*, trans. Lillian A. Clare (London: Allen and Unwin, 1923) and *How Natives Think*, trans. Lillian A. Clare (London: Allen and Unwin, 1926). Robinson acknowledged this debt in his *The Cross in the Old Testament* (1926; reprint, London: SCM, 1955), 76.

upon the children. Mozley had spoken of a "defective sense of individuality which marked that age."[27] Accordingly, Robinson named this "defect" "corporate personality" and defined it on one occasion this way:

> . . . There is a fluidity of conception, a possible transition from the one to the many, and vice versa, to which our thought and language have no real parallel. When we do honor to-day to the 'Unknown Warrior', we can clearly distinguish between the particular soldier buried in the abbey and the great multitude of whom we have consciously made him the representative. But that clearness of distinction would have been lacking to an earlier world, prior to the development of the modern sense of personality. The whole group is a unity, present in anyone of its members.[28]

Robinson based his view of "corporate representation" (another title he used for the same phenomenon) on models of primitive mentality. Allegedly, primitives, and therefore the Hebrews, thought in a prelogical way in which they were not able to distinguish between different objects or between objective and subjective experiences and thus they had no clear limits to their own personality within the group. Only from the eighth-century prophets onwards do we find the rise of individualism, according to Robinson.

Many of the facts of the Old Testament seemed to fit, but they fit in a different sense than that supplied by Robinson. Rogerson correctly observed, "By corporate responsibility he meant that a member of a group could be held fully responsible for an action of the group, though he personally had done nothing, because he was not regarded as an individual."[29] There was another difference when he linked the inability of an individual to recognize personal responsibility with an alleged inability of Hebrews to define the exact limits of an individual life.[30] Both of these protests against individuality were, as we shall see, without biblical support.

For these key reasons,[31] we cannot adopt any view of personality,

---

[27]Mozley, *Ruling Ideas*, 87.

[28]Robinson, *Cross in the Old Testament*, 77.

[29]Rogerson, "Hebrew Conception," 6.

[30]Rogerson, "Hebrew Conception," 7.

[31]There has arisen a large body of literature critiquing Robinson. Some are: Herbert May, "Individual Responsibility and Retribution," *Hebrew Union College Annual* 32 (1961): 107–20; Barnabas Lindars, "Ezekiel and Individual Responsibility," *Vetus Testamentum* 15 (1965): 452–67; J. R. Porter, "The Legal Aspects of the Concept of 'Corporate Personality' in the Old Testament," *Vetus Testamentum* 15 (1965): 361–80; M. Rodriguez, "Collective Responsibility," *New Catholic Encyclopedia* (New York: McGraw-Hill, 1967) III: 1002–3; and P. M. Joyce, "Individual Responsibility in Ezekiel 18?" in *Studia Biblica* (Sixth International Congress on Biblical Studies); ed. E. A. Livingstone (Sheffield, 1979): 185–96 [Journal for the Study of the Old Testament] Supplement Series, 11.

primitiveness, or conflicts between individualism and collectivism. In fact, there is no biblical case that can be built for a gradually emerging individualism that replaces or obscures the previous emphasis of the corporate group. Jeremiah and Ezekiel were not responsible for the start of individualism, for there had always been a case for both the individual and one's identity in the group throughout the whole Old Testament. Therefore, we will affirm both and use the term "corporate solidarity" instead of Robinson's "corporate personality."

There are at least three factors involved in defining solidarity. The first is *unity*. The whole group was often treated as a single unit as in 1 Samuel 5:10–11. There the people of Ekron in Philistia complained, "When the ark of God came to Ekron, the Ekronites cried out saying: 'The ark of the God of Israel has been brought around to *me* to slay *me* and *my* kin'" (italics added). The word "people" is treated in the Old Testament both as a singular and plural.[32]

The second factor can be seen in a single *representative* figure who often embodies the whole group. There are two extremes to be avoided here, the extreme of mere "collectivism" that is a simple combination of all the individuals, and the extreme of psychologism in which the individual is only a psychical whole who relates to the psychology of the group or the psychology of the individual. The most celebrated example of the legitimate use of this category is that of the Suffering Servant.

The third factor is the *oscillation* from the representative to the group where the individual was the embodiment of the group and the group was treated as an individual. The classic case of this phenomenon in Scripture is that of Achan who sinned when he took the banned items, yet the text clearly affirmed, "*Israel* has sinned" (Josh. 7:11; italics added) even though it is Achan who says, "*I* have sinned" (Josh. 7:20; italics added).

Thus the solidarity of the Old Testament must not be confused with: (1) a "collectivism" of a totalitarian type in which the individual is sacrificed for social ends or goals or (2) a "corporate personality" in which the individual has no consciousness of being an individual. Solidarity in the Old Testament is rather: (1) where the individual is able to implicate the whole group either in blessing or reprobation or (2) where the whole group is able to function as a single individual through one of its members who was designated as a representative of that group.[33]

Some examples of solidarity are: (1) of blessing because of the link between the one and the many—on Isaac for Abraham's sake (Gen.

---

[32]Cf. Lev. 17:4; 20:3, 6 for singular. For the plural cf. Gen. 17:14; Exod. 30:33, 38; Lev. 7:20.

[33]Note also the shifts from expected plural pronouns to singular pronouns in Gen. 44:4–9; Exod. 34:15; Num. 20:14–21; Deut. 7:25; 8:19; 14:21.

26:2–5); on Judah for David's sake (2 Kings 8:18ff.; 19:34); on Obed-Edom's household for the ark's sake (2 Sam. 6:11ff.); thus "the righteous man leads a blameless life; blessed are his children after him" (Prov. 11:21; 14:26; 20:7); (2) of reprobation because of solidarity—on the wives and children of Korah, Dathan, and Abiram (Num. 16:1–33); on the nation because of Saul's violation of the Gibeonite treaty (2 Sam. 21:1–13); and on whole cities because of an insufficient number of righteous men (Gen. 18:23–32); (3) of the interchange between the group and the representative individual in that group—in the "I" of many Psalms, the Servant of the Lord in Isaiah, and the "My Son, my Firstborn" of all Israel and Christ (Exod. 4:22; Hos. 11:1; and Matt. 2:15).

The ancient principle of Deuteronomy 24:16 ("Fathers shall not be put to death for their children, nor children put to death for their fathers: each is to die for his own sin") states the individual responsibility condition very clearly; however, since there are more factors in the outcome of virtue or calamity in a world of sin than just the nature or quality of a person or a nation, other aspects must be taken into account. "A single word, or a single incident, may bring out one side of the truth more than the other, but both sides must be remembered in any study of the thought and teaching of the Bible."[34]

Individualism

"The view that personal responsibility was originally unknown in Israel cannot . . . be considered correct: and a reference to the history of 2 Sam. xxiv, where the people were punished because of David's sin, is no proof, either; for 2 Sam. 9ff . . . makes it very clear . . . that David is certainly [also] punished individually. . . ."[35]

The central chapter usually raised in the discussion of individualism in Old Testament ethics is Ezekiel 18. This chapter, however, sets forth no new doctrine, but combats a fatalistic view of life engendered by self-pity and a one-sided emphasis of moral collectivism or corporate solidarity. The chapter opens with the famous proverb: "The fathers eat sour grapes, and the children's teeth are set on edge."[36] Verses 5–20 set forth alternative

---

[34]H. H. Rowley, "Individual and Community," *The Faith of Israel* (London: SCM, 1956), 106. See Rowley's excellent analogy of a fruit tree whose harvest depends on more than the nature or quality of the tree; there may be storms, frosts, or other things not of its own doing that circumvent the nature and quality of the tree and prevent it from bearing (p. 111).

[35]Th. C. Vriezen, *An Outline of Old Testament Theology*, 2d ed. (Newton; Mass.: Branford, 1970), 386.

[36]The sour grapes proverb of Jer. 31:29–30 makes a totally different point. There Jeremiah uses it to support his view of the present situation and then promises a removal of the basis for this complaint in the new age.

responses of three generations under the picture of three men in three different generations: (1) a righteous man (vv. 5–9), (2) his wicked son (vv. 10–13), and (3) his righteous grandson (vv. 14–17). From verses 21–29, Ezekiel examines what happens if: (1) the wicked man repents of his sins and does what is just and right (vv. 21–23, 27), and (2) a formerly righteous man turns to sin (vv. 24–26; cf. 33:10–16).

P. M. Joyce has set forth the position that the point being made in Ezekiel 18 is not a case for individual responsibility for sin. Instead, ". . . only the moral independence of generations is being asserted." "The message of Ezk. 18 is not 'Individual Responsibility' but the urgent need to accept responsibility as such. In fact, I would go further and say it is not a negative, retrospective concept of 'responsibility' which is in the author's mind at all, but rather the urgent need for response, in other words, repentance."[37] Joyce is not as convincing in answering the question why the argument of Ezekiel 18 happens to be developed in terms of examples given in the singular.[38] Vriezen's answer is to be preferred, ". . . a man may be held responsible both as an individual and as a member of the community, even if he is not directly guilty personally. . . . The two may be put on a level: the people may be considered as a unity and the individual members together may be addressed with a plural form."[39]

The idea that collectivism or group solidarity thinking dominated Israel's thought patterns until Ezekiel (18:20) and Jeremiah (31:29f.) abandoned these ways of thinking was, and still is, established dogma for most scholars. Some, however, have managed to break out of this mold and correctly argue that the individual always had a large place in the life and thought of the people.[40] Individual responsibility, value, worth, and importance is firmly grounded in the Old Testament doctrine of the image of God. Even though many place this doctrine late in the critical reconstruction of sources ("P"), in its canonical setting it comes at the head of the Old Testament texts and could explain why there is such a strong emphasis on God's interaction with individuals on a personal level—not just the heroes like Abraham, Isaac, Jacob, Moses, et al., but with his involvement with an

---

[37]Joyce, "Individual Responsibility," 187, 191. May, "Individual Responsibility," 110, says twenty of the twenty-three uses of שׁוּב, "repent" in Ezekiel are found in three passages, 3:17–21; 18:1–32; 33:1–20.

[38]Joyce, "Individual Responsibility," 187, 191. These represented a literary use of the terms of the priestly law . . . "to explore the problem of the suffering of the nation at the hands of the Babylonians," p. 192.

[39]Vriezen, *Outline of Theology*, 186–87.

[40]S. J. B. Wolk, "Individualism," *Universal Jewish Encyclopedia* (New York: Ktav, 1944), 5: 559–63 places the roots of individualism in the equality and human freedom in the desert, in the Sinai treaty, and experience of slavery in Egypt. See also Vriezen, *Outline of Theology*, 418–22.

Egyptian slave like Hagar (Gen. 16) and the righteous individuals in Sodom (Gen. 18). The existence of individual responsibility and value long before the age of the writing prophets is also seen in the Book of the Covenant where the death penalty was inflicted only on the offender (Exod. 21:12, 15, 16, 18, 20, etc.). Moreover, the principle of Deuteronomy 24:16 stated the general principle in most clear terms: "Fathers shall not be put to death for their children, nor children put to death for their fathers; each is to die for his own sin."

This rule was put into practice on at least one occasion. The Judean King Joash was assassinated in a palace conspiracy (2 Kings 12:20), but when his son Amaziah was firmly in control of the government, "he executed the officials who had murdered his father the king. Yet he did not put the sons of the assassins to death in accordance with what is written in the Book of the Law of Moses where the LORD commanded: 'Fathers shall not be put to death for their children, nor children put to death for their fathers: each is to die for his own sins'" (2 Kings 14:5–6).

Certainly, collective punishment involving group solidarity did appear, but these cases involved either collective guilt (where all the city is drawn into idolatrous worship by certain good-for-nothing fellows, Deut. 13:12–16), breaking of an oath (with the Gibeonites in 2 Sam. 21), or complicity and involvement in the crime of the royal house against Naboth with no repentance in the interim by any of the royal family (2 Kings 10:1–11; cf., 1 Kings 21). Both individual responsibility or worth and group solidarity must be understood and carefully defined in approaching Old Testament ethics.

Talion or Retaliation

Lex talionis, "law of the tooth," or the "law of retaliation" as many have referred to it, is the law found in the Pentateuch, "eye for eye, tooth for tooth" (Exod. 21:23–25;—its fullest statement; its shorter forms are, Lev. 24:19–20; Deut. 19:21). This enactment was never intended to give to individuals the right to work their own private justice and revenge for their own injuries. In Exodus, it is clear that this law had its setting in the covenant code (Exod. 21–23) which was addressed to the "judges" (Exod. 21:22, פְּלִלִים; or in 22:8, 9, אֱלֹחִים) who were to give "judgments" (Exod. 21:1, מִשְׁפָּטִים). These laws were given to the civil magistrates as precedents to guide them in cases of civil dispute.

The *talion* principle (Exod. 21:23–25) simply stated is "life for life." It is found in this stereotyped expression as a rule of thumb for civil magistrates to make sure that the restitution matched the loss perpetrated in the crime. It was simply to match the loss, but not to exceed it or fall short of it. "An eye for an eye and a tooth for a tooth" urged restitution; never retaliation. Commentators, both liberal and evangelical, err when they depict this principle as either a literal law or as allowing personal vendetta or retaliation. Rushdoony explains it this way:

> In modern law, the term restitution is usually replaced by "compensation" or "damages." But the significant difference is this: in Biblical law, the offender is guilty before God (and hence restitution to God, Num. 5:6–8), and before the offended man, to whom he makes direct restitution, whereas in modern law the offense is primarily and essentially against the state. God and man are left out of the picture in the main.[41]

Even in those cases where life was literally involved, Numbers 35:31 apparently permitted a substitution in order to ransom the offender's life in every capital punishment case except the one case of willful, premeditated murder. Since that involved such high despite to God and to his image in the offended victim (Gen. 9:6), capital punishment was necessary if men and women were to avoid offending God and ultimately demeaning the full value, worth, and dignity of persons made in his image.

It is to be granted that the principle of retaliation was known and apparently used by other Semitic peoples of the Ancient Near East. The Code of Hammurapi, for example, has a long section (laws 196–214) treating various cases of assault and injury. Some of these cases apply the talion principle, especially when the offense is against a nobleman, while the same offense (e.g., destroying an eye or breaking a bone) done against a commoner or slave only drew a small monetary punishment.

Interpreters must guard against two distortions in the *talion* principle: (1) the transfer to private life what belonged solely in the courtroom, and (2) the abuse of this provision to justify personal vindictiveness and aggrandizement.[42]

Vengeance

Vengeance and revenge are ideas popularly associated with the Old Testament and usually they are contrasted with the more enlightened conceptions of God and man in the latter prophets and especially in the New Testament. The most (and practically only) definitive study of vengeance and the Hebrew root for this word (נָקַם) was done by George E. Mendenhall.[43]

---

[41]Rousas John Rushdoony, *The Institutes of Biblical Law* (Nutley, N.J.: Craig, 1973), 274.

[42]John Murray, *Principles of Conduct*, 174.

[43]George E. Mendenhall, "The 'Vengeance' of Yahweh," *The Tenth Generation* (Baltimore: Johns Hopkins University Press, 1973), 69–104. See also now Elmer B. Smick, "Vengeance," *Theological Wordbook of the Old Testament*, ed. R. Laird Harris, Gleason L. Archer, Jr., and Bruce K. Waltke (Chicago: Moody, 1980) 2:599. Cf. on קָנְאָה, "zeal," Albrecht Stumpff, "Zeal in the OT and Judaism," *Theological Dictionary of the New Testament* 2:878–80: Henry McKeating, "Vengeance Is Mine: A Study of the Pursuit of Vengeance in the Old Testament," *Expository Times* 74 (1963): 239–45.

Of the seventy-eight passages in the Old Testament where the root נקם appears, fifty-one involve Yahweh as actor.[44] The classical statement of God's use of vengeance is in Deuteronomy 32:35,41: "It is mine to avenge . . . I will take vengeance on my adversaries."

Basically, there are two ways in which God takes vengeance with regard to his people. First, he is their champion against their enemies (Ps. 94). Second, he punishes the covenant-breaker (Lev. 26:24–25).[45] But what is common to both usages is his use of power,[46] whether internal or external, against all forms of unrighteousness and injustice. There was no idea of repayment in kind or of unrestrained human passion. Instead the germane idea is that of God's administration of justice is one in which he will vindicate his name, his holiness, and justice, as he rules the world with equity. In a triple statement of his vengeance, Nahum affirms that "the LORD is a jealous and avenging (נֹקֵם) God; the LORD takes vengeance (נֹקֵם) and is filled with wrath. The LORD takes *vengeance* (נֹקֵם) on his foes and maintains his wrath against his enemies. The LORD is slow to anger and great in power; the LORD will not leave the guilty unpunished." (Nah. 1:2–3, italics added). Thus, while God has held his ire in reserve for a long time, yet in this threefold mention of divine vengeance comes a warning that his holiness must finally express itself in disapproval of men and nations after they fail to live and act in his righteousness.[47] His anger is controlled; but he will direct it when, where, and against whom he will without indulging in carnal, hate-filled revenge. It will only vindicate his name. "The ascription to God of such anthropomorphic qualities as jealousy, vengefulness, and wrath, presupposes also a God who cares for his people. . . . The Israelites, knowing the human weakness for exacting a whole mouthful of teeth for a tooth [*Lex talionis*], asserted that 'vengeance belongs to God' (Deut. 32:35; Ps. 94:1; Isa. 34:8), because he alone was capable of repaying an injury with justice."[48]

חֵרֶם or the Ban

A most distinctive concept in the Old Testament was that of חֵרֶם, the "curse" or "thing dedicated to destruction." The word comes from the corresponding verb חָרַם, "separate"; hence a *ḥārem*, in Arabic, was an enclosure or a courtyard set aside for women; in Akkadian it was used to

---

[44]Mendenhall, "Vengeance," 82.
[45]Smick, "Vengeance," 599.
[46]Mendenhall, "Vengeance," 83.
[47]Walter A. Maier, *The Book of Nahum* (St. Louis: Concordia, 1959), 149–54.
[48]Joseph L. Michelic, "The Concept of God in the Book of Nahum," *Interpretation* 2 (1948): 203–4.

refer to a sacred prostitute. But it always carried the significance of a separation.[49]

חֵרֶם ("ban") occurs about eighty times in the Old Testament; it does not appear in Ugaritic, but all the other Semitic languages use it. For example, lines fourteen through seventeen of the Moabite Stone state that King Mesha of Moab "devoted" (*ḥārēm*) seven thousand inhabitants of the city of Nebo to his god Chemosh.

The spheres in which the "ban" or "thing(s) dedicated to God for destruction" operated were more than just in war. Exodus 22:20 declares "whoever sacrifices to any god other than the LORD must be destroyed [or 'be anathema']." Any object dedicated to the service of God was also חֵרֶם as can be seen from Leviticus 27:28. All such dedicated items were to be given to the priests or put in the sanctuary, but under no circumstances were they to be sold or redeemed by substituting something else for them (Num. 18:14; Ezek. 44:29). More frequently the idea is a compulsory dedication of that which impedes or opposes God's work. Accordingly, the Israelites promised to devote all the spoils of southern Canaan if God granted victory to Israel in Numbers 21:2–3. Other cities so "dedicated to destruction" in battle include Jericho (Josh. 6:21), Ai (Josh. 8:26), Makkedah (Josh. 10:28), and Hazor (Josh. 11:11). In fact, any city that harbored idolaters was to be anathematized or dedicated and put under the ban (Deut. 13:12–15). The rationale for such treatment of these cities is given in Deuteronomy 7:2–6.[50]

Since קָדַשׁ, "to be holy," also has the root idea of separation, חֵרֶם ("ban") and קָדַשׁ ("to be holy") must be distinguished. One text that brings both ideas together is Leviticus 27:28–29.[51] חֵרֶם ("ban") was set apart involuntarily and hence "put under the ban" for God's distinctive use while קָדַשׁ ("to be holy") was a voluntary setting apart, and therefore something that was holy. Malachi closes the Old Testament canon in English with חֵרֶם ("ban") as its final word. It is a warning, lest God must come and take a "forced dedication" for men and women who have refused to give a voluntary one.

LAW AND GRACE

Gerhard von Rad assessed our dilemma properly, "It is beyond question that God's will as expressed in law was announced to Israel. . . .

---

[49]Johannes B. Bauer, "Ban," *Sacramentum Verbi*, ed. Johannes B. Bauer (New York: Herder and Herder, 1970), 1:55–57.

[50]Abraham Malamat, "The Ban in Mari and the Bible," *Biblical Essays* 40–49.

[51]Leon Wood, "חָרַם," *Theological Wordbook of the Old Testament* (Chicago: Moody, 1980), 1:324–35.

But the question of how it is to be understood theologically, of how Israel herself understood this demanding will of God in the various phases of the history of her faith, is still far from being satisfactorily cleared up. Yet, for the value which Christianity has to put on the Old Testament much depends upon the answer."[52]

The most common misconception of the purpose of the law is that Old Testament men and women were brought into a redeemed relationship with God by doing good works, that is, by obeying the commands of the law, not through the grace of God. The truth of the matter is that this reading of the text will not fit the biblical evidence.

The history of the Old Testament revolves, for the most part, around three covenants: the Abrahamic, the Sinaitic, and the Davidic covenants. The substance of these three covenants occupy a great deal of the Old Testament writer's attention and exhibits common material and concerns. However, most Old Testament scholars link the Abrahamic and Davidic covenants on royal grant types of treaties.[53] Moshe Weinfeld demonstrated that the "royal [or divine] grants" made to Abraham and David with their promise of "land" and "house" (dynasty) were unconditional gifts that were protected and assured even if subsequent sins intervened. The gift might then be delayed or *individually* forfeited, but it had to be passed on to the next person in the line. Thus for Abraham and David, God's covenant was an "everlasting covenant" even though there might arise some undeserving rascals who would not be able to *participate* in the benefits of that covenant though they were obligated to *transmit* those same gifts on to their children.

But the Sinaitic covenant is placed on a different footing even though it shares much of the same substance with the Abrahamic and Davidic promises. It is not modeled on royal grant treaties, but on a vassal treaty form. To be sure, the vassal's obligations to obey in order to enjoy the benefits of this covenant are much more prominent.

Several cautions must be raised at this point. First, both the Abrahamic and Davidic covenants also required obedience: obedience was no spiritual luxury which the grace and goodness of the one bequeathing the grant had removed. While the recipients did not earn these benefits, neither did they participate in them if they sinned and fell out of favor with the grantor. The best they could do in that sad event was to pass on these

---

[52]Gerhard von Rad, *Old Testament Theology*, trans. D. M. G. Stalker (New York: Harper and Row, 1965) 2:390.

[53]Moshe Weinfeld, "The Covenant of Grant in the Old Testament and in the Ancient Near East," *Journal of the American Oriental Society* 90 (1970): 189–96. On this whole problem see W. C. Kaiser, Jr., *Toward an Old Testament Theology* (Grand Rapids: Zondervan, 1978), 59–63, 156–57.

gifts to their children. They would participate in them if they walked in truth, otherwise it could skip their generation also. Second, "obedience to the law is not the source of blessing, but it augments a blessing already given."[54] "Only after the historical preface to the covenant document has affirmed that Yahweh's grace came first, does the list of Yahweh's demands upon Israel begin."[55] The grace of God is the atmosphere and context into which the Decalogue is cast, for its prologue states: "I am the LORD your God, who brought you out of Egypt, out of the land of slavery" (Exod. 20:1). Likewise, before the specifications and stipulations of Deuteronomy 12–26 begin, Deuteronomy 1–11 lays the groundwork for such obedience by recording Moses' sermons on the great redemptive actions of God in history that brought this covenant into existence. Blessing would indeed come after obedience, but not as a "merited legal reward for the achievement of obedience to the law."[56] The pattern in the Sinaitic covenant was, as Gordon Wenham has observed, ". . . God's choice (1) precedes man's obedience (2), but man's obedience is a prerequisite of knowing the full benefits of election (3)."[57] Each of these three steps can be illustrated, as Wenham has, with a text like Exodus 19:4–5: "You yourselves have seen what I did to Egypt, and how I . . . brought you to myself" [(1) what God has done so far]. "Now if you obey me fully and keep my covenant" [(2) Israel's obligation], "you will be my treasured possession" [(3) a promise of fuller benefits is added for obedience, but in the context of a grace already received and begun].

Accordingly, "the priority and absoluteness of God's grace are constantly reiterated."[58] The law, then, must not be viewed as an abstract, impersonal tractate that stands inertly over the heads of men and women. It was, first of all, *intensely personal*. God spoke from heaven so all the people could hear his voice (Deut. 4:32–34: "Has any other people heard the voice of God speaking out of fire, as you have, and lived?"). The ultimate motivation for doing the law was to be like the Lord—in holiness (Lev. 20:26) and action (Deut. 10:17–19; 14:1–2; 16:18–20). The covenant aims to establish a personal relationship, not a code of conduct in the abstract.

The law, in addition, was that which *made living possible*. Without it, people could not live at all. They choose human laws, or the laws of the

---

[54]Gordon Wenham, "Grace and Law in the Old Testament," *Law Morality and the Bible*, eds. Bruce Kaye and Gordon Wenham (Downers Grove, Ill.: InterVarsity, 1978), 5.

[55]Norbert Lohfink, "Law and Grace," in *The Christian Meaning of the Old Testament*, trans. R. A. Wilson (London: Burns and Oates, 1968), 108.

[56]Lohfink, "Law and Grace," 108.

[57]Wenham, "Grace and Law," 6.

[58]Wenham, "Grace and Law," 10.

nations and thus they sinned against the Lord their God (2 Kings 17:7–8). And when Israel failed to live by this law, Yahweh graciously sent prophets as his representatives to urge the people to return not only to the "Law that I commanded your fathers to obey," but also the law "that I delivered to you through my servants the prophets" (2 Kings 17:13). There was a difference between having life and having and living it more abundantly.

Third, God loved the people he had redeemed from Israel so thoroughly that he attached *blessings and curses* (Lev. 26 and Deut. 28) to his law. His was no disinterested love, but one that seeks and finally turns the attention of his rebellious benefactors by the very circumstances of life. However, it would be well with them if they obeyed, for the extension of the benefits they were already receiving would increase and go beyond all they had received so far (Deut. 5:16). On the other hand, the curses were never God's final word. Even after Israel had broken the covenant and experienced the worse possible effects, Yahweh would ultimately restore the people yet once again (Lev. 26:40–45).[59]

Thus we see that grace is always the soil in which the law must take root, and law is the natural outcome and the only appropriate response to so high a calling and privilege. Even in the Abrahamic and Davidic covenants there were requirements laid down as the fruit of a resident faith. For example, circumcision became a sign of the covenant in which those who obeyed participated (Gen. 17), but circumcision never became the grounds or the meritorious basis on which faith or personal relationship with God was bestowed. Faith was or was not already present—circumcision did not change that fact.

---

[59]James Barr, "Some Semantic Notes on the Covenant," *Beiträge zur alttestamentlichen Theologie: Festschrift für W. Zimmerli*, ed. H. Donner (Göttingen: Vandenhoeck, und Ruprecht, 1977), 33 argues that *all* biblical covenants are eternal as cited by Wenham, "Grace and Law," 23. Cf., however, Ronald Youngblood, "The Abrahamic Covenant: Conditional or Unconditional?" in *The Living and Active Word of God: Studies in Honor of Samuel J. Schultz*, eds. Morris Inch and Ron Youngblood (Winona Lake, Ind.: Eisenbrauns, 1983), 31–46.

PART II
SUMMARIZING MORAL TEXTS
IN OLD TESTAMENT ETHICS

Chapter 5

The Decalogue: Exodus 20:1–17; Deuteronomy 5:6–21

It is difficult to exaggerate the importance and the significance of the Ten Commandments for Old Testament ethics. Its profundity can be easily grasped in its comprehensiveness and simplicity of expression. It is at once the very heart and kernel of a complex system of legislation that follows and elaborates on it.

This penchant for reducing a maze of moral details into a limited set of principles is not limited to the two accounts of the Decalogue in Exodus 20 and Deuteronomy 5. There are at least seven other summaries to which the Jewish community have regularly pointed. These are: the eleven principles of Psalm 15 (cf. Ps. 24:3–6);[1] the six commands of Isaiah 33:15; the three commands of Micah 6:8; the two commands of Isaiah 56:1; and the one command of Amos 5:4; Habakkuk 2:4; and Leviticus 19:2. Jesus himself continued this same tradition by summarizing the law in two principles, "'Love the Lord your God with all your heart and with all your soul and with all your mind'. . . . And a second is like it: 'Love your neighbor as yourself.' All the Law and the Prophets hang on these two commandments" (Matt. 22:37–40; Luke 10:26–28; cf. Deut. 6:5 and Lev. 19:18).

In spite of its marvelous succinctness, economy of words, and com-

---

[1]John T. Willis, "Ethics in a Cultic Setting," in *Essays in Old Testament Ethics*, ed. James L. Crenshaw and John T. Willis (New York: Ktav, 1974), 147–63.

prehensive vision, it must not be thought that the Decalogue was inaugurated and promulgated at Sinai for the first time. All Ten Commandments had been part of the law of God previously written on hearts instead of stone, for all ten appear, in one way or another, in Genesis. They are:

The first, Genesis 35:2: "Get rid of the foreign gods."

The second, Genesis 31:39: Laban to Jacob: "But why did you steal my gods?"

The third, Genesis 24:3: "I want you to swear by the Lord."

The fourth, Genesis 2:3: "God blessed the seventh day and made it holy."

The fifth, Genesis 27:41: "The days of mourning my father are near."

The sixth, Genesis 4:9: "Where is your brother Abel?"

The seventh, Genesis 39:9: "How then could I do such a wicked thing and sin against God?"

The eighth, Genesis 44:4–7: "Why have you stolen my silver cup?" (RSV)

The ninth, Genesis 39:17: "[Joseph] came to me to make sport of me . . . but . . . he ran. . . ."

The tenth, Genesis 12:18; 20:3: "You are as good as dead because of the woman you have taken; she is a married woman."

Of course, not every one of these illustrations are equally clear, for the text does not pause to moralize on the narratives, but each would appear to add to the orders of creation already given in the first chapters of Genesis.

INTRODUCTION TO THE DECALOGUE

The term "decalogue" can be traced to Exodus 34:28, "he wrote on the tablets the words of the covenant—the ten commandments," and to Deuteronomy 4:13, "he declared to you his covenant, the Ten Commandments." These "ten words" were distinguished from the rest of the law of God in that they were delivered in an audible voice by God himself and then later written by God on two tables of stone.

"The Reformed Churches regard verses 4–6 as the second commandment and verse 17 as the tenth, while the Lutheran and Roman Catholic communions consider verses 3–6 as the first commandment and divide verse 17 to obtain the ninth and tenth commandments. Jews have traditionally associated verse 3 with verses 4–6, as a part of the second commandment, regarding only verse 2 as the first." A small problem with this division of the tenth commandment arises when it is noted that in Exodus 20:17 the coveting of one's "house" occurs *before* the coveting of a "wife" whereas the order is reversed in Deuteronomy 5:21. Thus the ninth commandment in Lutheran and Catholic communions will vary depending on whether Exodus or Deuteronomy is used. There will also be a transposition of the sixth and seventh commandments in the Septuagint and Philo. In fact, Mark 10:19 and Luke 18:20 also place the prohibition on adultery (our seventh) *before* that of murder (our sixth). On the other hand, the Septuagint of Deuteronomy 5:17–18 and Matthew 19:18 preserve the usual Hebrew order of the text.[2]

INTERPRETATION OF THE DECALOGUE

The interpretation of the Decalogue is not especially difficult, but there are a few observations that should be borne in mind. They include:

(1) The law has a loving spirit in its prologue as well as in the main body of the commands. A course of action ought to be taken because it best reflects the character, nature, and will of God.

(2) The Decalogue could have been stated positively throughout as well as negatively, for moral law is always doublesided. Every moral act is at the same time also a refraining from a contrary mode of action that could have been taken.

(3) Merely omitting or refraining from doing a forbidden thing is not moral at all, otherwise a command could be fulfilled by sheer inactivity, which in the moral realm is just another name for death.

(4) Consequently, when an evil is forbidden in one of the commands, its opposite good must be practiced before one can be called obedient.

(5) To reject virtue is to choose vice, thus the absence of positive moral action has the force of rejecting that value or virtue.

(6) A command is never fulfilled either by the mere refraining to engage in an act (e.g., murdering) or by a single act of positive aid. Therefore we will not only refrain from injuring our neighbor, but we will do all that is in our power to contribute to the life and well-being of our neighbor.

(7) The command speaks not only to acts and attitudes, but to any and all incentives, enticements, or pressures that lead up to a thing forbidden.

(8) Since it is easier to state in fewer words a command in a negative form, and since that negative form strives to meet the strong current of evil in the human heart, most of the Dec-

---

[2]For more details see W. C. Kaiser, Jr., "Decalogue," *Baker's Dictionary of Christian Ethics*, ed. C. F. H. Henry (Grand Rapids: Baker, 1973), 165–67.

alogue takes this form. But our freedom in grace is so large that it would be difficult to give a set of moral prescriptions in the positive form with the scope and succinctness with which the Decalogue is presently cast.

These observations should protect us from being too provincial, too petty, or too literalistic in our interpretation of the Decalogue.

Perhaps it would be helpful to comment on the grammatical form of these commandments. There are only three positive statements in verses 2–17 of Exodus 20—all without a finite verb. These are:

v. 2 "I [am] the Lord your God."

v. 8 "Remember [זָכוֹר, an infinite absolute] the Sabbath Day."

v. 12 "Honor [כַּבֵּד, a piel infinitive absolute, though it could also be a piel infinitive construct or second person singular piel imperative] your father and mother."

John J. Owens[3] has suggested that these three clauses might serve as the basis for dividing up the Decalogue into three sections and govern the other seven commands. In fact, in Deuteronomy 5:6–21, the commands are connected (unlike Exodus 20:2–17) by the conjunction וְ ("and") that suggests that they are all governed by the fifth commandment. If adopted, the phrases might be rendered:

1. I *being* the Lord your God . . .
   [therefore observe commandments one to three],
2. *Remembering* the Sabbath day . . .
   [therefore do vv. 9–11], and
3. *Honoring* your father and mother . . .
   [therefore observe commandments six to ten].

It would seem appropriate, therefore, to use this outline for discussing the Decalogue: (1) Right Relations With God (vv. 2–7), (2) Right Relations With Work (vv. 8–11), and (3) Right Relations With Society (vv. 12–17).

ANALYSIS OF THE DECALOGUE

The Lawgiver and his gracious act of redemption provide the context and the backdrop against which the "ten words" are given. The "I" (אָנֹכִי) is both emphatic and the subject; "Yahweh your God" is the predicate. The promise of Israel's deliverance from Egypt had been tied to Yahweh's name in Exodus 3:14 and 6:2. Now that the promise had become a reality, he proclaims his name yet once again with the giving of the law. This phrase, in whole or in part, occurs in Exodus 15:26; 20:5, 7, 10, 12 and

---

[3]John J. Owens, "Law and Love in Deuteronomy," *Review and Expositor* 61 (1964): 274–83.

23:19; but it never occurs again in Exodus or Numbers while Deuteronomy will use it over two hundred times.

The rest of the statement is "who brought you up out of the land of Egypt, out of the land of slavery." That will become one of the great formulas of Scripture and will appear over 125 times. But it will also demonstrate that grace arrived before commandment, law, or obligation were demanded.

The reason why the Decalogue can bind the conscience of God's men and women is: (1) these are the words of God, and (2) these are of the words of "your God."

Right Relations With God (vv. 2–7)

The highest duty of man is given in the first commandment: "You shall have no other gods before [or beside] me." Here, also, is the foundation for all morality, for we shall define morality as our conformity to the character and will of God. If God is supreme and without any competitors, then there will be no higher standard of obligation or object of pleasure, service, or praise.

Internal Worship of God. The phrase "before [or beside] me" (עַל־פָּנָי) is a most difficult phrase to translate.[4] The phrase apparently does not mean "except" me. Such phrases do exist in Isaiah's vocabulary, but they are idioms such as: "There is no God *apart from me* (מִבַּלְעָדַי) . . . there is none" (אֵין זוּלָתִי, Isa. 45:21), and "none besides me" (וְאֵין עוֹד, Isa. 45:6). But not one of these expressions was chosen in the Decalogue. So wide is the usage of the Hebrew words in Exodus 20:3 that several possible translations can be suggested. For example, the words may take a hostile undertone when in Genesis 16:12 it is said of Ishmael, "He will live *over against* all his kinsmen" (cf. also, Gen. 25:18; Exod. 20:20; Deut. 21:16). William Foxwell Albright translated it, "Thou shalt not *prefer* other gods to me."[5] In any case, the result is the same, "I will not give my glory to another" (Isa. 42:8).

Thus the first "word" takes aim at atheism (we must have a God), idolatry (we must have Yahweh as our God), polytheism (we must have the Lord God alone), and formalism (we must love, fear, and serve the Lord God with all our heart, soul, strength, and mind). The ground of all morality begins here.

External Worship of God. The second precept takes up the *mode* of worship and ascribing worth to God, just as the first described the *object*

---

[4]See the full discussion in Johann J. Stamm and Maurice E. Andrew, *The Ten Commandments in Recent Research* (Naperville: Allenson, 1962), 79–81.

[5]William Foxwell Albright, *From Stone Age to Christianity*, 2d ed. (New York: Doubleday, 1957), 297, n. 29.

of worship and *source* of morality. This word has two parts: the precept (vv. 4–5) and the penalty (vv. 5–6). The prohibition is clearly aimed against idolatry. But idolatry can be twofold: spiritual and internal or material and external. The former is forbidden in the first commandment while the latter is taken up here.

There are fourteen Hebrew words for idols or images,[6] but פֶּסֶל, "idol" (v. 3) probably refers to "gods of silver or gods of gold" (Exod. 20:23) as well as images carved from stone, wood, and those that later are made from metal. On the other hand, תְּמוּנָה ("resemblance" or "form") applies to any real or imagined pictorial representations of deities. This latter word was not meant to stifle artistic talent, because the command has reference to religious worship: God himself commanded Moses to make many artistic representations on the curtains in the tabernacle.

The actual proscription, "You shall not bow down to them or worship them," takes the form of a figure of speech called hendiadys where the two expressions are used to convey a single idea, that is, "to offer religious worship" and is only used where worship of foreign deities is forbidden.[7]

The sanction attached to this command begins with the magisterial reminder that "I, the Lord [Yahweh] your God, am a jealous God." The term "jealous" or "zealous God" (אֵל קַנָּא) must not be connected with such popular misconceptions as: God is naturally suspicious, wrongfully envious of the success of others, or distrustful. When used of God it denoted: (1) the quality in his character that demands exclusive devotion in order to properly acknowledge with whom men and women are dealing (Exod. 34:14, Deut. 4:24; 5:9; 6:15); (2) the attribute of anger that he directs against all who oppose him (Num. 25:11; Deut. 29:20; Ps. 79:5; Ezek. 5:13; 16:38,42; 35:11; Zeph. 1:18); and (3) the energy that he expends on vindicating his people (2 Kings 19:31; Isa. 9:7; 37:32; Joel 2:18; Zech. 1:14; 8:2). Thus jealousy is that emotion by which God is stirred up and provoked against whatever hinders the enjoyment of that which he loves and desires. The greatest insult that can be done against love (in this case, God's love for us, his people) is to slight it and to embrace a lesser, more base love. Such idolatry is also labelled spiritual adultery elsewhere in Scripture because it breaks the covenant between God and his people just as an adulterous partner breaks the marriage covenant. Such a tragedy excites the zealousness of God for the consistency of his own character and being. Accordingly, every form of neglect, substitution, or contempt for

---

[6]Robert Baker Girdlestone, *Synonyms of the Old Testament* (Grand Rapids: Eerdmans, 1956), 303–8.

[7]Stamm and Andrew, *Ten Commandments*, 86.

public and private worship of God is rejected in this second commandment.

When children repeat the crimes and sin of their parents, they give evidence that they hate God and accordingly they will earn the same punishment as their God-hating fathers. However, "Fathers shall not be put to death for their children, nor children put to death for their fathers; each is to die for his own sin" as Moses made plain in Deuteronomy 24:16. No *eternal* condemnation can be laid on either the parents or the children by the other party, even though God does often allow some *temporal* punishments to come to children for the sake of parents when the sin involves: (1) national guilt and shame ("I will punish the Amalekites for what they did to Israel when they waylaid them as they came up from Egypt"; [1 Sam. 15:2; several hundred years after the Exodus in Saul's day]), (2) final religious rejection of his message or messenger ("And so upon you [the generation of Jesus' day] will come all the righteous blood that has been shed on the earth, from the blood of righteous Abel to the blood of Zechariah son of Berakiah [end of Old Testament canon in Judaism], whom you murdered between the temple and the altar," Matt. 23:35), (3) fraud and extortion of another man's good name and property as in the case of Ahab's filching of Naboth's name and vineyard ("The royal princes . . . these men took . . . and slaughtered. . . . The LORD has done what he promised through his servant Elijah," 2 Kings 10:1, 7, 10; cf. 1 Kings 21:21–22, 29), and (4) giving occasion to the enemies of God to blaspheme his name ("by doing this [David's sin with Bathsheba] you have made the enemies of the LORD show utter contempt, the son born to you will die," 2 Sam. 12:14).

However, God does not always take this route in avenging the offenses of the fathers. Many children of wicked parents (such as Hezekiah, son of wicked father Ahaz, or Josiah, son of Amon) refused to walk in the path set by their parents and received, instead, only the blessing of God. Mercy is the more usual trademark of Yahweh and its benefits are much more lasting—to a thousand generations—than any poisonous effects of God-hating parents. The key to this passage, when the *full* formula is pronounced, is that Yahweh visits the sins of the fathers to the third and fourth generation *of those who hate him*. But his חֶסֶד, "covenantal love, mercy, lovingkindness, or loyal love," extends to thousands of *those who love him*.

Verbal Worship of God. From internal (first word) and external (second word) worship, we move to the profession of the mouth (third word) in the adoration of God. To "take up" (נָשָׂא) the name (שֵׁם) of Yahweh on one's lips "in vain" (לַשָּׁוְא) meant to "misuse" it, or to use it for no real purpose.

But before we examine in detail these key expressions, it is well to notice that "the foundation for all legal procedure involving so-called civil disputes is clearly in the third commandment, and it would certainly carry over its importance into the realm of criminal law."[8] "Where there is no fear of God, then the sanctity of oaths and vows disappears, and men shift the foundations of society from the truth to a lie. . . . To despise, abuse, or profane the oath is therefore an offense which denies the validity of all law and order, of all courts and offices, and it is an act of anarchy and revolution."[9]

What then is involved in the "name" of God? His name includes: (1) his nature, being, and very person (Ps. 20:1; Luke 24:47; John 1:12; cf. Rev. 3:4), (2) his teaching and doctrines (Ps. 22:22; John 17:6, 26), and (3) his ethical directions and morals (Mic. 4:5).[10]

The "vain" or "empty purposes" to which God's name may be put are: (1) to confirm something that is false and untrue, (2) to fill in the gaps in our speeches or prayers, (3) to express mild surprise, and (4) to use that name when no clear goal, purpose, or reason for its use is in mind, whether it be in prayer, in a religious context, or absent-mindedly invoked as table grace when no real heart, thankfulness, or purpose is involved. When God's name is used lightly, what will we do in times of great distress? Proverbs 18:10 says "the name of the LORD is a strong tower; the righteous run to it and are safe."

This is not to say that all oath-taking is sinful and wrong. Many passages, like Deuteronomy 6:13, affirm that we must swear by his name ("Fear the LORD your God, serve him only and take your oaths in his name.")[11] But these lawful oaths must be made, as Jeremiah 4:2 teaches, "in a truthful, just and righteous way."

In all, we are to work at possessing our own heart and letting it be overawed with the greatness and majesty of God. The rudiments of unlawful oaths begin with by-words, idle talk, and requiring all of our words be confirmed by power(s) above and outside of ourselves—as if our word in itself were not sufficient.

---

[8]J. R. Ingram, *The World Under God's Law* (Houston: St. Thomas Press, 1962), 46 as cited by Rousas John Rushdoony, *The Institutes of Biblical Law* (Nutley, N.J.: Craig Press, 1973), 111.

[9]Rushdoony, *Institutes of Biblical Law*, 111–12.

[10]See W. C. Kaiser, Jr., "Name," *Zondervan Pictorial Encyclopedia of the Bible* (Grand Rapids: Zondervan, 1975), 4:360–66.

[11]Cf. also, Ps. 63:11; Isa. 45:23; Jer. 12:16; Rom. 9:1; 1 Cor. 15:31; Phil. 1:8; Rev. 10:5–6). The grand objection to all oaths based on Matt. 5:34–37 and James 5:12 miss the point that our Lord is refuting the false tradition of the scribes and pharisees who permitted oaths if they were by any creature, or if they did not expressly use God's name or true statements were involved. Jesus responded by saying, do not swear unnecessarily or arbitrarily unless some just and cogent necessity constrains you.

Right Relations With Work (vv. 8–11)

The fourth commandment poses more difficulties than the other nine, yet it was given for the liberation, not the bondage, of humanity. People are summoned "to rest" and "cease" from their labors so that they might be free from the tyranny of themselves and their work. Thus, the sabbath is primarily a day of "rest" and *then* a day of worship.

Many have attempted to derive the Hebrew Sabbath from the Babylonian *šapattu/šabattu* (on the first, seventh, fifteenth and twenty-eighth days of special sacrifice). Very little can be established with certainty except the fact that the Semitic world may have shared common word roots that give separate witnesses to the same socio-religious oral traditions in their backgrounds.

Ceremonial Aspect.   This command is mixed; it is both moral and ceremonial: moral in that it requires of men and women a due portion of their time set aside for rest, for worship, and service of God; ceremonial in that it fixed that day as the seventh day. There are a number of different kinds of sabbaths enjoined in the Old Testament, and to a degree this commandment is temporal and not permanent in its hold over men and women.

Moral Aspect.   Two reasons are given in the text for memorializing this seventh day: one retrospectively looks back to creation (v. 11) and points to a theology of rest; the other pointed to that final day when a new exodus and a redemption, like the previous exodus from Egypt, would occur (Deut. 5:15). Its essence is a time for the restoration of all mankind and creation. It is the recognition that work is a gift of God and not a tyrannical demon that rules us. It is also the recognition that all time belongs to God and therefore he is Lord over both his creation and time.

Right Relations With Society (vv. 12–17)

Once again the text begins without a finite verb, but the context in which commandments six through ten were to be placed is now set, "Honoring your father and mother . . . you shall not . . . kill, . . . commit adultery, . . . steal, . . . lie, . . . or covet. . . ." Next to loving God with all of one's being came loving one's neighbor as oneself.

Sanctity of the Family.   What does it mean to "honor" one's parents? Based on the usage of the verb in the Old Testament, we may say it involves: (1) "prizing [them] highly" (Prov. 4:8), (2) caring and showing affection to them (Ps. 91:15), and (3) showing them respect, reverence, and deference (Lev. 19:3). When Ephesians 6:1 urges, "obey your parents," instead of "honor" them, it immediately and necessarily qualifies it with "in the Lord." Parents are to be shown honor, but nowhere are their words, or wishes, to become a rival or substitute for the will or Word of God!

The promise connected with this commandment is unique even though there is a sense in which all the commandments of God have the promise of life standing over them (Deut. 4:1; 8:1; 16:20; 30:15–16). The specific promise of long life in the land refers primarily to the land of Canaan and the people of Israel, for the Babylonian captivity of the people would be brought on, in part, by this failure to honor parents (Ezek. 22:7, 12, 15). Thus, the promise briefly introduces, as in the last commandment, a ceremonial or nationalistic note in its promise. Nevertheless, the application of this promise to the present-day individual is meant to give a new quality of life without creating a merit system by which we can gain eternal life.

The "universalizability" of this particular command can be seen from the contextual and grammatical dependency that this law has to the five that follow it. Therefore, "this command is very large and comprehensive . . . [and] extends itself to all that are our superiors,"[12] including governors, magistrates, teachers, pastors, and counselors who surpass us in wisdom and years.

Sanctity of Life. The sixth commandment proscribes killing. While Hebrew possesses seven words related to "kill,"[13] the word used here, רָצַח, appears only forty-seven times in the Old Testament. רָצַח is almost always used of killing a personal enemy, but it does not appear to be confined to intentional and premeditated murder. Some of the instances relate to the avenger of the blood of one guilty of manslaughter in Numbers 35:16, 25; Deuteronomy 4:41–43 and Joshua 20:3. However, without exception in the later periods it carries the idea of murder with intentional violence (Ps. 94:6; Prov. 22:13; Isa. 1:21; Hos. 4:2; 6:9; and Jer. 7:9).

The principle that joins murder and manslaughter of Numbers 35:16, 25; Deuteronomy 4:41–43; and Joshua 20:3 is that both incur blood guilt, both pollute the land, and both require atonement: execution for the murderer and the death of the high priest (natural demise) for manslaughter. רָצַח refers to: killing for revenge (Num. 35:27,30), assassination (2 Kings 6:32) and even once of a lion killing a man (Prov. 22:13). But it does not apply to killing beasts for food (Gen. 9:3), to defending one's home against nighttime invasion by burglars (Exod. 22:2), to accidental killings (Deut. 19:5), to execution of murderers by the state (Gen. 9:6), or involvement in wars such as are sometimes described in Israel's history.

The prohibition against murder does apply, however, to self-

---

[12]Ezekiel Hopkins, *The Whole Works of Ezekiel Hopkins* (Edinburgh: Black, 1841), 77.

[13]They are: חָמִית, "put to death;" הָרַג, "wholesale or vengeful slaughter;" קָטַל, "kill or cut off;" טָבַח, "slay animals;" זָבַח, "sacrifice animals;" and שָׁחַט, "slaughter of sacrificial victim."

murder (i.e., suicide), to all accessories to the murder (2 Sam. 12:9), and to all those who have the authority of a magistrate or governor, but who fail to use it to punish known and convicted murderers (1 Kings 21:19).

So sacred was life, that all violent forms of snatching it away caused guilt to fall upon the land—whether in a manslaughter case or that of premeditated murder—and must lead to yielding up another life. In the case of premeditated murder, there would be no atonement, that is "substitute" or "ransom," for the life of the murderer (Num. 35:31). Genesis 9:6 would explain why this is so. This one capital offense required the death penalty, but was unlike the other crimes that also had a capital punishment which allowed substitution. It was because humans are made in the image of God that capital punishment for first degree murder became a perpetual obligation. To kill a person was tantamount to killing God in effigy. That murderer's life was owed to God; not to society, not to the grieving loved ones, and not even as a preventative measure for more crimes of a similar nature.

The laws of the Pentateuch show how the sixth commandment was applied in practice. A man or animal that caused the death of another person was to be put to death (Exod. 21:12, 28–32). In another law, when two men in a brawl caused the death of a woman's fetus when she tried to intervene in the fight, the fetus is fully regarded as human and viable, and the life of the murderer is required (Exod. 21:22–25).[14]

Accidental homicide or manslaughter can be and is distinguished from calculated and deliberate, premeditated murder (Exod. 21:13–14; Num. 35:11; Deut. 19:4–13). Included in this legislation are warnings about dangerous animals (Exod. 21:29, 36), the need for parapets around roofs to prevent people from falling off (Deut. 22:8), and digging pits without covers so that men or animals might fall in them (Exod. 21:33–34).

The crimes calling for the death penalty were:

(1) premeditated murder (Exod. 21:12–14),
(2) kidnapping (Exod. 21:16; Deut. 24:7),
(3) adultery (Lev. 20:10–21; Deut. 22:22),
(4) homosexuality (Lev. 20:13),
(5) incest (Lev. 20:11–12,14),
(6) bestiality (Exod. 22:19; Lev. 20:15–16),
(7) incorrigible delinquency and persistent disobedience to parents and authorities (Deut. 17:12; 21:18–21),
(8) striking or cursing parents (Exod. 21:15; Lev. 20:9; Prov. 20:20; Matt. 15:4; Mark 7:10),

---

[14]On the basis of the Job 10:8–12; Ps. 51:5–6; and Ps. 139:13–16, we conclude that the child in the womb was regarded and valued as a human person and under the protection of his or her Creator.

(9) offering human sacrifice (Lev. 20:2),

(10) false prophecy (Deut. 13:1–10),

(11) blasphemy (Lev. 24:11–14, 16, 23),

(12) profaning the Sabbath (Exod. 35:2; Num. 15:32–36),

(13) sacrificing to false gods (Exod. 22:20),

(14) magic and divination (Exod. 22:18),

(15) unchastity (Deut. 22:20–21), and

(16) rape of a betrothed virgin (Deut. 22:23–27).

Only for the first crime, premeditated murder, was there a "ransom" or a "substitute" payment unacceptable (Num. 35:31), but presumably all the other capital crimes could be commuted as the judges determined. The death penalty marks the seriousness of these errors.

It is interesting to note that Ancient Near Eastern cuneiform law prescribes capital punishment for crimes against property, but in the Old Testament no crime against property warrants capital punishment. Once again, the point is that life is sacred, not things. Anything that aims at destroying the sacred quality of life is a capital offense against God.

Sanctity of Marriage. The sanctity of marriage is laid down in the seventh commandment. The punishment for adultery was death (Deut. 22:22) while the penalty for seducing a virgin was either the offer of marriage or money (Exod. 22:16; Deut. 22:28–29); consequently, adultery was distinguishable from fornication in the Old Testament.

The question of adultery never was merely a matter of violating another person's property; it was primarily a question of morality. Joseph thought his offer of involvement with Potiphar's wife would be "a sin against God" as well as Potiphar (Gen. 39:9) and Abimelech called it "great guilt" (Gen. 20:9).

As early as Genesis 2:23–24 a strong and basic case for a monogamous relationship was announced. The departures from this divine standard come almost immediately with Lamech (Gen. 4:19) who marries two wives, but the exceptions in the Old Testament are not so numerous or as normative in their practice as first impressions are bound to imply. Clearly, polygamy is another evidence of the fall of man. After Lamech, we could list in order: Abraham (handmaid Hagar, Gen. 16:1–2), Nahor (concubine Reumah, Gen. 22:20–24), Esau's son Eliphaz (concubine, Gen. 36:11–12), Jacob married two sisters each with a handmaiden (Gen. 29:15–30; 30:1–9), Esau had three wives of equal rank (Gen. 26:34; 28:9; 36:1–5),[15] and Gideon had "many wives" and at least one concubine (Judg.

---

[15]On the problem of the Ancient Near East phenomena of renaming persons on important occasions, and for a general orientation to the problems of the names of these wives and their fathers see provisionally C. F. Keil and F. Delitzsch, *The Pentateuch* (Grand Rapids: Eerdmans, 1956) 1:321–22.

8:30–31). Nevertheless, the most common form of marriage in Israel continues to be monogamy. In the entire book of Samuel and Kings covering most of the united and divided monarchy, the only recorded case of bigamy among commoners was Samuel's father with his two wives Hannah and Peninnah (1 Sam. 1:2). The kings of Israel and Judah followed for the most part the precedent set by Saul, David, and Solomon.

All the while, the wisdom books held forth the model of the monogamous family. The best case for marital fidelity in a monogamous relationship can be made from the brief allegory on the same in Proverbs 5:15–19. Drinking water from one's own well (a delicate, but clear figure of speech for the coital act in marriage) was to be reserved for one person alone—this water was not to be put out on the street! Then in terms reminiscent of the greatest theological tractate ever composed on the purposes, joys, and sanctity of marriage—Song of Solomon, the text urged couples to delight in each other's love and beauty.

The same case could be made for the frequent warnings about the seductress in Proverbs 1–9. Better by far was the woman of virtue in Proverbs 31:10–31. Likewise, the prophets continued to hold forth the image of marriage to one wife just as the wisdom books did. Some of these texts are: Hosea 2:4ff.; Isaiah 50:1; 54:6–7; 62:4–5; Jeremiah 2:2; and the whole chapter in Ezekiel 16.

Marriage was prohibited for certain close relatives (Lev. 18:6–18; 20:10–21; Deut. 22:30; 27:15–26). While most scholars agree that these laws have perpetual sanctity and that principles can be drawn from them extending the relationships for which marriage was expressly prohibited, even when they are not explicitly listed, there is little agreement on how far the degree of kinship or blood is to be extended. John Murray, for example, states "there is no warrant from Scripture (. . . whatever biological or eugenical grounds [there may be]) for . . . prohibiting the marriage of first cousins . . . not to speak of the prohibition within degrees farther removed, as in some ecclesiastical canons."[16]

One phrase, in particular, has given rise to much dispute. In Leviticus 18:18 there is the prohibition against taking a woman as "a wife to her sister" (אִשָּׁה אֶל־אֲחֹתָהּ). Does this mean that a man should not be a bigamist and be married to two women who are sisters at the same time "in her lifetime" (בְּחַיֶּיהָ), that is, while the first sister is "still alive"?[17] Or does the

---

[16]John Murray, *Principles of Conduct*, 53, n. 8.

[17]See also Murray's discussion, "Appendix B: Additional Notes on Leviticus 18:16,18," *Principles of Conduct*, pp. 250–56; also Charles Hodge, *Systematic Theology* (Grand Rapids: Eerdmans, 1952), 3:415–18. See also S. E. Dwight, *The Hebrew Wife* (New York: Leavitt, 1836), 105–27.

phrase mean, as in the thirty-four other instances of its usage in the Old Testament, "one to another"? S. E. Dwight is just as sure as Murray was that "marriage is prohibited between all *lineals* and all *collaterals,* of the *first* and *second* degrees, both by *consanguinity* and *affinity.*"[18] He found seventeen cases *expressly* prohibited in the Old Testament and added another sixteen by *implication* because they represented the same degree of affinity. He also concluded that since the law expressly forbade the marriage of a man and his sister-in-law (brother's wife), it just as certainly forbade it between a woman and her brother-in-law (sister's husband).[19] The resulting translation, which we believe to be correct, is: "Neither shall thou take one woman, or one wife, to another, to vex her, to uncover her nakedness beside the other, in her life-time."[20]

Another well-known text is Deuteronomy 24:1–4. It provided for the *regulation* of divorce without thereby either condoning it or relinquishing God's original, monogamous purpose in marriage. But in order to prevent wife-swapping, men were obliged to put in writing their oral declarations about the breakup of their marriages. This in turn protected the woman and kept her from being mere chattel. It did not, however, provide a tacit approval to this practice.

Sanctity of Property. The eighth commandment prohibits theft. Property was viewed in the Old Testament as a gift and stewardship from God; the Lord owned everything in heaven and earth (Pss. 24:1; 115:16) and he it was who entrusted it to others. Hence, no one could despotically enslave another by kidnapping him or usurp his claim to goods over that of its rightful owner.

Wealth and goods were, on the other hand, to be shared with the poor and weaker members of society. Every third year tithes were to be given to the Levite, the orphan, the widow, and the resident alien or immigrant (Deut. 14:28–29). Indeed, the corners of the field were to be left unharvested so that the poor could glean them (Lev. 19:9–10; cf. Ruth).

Should anyone be so poor that they would be forced to sell their land or themselves into slavery for collateral, that person or land was to revert to its original status and ownership in the sabbatical year (seventh year) and jubilee year (fiftieth year; Exod. 21:1–2; Lev. 25; Deut.

---

[18]Dwight, *The Hebrew Wife,* 102. The terms used here can be confusing. Lineals are direct descendants (e.g., parents and children), collaterals are related by blood but from different lines (e.g., cousins), consanguines are those who are related by blood, and affines are people who are related by marriage.

[19]Dwight, *The Hebrew Wife,* 125.

[20]Dwight, *The Hebrew Wife,* 118, his italics omitted.

15:1–18). Thus the distribution and unnatural accumulation of wealth was kept in fairly balanced check since the land, with its means of producing food and surplus goods, was the base line for the whole economy and this was shared equally.

Sanctity of Truth. The ninth commandment is a call for the sanctity of truth in all areas of life even though the Hebrew vocabulary reflects the legal process in Israel, namely, "false witness" (עֵד שָׁקֶר, in Deut. 5:18 עֵד שָׁוְא), and "to answer" (עָנָה) as in response to legal questions posed at a trial.

To despise the truth was to despise God whose very being and nature was truth. The reference to "lying" (כַּחֵשׁ) in Hosea 4:2 shows that this commandment had a broad application. Prohibitions against other false or unfounded statements are given in Exodus 23:1–2,7; Deuteronomy 17:6; 19:15–21; and 22:13–21.

Sometimes the distinction is made between partial truth and untruth.[21] Using the case of Samuel's question to Yahweh about "How can I go? Saul will hear about it [that I have come to anoint David] and kill me" (1 Sam. 16:2). The Lord's answer was, "Take an heifer with you and say, 'I have come to sacrifice to the LORD.'" (1 Sam. 16:2). Apparently Saul had forfeited his right to know *all* the truth; nevertheless, Samuel had no right to speak an untruth. Lying is always wrong, whether it is the midwives' lie (Exod. 1:17) or anyone else's lie. Scripture repeatedly warns against all falsehoods and commends truth-telling (Pss. 27:12; 35:11; Prov. 6:19; 14:15). Even failure to come forward as a witness is severely condemned in Leviticus 5:1.

Sanctity of Motives. The tenth word turns its focus inward and speaks to a quality of inner contentment. The word in Exodus is חָמַד, "to desire earnestly, to long after, covet" while the parallel passage in Deuteronomy 5:21 is הִתְאַוָּה, "to set one's desire on something." Instead of taking up another outward action, this commandment appeals to a state of mind and the inner instinct that lies behind all acts, thoughts, and words. Thus as Jesus taught: "For out of the heart come evil thoughts, murder, adultery, sexual immorality, theft, false testimony and slander" (Matt. 15:19). The evil of greed, covetousness, and inordinate desire is treated frequently in the New Testament (Mark 7:22; Luke 12:15; Rom. 1:24; 2 Cor. 9:5; Eph. 5:3; Col. 3:5; 1 Tim. 6:9–10; 2 Peter 2:3). The truth taught here is the same as Paul will teach Timothy: "Godliness with contentment is great gain" (1 Tim. 6:6).

---

[21]Murray, *Principles of Conduct*, 140.

Chapter 6

The Book of the Covenant:
Exodus 20:22–23:33

The title "Book of the Covenant" for the section, generally taken to be from Exodus 20:22 to Exodus 23:33, comes from Exodus 24:7. In this section human values are consistently elevated over material ones. As opposed to the apodictic formulation of the Ten Commandments ("thou shall . . .), Albrecht Alt[1] pointed out some years ago that these laws are mainly cast into a casuistic or case law form. Their key formal distinguishing marks are the use of the conditional particle, "if" or "when" (כִּי) followed oftentimes by an additional subheading introduced by "if" (אִם) and concluded with the apodosis. Besides the apodictic and casuistic law forms, some scholars have isolated a third type from among Alt's apodictic group. These are the "Hebrew participial laws," but they are actually unconditional and apodictic in function. They all begin with a Hebrew participle, are usually very brief (about five short words), and carry a capital punishment. They are found in Exodus 21:12, 15, 16, 17; 22:19, 20.[2]

---

[1]Albrecht Alt, *Essays on Old Testament History and Religion*, trans. R. A. Wilson (Oxford: Blackwell, 1966), 81–132.

[2]For example, see J. Philip Hyatt, *Commentary on Exodus* (Greenwood, South Carolina: Attic Press, 1971), 220–21. Julian Morgenstern, "The Book of the Covenant," *Hebrew Union College Annual* 7 (1930): 19–258 has four categories: (1) The דָּבָר ("speech") type which is concise, direct, in second person singular and deals with ritual principles (Exod. 20:23–26; 22:27–30; 23:10–19), the (2) מִשְׁפָּט ("judgment") type introduced by כִּי in the main condition with אִם for subordinate conditions and in the third person singular

Every indication is that the "Book of the Covenant" is very early, for they breathe the same ethos as that of several other ancient Near Eastern law codes. Yet, many of the biblical laws differ markedly from these parallel law codes[3]—especially in its use of the apodictic laws in the Ten Commandments and the heavy use of motive clauses.

There is no easy outline for dividing up the topics and sections of the covenant code. Probably the prologue (20:22–26; 21:1) and the epilogue (23:20–33) are most easily separated from the main body of material. My suggestion is that there are seven parts of the main body with this type of outline:

(1) Cases Involving Slaves (21:2–11),
(2) Cases Involving Homicides (21:12–17),
(3) Cases Involving Bodily Injuries (21:18–32),
(4) Cases Involving Property Damages (21:33–22:15),
(5) Cases Involving Society (22:16–31),
(6) Cases Involving Justice and Neighborliness (23:1–9), and
(7) Laws on Sacred Seasons (23:10–19).

THE PROLOGUE (20:22–26; 21:1)

Once again it is stressed that the fountainhead of law is God himself:[4] "I have spoken to you from heaven" (v. 22). A number of consequences flow from this basic observation: (1) all crimes against law that is an expression of the divine will is "sin"; (2) Israel is responsible not to a legislative body nor a human ruler, but to the sole legislator, God; (3) man's civil, moral, and religious obligations all are combined in a single corpus since all stem from God; and (4) life is not commensurate with property (since man was made in the image of God) and thus monetary

---

dealing with civil matters (mainly Exod. 21:1–22:13,16), (3) the חֹק ("decree") type which uses a participle in the protasis of the condition often with the third person singular imperfect strengthened by an infinitive absolute in the apodosis and dealing mostly with crimes or sins requiring the death penalty (Exod. 21:12–17; and 22:17–19 in a pseudo-חֻקִּים type) and (4) the מִצְוָה ("commandment") type which is usually in direct second person singular form amplified by an explanatory statement or motive clause and dealing with ethical matters or a civil law having ethical connotations to it (Exod. 22:20–23:9). M. G. Kyle, "A New Solution of the Pentateuchal Problem," *Bibliotheca Sacra* 75 (1918): 32–54 also distinguishes four types of law. It is apparent that Morgenstern's מִשְׁפָּט and חֹק types are Alt's casuistic and participial forms respectively. His first and fourth types are interesting, but not as clearly isolated in form so much as in subject matter.

[3]The most recent and comprehensive commentary on the covenant code is from Shalom M. Paul, *Studies in the Book of the Covenant in the Light of Cuneiform and Biblical Law* (Leiden: Brill, 1970).

[4]See Paul, *Covenant in Light of Cuneiform*, 37–40, for a fine discussion on this point and similar ones.

compensation or property settlements are absent from biblical legislation, but present in extrabiblical legal corpora.

It would appear to be odd to have a ritual or cultic law included in the prologue until this connection is observed: "since all of you heard me speaking from heaven, yet saw no visible form or representation: therefore totally abandon any thought of trying to embody me in any material image." Law, like life, begins with the worship of God and apart from any idols (cf. the second commandment). This was true not only for verse 23, but also the injunction against using a "tool" (literally "sword," חֶרֶב) to hew a stone altar—apparently to prevent anyone from turning it into an image or some other rival superstition.

The title of 21:1 came after the altar law (20:22–26). Since Exodus 22:18–23:19 consists both of moral and sapiental exhortations, along with ritual instructions, many limit this title to 21:2–22:17. But why not take it all the way up to 23:10?

It is clear that what is included in this section are "judgments" or "precedents" (מִשְׁפָּטִים) given for the magistrates to use in civil disputes. Set alongside of the Decalogue in the text, as we have it before us, the covenant code deals with the expression of the moral law as it was applied to temporal matters. Moreover, they were "set before" the people so that there was an openness in its promulgation designed to prevent the emergence of a special class of judges or jurists who could hold a corner on its substance and interpretation.

CASES INVOLVING SLAVES (21:2–11)

People, not property, were at the heart of Old Testament legislation. A good part of this legislation is concerned about the rights, limits of control, and personhood of slaves. Slavery in the Old Testament is not the horrible institution known by the same name in the modern western countries, for it often approximated employer and employee relationships, but there were aspects of it that were subject to abuse and the law spoke to these. Beside verses 2–11, 20, 26–27 in this chapter, significant teaching blocks of material on slaves also appear in Leviticus 25:39–43: Deuteronomy 15:12–18; and Jeremiah 34:8–22. Each has a slightly different set of circumstances: in Deuteronomy 15:12 the male or female slave is sold, while the slave sells himself into servitude in Leviticus 25:39 until the Year of Jubilee. That servitude is limited to six years in Exodus 21:6 and Deuteronomy 15:17.[5]

---

[5]The Hammurapi Law Code (No. 117) limits bondage to three years on an apparently higher standard of living and more productive economy.

Since the land could not be sold, it meant that the only collateral available to the Hebrews was their labor power. The debt could not extend beyond six years, when the sabbatical year came, and thus a limit was placed on debt ceilings and bondage service. After six years of service, the Hebrew (עִבְרִי)[6] went out "free" (חָפְשִׁי).[7] He or she was once again a "freeman" and "citizen" after the mandatory emancipation.

The juridical terms in this legislation can also be seen in "buy" (תִּקְנֶה, i.e., to acquire as one's own property),[8] "coming" (בּוֹא), and "going" (יָצָא), terms used for entering and leaving the status of a slave, as well as in the fact that a slave must leave slavery in the same marital status he entered or else the wife given to him while in slavery and any children coming from that union belonged to the master.[9] Another juridical term is "love" for one's master (cf. its juridical antonym in Deuteronomy 21:15–17 "hates"). If the servant prefers to remain in the working relationship he finds himself in, he may voluntarily request that the "judges" (הָאֱלֹהִים)[10] make this a permanent arrangement by a ceremony at the doorpost of the master's house in which his ear was perforated as a sign of this perpetual voluntary relationship.

Another pericope (21:7–11) dealt with a girl who was sold by her father, not for slavery, but for marriage. All the same, she was designated a

---

[6]Whether "Hebrew" is gentilic (see Moshe Greenberg, *The Ḥab/piru* [New Haven: 1955]), an ethnic name for a fellow Israelite (J. Philip Hyatt, *Commentary on Exodus*, 228), an appellative denoting a member of a social class, e.g., a foreign mercenary (M. P. Gray, "The Hâbirū-Hebrew Problem," *Hebrew Union College Annual* 29 [1958]: 135–202, Umberto Cassuto, *A Commentary on the Book of Exodus*, trans. Israel Abrahams [Jerusalem: Magnes, 1967], 265–66) is difficult to say for certain. If the term is related to Eber (Gen. 11:16) then it is "Hebrew."

[7]As early as 1926, J. Pedersen ("Note on Hebrew *ḥofšī*," *Journal of the Palestine Oriental Society* 6 [1926]: 103–5) saw a connection between Hebrew *ḥopši* and the social class *hupšu* found in the Rib-Addi Amarna correspondence from Byblos. See also I. Mendelsohn, "New Light on the *Ḥupšu*," *Bulletin of the American Schools of Oriental Research* 139 [1955]: 9–11 and N. P. Lemche, "The Hebrew Slave," *Vetus Testamentum* 25 [1975]: 139–42. They translate it as "freeman" or "citizen of a city-state." In note 63 Lemche conjectures that *hupšu* may be West Semitic for *muškēnum*, another client class.

[8]Paul, *Covenant in Light of Cuneiform*, 46, n. 7.

[9]Paul, *Covenant in Light of Cuneiform*, 48, n. 5. An exact parallel to v. 4 exists at Nuzu.

[10]See Cyrus M. Gordon, "אֱלֹהִים in its Reputed Meaning of Rulers, Judges," *Journal of Biblical Literature* 54 [1935]: 134–44 and A.E. Draffkorn, "Ilāni:/Elohim," *Journal of Biblical Literature* 76 [1957]: 216–24. The background for the Hebrew use of this word to mean "judges" reflects the quasi-juridical function of the house gods, *ilāni* at Nuzi where a person in Nuzi society had to swear before the household gods. Thus, it became a stereotyped formula for the court on those before whom the witnesses appeared in that court. F. Charles Fensham, "New Light in Exodus 21:7 and 22:7 From the Laws of Eshnunna," *Journal of Biblical Literature* 78 [1959]: 160–61 unconvincingly argued that the הָאֱלֹהִים was Yahweh and this ceremony took place at the door of the sanctuary.

"servant" (אָמָה)! Should the terms of this marriage not be fulfilled, the purchaser must allow the girl to be redeemed; she was not to be sold outside that family. Furthermore, she must always be treated as a daughter and a free-born woman[11] or a forfeiture clause was invoked in this breach of contract.

Truly, personhood is upheld and the institution of indentured slavery, indebtedness, and marriage contracts are all subject to the rights, worth, and value of a person.

CASES INVOLVING HOMICIDE (21:12–17)

Human life is so sacred that whoever assails it is subject to forfeiting his or her own life. Five different situations involving the value of another person's life are examined: unintentional manslaughter (v. 12), premeditated murder (vv. 13–14), striking a father or mother (v. 15), kidnapping (v. 16), and dishonoring one's father or mother (v. 17).

Again, it is because men and women are made in the image of God that these assaults on human dignity, worth, and life itself are viewed so seriously. They clearly contravene the divine order established by God. This does not argue, however, that the life of the accused is not also sacred. That is why the text insists on establishing intentionality as its criteria before deciding whether a person has deliberately plotted against the divinely esteemed and prized life of another person.

Accidental death (grievous and as blameworthy as it too may be in a different sense) is sharply distinguished from intentional murder in verses 13–14. The expression used in verse 13 is unusual: "But God lets it happen" (וְהָאֱלֹהִים אִנָּה לְיָדוֹ). Here is an event beyond direct human control, "an act of God," as it were.[12] Similar expressions of unintentionality can be found in Numbers 35:22–23, "without design" (בְּלֹא צְדִיָּה), "without seeing," or "inadvertently" (בְּלֹא רְאוֹת), "[though he was] not an enemy (לֹא־אוֹיֵב) and in Deuteronomy 19:4–5 "without knowledge" or "unwittingly" (בִּבְלִי־דַעַת). For all of these cases, there were places of asylum that later became cities of refuge (Num. 35:10–34; Deut. 19:1–13).

So serious, on the other hand, is deliberate murder that the unusual

---

[11]She must always be provided her "food, clothing, and marital rights" (עֹנָתָה). This third element is a *hapax legomenon*. S. M. Paul, "Exodus 21:10: A Threefold Maintenance Clause," *Journal of Near Eastern Studies* 28 [1969]: 48–53 suggests "oil or ointments" since this is the third item in many Sumerian and Akkadian lists. Cassuto (*Exodus*, 269) disputes the tradition "times of cohabitation" (cf. Greek τὴν ὁμιλίαν αὐτῆς) and conjectured instead "the conditions of her abode," or "her quarters."

[12]There is a similar expression for acts of providence in the Hammurapi Law Code: 249:38–39; 266:77.

first person reference intrudes into the code: "I will designate" (v. 13) and "my altar" (v. 14) Thus the gravity of the issue is further underscored since the only other place where direct address appears in the biblical corpus is in Exodus 20:2, 23.[13] Not even the sanctuary or God's altar were safe places of asylum for those guilty of first degree murder.[14]

The fifth commandment is reinforced in verses 15 and 17. The honor that was due one's mother or father was violated by any act of striking or cursing either one or both parents. The fact that both parents are mentioned together stresses their basic equality. The law did not allow more liberty in striking or cursing one's mother, under the pretense that she was a woman whose state allegedly was more demeaning in the Old Testament, than in striking one's father. No, both parents were owed equal respect and equal worth. To violate this commandment was to forfeit one's right to life—it was that serious a matter.

The fifth offense that was serious enough to call for the death penalty was kidnapping (v. 16). Notice that this was not a crime against property and is not listed in that section. Instead, it is an attack on life and ultimately on the image of God. To steal is bad enough; but to steal a human being is so wicked that it violates the basis of life itself.[15]

All five cases presumed on the abiding moral law that was announced in Genesis 9:6. An attack on man's blood, or for that matter his dignity, worth, and personhood, was an attack on the image of God, and this image set the standard and the value. In every case, except murder, however, there appears to have been a "substitute" or "ransom" since the former case is singled out as not being worthy of such an exception (Num. 35:31).

CASES INVOLVING BODILY INJURIES (21:18–32)

Five more cases are introduced in which the assault has left bodily injuries. It is once again apparent that the concern is with people and the value they possess as individuals. The cases involve: a debilitating injury as a result of two men fighting (vv. 18–19), a master striking his slave (vv. 20–21), a pregnant woman's labor that is prematurely induced when hit by two quarreling men (vv. 22–25), a permanent injury to a slave (vv. 26–27), and an ox goring people (vv. 28–32).

In the first example, a dispute between two men lead to one man

---

[13]As observed by Paul, *Covenant in Light of Cuneiform*, 64. He said 21:2, 23 [sic] is an obvious typographical mistake.

[14]See the illustration in 1 Kings 1:51; 2:28–34.

[15]Cf. Hammurapi Code, No. 14.

being confined to his bed and only later able to walk outdoors with the help of a cane or crutches. This injury will not carry the telionic punishment (Exod. 21:23–25) but the assailant must indemnify his opponent for his "loss of time" (שִׁבְתּוֹ, literally, "his sitting" or "his cessation"), loss of income, and all medical expenses.[16]

Another instance of an injury is the problem of a slave being chastised by his or her master (vv. 20–21). This law relates only to the legitimate use of the rod: should the master use any other instrument of chastisement, say a lethal weapon, the case would be treated under different laws and might result in the master being tried for murder.

The aim of this law was not to place the slave at the mercy of the master, but to *restrict* the master's power over his slaves. Simply put, proof was needed only of a master's malice or of his murderous intent. In cases where the slave lived "a day or two" after the chastisement, the benefit of doubt was given to the master only because proof became more difficult. But if the slave died immediately, no more proof was needed and presumably laws such as Exodus 21:12 would be operative.

The mere risk of jeopardizing one's investment—for it must not be forgotten that in the case of a fellow Hebrew, this was like a bank loan situation ("he is his property [or money]," v. 21)—was a powerful deterrent. Even the slightest injury to one part of the body entitled the slave to his full freedom and exemption from any further obligation to pay back the debt with his labor power (Exod. 21:26–27). Thus all disciplinary actions by a master had better be held in check or some would come within a hair's-breadth of loosing their shirts in a fit of temper! Hitting a master where it hurt—in the pocketbook—reinforced the value system that said people were more important than investments.[17] This law is almost unprecedented in the ancient Near East where men usually treated their slaves as they pleased. But brutality and contempt for human life was an offense to God and his law.

A third type of injury raises some extremely difficult exegetical questions. In a fight[18] between two men, a pregnant woman intervened (perhaps the concerned wife of one of them) and was struck, thus inducing

---

[16]Cf. similar Code of Hammurapi, 206. He must pay the costs of the physician if he swears: "I did not strike him deliberately." The Hittite Laws, No. 10, requires the assailant to care for the injured man until he recovers, then pay him six (later edition, ten) shekels of silver in addition to the doctor's fees!

[17]Some similar notions in Code of Hammurapi, Nos. 196–97, 200.

[18]The Niphal form of יִנָּצוּ emphasizes blows were being traded back and forth. The difference between the verb נָצָה, "to strive, quarrel" in v. 22 and רִיב, "to content, strive, quarrel" (v. 18) is that the latter is mainly entirely vocal and verbal while the former is almost always physical.

labor immediately. Two different alternatives are envisaged as a result of this blow: (1) "her children come out" (וְיָצְאוּ יְלָדֶיהָ) with the plural allowing for several children and either sex) with the result that "there is no harm" (וְלֹא יִהְיֶה אָסוֹן)[19] or (2) "if there is harm" (וְאִם־אָסוֹן יִהְיֶה)— either to her or her child(ren). The key question, however, is this: is this law similar to the numerous cases of miscarriage in such law codes as: the Sumerian Laws 1–2; Lipit Ishtar (?) Laws iii, 2–13; Code of Hammurapi 209–14: Middle Assyrian Laws A 21, 50–52, and the Hittite Law Code 17–18?

We cannot agree that these laws are the proper background for this law. While it is true that the Septuagint distinguishes here between a fetus not fully formed (ἐξεικονισμένον) and one that is fully developed, and while Philo took the same tack,[20] this will not fit the evidence here. The unspecified "harm" would appear to include both the mother and/or the child(ren). The most that would be required of the assailant in this case would be a sort of inconvenience fee as determined by the judges (בִּפְלִלִים וְנָתַן). Those who argue that the harm done is only a miscarriage of a partially formed fetus usually attempt to emend this last phrase to say "he shall pay for the fetus or abortion" (וְנָתַן בַּנְּפָלִים; from the verbal root נָפַל, "to fall").[21] The emendation would not explain why the plural of fetuses was used, nor why one would have a tautological saying at the end of what is otherwise a concise form of legal writing where every word is important and is indispensable for understanding the law. Moreover, no versions or manuscripts of the Masoretic text support this emendation or others such as "according to the decision."

We conclude that in this case of assault, the offender must still pay some compensation even though the mother and her child(ren) survived (vv. 18–19). The fee would be suggested by the woman's husband and approved by a decision of the court. But in the event that "harm" comes either to the pregnant woman or to her child(ren) and either or both die, then the principle of *talio* would be invoked demanding "life for life" (v. 23).

However, that raises a problem. If this were an accidental fatality, would not that assailant be protected as he was in verse 13 and thus

---

[19]אָסוֹן, "mischief, harm." Cf. Gen. 42:4, 38; 44:29.

[20]Philo, *On Special Laws*, 3:108–9.

[21]So Budde as early as *Zeitschrift für die alttestamentliche Wissenschaft* 11 (1891), 107 cited and refuted by Morgenstern, 66ff. See Ephraim Speiser, "The Stem PLL in Hebrew," *Journal of Biblical Literature* 82 (1963): 301–6, especially p. 303. Paul, *Covenant in Light of Cuneiform*, 72, suggests another translation, "The payment to be based on reckoning," i.e., reckoning the estimated age of the embryo. But this does not explain the plural and the phrase is much too eliptical for legal documents.

exempted from the death penalty? The response would seem to be: (1) the *talion* principle (vv. 23–25) is a stereotyped formula[22] that only states that the punishment must match the crime, but not exceed the damage done, and (2) Numbers 35:31 permitted a "substitute" or "ransom" for all capital offenses except those where it could be demonstrated that willful and premeditated murder was involved. Accordingly, the defendant would have to surrender an appropriate monetary value for each life (cf. v. 30) harmed to the deceased wife's husband or deceased child's father.

The *lex talionis* of vv. 23–25 imposes only a strict limit on the amount of damages that were collectible. "An eye for an eye" might now read: "a bumper for a bumper, a fender for a fender; don't try to get tuition money or cash for a boat." Furthermore, this was a rule for the judges and not an authorization for individuals to tell their opponents to hold still while they tried to even the score and punch out an equal number of their teeth. Contrary to Oriental jurisprudence, where the wealthy and social elite only paid fines, thus escaping punishment, biblical *lex talionis* made the principle of equal justice for all the rule and not the exception. In briefer form, the *lex talion* was repeated in Leviticus 24:19–20 and Deuteronomy 19:21.

We have already seen this fourth case in our discussion of the master disciplining his slave. The point to be made about permanent injuries inflicted by capricious owners (vv. 26–27) is that these strong economic sanctions against the master were designed to stop any tendencies in that direction. If he would not stop out of consideration for the worth of the individual, then there were additional financial reasons why such abusive tactics should never be tried.

The fifth, and final, case of injury involved men and women being gored by oxen. These laws (vv. 28–32) are paralleled very closely by the Eshnunna Law Code (Nos. 54–55) and the Code of Hammurapi (Nos. 250–52). While all three law codes share the same culture, times, and historical setting, the motivation in the biblical text is moral and religious, once again, rather than societal or economic. What is more, the ox alone in verse 28 is guilty, but the ox and its owner were guilty when the ox was previously proven guilty of taking another person's life in verses 29–30. Genesis 9:5–6 required that the life of a beast be surrendered when it killed a man made in the image of God just as it required the same of

---

[22]I fail to see evidence for a *talion* which *literally* demanded that one "pay" with the identical part that was injured, e.g., a rich man would "pay" with his "arm" for injuring another man's arm. Why argue that there was no fixed composition or substitution? Did not the death of the high priest function as a "substitute" for all previous homicides? See Moshe Greenberg, "The Biblical Conception of Asylum," *Journal of Biblical Literature* 78 (1959): 125–32.

mankind. The age, social status, gender, or title of the person gored made no difference (vv. 31–32), all—male and female, slave and free, boys and girls—were made in the image of God.

CASES INVOLVING PROPERTY DAMAGES (21:33–22:15)

Five types of property damage are now examined: culpable negligence (21:33–34), loss from animals fighting each other (35–36), loss from theft (22:1 [21:37] – 4 [3]) more negligent acts leading to losses (22:5[4] – 6[5], and losses from goods entrusted to another's custody (22:7[6] – 15[14]). The concern in every case is the eighth commandment.

First, in such negligence as leaving a pit uncovered so that loss or damage is sustained by another, full and equal restitution is demanded to cover only the loss (vv. 33–34). Should it involve an ass or ox, the dead animal will be turned over to the negligent person and full compensation shall be paid. This is especially critical in the case of these two animals since they could well be the means of the man's livelihood—equivalent to his tractor or truck.

In a second situation, when cattle fight and one kills the neighbor's animal, the law specifies that the live animal be sold and the money with the dead animal be divided between both neighbors. However, should the surviving animal have the reputation of being a gorer, his owner must assume full responsibility for restoring the dead animal. The Eshnunna Law Code (No. 53) is exactly the same in principle: "If an ox gores to death another ox, both owners shall divide the price of the live ox and the flesh of the dead ox."

The third set of examples has a group of five cases. The subject is introduced by the first "if" (כִּי) and continues with four special instances prefaced by the word "if" (אִם). The morality of the eighth commandment stands behind this injunction in verse 1.

A fivefold penalty is invoked against stealing an ox. This is probably because this was that man's source of livelihood. The Hittite laws (Nos. 57–59) and Hammurapi Code (No. 8) went as high as a thirtyfold penalty which later was reduced to fifteenfold, but the maximum in the Bible is fivefold. This is assuming that the "sevenfold" of Proverbs 6:31 is a figurative expression for complete or full repayment (cf. Gen. 4:24; Pss. 12:6; 79:12). Lesser offenses draw lesser restitution amounts: fourfold for a sheep, twofold for retrieval of a stolen live ox or ass.

In the case of "breaking in" (בַּמַּחְתֶּרֶת, literally "digging through" since homes were frequently made of thick dried mudwalls, cf. Job. 24:16; Ezek. 8:8) and entering (vv. 2–3), the thief was exposed to the loss of his life as the householder defended himself, his family, and his home by delivering a lethal blow. This was especially true at night when the thief's intentions (whether to steal, kill, or both) could not be easily and quickly determined. This same distinction between day and night entry was made in Eshnunna Law 13.

After the thief had "fenced" his goods and his crime had been discovered, but he had nothing left to repay his crime, nothing was left except to sell the thief into servitude to repay the debt. When the goods were still in his possession, however, then there was alway hope of repentance and voluntary restitution. In such cases of voluntary confession (Lev. 6:4–5), the thief had only to add one-fifth to the theft (Num. 5:6–7).

A fourth property damage case discussed: (1) letting livestock graze on another man's property (v. 5) and (2) letting a fire get out of control so that it burned over into a neighbor's field.[23] Both the harm men actually *do* and the damage they *occasion* is subject to the law. Restitution must be based on full parity of the best yield that field has ever had or an equivalent amount to the choicest sections still left standing.

The last section raises four examples of goods entrusted to another person for their custody or use (vv. 7–15). One involves money (כֶּסֶף), articles or goods (כֵּלִים) left for safekeeping only to find a thief has stolen them. The thief is required to make double restitution (v. 4). In the same situation, where there is suspicion that the keeper may have embezzled these securities (vv. 8–9), and not some unknown thief, the bailee must appear before "the judges" (הָאֱלֹהִים)[24] and give a deposition of innocence as an oath[25] in court. A second instance (vv. 10–11) involved entrusted animals that were either mutilated in the pasture, injured themselves, or were driven off by robbers. The same oath was required in court, since there were no witnesses and only God could decide the keeper's culpability. Interestingly enough, the name of "Yahweh" was invoked in the oath (v. 10). In yet again another situation (vv. 12–13), the animal given for safekeeping was stolen and it was determined that the bailee was negligent in guarding the animal. He must then replace the stolen animal. No payment would be required if the keeper could present evidence that the animal left for safekeeping had been torn to pieces by wild animals.[26]

---

[23]Hittite Laws 105–106 and 107 take up identical situations, only in reverse order of the covenant code.

[24]See our discussion on this word in Exod. 21:6; footnote 9 above; also note Exod. 22:7,8,27; Ps. 82:1,6.

[25]While no oath is specifically mentioned, the phrase אִם־לֹא, literally "whether not" is elsewhere frequently used as an oath formula.

[26]Hammurapi Law Code, Nos. 266–67 is similar, but it dealt with an outbreak of infections calling them "the stroke of a god"; but the keeper was exempted of all responsibility. See other laws on livestock being devoured by wild beasts: Hammurapi Code Nos. 75 and 244; Sumerian Law 8; New Sumerian Fragments 3:9–11.

And in the fourth case (vv. 14–15), a hired animal was either injured or died while the owner was not present. In this case, neglect is presumed and full repayment is required. However, if the owner were present, the agreed upon wages would be sufficient to offset the hazard run by the owner in renting out his property, and his presence and firsthand witness to the deed would remove all suspicion of negligence.

CASES INVOLVING SOCIETY (22:16–30)

The theme underscoring this whole section comes in the last verse: "You are to be my holy people" (אַנְשֵׁי קֹדֶשׁ) (v. 30). As God's "treasured possession, kingdom of priests and a holy nation" (Exod. 19:5–6) and his "firstborn," his "son" (Exod. 4:22), Israel was expected to match her noble calling with noble living. The very fabric of society itself was to be infused with holiness, righteousness, and justice. This program is laid out in approximately eight laws.

The first law affects the family. Exodus 22:16–17 takes up the problem of the seduction of a maiden who was not engaged, therefore this law is different from the one in Deuteronomy 22:23 where she was betrothed and where violence was also involved. Here the seducer must pay the "bride-price" (מֹהַר)[27] and agree to marry her. Such a payment and offer of marriage did not clear the guilt of the sin and should the offer of marriage be rejected by the girl's father, the bride-price still must be paid.

Verse 18 outlawed sorcery. The word, "sorceress," (מְכַשֵּׁפָה) is the feminine form of the word for "magician" or "sorcerer." Each use of magic, sorcery, incantations, or arts of witchcraft[28] demeaned Israel's standing as a holy people. The expression, "not allow to live" (לֹא תְחַיֶּה) becomes a technical term for placing something under the ban.[29] Sorcery was likewise punished in the Hammurapi Code (No. 2) by drowning and by death in the Middle Assyrian Laws (No. A. 47). Hittite Laws (Nos. 9–10) required a cash settlement to be made to the one bewitched and to pay for a physician if he or she were ill from the bewitchment.

Bestiality was also forbidden in the next law (v. 19) as it was also in Leviticus 18:23; 20:15–16 and Deuteronomy 27:21. The Canaanites practiced this offensive sex act. The Hittites proscribed it with sheep, cows, or pigs, but not with horses or mules.[30] Once again, the sanctity of the human

---

[27]See Loewenstamm, "מהר," *Entsiklopedyah Mikra'it* (Jerusalem: 1962), 4:702–6.

[28]English "witch" may be related to "to wit," i.e., "to know" and the adjectival wittig or wittich may be contracted to witch. The Greeks rendered it φάρμακοί, "poisoners" since sorcerers and sorceresses dealt in drugs and pharmaceutical potions.

[29]Cf. Num. 31:15; Deut. 20:16; 1 Sam. 27:9–11.

[30]Cf. Hittite Laws 187–188,199:16–18 for threat of death or the need of a royal pardon; but see Hittite Laws 199:20–22 for permissiveness.

person, marriage and human sexuality called for a separateness from a sensate and self-destroying culture. Israel was to be holy as Yahweh was.

Violation of the first and second commandments in verse 20 drew the sharp judgment of being "dedicated for destruction (יָחֳרַם). This was not a voluntary offering; it was an involuntary dedication. That person was now set aside to be anathematized from the earth, for he had given up his rights in refusing to acknowledge his maker, sustainer, and judge.[31]

Next comes a whole series of laws aimed at the oppression perpetrated against those without natural protectors: the poor, the widow, the orphan, and the immigrant (vv. 21–27). God called on Israel to awaken her social conscience in protecting and caring for these weak and helpless persons. Two dramatic shifts occur in these laws: (1) there is a shift to first person pronouns in which God himself becomes a special protector and advocate for these underprivileged people and (2) there is a shift to the second person plural pronoun in verses 22–24 much like the style of Deuteronomy. The cry of the weak came directly up to God (cf. Jacob in Gen. 31:42), therefore the immigrant or resident alien (v. 21) was to be protected like the widows and orphans (vv. 22–24).[32] Acts of responsible love were: to leave the corners of the field and the remaining fruit on the trees for them to glean free of charge (Lev. 19:9,10; Deut. 24:21; Ruth 2:6,8–9; hence the proverb in Judg. 8:2; see also Isa. 17:5–6; Jer. 49:9: Mic. 7:1); to leave a forgotten sheaf in the field for the orphan, widow, or stranger to pick up (Deut. 24:19); to allow the traveller through a field or vineyard to eat at their pleasure (Deut. 23:24–25); to give a tenth of one's income every three years to the poor (Deut. 14:28–29); to let them take their portion from the fields even in the sabbatical year (Exod. 23:11; Lev. 25:6), and to allow them to partake in the festivals such as Feast of Weeks, Tabernacles, and Passover (Exod. 23:14; Deut. 16:11,14; Neh. 8:14).

The poor were especially vulnerable when it came to borrowing money (25–27). God did not want his people in bondage because of debts; in fact, the righteous man may be defined as the one "who lends his money without usury" (נֶשֶׁךְ, Ps. 15:5). This law is dealt with more fully in Levi-

---

[31]See discussions on חֶרֶם in earlier and later chapters. Cf. Deut. 17:2–5 for a similar law.

[32]Among the long list of Old Testament passages dealing with this subject, some are: Exod. 23:11; Lev. 19:9–10; Deut. 14:29; 16:11,14; 24:19–21; 26:12–13; Ps. 94:6; Isa. 1:23; 10:2; Jer. 7:3–6; 22:3; Zech. 7:10; Mal. 3:5. See Charles F. Fensham, "Widow, Orphan and the Poor in Ancient Near Eastern Legal and Wisdom Literature," *Journal of Near Eastern Studies* 21 (1962): 129–39: Richard D. Patterson, "The Widow, The Orphan and the Poor in the Old Testament and Extra-Biblical Literature," *Bibliotheca Sacra* 130 (1973): 223–35; N. W. Porteous, "The Care of the Poor in the Old Testament," in *Living the Mystery*, ed. J. I. McCord (London: Blackwell and Mott, 1967).

ticus 25:35–37 and Deuteronomy 15:7; 23:19–20.[33] While Deuteronomy 23:20 allowed that "You may charge a foreigner interest (נֶ֫שֶׁךְ)," one must not charge a fellow Israelite. To charge interest was a way of avoiding one's responsibility to the poor and to one's fellowman. In a similar manner, retaining one's outer garment overnight for temporary collateral was also strictly forbidden (vv. 26–27), since even interest-free loans must have required some small type of security. But to take a man's cloak or poncho, which doubled as his blanket for the night, was striking at the very being and essentials of personhood and so it was ruled illegal.

The third commandment is reflected in verse 28. All reviling of God, in word or deed, was a detraction from the high worth of his name. Also, to curse the authorities (נָשִׂיא, "ruler"), was to fail to honor them as the fifth commandment implied.

Society would also be benefited when it appropriately honored God with the offering of its firstfruits (vv. 29–30). Here morality, social conscience, and ritual come together into a single whole. Out of the fullness of their winepresses, olivepresses, large families, increased flocks and herds, they were to honor him. The children could be redeemed by the substituted service of a Levite for each firstborn or by a money payment (Exod. 13:13; Num. 3:46–48). Since men and women have such a natural reluctance to offer freely to God out of their fullness, they are urged not to "hold back" or "delay" in doing these things. The reason for doing so is theological (as Exod. 4:22–23 shows) and moral.

Finally, verse 31 warns that animals killed by another beast were unclean since the carnivorous beasts were themselves unclean and the blood of the slain animal would remain in its tissues making it unclean. This meat was only fit for dogs. God's society was to be separate in inward principle and outward practice: his new society of clean, caring, sharing, and worshiping men and women.

CASES INVOLVING JUSTICE AND NEIGHBORLINESS (23:1–9)

Whereas the previous parts of the covenant code stressed love and compassion towards the weak, poor, widow, and immigrant, this section[34] will exhort Israel to practice another virtue: justice.

---

[33]This same negative stance on usury is continued in Job 24:9; Prov. 28:8; Ezek. 18:13; 22:12; and Neh. 5:6–12. See below for fuller discussion and bibliography.

[34]The attempt by J. W. McKay ("Exodus XXIII 1–3, 6–8: A Decalogue For Administration of Justice in the City Gate," *Vetus Testamentum* 21 [1971]: 311–25) to organize vv. 1–3, 6–8 into another decalogue of laws is not convincing since he depends on heavy emendation and deletion without any manuscript or evidential warrants.

Justice can only take place in an environment of truth-telling, therefore the ninth commandment is amplified in this prohibition on slander (v. 1).[35] Justice also demands impartiality; not compliance with the masses (רַבִּים, "crowd," "many"; v. 2) or favoritism to the poor (v. 3; cf., Lev. 19:15). Justice would also best be served by extending that same spirit of impartiality even to one's enemies (vv. 4–5; cf. Deut. 22:1–3). Regardless of the fact that a man was your enemy (v. 4) or if he even hated you (v. 5), kindnesses were still obligatory even as Job 31:29, and Proverbs 25:21–22 argued. Nowhere in the Old Testament was anyone allowed or even commanded to "hate your enemy." Only a lax oral tradition could have added that (Matt. 5:43, "You have heard that it was said"). Justice also meant avoiding discriminating against the poor (v. 5) or joining in and sponsoring slanderously false statements against others, even as Jezebel did against Naboth (1 Kings 21:10–13). The use or acceptance of bribes in verse 8 (almost verbatum law in Deut. 16:19) was odious and reprehensible to God and society. The motivation for feeling so strongly about the principle and practice of justice is given in verse 9: remember you too once were aliens in Egypt: you should know what it feels like and therefore act differently; besides, you know God who himself is just. The moral aspect of the law is never far behind the external demands in society, politics, or ritual.

LAWS ON SACRED SEASONS (23:10–19)

Just as the Decalogue has the fourth commandment placed as a sort of pivot point in the center of its concerns for God, on the one hand, and society on the other, so the covenant code appropriately includes these further elaborations on rest for people, fields, and servants and their worshipful service to God. In fact, verse 12 repeats the fourth commandment with an additional reason for its observance being supplied: so that man and beast might "be refreshed" (יִנָּפֵשׁ). There is a strong humanitarian reason, then, for this law and these illustrations of it. The law of the sabbath year begins the section (vv. 10–12). It was to be a time of letting the land rest (שָׁמַט) and lie fallow (נָטַשׁ): a time of favoring the poor and the wild animals with what was left in the field and on the trees (v. 11). Furthermore, three times a year Israel was to drop everything and go to the three great pilgrimage feasts in Jerusalem (vv. 14–19). The principle of rest and service to God remains the hallmark of the moral man who wants to enjoy the good life.

---

[35] Cf. the injunctions of Lev. 19:16; Deut. 22:13–19; and the case of Naboth in 1 Kings 21:10–13.

THE EPILOGUE (23:20–33)

An angel is promised for Israel's protection and success. This appears to be no ordinary angel, for God's "Name is in him" and he can "pardon [their] transgression" (v. 21; "Who can forgive sin but God alone?"). This must be "the angel of the covenant" (Isa. 63:9; Mal. 3:1), the pre-incarnate Christ[36] himself who now attends his law.

Obedience, then, was not to a dead law, but obedience to the angel, Christ himself. Obedience would result in blessing; therefore, "Do not rebel against him" (v. 21); but, rebel Israel did (Num. 14:11; Ps. 78:17, 40, 56).

Besides "sending" his angel, God would "send" panic and confusion (v. 27) to every nation they had to face up to in military action. First, they must disavow as firmly as possible every pagan rival to God in the land of Canaan (vv. 23–26). God, in turn, would send "the hornet" (הַצִּרְעָה; also in Deut. 7:20 and Josh. 24:12) to drive out the Canaanites. Just as "fly" and "bee" were symbols of Egypt and Assyria respectively, (Isa. 7:18), so God would perhaps use national instruments to accomplish some of his purposes for an obedient nation. Their borders would extend from the Gulf of Aqabah (יַם־סוּף) on the east to the Mediterranean Sea ("Sea of the Philistines") on the west, and from the desert (נֶגֶב) on the south to "the river" (הַנָּהָר), that is, Arabic *Nahr el-Kebir,* "The Great River"[37] in the valley north of the Lebanon mountains, currently in the boundary between Lebanon and Syria on the north.

No religious compromise or covenant must be made with the Canaanites,[38] for the potential snare of their gods, practices, and morals was all too great. Israel was to know that there was no one else beside the Lord her God. And that God was holy, just, and true; therefore they too had to be the same.

---

[36]See W. C. Kaiser, Jr., *Toward an Old Testament Theology* (Grand Rapids: Zondervan, 1978), 120 for a discussion on Exodus 33 and this issue of Christophanies.

[37]Cf. the same name in Hebrew in Gen. 15:18; Deut. 1:7; and Josh. 1:4. For elaboration see W. C. Kaiser, Jr., "The Promised Land: A Biblical-Historical View," *Bibliotheca Sacra* 138 (1981): 302–12, especially pp. 303–4.

[38]Though the Gibeonites did succeed in doing just that, Josh. 9:3–15.

Chapter 7

The Law of Holiness: Leviticus 18–20

Old Testament ethics cannot be properly grasped apart from some understanding of the holiness of God. One large teaching block of Scripture eminently qualifies in filling in this gap in our approach to Old Testament ethics, namely Leviticus 18–20. Since Israel's ethical conception of Yahweh formed both the grounds and the starting point for all her ethical and moral teaching, it is fitting that we examine this doctrine of the holiness of Israel's God.

It was A. Klostermann who first coined the name *Das Heilig-Keitsgesetz,* "The Law of Holiness," in 1877 for the section stretching from Leviticus 17 to 26; a term that has been widely used ever since. However, there is no such label in the text as there was for the "covenant code" nor can such a formal unit be distinguished by any clear textual indicators. The one great feature that many of these chapters have in common is the repeated emphasis on holiness. Therefore the designation is a helpful subject or topical indicator, but it will hardly serve the heavy duty assigned to it by the Graf-Wellhausen theory of Pentateuchal composition, namely that is was added as a separate source to the priestly "document" shortly after the time of Ezekiel. Furthermore, Leviticus 17 has, in some ways, more affinities with the first sixteen chapters than it has with what follows.[1]

---

[1] Gordon Wenham, *The Book of Leviticus* (Grand Rapids: Eerdmans, 1979), 7, points to the studies of Hoffmann and R. Kilian on this last point. There is a way in which it does tie in with chapters 18–20 that we will discuss later in this chapter.

Chapters 18 to 20 are a distinct section with a formal introduction in 18:1–5 and a formal closing in 20:22–26. We may call this section the "Law of Holiness." In these three chapters, the first two mainly contain *moral* prohibitions and precepts while the third chapter has penal sanctions. The features that attract our attention from the standpoint of Old Testament ethics in these chapters is the introductory formula of Leviticus 18:2: "I am the LORD Yahweh your God" (a feature that is almost identical to the one that introduces the Ten Commandments, Exod. 20:2: Deut. 5:6), the formula "Be holy, because I, the LORD your God, am holy" is repeated four times in this section (19:2; 20:7, 26; 21:8, but it had appeared twice earlier in 11:44–45), and the words "I am the Lord your [or their] God" occurs nearly fifty times in these chapters beginning with Leviticus 18:2. These chapters set out:

> The foundation principles of social morality. The first place among these is given to the institution of marriage . . . the cornerstone of all human society . . . Any violation of the sacred character of marriage is deemed a heinous offence, calling down the punishment of Heaven both upon the offender and the society that condones the offence.[2]

Leviticus 17 is difficult to classify. While the first sixteen chapters have dealt only with sacrificial worship and ceremonial laws, chapter 17 focuses on applying holy living to the use of food. At first glance, it might appear that this chapter is also more ceremonial than moral law, but the injunctions found here have special reference to the problem of idolatry— and thus the law of holiness begins where the first and second commands began. Leviticus 12 had asked the true Israelite to abstain from prohibited foods, but now Leviticus 17 asks that all the permitted foods be used in a way that pleases God and in a way that avoids all appearance of agreeing with or participating in idolatry.

Leviticus 17:1–9 regulates the use of clean animals that also could be offered to God in sacrifice while 17:10–16 regulates permitted food not allowed for sacrifice.[3] Apparently the ordinary slaughter of animals for food

---

[2]J. H. Hertz, *Leviticus* (London: Oxford University Press, 1932), 172 as cited by Wenham, *Leviticus*, 250.

[3]The comment of S. H. Kellogg, *The Book of Leviticus*, 3d ed. (1899; reprint, Minneapolis: Klock & Klock, 1978), 369 is pertinent to the dating question. ". . . How manifest is the Mosaic date of this part of Leviticus? The terms of this law suppose a camp-life; indeed, the camp is explicitly named. . . . The modified law of Deuteronomy (xii. 15, 16, 20–24), assuming the previous existence of this earlier law, explicitly repeals it. To suppose that forgers of a later day, as, for instance, of the time of Josiah, or after the Babylonian exile, should have needlessly invented a law of this kind, is an hypothesis which is rightly characterized by Dillmann as 'simply absurd.'"

was often connected with the idolatrous goat-worship perhaps from Egypt (Lev. 17:7; cf. 2 Chron. 11:15; Isa. 13:21; 34:14). The repeated reference to the idols of Egypt (e.g., Ezek. 20:6–7,15–18) along with Israel's "prostituting themselves" (Lev. 17:7) demonstrated that the issue in this chapter was holiness of life, even in the eating and preparing of food.

The moral and spiritual purpose of this law, then, was to teach holiness even in the mundane aspects of life; to avoid all appearances of idolatry by not sacrificing out in the open field; to eat as unto the Lord; to educate the people in reverence for life; and to develop a sensitivity for all that is associated with holy things, especially the sacredness of blood which was God's appointed means for expiation of sin.

But our main concern is with Leviticus 18–20. We will treat this section under these divisions: (1) Holiness in Sexual Behavior (18); (2) Holiness in Social Ethics (19); (3) Holiness in Worship (20:1–8, 27); and (4) Holiness in Family Relations (20:9–26).

HOLINESS IN SEXUAL BEHAVIOR (18:1–30)

This chapter has four sections: (1) a warning about the customs of the pagan nations (1–5), (2) a warning against incestuous and illicit sexual unions (6–20), (3) a warning against Canaanite deviations (21–23), and (4) a warning about the consequences of neglecting these rules (24–30).

The Customs of Pagan Nations

The formal introduction (18:1–5) repeats the solemn words of Israel's covenantal relationship three times, "I am the LORD your God" (vv. 2,4 and in shorter form, v. 5). Obviously, the writer is alluding to Exodus 3:15 and 6:2–4 where God revealed his character in his name Yahweh, and to Sinai where God had called his people to be a "holy nation" and a "kingdom of priests." But this introduction also warned about the customs of the pagan nations Egypt and Canaan. The Canaanite Ugaritic texts even speak of gods copulating with animals, much less referring to bestiality among men. In fact, in Egypt, Rameses II claimed to be the son of the goat-god Ptah. Moreover, incestuous relationships abounded, as the Hammurapi Code and the Hittite laws indicate by the fact that it is necessary to prohibit some of the same relationships banned in Leviticus 18. Homosexuality was also attested in Canaan (Gen. 19) and in Mesopotamia.

Instead of becoming involved with these wicked practices, men and women would fare much better if they followed God's laws, for they would "live by them" (v. 5). Keeping the law did not lead to eternal life; but it did lead to happiness and fulfillment in the present life.[4]

Incestuous and Illicit Sexual Relations

Verse 6 begins this section (vv. 6–20) with a general statement which underlies all prohibitions on all incestuous and illicit sexual relations: "No one[5] is to approach[6] any close relative[7] to have sexual relations";[8] and for the fourth time, these words are almost sealed with a signature to underscore the importance and authority of what has just been said, "I am the LORD."

Because the husband and wife are "one flesh" (Gen. 2:24), to uncover the nakedness of one partner was equivalent to exposing the other partner. Thus verse 7 literally says, "The nakedness of your father, *even* (Hebrew ‏וְ‏) the nakedness of your mother you shall not uncover; she is your mother." The husband and wife are completely identified in marriage and no longer two. "She is your mother" shows that only the *mother's* nakedness was meant even though it was called the *father's* just as it was in Deuteronomy 27:20: "Cursed is the man who sleeps with his father's wife, for he dishonors his father's bed" (‏כְּנַף אָבִיו‏). Consequently, the flesh of one was the flesh of the other. Likewise in Leviticus 18:16; the nakedness of a brother's *wife* also was the *brother's* nakedness. Truly they were "one flesh."

Incest was forbidden with one's own mother (v. 7), step-mother[9] (v. 8), sister (v. 9), grand-daughter (v. 10), half-sister on the father's side (v. 11), paternal aunt (v. 12), maternal aunt (v. 13), paternal uncle's wife (v. 14), daughter-in-law (v. 15), brother's wife (v. 16), step-daughter or grand-daughter (v. 17), or wife's sister (v. 18).

---

[4]For a full discussion of this statement, see W. C. Kaiser, Jr., "Leviticus 18:5 and Paul: 'Do This and You Shall Live' (Eternally?)," *Journal of the Evangelical Theological Society* 14 (1971): 19–28; also *idem, Toward an Old Testament Theology*, 110–13.

[5]"No one" (‏אִישׁ אִישׁ‏, "man, man"), i.e., "none of you." Some insist this is equivalent to all mankind, "no one," neither Jew nor Gentile.

[6]"You shall not approach" (‏לֹא תִקְרְבוּ‏) is a euphemism for sexual intercourse: "Abimelek had not come near her" (Gen. 20:4) and Isaiah "approached the prophetess and she conceived" (Isa. 8:3). "To approach" is explained by "to lie with" in Lev. 20:11 and "to take" (or "marry a wife") in Lev. 20:21 and "to uncover the nakedness" in Lev. 18:14. All four phrases have the same meaning.

[7]Literally, "to all (any) remainder of his flesh" (‏אֶל־כָּל־שְׁאֵר בְּשָׂרוֹ‏). Thus, so close were the parties listed here, that one was the remainder of the other.

[8]Literally, "to uncover the nakedness of" (‏לְגַלּוֹת עֶרְוָה‏), a phrase describing intercourse within marriage and outside of it.

[9]Reuben with Bilhah (Gen. 35:22) and Absalom with David's wives (2 Sam. 16:21–22) were guilty of this act.

The most hotly contested interpretation of this law is Leviticus 18:18.[10] The phrase "a woman to her sister" (אִשָּׁה אֶל־אֲחֹתָהּ) is taken by many interpreters in its usual idiomatic sense, "one to another" to outlaw the bigamy of marrying two sisters at the same time while they both are living. Charles Hodge affirmed this: "All that the passage teaches is, that if a man chooses to have two wives, at the same time, which the law allowed, they must not be sisters; and the reason assigned is, that it would bring the sisters into a false relation to each other."[11] Keil made the same assessment: "It was forbidden to take a wife to her sister . . . After the death of the first wife a man was at liberty to marry her sister."[12]

But I cannot agree. In every case, except the case of Leviticus 18:18, the phrase is an idiomatic expression for "one to another," but it cannot be so here. In every other case where it is idiomatic,[13] the things added to each other are inanimate objects of a feminine gender; in Leviticus 18:18 we have persons, not things, being spoken about in a context where other relationships by blood are mentioned. Furthermore, in all other nine instances of the feminine idiomatic use of this phrase, the subject of the sentence is mentioned, but should we take our phrase idiomatically here it would be translated: "You shall not take one to another to vex . . . ." The question is, one what? If we supply "one [woman]" to answer this question, this will be extending the idiom way beyond its usual force as an idiom. In all other instances this idiom entails a reciprocal relationship, but what would the reciprocal relationship be in this rendering? Therefore, the best rendering is "You shall not take a wife to her sister." That, also, is the conclusion of all the ancient versions including the Septuagint, the Samaritan, Syriac, Arabic, and Targum of Onkelos.

What this text forbids then, is not polygamy (although polygamy is contrary to the original institution of marriage and never was sanctioned, even though it was protected from abuses by divine legislation), but it forbids marriage simultaneously to two sisters. The spectacle of two natural sisters, who should be bound together in tenderness by blood, now vying with one another is anathema to Scripture. Nor must we take the force of

---

[10]See the discussion in chapter 5.

[11]Charles Hodge, *Systematic Theology*, (Grand Rapids: Eerdmans, 1952), 3:416. Also see chapter 5 for John Murray's agreement.

[12]Carl F. Keil and Franz Delitzsch. *The Pentateuch*, trans. James Martin (Grand Rapids: Eerdmans, 1956) 2:416.

[13]These instances are: Exod. 26:3 (twice), 5; 26:6, 17; Ezek. 1:9, 11, 23; 3:10. I am indebted to George Bush, *Leviticus* (New York: Newman and Ivison, 1852), pp. 193–98 for this extended discussion. He in turn seems to have assimilated the arguments of S. E. Dwight, *The Hebrew Life* or *The Law of Marriage* (New York: Leavitt, 1836), 105–27, though Dwight understands Lev. 18:18 as a simple prohibition on polygamy.

"in her lifetime" as implying that upon her decease there is no problem with her husband marrying her sister. "The expression [in her lifetime] . . . is too slight to be allowed to vacate the force of all the considerations which [are] . . . adduced in proof of the implied prohibitions contained in the preceding verses."[14] Thus the expression means "as long as she lives" without attempting at all to answer what comes after she dies.

Another area of illicit sex is found in having sexual relations during the menstrual cycle. When the cycle appears unexpectedly or prematurely (Lev. 15:24), it is a ritual impurity and not a moral offense. But deliberate acts (Lev. 18:19; 20:18; Ezek. 18:5–9) are characterized as aggressive acts that pollute the land and often are done to humble or sin against those with whom it is performed.[15] It is an exposing of her fountain of blood or uncovering the springs (Lev. 20:18). Perhaps it is because of the sacredness of the blood (as seen in our discussion of Leviticus 17) and the fact that God is total Lord of persons that no man can claim total rights to a woman without limitations. This would act, then, as God's sign that he is the ultimate source of life and Lord over domains into which no one can transgress.

Pagan Deviations

The Canaanites freely indulged in human sacrifice, profanation, homosexuality, and bestiality. This section, verses 21–23, warns about each of these aberrations. Child sacrifice to the god Molech was repeatedly condemned in Israel's history.[16] Traces of this form of infanticide were found in Carthage, North Africa,[17] having arrived there from Phoenicia. Now evidence of child sacrifice is known from a temple in Amman, Jordan. During the reigns of Manasseh and Amon, kings of Judah, Molech worship was practiced just outside Jerusalem at Topheth, in the valley of Hinnom. Manasseh even sacrificed his own children to this god (2 Chron. 33:6)! So despicable and disgusting was this cult that King Josiah, Manasseh's grandson, ordered the Molech installation razed to the ground, and the place was subsequently renamed Gehenna, the awful symbol of hell.

Another deviation was profaning God's name (Lev. 18:21b). To profane (חלל) meant to make something unholy; for example, God's house

---

14Bush, *Leviticus*, 195.

15See the discussion of Rousas John Rushdoony, *The Institutes of Biblical Law* (Nutley, N. J.: Craig, 1973), 427–30.

16Cf. Lev. 20:2–5; 1 Kings 11:7; 2 Kings 23:10; Jer. 32:35.

17Cf. Roland deVaux, *Studies in Old Testament Sacrifice* (Cardiff: University of Wales Press, 1964), 73–90; also N. H. Snaith, "The Cult of Molech," *Vetus Testamentum* 16 (1966), 123f.

(Lev. 21:12,23), God's name in false oaths (Lev. 19:12), by disfiguring one's own body (Lev. 21:5), or by idolatry (Ezek. 20:39).

Homosexuality[18] also carried strong disapproval of Scripture. It is labelled an "abomination" (תּוֹעֵבָה) five times in this chapter (vv. 22, 26, 27, 29, 30) and in Leviticus 20:13. The root meaning of "abomination" is "to detest," "to hate," or "abhor." It is that which is hated and detested by God and is therefore degrading and offensive to the moral sense.

Some would attempt to classify the prohibition against homosexuality along with the other parts of the ceremonial law which were dispelled in Christ's death and resurrection. To prohibit homosexuality today, some would argue, would be like forbidding unclean meats. It is admitted, of course, that there is a category of temporary ceremonial laws, but I do not agree that homosexuality is among them. Nothing in its proscription points to or anticipates Christ, and the death penalty demanded for its violation places it in the moral realm and not in temporary ceremonial legislation. As Bahnsen[19] correctly argued, the predominate character of the law of holiness is moral and its content is still binding today (e.g., prohibiting incest, adultery, child sacrifice, idolatry, oppression of the poor, slander, hatred, unjust weights and measures). Bahnsen goes on to say:

> Christ himself appealed [to the contents of Lev. 18–20] as summarizing all the law and the prophets (Lev. 19:18; cf. Matt. 22:39,40). . . . The defender of homosexuality must produce a viable criteria for distinguishing between moral and ceremonial laws, or else consistently reject them all (contrary to the emphatic word of Christ). We have the New Testament warrant for discontinuing obedience to the sacrificial system (Heb. 10:1–18), . . . However, the Scriptures never alter God's revealed law regarding homosexuality, but leave us under its full requirement (cf. Deut. 8:3; 12:32; Matt. 4:4). Indeed, the Bible repeatedly condemns homosexuality, the New Testament itself stressing that it is contrary to God's law (I Tim. 1:9,10), bringing God's judgment and exclusion from the kingdom (Rom. 1:24ff.; I Cor. 6:9,10). Therefore, the prohibition against homosexuality cannot be viewed as part of the ceremonial system prefiguring Christ or as a temporary in its obligation.[20]

Neither will it solve the problem by attempting to associate homosexuality with ancient cultic fertility rites or the like as if they were actually

---

[18]Homosexuality is condemned elsewhere in Scripture: Gen. 19; Lev. 20:13; Judg. 19:22–26; Rom. 1:27; 1 Cor. 6:9; Rev. 22:15. See Greg L. Bahnsen, *Homosexuality: A Biblical View* (Grand Rapids: Baker, 1978); David Field, *The Homosexual Way—A Christian Option?* (Downers Grove, Ill.: InterVarsity, 1979).

[19]Bahnsen, *Homosexuality,* 38–47.

[20]Bahnsen, *Homosexuality,* 40–41.

warning about avoiding procreation, dishonoring the superior [?] male gender, or contact with idolatrous religions that had this act as part of their ritual. Such a circumstantial or cultic interpretation seeks to place homosexuality in the same class as the prohibition against boiling a goat in its mother's milk (Exod. 23:19). The problem with this suggestion is that there are no references to the cult, prostitutes, or the like: the *act itself* is an "abomination." Its setting is in a context of holiness of life; only in Leviticus 21 does the text resume the ceremonial and ritual legislation observed in Leviticus 1–16. When the New Testament arguments are added to these hermeneutical observations, it is extremely difficult to deny that the prohibition against homosexuality is based on moral reasons and not ceremonial or circumstantial ones.

Bestiality[21] is both condemned and named a "confusion" (תֶּבֶל). To cross over the boundaries set by God between man and animal is to act in an unholy way. Such confusions and mixtures are condemned as unnatural.

Consequences of Neglecting These Warnings

To avoid being "vomited out" of the land in which they are currently living, it would be well for men and women to live holy lives and heed the moral injunction listed here. Just as the Canaanites were expelled out of the land for their wickedness, so will all others be for practicing "abominations" and "confusions." The section ends with God's signature: "I am the LORD."

HOLINESS IN SOCIAL ETHICS (19:1–37)

In order to illustrate the standard that stands at the head of the chapter, namely, "Be holy because I, the LORD your God, am holy" (v. 2), a list of illustrations from everyday life are given. No less than fourteen times does this refrain appear: "I am the LORD [Yahweh] (your God)." It marks the end of almost every paragraph, since the chapter falls into sixteen paragraphs.

Once again, reverence and fear of God heads the list. Instead of using a direct injunction that urges men to sanctify God as supreme in their hearts and lives, it urges them to demonstrate the same by observing four injunctions: (1) "respect . . . mother and father" (v. 3; God's representatives); (2) "observe my Sabbaths" (v. 3; he is the Lord of time); (3) "Do not turn to idols" (v. 4; he is Lord alone); and (4) bring the peace or fellowship offerings (vv. 5–8; be careful to perform all service due to God in the prescribed manner).

---

[21]It is condemned also in Exod. 22:19 [18], Lev. 20:15–16; Num. 35:16–21; Deut. 27:21.

The second section (vv. 9–18) consists of five sections, each with five precepts, all relating to what expressing the holiness of God in everyday affairs would mean. Each pentad ends with the refrain, "I am the LORD".

Regard for the Poor (vv. 9–10)

The first pentad seeks not only to aid the poor by legislating that some of the three chief products of agriculture, the grain, grapes, and olives and fruit, were to be left for their benefit, but it also seeks to demonstrate that the earth belongs to the Lord. Land owners were not to become selfish and overly possessive of the ground nor of what it produced, for the real owner was the Lord, people were only its stewards. Likewise, strangers were to be helped by the same provisions. The effect was to inculcate a liberal, kind, and generous attitude. Grasping, covetous, and stingy personalities were not holy persons; piety began with one's treatment of the poor and the immigrant.

Regard for the Truth (vv. 11–12)

The second pentad is closely connected with the first, for those who are grasping and uncharitable to the poor and stranger will also try to profit from their neighbor by lying. And when challenged about such lies, they will brace up their lies with an oath to God as witness for the truthfulness of their lie. What had started as a disregard for people ended up being an abuse of God's name and person. Thus three of the Ten Commandments are raised in this pentad, the third (name of God), the eighth (stealing), and the ninth (false witness). Again the motivation for observing these five injunctions is: "I am the LORD."

Regard for the Employee and the Helpless (vv. 13–14)

With another five injunctions, the law of holiness warns: "Do not defraud" (לֹא־תַעֲשֹׁק—using fraud to oppress the helpless or the wage-earner) and "do not rob" (לֹא תִגְזֹל—using violence as the means of oppression). Time and again the prophets lashed out against such robbery and fraudulent practices among Israel's populace (e.g., Isa. 3:14; Jer. 22:3). Taking advantage of people to get them at lower wages when they are hard pressed for work or calling in a mortgage for the slightest legal loophole or momentary lapse in payments are some of the things this passage rebukes. Likewise, retaining one's daily wages was enough to attract the special attention of God (Deut. 24:15; James 5:1,4). Those who live "from hand to mouth" are especially hard pressed when insensitive employers delay in giving them their daily wage. Others are helpless by no reason of their own doing; the deaf and blind are not to be vilified, defamed, or treated with contempt or in a disparaging way. George Bush comments this way on the "stumbling block" placed in front of the blind:

> The spirit of these precepts is to forbid not only the ridiculing the bodily infirmities, but the taking advantage, in any case, of the ignorance, simplicity, or inexperience of others, particularly the giving of bad counsel to those that are simple and easily imposed upon, by which they may be led to do something to their own injury.[22]

While people may not fear the deaf and the blind, they should "fear [their] God." "I am the LORD," concludes the third pentad with all of its majestic and ominous implications.

Regard for the Rich (vv. 15–16)

To prevent the false inference that God is only concerned for the poor, helpless, and disabled, this pentad warns against violating the rights of the rich and from indulging in slander against people. Justice can be easily perverted when class or special concerns of the day are made to the norm rather than righteousness and truth. Therefore, God's people are strictly warned against "lifting up [or 'accepting'] the face of the poor (לֹא־תִשָּׂא פְנֵי־דָל) or of the great." Kellogg has this interesting comment:

> A plain warning lies here for an increasing class of reformers in our day, who loudly express their special concern for the poor, but who in their zeal for social reform and the diminishing of poverty are forgetful of righteousness and equity. It applies, for instance, to all who would affirm and teach with Marx that "capital is robbery;" or who, not yet quite ready for so plain and candid words, yet would, in any way, in order to right the wrongs of the poor, advocate legislation involving practical confiscation of the estates of the rich.[23]

In a similar manner, verse 16 warns those who travel up and down the land dealing in slanders, distorting the facts, and coloring the truth out of dishonest motives. Such tale-bearing and sowing of discord often leads to an embroiled society ultimately with some even losing their lives. Whether this loss results from slander or from a conspiracy of silence ("stand against: לֹא תַעֲמֹד עַל) when the neighbor is in need of a testimony to save his life is difficult to say. The section ends with the reminder that the judge of every seen and unseen act is present in all such deliberations: "I am the LORD." All earthly actions and decisions will be reviewed in "that day" by the chief magistrate whose name is "I am."

---

[22]Bush, *Leviticus*, 204.
[23]Kellogg, *Book of Leviticus*, 400.

Regard for One's Neighbor (vv. 17–18)

The final pentad focuses on the state of one's heart towards his neighbor that the law of holiness requires. Kellogg says:

> It closes with the familar words, so simple that all can understand them, so comprehensive, that in obedience to them is comprehended all morality and righteousness toward man . . .
>
> Most instructive it is to find [in the order of the pentad that] . . . the best evidence of the absence of hate, and the truest expression of love to our neighbor, [is] that when we see him doing wrong we rebuke him.[24]

Nevertheless, even as Paul warned in Galatians 6:1, such a rebuke is to be given "gently [watching ourselves]." If a neighbor fails to rebuke a wrong-doer, then the neighbor will also bear the sin (v. 17).[25] People become guilty, to a degree, of the sin they did not in any way seek to restrain, rebuke, or hinder. But such rebuke of the wrong-doer must not lead to vigilantee action wherein they take the law into their own hands and personally begin to avenge the wrongs that they or others have suffered. What is owed, however, is to "love your neighbor as yourself." It was this injunction that our Lord used to summarize the entire scope of the law's teaching on our responsibility to each other and society (Matt. 19:19: 22:39; cf. also Rom. 13:9; Gal. 5:14; James 2:8). Thus the law and the gospel are alike in their aim and goal. Moses said, "Be holy because I, the LORD your God, am holy." Jesus said, "Be perfect, therefore, as your heavenly Father is perfect" (Matt. 5:48). The section concludes, "I am the LORD."

The third section of this chapter (vv. 19–32) groups nine areas under the general heading of "keep my decrees" (v. 19).

The first warns against mixing cattle, seed, or materials in garments (v. 19). Whether these rules were to call for a reverence for the order in nature set by God or to prevent sterility that comes with some hybrids is difficult to say. Perhaps the best answer for this ban on all mixtures is that Israel must keep separate these things as God had kept her separate from the nations (Deut. 7:3–6) as an object lesson.

Two institutions, slavery (with its potential evil) and concubinage, were given regulation in the case of the engaged slave girl (vv. 20–22). Kellogg has a most interesting comment on this point:

> By thus appointing herein a penalty for both the guilty parties such as the public conscience would approve, God taught the Hebrews

---

[24]Kellogg, *Book of Leviticus*, 401–2.

[25]וְלֹא־תִשָּׂא עָלָיו חֵטְא, "You will share in his guilt," i.e. you shall not, on account of neglecting your duty to him, contact guilt for yourself (cf. Lev. 22:9; Num. 18:32).

the fundamental lesson that a slave-girl is not regarded by God as a mere chattel: and that if, because of the hardness of their hearts, concubinage was tolerated for a time, still the slave-girl must not be treated as a thing, but as a person, and indiscriminate license could not be permitted. . . .

. . . There are many who think that if once it be proved that a thing is wrong it follows by necessary consequence that the immediate and unqualified legal prohibition of that wrong . . . is the only thing. . . . That is not always the best law practically which is the best law abstractly. That law is the best which shall be most effective in diminishing a given evil, under the existing moral condition of the community . . . Remembering this, we may well recommend the duty of a more charitable judgment, in such cases, than one often hears from such radical reformers, who seem to imagine that in order to remove an evil all that is necessary is to pass a law at once and for ever prohibiting it. . . .[26]

While I cannot agree with the utilitarian based rationale Kellogg uses here, the distinction that he makes between maintaining the principle and moderating the application of that principle while the people come to maturation is well worth observing.

The third law (vv. 23–25) requiring that the fruit of fruit trees be left alone for three years and be given to the Lord in the fourth year also has a moral foundation behind it. It is this: God is to be served before we serve ourselves! "I am the LORD" (v. 25) appropriately reminds us that Yahweh is the God of nature with power to send fruit on the trees in their season.

The next six commands all refer to various heathen practices that holy men and women are to avoid. The prohibitions are against: (1) eating blood (v. 26), (2) practicing divination (v. 26), (3) or sorcery (v. 26), (4) cutting the hair and beard in connection with pagan mourning rites (v. 27), (5) cutting or tattooing the flesh for the dead (v. 28), and (6) hiring one's daughter out as a prostitute (v. 29). It is the idolatrous roots of these customs that cause these actions to be singled out and condemned by God.

The last major division of Leviticus 19 begins by repeating the command to keep the Lord's sabbaths and to reverence his sanctuary (vv. 30–37). Both of these promote the holy life, therefore the chapter returns to them in verse 30. Four more injunctions are added. The children of Israel are cautioned to avoid consulting mediums and spiritists (v. 31), to have respect for the aged (v. 32), never to oppress the stranger (vv. 33–34), and to use honest scales and weights (vv. 35–36). All four injunctions have the majestic refrain of this chapter, "I am the LORD" and verse 37 summa-

---

[26]Kellogg, *Book of Leviticus*, 405–6.

rizes the whole chapter: "Keep all my decrees and all my laws and follow them. I am the LORD."

HOLINESS IN WORSHIP (20:1–8, 27)

It has always been necessary in every age to have penal sanctions attached to commands to insure their observance. It is not enough to appeal to the attached motive clauses in these laws or to the consciences of men. Leviticus 20 is mainly that, a penal code. It can be divided into two sections: the penalty for Molech worship or going to mediums and spiritists (vv. 1–8, 27), and penalties for sinning against the family (vv. 9–26). Both sections conclude with a strong exhortation for holiness of life (vv. 7–8 and vv. 22–26). And while the laws in chapters 18–19 were apodictic in form, this chapter will use the casuistic form and state the penalty for those who break the apodictic commands listed in chapters 18–19.

The death penalty was prescribed for those who fell into Molech worship proscribed in Leviticus 18:21. Likewise, turning to mediums and spiritists to prostitute oneself earned a similar judgment. The fact was that people must consecrate themselves to God and be holy. It was the Lord who set Israel apart as holy and that demanded a corresponding holiness of life and worship.

HOLINESS IN FAMILY RELATIONS (20:9–26)

Just as death was the prescribed penalty in the last section for offering one's child to Molech (vv. 2–5), professing to be a medium (v. 6), or having any dealings with a medium or spiritist (v. 27), so death is the penalty in this section for adultery (v. 10), incest with a mother, step-mother, daughter-in-law, or mother-in-law (vv. 11–12,14), homosexuality and sodomy (v. 13), bestiality (vv. 15–16), incest with a full or half-sister (v. 17), and relations with a woman during her menstrual cycle (v. 18). A lesser penalty is attached to an alliance with an aunt by blood (vv. 19–21), but "they will be held responsible." God will hold them accountable for such an act.

The issue at stake in every one of these crimes is the holy status of the family. Every assault against an individual here is simultaneously an attack on the very existence of the family. Said Kellogg, "where there is incest or adultery, we may truly say the family is murdered; what murder is to the individual, that, precisely, are crimes of this class to the family."[27] In God's sight, the sins against the seventh commandment are not com-

---

[27]Kellogg, *Book of Leviticus*, 426–27.

paratively less heinous than the apparently grosser sins of bestiality, incest, and sodomy. They all rate the same degree of severity in their punishments. Therefore, we may not treat these attacks on the family as relatively slight and somewhat more trifling than we regard murder and similar crimes. The gravity of the punishment ought, instead, to indicate the importance and the significance of the family in any kind of holy living and responsible biblical system of ethics. Not only was the intrinsic seriousness of these sins against the family indicated by the death penalty, but a signal was also given of the danger such crimes posed to the moral and spiritual well-being of the community. The family was as central to the ethical development and management of the community as was the vitality and worth of the individual.

This section closes with one more strong invitation to holiness of life (vv. 22–26). God wanted "wholeness": men and women, families and institutions that were set apart in a new relationship and belonging totally to Yahweh. The opposite of holiness was חֹל "profane," "common," or that which was taken from the temple.[28] In fact, "within the one term קָדוֹשׁ ['holy'] Israelite and heathen conceptions of holiness are brought into mortal combat, since in the עַם קָדוֹשׁ ['holy people'] there must be neither קָדֵשׁ ['male prostitue'] nor קְדֵשָׁה ['female prostitute'] (Dt. 23:18)."[29] Both the heathen and the Israelite קָדוֹשׁ ("holy") one was "set apart," but the object and person or task to which they were set apart in each case were at opposite ends of the scale.

SUMMARY

No better summary can be given than S. H. Kellogg gave:

. . . The Church needs to come back to the full recognition of the principles which underlie the Levitical code; especially of the fact that marriage and the family are not merely civil arrangements, but divine institutions; so that God has not left it to the caprice of a majority to settle what shall be lawful in these matters. . . .

God has declared not merely the material well-being of man, but *holiness*, is the moral end of government and of life; and He will find ways to enforce His will in this respect. 'The nation that will not serve Him shall perish.' All this is not theology, merely, or ethics, but history. All history witnesses that moral

---

[28]On the words "holy" and "profane," see A. B. Davidson, *The Theology of the Old Testament* (Edinburgh: T. & T. Clark, 1904), 144–60; Norman H. Snaith, *The Distinctive Ideas of the Old Testament* (London: Epworth, 1944), 21–50; Otto Procksch, "The Use of the Term Holiness in the Old Testament," in *Theological Dictionary of the New Testament*, 1:89–97.

[29]Procksch, "Use of Term Holiness," p. 92.

corruption and relaxed legislation, especially in matters affecting the relations of the sexes, brings in their train sure retribution, not in Hades, but here on earth. Let us not miss taking the lesson by imagining that this law was for Israel, but not for other peoples. The contrary is affirmed in this very chapter (vv. 23, 24), where we are reminded that God visited His heavy judgments upon the Canaanitish nations precisely for this very thing, their doing of these things which are in this law of holiness forbidden. Hence, the land spued them out! Our modern democracies, English, American, French, German, or whatever they be, would do well to pause in their progressive repudiation of the law of God in many social questions, and heed this solemn warning. For, despite the unbelief of multitudes, the Holy One still governs the world, and it is certain that He will never abdicate His throne of righteousness to submit any of His laws to the sanction of a popular vote.[30]

---

[30]Kellogg, *Book of Leviticus*, 430–31.

Chapter 8

The Law of Deuteronomy

All too frequently in the past, contemporary biblical scholars have tended to regard the laws of Deuteronomy 12–25 as a disparate collection of legal stipulations without any visible structure, unity, or order. A. C. Welsh's comment summarized the overwhelmingly prevalent appraisal of the structure of the Law of Deuteronomy in critical scholarship: "While any order into which these laws may be placed is sure to be unsatisfactory, none can be quite so bad as the order in which they appear in Deuteronomy today."[1]

Not all commentators have shared this pessimistic view, for there has been a long line of biblical commentators, stretching from the Rabbis and Philo down to Calvin and the other Protestant reformers, who sought to group the various laws in Deuteronomy 12–25, in a rather general way, under one of the commandments in the Decalogue. But in 1859, Father W. Schultz[2] argued in his commentary on Deuteronomy that the specific order of the laws in Deuteronomy 12–25 was dictated by the order of the commandments in the Decalogue. His arrangement was as follows:

---

[1]A. C. Welsh, *The Code of Deuteronomy: A New Theory of Its Origin* (London: Clarke, 1924), 23 as cited by Stephen A. Kaufman, "The Structure of the Deuteronomic Law," *MAARAV* (1978–79): 107.

[2]W. Schultz, *Das Deuteronomium* (Berlin: G. Sclawitz, 1859): 13ff. as cited by Kaufman, "Structure," 111, 151.

Commandment	Deuteronomy
1–2	6–11
3	12–14
4	15–16:17
5	16:18–18:22
6	19:1–21:9
7	21:10–23
8	22
9–10	23–25

It was in the latter half of the Deuteronomic laws (chapters 19–25) that any criticism was focused on Schultz's theory. Few, however, gave his theory any attention, presumably because he argued for the Mosaic authorship of Deuteronomy; but C. Steurnagel[3] did see some merit in his suggestion. C. F. Keil also rejected Schultz's arrangement, but he did allow some connection between the first table of the Ten Commandments to be traced in Deuteronomy 12:1–18:22. It was his judgment that:

> So far as the arrangement of this address is concerned, the first two series of these laws [religious laws in 12:1–16:17; and the rights and duties of civil and religious leaders in 16:18–18:22] may be easily regarded as expositions, expansions, and completions of the commandments in the decalogue in relation to the Sabbath and to the duty of honoring parents; and in the third series [19:1–26:19] also there are unquestionably many allusions to the commandments in the second table of the decalogue. But the order in which the different laws and precepts in this last series are arranged, does not follow the order of the decalogue, so as to warrant us in looking there for the leading principle of the arrangement, as Schultz has done. Moses allows himself to be guided much more by analogies and free association of ideas than by any strict regard to the decalogue; although, as Luther says, as "a very copious and lucid explanation of the decalogue, an acquaintance with which will supply all that is requisite to a full understanding of the ten commandments."[4]

Stephen Kaufman noted that D. Hoffman's[5] 1913 commentary on Deuteronomy was the most receptive of those earlier commentators to

---

[3]C. Steurnagel, *Die Enstehung des deuteronomischen Gesetzes* (Halle: J. Krause, 1896), 10 as cited by Kaufman, "Structure," 111, 151.

[4]C. F. Keil and F. Delitzsch, *Biblical Commentary on the Old Testament: The Pentateuch.* trans. James Martin (Grand Rapids: Eerdmans, 1956), 3:351–52.

[5]D. Hoffman, *Das Buch Deuteronomium* (Berlin: M. Poppelauer, 1913), 131 as cited by Kaufman, "Structure," 111, 151.

Schultz's position, but he too limited its validity to the first table of the Decalogue up to Deuteronomy 18:22.

Schultz's theory was revived in a 1966 Marburg dissertation on capital punishment in the Old Testament by Hermann Schulz.[6] He argued that Deuteronomy 12–18 followed the outline of the Decalogue only in its larger outline, but not in its details and not without major transpositions and additions to what was the original order of Deuteronomic law.

But the most valuable contribution to this discussion is, by all odds, the remarkable article by Stephen Kaufman in 1979.[7] His thesis is that Deuteronomy 12–26 ". . . is a highly structured composition whose major topical units are arranged according to the order of the laws of the decalogue . . . as it appears in chapter 5 of [Deuteronomy]. . . ."[8] The following structure emerges:

Deuteronomy 5	Commandment	Deuteronomy	Description
5:6–10	1–2	12:1–31	Worship
5:11	3	13:1–14:27	Name of God
5:12–15	4	14:28–16:17	Sabbath
5:16	5	16:18–18:22	Authority
5:17	6	19:1–22:8	Homicide
5:18	7	22:9–23:19	Adultery
5:19	8	23:20–24:7	Theft
5:20	9	24:8–25:4	False Charges
5:21	10	25:5–16	Coveting

I am persuaded that the Decalogue forms the proper structuring outline for the order and sequence of the stipulations in this part of Deuteronomy. In fact, the entire second discourse of Moses (Deut. 5–26) is a single literary unit that convincingly demonstrates that the moral law informs the statutes, judgments (מִשְׁפָּטִים), and commands of God.

This connection between the Decalogue (what I am here calling God's moral law) and the law of Deuteronomy may be argued in two ways. The centrality of the Decalogue for Deuteronomy 12–26 may be expanded to Deuteronomy 5–26, for scholars have readily acknowledged that Deuteronomy 5–11 is a "parenetic expansion of and commentary on the first commandment of the Decalogue."[9] N. Lohfink referred to Deuteronomy 5

---

[6]Hermann Schulz, "Das Todesrecht im Alten Testament" (Dissertation: Marburg, 1966), 151–57 as cited by Kaufman, "Structure," 112, 151.

[7]Stephen Kaufman, "Structure," 105–58. I owe this reference to Dale M. Wheeler.

[8]Kaufman, "Structure," 108–9.

[9]Kaufman, "Structure," 110.

as the "Hauptgebot"[10] ("The Great Commandment") of the book and the one for which all of the laws that followed in Deuteronomy were only expansions and expositions. Said Lohfink:

> It is clear . . . that these passages of "parenesis" are nothing other than elaborations of the theme of the great commandment. . . . It is possible to make out Israel's theology of the principal commandment from the exhortatory passages in chapters 1–11 of Deuteronomy.[11]

What is true of the early chapters of Deuteronomy can also now be shown to be true for chapters 12–25 in what follows below.

There is also a historical connection that points to the centrality of the Decalogue for this second Deuteronomic discourse of Moses. What Moses would now deliver to Israel in this long second speech was what he had received while he was on the mount in Sinai (Deut. 6:1). Thus Moses waited until the people had arrived in the Plain of Moab before he rehearsed these explanations of God's law along with the covenant Yahweh had made with Israel while they were at Horeb (Deut. 29:1 [28:69]).

The only reason Moses had intervened in this process of communicating God's law to his people, instead of the people hearing all of these laws directly from the audible voice of God, was that the people had panicked and feared for their own lives when God began to speak to them from heaven (Deut. 5:25). Instead, they begged Moses to represent them and be their intermediary (Deut. 5:27). When Moses did enter into God's presence on the mount he was instructed: ". . . stay here with me so that I may give you all the commands, decrees and laws you are to teach them to follow in the land I am giving them to possess" (Deut. 5:31). Accordingly, on the grounds of the role of the first commandment in chapters 5–11 and the historical connection between the revelation of the law to Moses on Sinai and the laws given here in chapters 5–25 in the Plain of Moab, there is more than a high degree of probability that the Decalogue itself may be the central structuring device for these laws.

Kaufman lays down "five major interacting principles of arrangement"[12] that he contends are operative in Deuteronomy 12–25. They are:

(1) These laws are grouped together according to general topics.

(2) In each topical unit, there is an observable principle of priority that dictates the sequence and order of the laws of that topic.

---

[10]N. Lohfink, *Das Hauptgebot: eine Untersuchung literarischer Einleitungsfragen zu Dtn 5–11* (Rome: Pontifical Biblical Institute, 1963). See now Norbert Lohfink, S.J. "The Great Commandment," in *The Christian Meaning of the Old Testament*, trans. R. A. Wilson (London: Burns & Oates, 1969), 87–102.

[11]Lohfink, "The Great Commandment," 92–93.

[12]Kaufman, "Structure," 115.

(3) The transitions between subunits within the topics or frequently between some of the topical units are ordered not on the basis of what has been labelled as "free association," but on the basis of the ancient Near Eastern method of a "concatenation of ideas, key words and phrases and similar motifs"[13] that capture the attention of the eye or ear.

(4) The sequence of the topics is determined by the order of the commandments of the Decalogue.

(5) Since the presumption is that the Decalogue is already operative, these commandments are not repeated at the head of each topic in the law of Deuteronomy.

It remains to show how these "interacting principles of arrangement" apply to Deuteronomy 12–25.

THE FIRST AND SECOND COMMANDMENTS (12:1–31)[14]

Of course, it is not fair, in one way, to just jump into the discussion at Deuteronomy 12, for already the first commandment (and in part, the second commandment) has received a full treatment in chapters 5–11. But it is also true that the intermingling of instructions on right worship and the prohibition against false worship is the hallmark of Deuteronomy 12.

The order of the subunits within this injunction on the proper and improper worship of God is as follows:

(1) The title or preface statement for the whole section incorporating the law of Deuteronomy, 12:1;

(2) The destruction of all pagan altars as the grounds for establishing the true means and place for worshiping Yahweh, 12:2–3;

(3) The establishment of the true place for the worship of Yahweh, 12:4–12;

(4) The provision for sacrifices in this place of worship;
  (a) general concerns, 12:13–19;
  (b) special concern for the blood, 12:20–28; and

(5) The prohibition against false gods, 12:29–31
  (a) transitional word to the next topic on apostasy and holy peoplehood.

---

[13]S. M. Paul, *Studies in the Book of the Covenant in the Light of Cuneiform and Biblical Law, Vetus Testamentum Supplement*, 18 (Leiden: Brill, 1970), 106.

[14]As already indicated in chapter 5, there are at least three ways in which the first commandment has been divided: (1) Deut. 5:6=1, 5:7-10=2; (2) v. 6=prologue, v. 7=1, vv. 8-10=2; or (3) v. 6=prologue, vv. 7-10=1 and v. 21 is divided into two=9 and 10. For our own purposes and for reasons briefly indicated above, we have chosen the first alternative here. Once again, let it be noted that I am indebted to S. Kaufman for the discussion that follows in this chapter.

Clearly, each of these subsections only enlarges on the fact that there is no other god beside the LORD God. Therefore, Israel's worship of him ought to be as unique as he himself is.

THE THIRD COMMANDMENT (13:1–14:27)

Deuteronomy 13:1 to 14:27 are expansions of the injunction not to take the name of the LORD God in vain. Of all the sections in Deuteronomy 12–25, this one is the most difficult to associate with the Decalogue. Kaufman's rejoinder to this problem is to acknowledge that on the surface there is some validity to this complaint. But, he argues, instead of regarding Deuteronomic law as a direct commentary or sermon on each commandment in the Decalogue, the case presented here is that Deuteronomy contains "statutes" and "judgments" "designed to provide divine authority for the religious and social reforms it proclaims."[15]

Using the principles of "concatenation" characteristic of that era and the inner Deuteronomic logic, Kaufman establishes a double connection between the third commandment and Deuteronomy 13: (1) by a literary link with the prohibition against false witnesses in Deuteronomy 19 and (2) by a paronomastic and associational link between "name" (שֵׁם) and "hear" (שָׁמַע). He explains these in this manner. There is a close association between the third and ninth commandment: the third prohibits swearing a false oath in the Lord's name (emphasizing a relationship between God and his people) and the ninth prohibits false witness between persons. The passage on false witnesses in Deuteronomy 19:16–21 shares these expressions with Deuteronomy 13:2–19: (1) speaking or acting "falsely" (סָרָה; 13:6; 19:16); (2) requiring a "thorough investigation" (דָּרַשׁ הֵיטֵב; 13:15; 19:18); (3) demanding that no pity be shown (לֹא תָחוֹס עֵינְךָ; 13:9; 19:13, 21; see also 25:12); and (4) the sole use of the same motivational clause in both units, "so that all Israel [or in chapter 19, "the rest of the people"] will hear of this and be afraid, and never again will such an evil thing be done in your midst" (13:12; 19:20). The other principle of "concatenation" is the nearly homophonous link between the repeated word "hear" (שָׁמַע) in each of the three paragraphs in Deuteronomy 13:4, 9, 13 and the law of Exodus 23:1, לֹא תִשָּׂא שֵׁמַע שָׁוְא, "Do not spread false reports."

The sanctity of God's name is taught by warning Israel against:

(1) The word of apostasy from a prophet: 13:2–6,
(2) The word of apostasy from a brother: 13:7–12, and
(3) The word of apostasy from a scoundrel: 13:13–19.

Note the principle of priority reflecting a type of socio-stratification of

---

[15]Kaufman, "Structure," 125.

society that moves from prophet to brother and, finally, to the sons of Belial (scoundrels).

Chapter 14 continues the condemnation of apostasy with an emphasis on holiness. The paragraphs continue:

(4) A prohibition on pagan rites: 14:1–2,

(5) A prohibition against eating unclean flesh which is here called an abomination (תּוֹעֵבָה): 14:3–20, and

(6) Transitional laws against pagan customs of the Canaanites (14:21; a law that comes at the end of the laws on festivals in the covenant code, Exod. 23:19) and the law of the tithes (Deut. 14:22–29).

The unifying theme throughout is the holiness and sanctity of God's name and the people of his name. The significance of Deuternomy 14:2 ("For you are a people holy to the LORD your God. Out of all the peoples on the face of the earth, the LORD, has chosen you to be his treasured possession") is that it connects "sonship" with the warnings against apostasy (even as Deut. 7:1–6 does)—especially that form of apostasy practiced in pagan priestly circles, such as cuttings and tatooing. The association of a "holy people," a "treasured possession," and "a kingdom of priests" is reminiscent, as Kaufman reminds us, of Exodus 19:5–6.

THE FOURTH COMMANDMENT (14:28–16:17)

The connection between the Sabbath law and the seventh year of sabbatical rest, or the great pilgrimage festivals, are already known from the similar association in the covenant code (Exod. 23:10–14) and the law of holiness (Lev. 23 and 25:3–8).

The sequence and inner logic within this topic proceeds in this manner:

(1) The triennial tithe for the indigent Levite, alien, orphan, and widow (14:28–29) is identical in form to the sabbatical year regulations of 15:1–11;

(2) Sabbatical year regulations: 15:1–11;

(3) Release of all Hebrew slaves in the sabbatical year: 15:12–18;

(4) The law of firstlings that are not to be worked (a theme of the sabbath): 15:19–23 (note the principle of priority in chapter 15 moving from freeman to slaves, to animals); and

(5) The festivals of the Passover (16:1–8), Feast of Weeks (16:9–12), and the Feast of Booths (16:13–17) with the principle of priority repeated in verses 11 and 14 (son and daughter, male and female servants, Levite, stranger, father, and widow).

THE FIFTH COMMANDMENT (16:18–18:22)

That the scope embraced in the fifth commandment is more than parents can be seen in the inclusiveness of Deuteronomy 16:18–18:22. These chapters embrace the following authority figures in the nation:
(1) The judges: 17:2–13,
(2) The king: 17:14–20,
(3) The priesthood: 18:1–8, and
(4) The prophets: 18:9–22.

The transitional verses of 16:18–17:1 are not as immediately apparent. Certainly the first paragraph in 16:18–20 is introductory. It is a call for the appointment of judges and officials who will exercise an impartial justice. But the two paragraphs of 16:21–22 (a prohibition against planting Asherah and erecting a pillar) and 17:1 (a prohibition against sacrificing to God a defective or flawed ox or sheep) seem to be intrusive. But these laws on altar and sacrifice are two case laws that introduce the need for the judicial procedures that 17:2–13 provide. Kaufman also notes that the "concatenation" of ideas is served by the expression "evil thing" (דְּבַר רָע) appearing in 17:1 and 5 along with "abomination" in 17:1 and 4.

Accordingly, all divinely ordered structures of authority in society were intended to be embraced in the command to honor one's father and mother.

THE SIXTH COMMANDMENT (19:1–22:8)

The longest and most complicated of the laws in the deuteronomic legislation is the word on taking a life (רָצַח), extending from Deuteronomy 19:1 to 22:8. There are thirteen subunits within this topic. The first five deal with those institutions discussed in the fifth commandment, namely, civil judicial procedures (paragraphs 1–3), the state (4), and priests (5); thereafter the priority principle moves from these institutions to free citizens (6–8), criminals (9), and animals (10, 12). The last paragraph on manslaughter forms a kind of inclusion balancing off the opening paragraphs on taking life with this final paragraph on the need to save life by building protective parapets on the roofs of homes. Only the eleventh paragraph on transvestism (22:5) appears to be displaced. But a "concatenation" of ideas seems to be present, for Kaufman points to the connection between "garment" (שִׂמְלָה) in the previous paragraph (22:3) and in verse 5 as well as a concern for separation between male and female in verse 5 with the separation of mother and "sons" (בָּנִים) in the paragraph that follows (22:6–7).

The paragraphs then are these:
(1) Accidental or intentional homicide and cities of refuge: 19:1–13,
(2) Respect for neighbor's boundaries: 19:14,
(3) Laws of evidence and testimony at civil trials: 19:15–21,
(4) Law of war: 20,
(5) Law of untraced homicide: 21:1–9,
(6) Law of a wife captured in war: 21:10–14,
(7) Law of loved and hated wives and their sons: 21:15–17,
(8) Law of a rebellious son: 21:18–21,
(9) Law of public display of executed criminals: 21:22–23,
(10) Law of respect for the property of one's fellow: 22:1–4,
(11) Law on transvestism: 22:5,
(12) Law on protecting birds' nests: 22:6–7, and
(13) Law on requiring parapets on homes: 22:8.

It remains only to say that the laws on criminal justice (paragraphs 3, 8, 9) are probably included here since provision is made for the only legitimate method for taking life and paragraph 10 is included because it sought to prevent the "unnecessary loss of life through intentional oversight."[16]

THE SEVENTH COMMANDMENT (22:9–23:19)

The connection between the commandment on adultery and the seven paragraphs of Deuteronomy 22:9–23:19 are fairly transparent with the exception of the sixth paragraph on the escaped slave (23:16–17). But if this slave fled to Israel in wartime, then its association with the seventh paragraph and the presence of foreign cultic prostitution is clear.

The seven paragraphs are:
(1) A transitional paragraph bridging commandments six and seven on unnecessarily exposing the life of crops, and two unequally yoked animals: 22:9–11,
(2) A transitional connection between paragraphs 1 and 3 involving cloths and clothing: 22:12,
(3) Laws on improper sexual relations: 22:13–23:1,
(4) Sexual wholeness and purity: 23:2–9,
(5) Sexual purity and cleanness in military camps: 23:10–15,
(6) The escaped slave: 23:16–17, and
(7) Laws on cult prostitutes: 23:18.

---

[16]Kaufman, "Structure," 135.

THE EIGHTH COMMANDMENT (23:20–24:7)

Every form of stealing or withholding property that rightfully belonged to someone else is condemned in Deuteronomy 23:20–24:7 just as the eighth commandment forbade. The first three paragraphs (23:20–21; 23:22–24; 23:25–26) deal with the theft of property and the last three with the theft of "life" (נֶפֶשׁ; 24:1–5; 24:6; 24:7).

THE NINTH COMMANDMENT (24:8–25:4)

Fairness is the hallmark of the ninth commandment and of these laws in Deuteronomy 24:8–25:4. All forms of mockery or belittling people are ruled out as being a form of bearing a false witness.

The paragraphs may be summarized as:
(1) Do not speak libelously as Miriam did: 24:8–9,
(2) Treat debtors justly: 24:10–13,
(3) Treat employees fairly: 24:14–15,
(4) Hold only the guilty persons responsible for their crimes and not their relatives or family members: 24:16,
(5) Dispense justice and charity to the stranger, orphan, and widow alike: 24:17–22,
(6) Exercise justice in corporal punishment even to criminals: 25:1–3, and
(7) Treat even animals mercifully: 25:4.

The point is that the result on the person exercising such fairness is as important, if not more so, than the one receiving such mercy; for God is desirous of inculcating merciful attitudes and marks of truthfulness in his people.[17]

THE TENTH COMMANDMENT (25:5–16)

The final section appears in Deuteronomy 25:5–16. The three issues dealt with are:
(1) The levirate marriage: 25:5–10.
(2) The law of a wife's non-interference in a fight between two men: 25:11–12, and
(3) The law of just weights for buying and selling: 25:13–16.

The logic that brings these laws together is as Kaufman argues: a social institution that provides a legitimate exception to the prohibition of

---

[17]W. C. Kaiser, Jr., "The Current Crisis in Exegesis and the Apostolic Use of Deuteronomy 25:4 in I Corinthians 9:8–10," *Journal of the Evangelical Society* 21 (1978):13–18.

coveting what belongs to another person (levirate marriage), and another law on two "brothers," a subject shared by both paragraphs 1 and 2.

The third paragraph is a most interesting commentary on the tenth commandment. The verb, "covet" (חָמַד) does not stress the act of taking something, as most scholars have argued, but "תִּתְאַוֶּה in Deut. 5:21 can only refer to mental processes."[18] Thus what was discouraged here was "even the patterns of thought that might lead a man to commit any of the civil crimes subsumed under the preceding rubrics of murder, adultery, theft, and false witness."[19] The interesting point is that this law prohibits not only the use of all weights and measures that are false, but even their possession! Israel was urged to "avoid tempting situations" (לֹא תַחְמֹד)[20] as well as the actual acts themselves.

SUMMARY

The amazing result of Steven Kaufman's article, which we have surveyed in this chapter, is that he convincingly demonstrates that the Deuteronomy law depends on the Decalogue both in its general structure and specific details. He also settles the distinction A. Alt blurred between the eighth commandment (לֹא תִּגְנֹב, "thou shalt not steal," the act of stealing anything and not just kidnapping or man theft) and the tenth (לֹא תַחְמֹד, "thou shall not covet," a mental state and not an act).

Even more surprising is Kaufman's final estimate: "The efforts of a century of scholarship to propose elaborate redactional histories for [the Law of Deuteronomy, 12–25] must be deemed fruitless. [It] did not grow in stages as these scholars would have us believe. It is rather a unified masterpiece of jurisprudential literature created by a single author . . . . . into . . . . an expanded Decalogue."[21]

---

[18]Kaufman, "Structure," 143.
[19]Kaufman, "Structure," 143.
[20]Kaufman, "Structure," 144.
[21]Kaufman, "Structure," 147.

PART III
CONTENT OF
OLD TESTAMENT ETHICS

Chapter 9

Holiness As a Way of Life

In the Old Testament, holiness lays claim to the entirety of a person's life. It is impossible to exclude anything from the potential sphere of God's own holiness. Religious objects and material things are all potentially holy in so far as they are associated with a holy God. It is difficult to the point of being impossible to escape God's holiness, for "the Law of Holiness" (Lev. 18–20) easily illustrates how comprehensive and pervading is the model of God's holiness, and his demand for the imitative holiness of men and women includes the smallest details of human life.

HOLINESS AS THE CENTRAL FEATURE
IN OLD TESTAMENT ETHICS

Here, then, is the central organizing feature of Old Testament ethics: holiness.[1] To inquire what is the supreme human good is to hear the definite challenge that comes to formal expression in Leviticus 11:45: "I am the LORD who brought you up out of Egypt to be your God; therefore be holy, because I am holy."[2]

---

[1]See Elpidius Pax, "Holy," in *Sacramentum Verbi: An Encyclopedia of Biblical Theology*, ed. Johannes B. Bauer (New York: Herder and Herder, 1970), 1:372–75.

[2]This is one of the great formulae of Old Testament theology and connected with the integrating theme of the promise. See W. C. Kaiser, Jr., *Toward an Old Testament Theology* (Grand Rapids: Zondervan, 1978), 32–35.

But it is not only in the context of history, grace, and redemption that Old Testament ethics finds their ground. This might have led to a teleological and pragmatic basis for ethics. We perceive Old Testament ethics to be deontological (from the Greek word δέον, the "ought" or "binding" wherein the rightness or wrongness of an action or rule was contingent not on its results, but on the specific command or person of God). Leviticus 11:44 boldly grounds Old Testament ethics in the normativeness of Yahweh's moral nature, character, and commands which express his "wholeness." It simply affirms: "I am the LORD your God; consecrate yourselves and be holy, because I am holy."[3] Repeatedly, the very grounds for calling humanity to obedience and moral action are to be found in one simple, but awesome, statement: "I am the LORD (your God)." See this frequent use in Leviticus 18:2, 4, 5, 6, 21, 30; 19:2, 4, 10, 12, 14, 16, 18, 25, 28, 30, 31, 34, 37.

More than any other attribute, holiness is the one quality in God's character that describes the essential nature of God in all his fullness. While God's awesomeness, greatness, power, fiery judgment, and wrath are easily comprehended in his holiness, yet this attribute carries a clear ethical significance in the complex of ideas that belongs to it. Holiness includes Yahweh's *uniqueness*, the thrice Holy One (Isa. 6:3), to whom no human can compare and no idea or value compete (Isa. 40:25). "[He is] God, and not man—the Holy One among you" (Hos. 11:9). Thus he is *altogether different* from mortals, but still present *in the midst of them.* There is both a model of transcendence and immanence—all expressed in the attribute of holiness!

Especially significant for ethical modeling is the fact that God's holiness means that he is free from the frailties and moral imperfections common to mankind (Hos. 11:9) and therefore can be counted on to be consistent in his dealings with people (Hab. 1:12). Accordingly, holiness laid a claim to the entirety of a person's life. This can be illustrated by the thought expressed in Psalm 24:3–4, ". . . who may stand in his holy place? He who has clean hands and a pure heart, who does not lift up his soul to an idol or swear by what is false." Rather than being purely ritualistic, holiness was concerned with the whole of a person and his or her way of life.

Israel and the believing community had been called to be a "holy nation," a "kingly priesthood" and a "special treasure" in Exodus 19:5–6. Thus, as God's possession, they were to be a "holy people" or "a people holy to the LORD your God" (Deut. 7:6; 14:2, 21; 26:19). In the last analysis, that was what distinguished Israel from the nations: their call to

---

[3]Cf. also Lev. 19:2.

holiness had separated them from the nations and from all that was "common" or "profane" (חל; cf. חָלַל, "to defile").[4]

Having said all of this by way of definition, it is still difficult to embrace everything holiness is in one comprehensive statement. Certainly James Muilenberg was correct when he stated that holiness was:

> The "given" undergirding and pervading all religion; the distinctive mark and signature of the divine. More than any other term, "holiness" gives expression to the essential nature of the "sacred." It is therefore to be understood, not as one attribute among other attributes, but as the innermost reality to which all others are related. Even the sum of all the attributes and activities of "the holy" is insufficient to exhaust its meaning, for to the one who has experienced its presence there is always a plus, a "something more," which resists formulation or definition.[5]

Many contemporary biblical ethicists agree that "holiness" is *one of* the mainsprings and central organizing themes of Old Testament ethics, but they vigorously deny holiness could ever stand as a single theme for all ethical action. Such a suggestion, they complain, is reductionistic and depends too much on an unachievable concept of the "wholeness" or even "a unitary whole" for all the Old Testament or even for both testaments. Instead, many scholars insist that the Scriptures themselves give evidence of a great variety of values, norms, principles and perspectives.[6]

In 1957 Carl F. H. Henry had already taken the opposite point of view and cautioned:

> While the Bible does not give us ready-made a system of ethics, the growing distrust of a systematic biblical ethics is unjustified. . . . While the Bible is no systematic ethics text, it contains revealed ethical truths capable of systematic correlation. There are also whole blocks of extended moral instruction, in New Testament as well as Old. Not only are these passages capable of reconciliation, but they form a unitary whole, mirroring the revelation of a single Divine will for man.[7]

4Cf. the essays on holiness by Thomas E. McComiskey, "קָדַשׁ" in *Theological Wordbook of the Old Testament*, ed. R. Laird Harris, Gleason Archer, Jr., and Bruce K. Waltke (Chicago: Moody Press, 1980) 2:786–89; Horst Seebass, "Holy," *The New International Dictionary of New Testament Theology*, ed., Colin Brown (Grand Rapids: Zondervan, 1979), 2:224–29.

5James Muilenberg, "Holiness," *Interpreter's Dictionary of the Bible*, ed. George A. Buttrick (Nashville: Abingdon Press, 1962), 2:616.

6See for example, James Gustafson, "The Place of Scripture in Christian Ethics: A Methodological Study," *Interpretation* 24 (1970): 444.

7Carl F. H. Henry, *Christian Personal Ethics* (Grand Rapids: Eerdmans, 1957), 346–47.

It is also possible today to look at the Scriptures as a whole—if not in their origin and source, then certainly in their "final shape." A small ground swell is beginning to shake the scholarly landscape with the thought that perhaps "it is time that we ignored the sources—hypothetical as they are—for a little, and asked what the Pentateuch [or the Old Testament] as a whole is about. . . ."[8] This is not to say that higher criticism as a discipline has no place in the study of Scripture or biblical ethics—it has! But scholars must not insist upon prior acquiescence to the so-called assured results of the last two hundred years of biblical scholarship as the basis for acceptance into the ranks. Surely it is well known by now that there is a babel of voices on the question of sources with very few agreeing to the source of any selected verse or group of verses.

But even more devastatingly, this whole process has led to two major tendencies in Old Testament research: *atomism* and *geneticism*. David Clines[9] was the first scholar, to my knowledge, to put his reputation on the line and to point to the severe restriction that these two tendencies have left on current Old Testament studies. Clines asks, in effect, is it always true that a text is best understood when its origins are uncovered? Are there no other ways of doing Old Testament study? Is not a holistic approach just as valid as an atomistic one? Can a subject in the humanities, like Old Testament research, be totally built on a "pyramid view" of the growth of knowledge such as is used in the natural sciences? Clines's protest, like mine, is against "the dominance" of these two tendencies to the exclusion of other models. Clines's citation of von Rad's comment on Genesis 2–3 is apropos to the stance we are taking for developing a holistic approach to Old Testament ethics. Von Rad thundered:

> Reconstruction of the original texts . . . is not the primary task of exegesis . . . No matter how much a knowledge of the previous stages of the present text can preserve us from false exposition, still . . . the narrative . . . , in spite of certain tensions and irregularities, is not a rubble heap of individual recensions, but it is to

---

[8]David J. A. Clines, *The Theme of the Pentateuch* (Sheffield: Sheffield University, 1978), 5. See also the amazing statements by Walter Wink, "How I Have Been Snagged By the Seat of My Pants While Reading the Bible," *Christian Century* 24 (1975): 816. ". . . the historical-critical approach to biblical study had become bankrupt . . ."; O. C. Edwards, Jr., "Historical-Critical Method's Failure of Nerve and a Prescription for a Tonic: A Review of Some Recent Literature," *Anglican Theological Review* 59 (1977): 116. ". . . today the historical-critical method is in trouble"; and James N. Sanders, "The Problem of Exegesis," *Theology* 43 (1941): 325. ". . . historical criticism . . . is proving to be inadequate to . . . understanding and expounding [the text]."

[9]Clines, *Theme of Pentateuch*, 7–10. He also pointed to the structuralist, and men like Brevard Childs of Yale, Luis Alonso Schökel of the Pontifical Biblical Institute in Rome, Walter Wink, and an unusual quote from Gerhard von Rad's commentary on Genesis.

be understood as a whole with a consistent train of thought. Above all else, the exegete must come to terms with this existing complex unity.[10]

Therefore, we choose to follow the route of taking a holistic view (while being mindful of all the atomistic and genetical studies and standing ready to engage in the legitimate tools of higher criticism where they are needed). But this will not automatically establish the view that "holiness" was the Old Testament's own way of organizing a systematic approach to biblical ethics.

The case for holiness is to be found at three levels: (1) the explicit statements in "The Law of Holiness" (Lev. 18–20), (2) the definition of holiness as being a term practically equivalent for the "Godhead" itself in all its attributes as well as a standard for what is spiritual, moral, and ethical, and (3) the normativeness of the person, actions, and will of God for what is a good, just, right, and appropriate standard for men and women—all of which can be and is summarized in the one word, "holiness." Briefly stated, the mainspring of Old Testament ethics is: "Be holy because I, the LORD your God, am holy." It is an *imitatio Dei* even as the constant reminder of that oft repeated phrase captures it—"I am the LORD your God."

One more significant fact may be brought forward in favor of using holiness as our organizing concept in Old Testament ethics. The Hebrew word קָדוֹשׁ, "holy," and its family are used over six hundred times in the Old Testament to indicate moral perfection. Almost everywhere in the testament, men and women are reminded of God's holiness as their only true standard. For example: "There is no one holy like the LORD, there is no one besides you; there is no Rock like our God. . . . and by him deeds are weighed" (1 Sam. 2:2–3; cf. Job 6:10; Pss. 22:3; 145:17; Isa. 52:10). The goal of life was this: "Blessed is the man who does not walk in the counsel of the wicked, or stand in the way of sinners or sit in the seat of mockers. But his delight is in the law of the LORD; and on his law he meditates day and night" (Ps. 1:1–2). The result was "I—in righteousness I will see your face; when I awake, I will be satisfied with seeing your likeness" (Ps. 17:15).

God's holiness had two distinct sides. One stressed his otherness, his so-called numinous character. This was picked up in the ceremonial and ritual laws of Israel. The other side of holiness expressed the righteousness and goodness of Yahweh and that became the basis for the morality and ethics taught in the Old Testament.

---

[10]Clines, *Theme of Pentateuch*, 10, citing Gerhard von Rad, *Genesis: A Commentary*, trans. J. H. Marks, rev. ed. (Philadelphia: Westminster, 1972), 75.

HOLINESS IN WORSHIP

We begin our case for the contents of Old Testament ethics with worship, for that is where all four summarizing ethical texts of the Old Testament began (see above chapters 5–8). Worship of God was a holy meeting of God and his people. Israel's response in worship was, "The LORD our God is holy" (Ps. 99:9).

When Jesus gave his famous summary of the law, he too began it with, "Love the Lord your God with all your heart and with all your soul and with all your mind" (Matt. 22:37; Mark 12:30; Luke 10:27; cf. Deut. 6:5). Yahweh alone was Lord, and in no way was his lordship to be usurped by any idol, man, idea, institution, or competing loyalty. In fact, such competition and replacement of what was real and right with what was false excited the zeal and jealousy of God. All denials of Yahweh's claim for exclusive service and loyalty aroused his zeal. All such competing constraints were nothing more than idols (Num. 25:1–13; 1 Kings 14:22–24; Ezek. 36:5–7; 38:19; 39:25–29). His was the sole right to be praised and adored by all living creatures, because there is no one like him among all the gods in his holiness (Exod. 15:11; 1 Sam. 2:2; Ps. 77:13; Isa. 40:18–20, 25–26). Comparisons are worthless and futile.

The first commandment of the Decalogue was closely connected with the "*Shema* Israel" [i.e., "Hear, O Israel"] of Deuteronomy 6:4–5.

> "Hear, O Israel: The LORD our God, the LORD is one. Love the
> LORD your God with all your heart and with all your soul and with
> all your strength."

The Rabbis considered the *Shema* "to contain the principles of the Decalogue."[11]

One of the most important consequences of the absolute unity of the Godhead is that law, morality, and ethics of this one Lord is also single. Only in a society that embodies a real or practical polytheism can the existence of an absolute be denied. The only other alternative to these two options is a human imperialistic government.[12] But the first principle of the first commandment and the *Shema* is one God and *one law*.

Moreover, because God is one and his truth and law is one, that one law has an *inner coherence*. God's unity speaks both to the ultimacy, singleness, and coherence of all that he commands. Rushdoony warns that "To hold, as the churches do, Roman Catholic, Greek Orthodox,

---

[11]*Seder Nezikim, Babylonian Talmud,* ed. I. Epstein (London: Soncino Press, 1935) 4:22, n. 8 as cited by Rousas John Rushdoony, *The Institutes of Biblical Law* (Nutley, N.J.: Craig Press, 1973), 16.

[12]See Rushdoony, *Biblical Law,* 17–18 for enlargement of these ideas.

Lutheran, Calvinist, and all others virtually, that the law was good for Israel, but that Christians and the church are under grace and without law, or under some higher, newer law, is implicit polytheism."[13]

Such reasoning has a touch of the Joachimite heresy[14] and a partial antinomianism.[15] God's one law cannot be pitted either against himself or his grace. It is true that the apostle Paul consistently rejected the law as a means of salvation; nevertheless, he affirmed just as vigorously the continuing validity of the moral law for the believer (Rom. 3:31; 8:4). Patrick Fairbairn spoke out on this unnatural division of the unity of the Godhead and his law.

> *Antinomianism* . . . is the view of men, evangelical indeed, but partial and extreme in their evangelism—who, in their zeal to magnify the grace of the Gospel, lay stress only upon a class of expressions which unfold its riches and its triumphs, as contrasted with the law's impotence in itself . . . and silently overlook, or deprive of their proper force, another class, which exhibit law in living fellowship with grace. . . . Some so magnify grace in order to get their consciences at ease respecting the claims of holiness, and vindicate for themselves a liberty to sin that grace may abound. . . . These are Antinomians of the grosser kind, who have not particular texts merely of the Bible, but its whole tenor and spirit against them. Others, however, . . . are advocates of holiness after the example and teaching of Christ. They are ready to say, "Conformity to the Divine will, and that as obedience to commandments, is alike the joy and the duty of the renewed mind". . . . So far excellent; but then these commandments are not found in the revelation of law, distinctively so called. The law, it is held, had a specific character and aim, from which it cannot be dissociated, and which makes it for all time the minister of evil. [An illustration of this type of antinomianism can be found in J. N. Darby, "On the Law," pp. 3–4. He also taught in addition to the previous quote which Fairbairn judged to be excellent that] "It is a principle of dealing with men which necessarily destroys and con-

---

[13]Rushdoony, *Biblical Law*, 18.

[14]The Joachimite heresy [Joachim of Fiore (c. A.D. 1135–1202)] had all of history divided into three ages: The Age of the Father and the Old Testament was the age of justice and law; the second age was the Age of the Son, of the Church, the New Testament, and of grace, while the third and last was the Age of the Spirit when men became gods and were their own law beginning about A.D. 1260.

[15]Antinomianism was a term first used by Luther in his debate with Johann Agricola to describe any rejection of the moral law as relevant to the Christian. Some antinomians reject all use of the moral law even in bringing the sinner to repentance while others accept only a pedagogical use of the law to convince sinners of their sin and need of Christ. However this second group insists that the moral law has no place in the life of a Christian who is under grace and not under law.

demns them. This is the way the Spirit of God uses law in contrast with Christ, and never in Christian teaching puts men under it. Nor does Scripture ever think of saying, You are not under the law in one way, but you are in another; you are not for justification, but you are for a rule of life. It declares, You are not under the law, but under grace; and if you are under law, you are condemned and under a curse. How is that obligatory which a man is not under— from which he is delivered?"[16]

Fairbairn did not agree with Darby, nor can we. He responded to Darby and this partial antinomianism that continues to cripple the church by saying:

> Antinomianism of this description—distinguishing between the teaching or commandments of Christ and the commandments of the law, holding the one to be binding on the conscience of Christians and the other not—is plainly but partial Antinomianism; it does not, indeed, essentially differ from Neonomianism,[17] since law only as connected with the earlier dispensation is repudiated, while it is received as embodying the principles of Christian morality. . . .[18]

Deuteronomy 6:4–5 connect the *"Shema* Israel" and the priority of the first commandment with obedience to the words and commands that God had given them (Deut. 6:6; note that the Decalogue had just been given in Deut. 5:6–21). These commandments were to be stored in one's heart (Deut. 6:6) and taught to one generation after another (Deut. 6:7–9, 20–25). Only in observing and obeying these precepts would Israel enjoy life to its fullest. (Note the three purpose clauses in Deut. 5:33).

The centrality of the law in all of life and worship can also be seen from the fact that the Decalogue was placed in the ark of the covenant in the Holy of Holies of the tabernacle. Accordingly, the most sacred room with the most sacred piece of furniture that formed the very throne for the presence and glory of Yahweh's rule and reign contained the tables of the law (Exod. 25:10–20; especially v. 16, "the Testimony"; cf. Deut. 10:5). Rushdoony wisely observes that "God did make the altar his throne, because the altar, however important, set forth atonement, the beginning of new life for God's people. . . . [But] it is truncated and defective faith which stops at the altar. The altar signifies redemption. . . . But rebirth

---

[16]Patrick Fairbairn, *The Revelation of Law in Scripture* (1869; reprint, Grand Rapids: Zondervan, 1957), 29–30.

[17]Neonomianism is the doctrine that a new law, opposed in some respects to the old law is a law of principles rather than precepts, especially the law of love and faith and is therefore higher than the former. This view was first propounded by the Socinians. See Fairbairn, *Revelation of Law*, 27–28.

[18]Fairbairn, *Revelation of Law*, 30–31.

for what? Without the dimension of law, life is denied the meaning and purpose of rebirth."[19] The center for all fellowship, growth, and enjoyment of the new life found in the atonement of the altar can only be located in the holiness where God dwells and where the law is contained in the context of covenant.

This does not mean that the altar has no part in any discussion about law or the life of holiness. The central fact about the altar is that it is the place where atonement and acceptance can be found in the gracious provision and foreshadowing of that final act of sacrifice in Christ.[20] Christ's death was a substitutionary and vicarious atonement. That is one great truth found in the altar typology.

But there is what Fairbairn calls a second, but too frequently neglected, aspect of the altar.

> Christ bore a judicial death . . . [was] made a curse, that He might redeem men from the curse of the law. . . .

> There are those who cannot brook the idea of these legal claims and awful securities for the establishment of law and right in the government of God. . . ."

Fairbairn was even more specific:

> . . . the sufferings and death of Christ [are] as a satisfaction to God's justice for the offense done by our sin to His violated law. *Satisfaction*, I say emphatically, to God's justice—which some, even evangelical writers, seem disposed to stumble at; they would say, satisfaction to God's honour, indeed, but by no means to God's justice. What, then, I would ask, is God's honour apart from God's justice? His honour can be nothing but the reflex action or display of His moral attributes; and in the exercise of these attributes, the fundamental and controlling element is justice. Every one of them is conditioned; love itself is conditioned by the demands of justice; and to provide scope for the operation of love in justifying the ungodly consistently with those demands, is the very ground and reason of the atonement—its ground and reason primarily in the mind of God, and because there, then also in its living image, the human conscience, which instinctively regards punishment as "the recoil of the eternal law of right against the transgressor," and cannot attain to solid peace but through a medium of valid expiation. So much so, indeed, that wherever the true expiation is unknown, or but partially understood, it even goes about to provide expiations of its own. Thus has the law been

---

[19]Rushdoony, *Biblical Law*, 73.
[20]See W. C. Kaiser, Jr., *Toward an Old Testament Theology* (Grand Rapids: Zondervan, 1978), 115–19.

most signally established by that very feature of the Gospel, which specially distinguished it from the law—its display of the redeeming love of God in Christ.[21]

It must be noted that the "covenant code" began its legal provisions with a prologue on the altar law (Exod. 20:22–26) just as "The Law of Holiness" had Leviticus 17, if not all of the first sixteen chapters on the sacrifices and worship of God as a backdrop for the precepts which followed in both codifications. Once again it must be stressed that grace does not set aside law nor can the law be properly appreciated without the priority of grace being evidenced.

The necessity for blood to be shed in death at the altar also reminds us that capital punishment is not an optional feature in a truly moral and ethically obedient society. As Rushdoony succinctly states it, "To oppose capital punishment as prescribed by God's law is thus to oppose the cross of Christ and to deny the validity of the altar."[22] In the case of first degree murder, Numbers 35:31 specifically requires that there be no remission from the penalty of death. If we are to prevent the very ground itself from vomiting forth its inhabitants in order to cleanse its defilement with innocent blood (Lev. 18:25), then there had better be a godly exercise of capital punishment against all murderers. To extend love or mercy in exchange for justice at this level is to despise both the image of God in the one who has been suddenly felled (Gen. 9:6) and, more importantly, to despise the very basis by which we received new life in Christ by the death of the Lamb of God.

Holiness, then, is integrally related to God's law. The holiness enjoined in the Old Testament is first of all a transcendental attribute of God. Then it is the "separateness" and "otherness" of God which manifests itself in exclusive devotion to him. Thus every law of the Old Testament, whether it was civil, ceremonial, or moral, was concerned at its very root with holiness. There was to be a separation, whether in symbol or in literal action, from everything that God was not: disease, death, putrification, paganism, idolatry, covetousness, and confusion in the orders of creation. A clear line had to be drawn between all that was holy and all that was common or profane.

Profanity covers all speech, action, and living that is outside of and apart from God. The word profane comes from the Latin *pro*, "before," and *fanum*, "temple"; hence, "before or outside the temple."

The third commandment proscribed all profanity. Such swearing,

---

[21]Fairbairn, *Revelation of Law*, 247–48 and 250–52.
[22]Rushdoony, *Biblical Law*, 77.

or taking the name of God (in all that that rich term stood for[23]) "for no purpose" or in a slight, trivial, or unthinking (much less in a vilifying, ridiculing, or blasphemous) way was a species of false worship of God. To reduce the greatness of God's person, his teaching or doctrines, his attributes, or his ethical directives to trivialities or to open contempt is to indulge in blasphemy. Many acts that are overly pious in their intention (such as public prayers, evangelical preaching, ministry to the sick or the body of Christ) can and often are profane and blasphemous in their execution because they treat so lightly or with such little or no content and majesty the grandeur of the one whom they pretend to serve. Calvin[24] noted this connection between real worship of God and taking God's name on one's lips and life for a stated purpose that was in keeping with the holiness of the "name" of God. Calvin based his argument in part on Isaiah 45:23: "By myself I have sworn, my mouth has uttered in all integrity a word that will not be revoked: Before me every knee will bow." Anything less was treason on the part of those who claimed to be a "holy people," God's "special possession," or "moveable treasure" (Exod. 19:5–6). Holy men and women will worship in the "beauty of holiness" (1 Chron. 16:29; 2 Chron. 20:21; Pss. 29:2; 96:9; 110:3).

HOLINESS IN WORK

Work is a holy calling from God given to men and women since the days of Adam and Eve. In Genesis 2:15 a divine mandate was given to cultivate and care for the Garden of Eden. Man was also called to name the creatures brought before him. Hence, we may affirm that labor and knowledge that tenderly subdues the earth and exercises sensitive dominion over the created order is a holy calling from God.

The whole created order was made by God for his use and pleasure. But he also made people, surprisingly in his own image, to be his vicegerent over that whole created realm under the scrutinizing eye of its owner—the living God. There is no truth to the charge that biblical Christianity gave rise to the abusive use of the ecology since it commanded men to "subdue" and "have dominion" over the earth. No person may ruthlessly "trample" under foot God's creation in order to wrench from the earth every last penny. That would be to invite the judgment of God and

---

[23]See our discussion in chapter 5 under the third commandment.

[24]John Calvin. *Commentaries on the Four Last Books of Moses in the Form of a Harmony* (Grand Rapids: Eerdmans, 1950), 2:408 as cited by Rushdoony, *Biblical Law*, 115.

the dispersement and disappearance of any or all wealth obtained in such fraudulent means.

Work, however, was never meant to be a strain or a curse. True, a curse was *connected* with labor after the fall in Genesis 3:17–19, but it never was put on work itself. The curse was to be found in the pain, frustration, and strain that now accompanied work. God's intention from the very beginning was that people would find joy, fulfillment, and blessing in the fact and constancy of work. Six days they were to work and then, like their Lord, they and their households were to rest.

Proverbs frequently stresses the significance and dignity of work:

> "Diligent hands will rule, but laziness ends in slave labor" (Prov. 12:24).
> "Dishonest money dwindles away, but he that gathers money little by little makes it grow" (Prov. 13:11).
> "Do you see a man skilled in his work? He will serve before kings" (Prov. 22:29).

Behind the whole institution of labor lies the principle of human vocation. Calvin, like several of the reformers, gave special emphasis to this biblical doctrine.

> It is to be remarked that the Lord commands every one of us, in all the actions of life, to regard his vocation. For he knows with what great disquietude the human mind is inflamed, with what desultory levity it is hurried hither and thither, and how insatiable is its ambition to grasp different things at once. Therefore, to prevent universal confusion from being produced by our folly and temerity, he has appointed to all their particular duties in different spheres of life. And that no one might rashly transgress the limits prescribed, he has styled such spheres of life *vocations*, or *callings*. Every individual's line of life, therefore, is, as it were, a post assigned to him by the Lord, that he may not wander about in uncertainty all his days . . . It is sufficient if we know that the principle and foundation of right conduct in every case is the vocation of the Lord, and that he who disregards it will never keep the right way in the duties of his station. He may sometimes, perhaps, achieve something apparently laudable; but however it may appear in the eyes of men, it will be rejected at the throne of God; besides which there will be no consistency between the various parts of his life.[25]

Not only is work or labor a vocation from God, but it is one of God's good gifts. The writer of Ecclesiastes repeats the fact that things as mundane as eating, drinking, and finding enjoyment in one's labor are all gifts

---

[25]John Calvin, *Institutes* 3, 10, 6.

from the hand of God (Eccl. 2:24–26; 3:22; 5:18–20; 8:15). Since work is a gift as much and as real as are wealth, possessions, honor (Eccl. 6:2) and one's wife (Eccl. 9:9), "the Preacher" urges "whatever your hand finds to do, do it with your might" (Eccl. 9:10). The apostle Paul will add to this citation from the Preacher "work with all your heart, as working for the Lord, not for men." Work, in the biblical model of holiness, is a heavenly vocation, received as a gift, and is performed not with an eye primarily to pleasing men, but as unto the Lord.

Holiness, then, permeated the whole tenor and fiber of Israel's life, whether it involved worship of the living God or their day to day employment. The whole of life involved a constant dedication and consecration of all of its components as a holy people set themselves apart to live in communion with a holy God.

Chapter 10

Holiness in the Family and Society

"The first means to attain to holiness, which is to make the Israelite reflect the holiness of God, is uniformly to reverence his parents."[1] Thus Leviticus 19:1–3 affirmed:

> The LORD said to Moses, "Speak to the entire assembly of Israel and say to them: 'Be holy, because I, the LORD your God, am holy. Each of you must respect his mother and father, and you must observe my Sabbaths: I am the LORD your God.'"

Ginsburg noted that only twice in the whole law had this introductory formula been used, "Speak to the entire assembly of Israel": here in Leviticus 19:2 and in Exodus 12:3 at the institution of the Passover. Ginsburg went on to comment:

> Thus the group of precepts contained in [Leviticus 19] opens with the fifth commandment in the Decalogue (Exod. xx.12), or, as the Apostle calls it, the first commandment with promise (Eph. vi.2). During the second Temple, already the spiritual authorities called attention to the singular fact that this is one of the three instances in the Scriptures where, contrary to the usual practice, the mother is mentioned before the father; the other two being Gen. xliv. 20 and Lev. xxi.2. As children ordinarily fear the father and love mother, hence they say that precedence is here given to the

---

[1]Christian David Ginsburg, "Leviticus," as cited in Charles J. Ellicott, ed. *Ellicott's Commentary on the Whole Bible* (1897; reprint, Grand Rapids: Zondervan, 1959), 1:421.

152

mother in order to inculcate the duty of fearing them both alike. . . . The parents, they urge, are God's representatives upon earth; hence as God is both to be "honored" with our substance (Prov. iii.9), and as He is to be "feared" (Deut. vi.13), so our parents are both to be "honored" (Exod. xx.12), and "feared" ([Lev.] xix.3); and as he who blasphemed the name of God is stoned ([Lev.] xxiv.16) so he who curses his father or mother is stoned ([Lev.] xx.9).[2]

Accordingly, both God and parents were to be honored and revered; for rebellion or an assault on one or the other was an attack on God's fundamental structure for order and responsibility in society.

THE OLD TESTAMENT FOUNDATIONS OF THE FAMILY

A family consists of all who are united by blood and are usually living in a common dwelling. In fact, one of the Semitic terms[3] for a "family" is "house" (בַּיִת; Ruth 4:11; Ps. 68:6[7]) and to found a family was "to build a house" (Neh. 7:4).

The Institution of the Family

The first and the seventh ordinance in the usual list of creation mandates[4] extending from Genesis 1:28 to Genesis 2:23–24 are closely related and bear directly on the subject of the family. God ordained the union of male and female in marriage to meet their personal need for companionship, to multiply the human race, and to be the main unit and central authority for responsibly subduing the earth and exercising control over it. Human family life, then, constituted God's norm for meaningful existence as the pattern is set forth in Genesis 2:4–5:1.

The monogamous relationship was likewise set forth as the normal intention for marriage—the foundation and cornerstone of the family (Gen. 2:23–24). Only a man's or woman's relationship to God superseded this relationship (Deut. 13:6–10; Luke 14:26). The family is a divine institution and not: (1) a stage in human evolution (as William Robertson Smith or Sir James G. Frazer taught); (2) a derivative from the psychoanalytical observation of spin-offs from the Oedipus Complex (Freud); or (3) something

---

[2]Ginsburg, "Leviticus," 421–22.

[3]There are two other Hebrew words that are not used very frequently at all in the sense of family: אֶלֶף, "thousand" or "family" in Judg. 6:15 and מִשְׁפָּחָה, "clan" or larger family group in Gen. 24:38. This latter term does appear in Ugaritic as a noun meaning "family."

[4]See John Murray, *Principles of Conduct* (Grand Rapids: Eerdmans, 1957), 27–44. Murray lists: procreation, replenishing the earth, subduing the earth, dominion over the creatures, labor, weekly sabbath, and marriage as the seven. The texts he gives are Genesis 1:27, 28; 2:2, 3, 15, 24.

that originated in the fertility cults of mother religion and father religion (Gerhardus Van den Leeuv).[5] In God's plan for the family its origin, function, and perpetuity are measured not by humanistic or societal conventions, but by the counsel and word of God. The quality, meaningfulness, and productivity of life were best when God's order and purpose for the family were recognized.

When God created man in his image, he also created woman in his image (Gen. 1:27). Even though man had a chronological priority in his appearance on the scene, the biblical text takes special pains to raise the woman to an equal level: she was a fitting complement to assist him (כְּנֶגְדּוֹ עֵזֶר; "suitable helper," Gen. 2:20). She was not only to be the one who put an end to his solitude, she was also to be a helpmate especially endowed by God to aid man in fulfilling his calling of tilling and keeping the ground (Gen. 2:15). As helper, Eve was not a hired hand; on the contrary she was more of a wonderwoman as can be seen from the joyous exclamation of Adam when she was presented to him. He responded in bubbly excitement (if I may paraphrase it), "Now, at last; there she is: Miss Eden: my very own, my special friend." Some of that rendering may include dubious marginal readings (I write playfully), but the substance is on target.

Immediately after this recognition, "God emphasizes that man is fulfilled in his wife, in the sense that he becomes truly *adult* through her: 'Therefore a man leaves his father and mother [a symbol of the passage to adulthood] and cleaves to his wife [to cleave is not to possess, the word indicating a relationship of interpersonal fidelity] and they become one flesh' (v. 24). The fulfillment is in this appearance of one flesh. One could not underline more clearly the equal ontological dignity of man and woman, called to constitute together the human unity upon which the blessing of God rests."[6]

The Role of the Family

From the institution of marriage comes a "house" or "family" with the husband and father as its head, the wife as an equal and a most fitting helper in fulfilling the cultural mandate (Gen. 2:20, 24, 25), and children

---

[5]For a discussion and bibliography on these positions, see R. J. Rushdoony, *The Institutes of Biblical Law* (Nutley, N.J.: Craig, 1973), 159–61.

[6]Roger Mehl, *Society and Love: Ethical Problems of Family Life*, trans. James H. Farley (Philadelphia: Westminster, 1964), 72–73. R. David Freedman, "Woman, a Power Equal to Man," *Biblical Archaeology Review* 9 (1983): 56–58, argued as this book went to press that there were two Hebrew roots for עֵזֶר, one to help and the other (*ǵzr*) to be strong. The second is the more frequent meaning of the noun (thirteen of the twenty-one instances). The other term כְּנֶגְדּוֹ only appears here in Gen. 2:18 and is translated in later Hebrew as "equal." The resulting translation instead of "a suitable helper" is "a power (or strength) equal to him." This translation may now be the preferred one.

who honor and respect both father and mother (Exod. 20:12; Deut. 5:16). This three-way mutual responsibility of father, mother, and children was the hallmark of successful and biblical families.

Husband and wife were to be equals before God, deeply devoted and in love with each other, sharing together with one voice in training of their children. Proverbs speaks with special emphasis on all these matters. The husband was to be "captivated by her [his wife's] love" (Prov. 5:19) and ardently devoted to "the wife of [his] youth" (Prov. 5:18). Conjugal fidelity and the monogamous relationship is taken so seriously as the only norm for marriage and sexual relationships that it has been immortalized in an allegory on marital fidelity in Proverbs 5:15–21 and made the grounds for the most frequent warnings against the loose woman or seductress in Proverbs 2:16–19; 5:3–14; 6:24–29, 32–36; 7:6–27; and 9:13–18. To court this kind of woman and to indulge in sexual sin is to flirt with death itself (Prov. 2:18–19) and social disgrace (Prov. 6:26, 32–35). Why, asks the writer of Proverbs, should "you give your best strength to others and your years to one who is cruel?" (Prov. 5:9). Such violent action against your "partner" and "closest friend" (אַלּוּף; Prov. 2:17) is a violation of a "covenant" "made before God" (Prov. 2:17; Mal. 2:14). Therefore, marriage is more than a social convention or a horizontal agreement between a man and a woman; it has a vertical aspect. God is a "witness" to all marriage agreements (Mal. 2:14). And marriage is a covenant made not only before mortals, but before God and as such it is a "covenant" and not a social contract that can be broken when one or both human parties want it dissolved.

The wife is never a mere possession, chattel, or solely a child-bearer. She is "from the LORD" (Prov. 19:14). Finding a wife is like "receiv[ing] favor from the LORD" (Prov. 18:22). She can be either her husband's pride and joy ("crown," Prov. 12:4) or like "rottenness" or "decay in his bones" (Prov. 12:4). The model for the godly wife is given in Proverbs 31:10–31. There she is depicted as a competent manager of goods and real estate, an expert businesswoman in a cottage industry, a competent mother and wife, and a person with a strong sense of personal worth able to carry out her sphere of authority with resoluteness and great efficiency! She is no "helpless slave" or "pretty parasite";[7] she is "woman of valor" (אֵשֶׁת־חַיִל).

Children, on the other hand, were to honor their parents as God's representatives on the earth. We have already seen how significantly the text stressed that both parents were to be respected and how it linked rebellion against them with rebellion against God. Uppermost in this role

---

[7]See Rushdoony, *Biblical Law*, 164. Terms are his.

of respect for parents is the child's responsibility to learn the law of God from his or her parents: "These commandments that I give you today are to be upon your hearts. Impress them on your children. Talk about them when you sit at home and when you walk along the road, when you lie down and when you get up" (Deut. 6:6–7; cf. Deut. 4:7–9). Moral and religious education, then, was a family-centered responsibility.

The child, on his or her part, was to "honor" the parents. This honoring, if we are to judge on the basis of the usage of the verb "to honor" in the Old Testament, involved: (1) highly prizing them (Prov. 4:8); (2) caring and showing affection for them (Ps. 91:15); and (3) showing respect, fear, and reverence to them (Lev. 19:3). When Ephesians 6:1 uses the word to "obey," it immediately qualifies it with "in the Lord." Parents then, are to be shown honor, but nowhere was their word to become a rival or substitute for God's Word.

But another, but less pleasant aspect of education and discipling involved chastisement. Sparing the rod, advises Proverbs 13:24, was equivalent to hating one's son. As Derek Kidner observed, ". . . If wisdom is life itself ([Prov.] 8:35, 36), a hard way to it is better than a soft way to death ('Thou shalt beat him with the rod, and shalt deliver his soul from Sheol,' [Prov.] 23:14; cf. 19:18)."[8] Chastening is sometimes necessary, continued Kidner because:

> First, 'foolishness is bound up in the heart of a child'; it will take more than words to dislodge it ([Prov.] 22:15). Secondly, character (in which wisdom embodies itself) is a plant that grows more sturdily for some cutting back (cf. [Prov.] 15:32, 33; 5:11, 12; Heb. 12:11)—and this from early days . . . In 'a child left to himself' the only predictable product is shame ([Prov.] 29:15).[9]

Unfortunately, not always can success be guaranteed from either approach or even a combination of teaching and chastening. Kidner said it well.

> . . . Even the best training cannot instil wisdom, but only encourage the choice to seek it (e.g. [Prov.] 2:1ff.). A son may be too opinionated to learn ([Prov.] 13:1; cf. 17:21). A good home may produce an idle ([Prov.] 10:5) or a profligate (29:3); he may be rebel enough to despise (15:20), mock (30:17), or curse (30:11; 20:20) his parents; heartless enough to run through their money (28:24), and even to turn a widowed mother out of doors (19:26). While there are parents who only have themselves to thank for

---

[8]Derek Kidner, *The Proverbs: An Introduction and Commentary* (London: Tyndale Press, 1964), 51.
[9]Kidner, *Proverbs,* 51.

their shame (29:15), it is ultimately the man himself who must bear his own blame, for it is *his* attitude to wisdom (29:3a; 2:2ff.), *his* consent given or withheld (1:10) in the face of temptation which sets his course.[10]

The Promise of Long Life

The fifth commandment is the first, as the apostle Paul observed in Ephesians 6:2, to have a promise attached to it. In one sense, the promise of life stood over against all the commandments (Deut. 4:1, 40; 5:29, 33; 7:12–16; 8:1; 16:20; 28:58–63; 30:15–16; 32:46–47). Even Proverbs urges, "Listen, my son, accept what I say, and the years of your life will be many" (Prov. 4:10 *et passim* in Proverbs on "life"). Yet, in another sense, this commandment was particularly marked and therefore seems to have a certain primacy.

The same promise that is found with the fifth commandment explicitly appears in Deuteronomy 22:6–7 where birds' eggs or newly hatched birds were not to be separated from the hen who was their source of life. Likewise, although with the explicit promise of life attached, Leviticus 22:28 and Exodus 23:19 prohibits killing a cow, ewe, or goat with their young in the same day or boiling the young in its mother's milk. Certainly, these injunctions were given to foster humane sensitivities in people[11] but they were also aimed at fostering a regard for life. Thus, what happened in these "minimal cases . . . illustrate[d] the maximal reach of the Law."[12]

Does this promise have permanent value or was it directly linked with the land of promise and theocratic in its form? Certainly one of the reasons for the Babylonian captivity was the dishonoring of one's parents (Ezek. 22:7, 15; note also the national character of the promise in Deut. 4:26, 40; 32:46–47).

But it is also true that the apostle Paul left off the concluding words referring to the nation and made the promise refer to more than one land and one people in Ephesians 6:2. Thus, we conclude that the promise applies directly to the nation Israel and as a general principle to all individuals. Here again we find what was given in a concrete form was also universalized (see chapter 2).

But if the promise exceeds theocratic and nationalistic boundaries, can we affirm that children who show respect and honor to their parents

---

[10]Kidner, *Proverbs*, 51–52.

[11]See W. C. Kaiser, Jr., "The Current Crisis in Exegesis and the Apostolic Use of Deuteronomy 25:4 in I Corinthians 9:8–10," *Journal of the Evangelical Theological Society* 21 (1978): 11–18, for development of this case for inculcating a spirit of gentleness and regard for life.

[12]Rushdoony, *Biblical Law*, 169.

are invariably favored with long life and prosperity? Does it ever happen that some properly obedient children nevertheless die young and poor? These questions raise the issue of the moral interpretation of Scripture (see chapter 4). Since we live in a fallen world and are involved with more issues and influences than just this one named in the fifth commandment, some respectful children have died young—sometimes due to no fault of their own. Furthermore, universal or indefinite moral statements often denote only what generally or normally takes place. In that sense, many moral propositions are cast in a proverbial form which, by their very nature and definition, gather up only the greater number of instances without pausing, at that point, to qualify the statements with a *ceteris paribus*, "all other things being equal."

But so significant is the matter of *ceteris paribus* attached to the promise with honoring one's parents that we must comment further. H. H. Rowley, in another connection, dealt deftly with this same issue. He counseled:

> That virtue leads to well-being is firmly believed to be one side of the truth . . . ; but it is not the whole of the truth. . . . Because here and now there is sin, the fruits of virtue may not always be reaped . . . the man who plants a fruit tree may not gather the fruit. The frosts may carry off the blossom or the storms the fruit and the tree yield no harvest, since the harvest depends not merely on the nature and quality of the tree but on other factors. But no wise man would conclude that the nature and quality of the tree were of no moment. [13]

A promise of physical and material, if not national, life is clearly promised then. Not only is the quality of a person's life in every nation and every age connected with the way individuals respond, first of all, to parents and then to all who are in authority, but also all of life. Since humans were made from "the dust of the earth," the dirt is affected by their spiritual progress or decline. So one of the great bulwarks against disease, infertility of the soil and herds, and ecological disaster is for children to honor their parents and, correspondingly, all who have legitimate authority over them.

THE OLD TESTAMENT FOUNDATIONS OF SOCIAL JUSTICE

The command to honor one's parents is large and comprehensive—as can be demonstrated from the universality of Old Testament moral propositions or narratives and from the unusual grammatical form of using

---

[13]H. H. Rowley, *The Faith of Israel* (London: SCM, 1956), 111.

no finite verbs in which the Decalogue is cast (see above our discussion on the Decalogue). Thus it is not limited to the immediate superiors under view—one's parents, but it extends to all that are our superiors: governors, magistrates, teachers, leaders in the house of God, and all who are superior by virtue of the gifts of divine providence, whether of age, riches, or knowledge.

The fabric of society, insofar as it represents individuals who are made in the image of God, or is made up of human institutions that had their origins in the word of God, is of great concern to our holy God. Neither individualism or communal relationships can be sacrificed for the sake of the other. Western civilization tends to value individualism more than corporate solidarity, but both have their proper place in the economy of God. Holiness and justice must permeate not only such personal topics as sex, truthfulness, and financial integrity, but also such social issues as the needs of the Third World, racism, and nuclear holocausts. The concerns of the Old Testament world may now be investigated as a basis for making the social responsibilities of this question universal.

Social Responsibility to the Poor and Needy

Hardening one's heart or shutting up one's hand against a brother who was poor was a sin[14] against God (Deut. 15:7–11). Instead, "blessed is he who is kind to the needy. He who oppresses the poor shows contempt for their Maker; but whoever is kind to the needy honors God" (Prov. 14:21, 31).

There are over a dozen Hebrew words for the "poor" and almost three hundred instances in the Old Testament where they are mentioned.[15] The Old Testament could be very specific about the community's social responsibility for the poor. Leviticus 25:35 bluntly advises, "If one of your countrymen becomes poor and is unable to support himself among

---

[14]A huge bibliography exists on this topic. Some key pieces are: Norman W. Porteous, "The Care of the Poor in the Old Testament," *Living the Mystery*, ed. J. I. McCord (London: Blackwell, 1967), 143–55; F. C. Fensham, "Widow, Orphan and the Poor in Ancient Near Eastern Legal and Wisdom Literature," *Journal of Near Eastern Studies* 21 (1962): 129–39; Ernest Bammel, "The Poor in the Old Testament," *Theological Dictionary of the New Testament* 6:888–94; G. J. Botterweck, "אֶבְיוֹן," *Theological Dictionary of the Old Testament*, ed. G. Johannes Botterweck and Helmer Ringgren, tr. John T. Willis (Grand Rapids: Eerdmans, 1974), 1:27–41; Richard D. Patterson, "The Widow, the Orphan and the Poor in the Old Testament and Extra-Biblical Literature," *Bibliotheca Sacra* 130 (1973): 223–35; John T. Willis, "Old Testament Foundations of Social Justice," *Restoration Quarterly* 18 (1975): 65–87 also in *Christian Social Ethics*, ed. Perry C. Cotham (Grand Rapids: Baker, 1979), 21–43; and C. Brown, *New International Dictionary of New Testament Theology* 2: 820–28; Rushdoony, *Biblical Law*, 246–53.

[15]Botterweck, 29.

you, help him." All who are "kind to the poor" "lend to the LORD" (Prov. 19:17). Such deeds did not go unnoticed or unrewarded by God. The psalmist pronounced a beatitude over all such: "Blessed is he who has regard for the weak" (Ps. 41:1).

The law required that the corners and the gleanings of the fields, fruit trees and vines be left for the poor and the strangers (Lev. 19:9–10; 23:22; Deut. 24:19–22; Judg. 8:2; Ruth 2:6, 8, 9; Isa. 17:5–6; Jer. 49:9; Mic. 7:1). Every seventh year, the fields and orchards were to be left fallow and what grew on its own in fields was to be given to the needy (Exod. 23:10–11; Lev. 25:2–7).

Likewise, in the Old Testament narratives injustice and acts of taking unfair advantage of the poor drew the quick rebuke of God's servants, the prophets. In Nathan's parable about the rich man who arbitrarily expropriated the poor man's ewe lamb, both a sense of fairness, pity, and compassion for the poor were in evidence (2 Sam. 12:5–6). No less stinging was the indictment given by the prophet Elijah against Ahab for moving in such a violent and unjust manner against a poorer farmer, Naboth (1 Kings 21:1–21).

But it was the writing prophets who gave some of the severest rebukes in Scripture against exploiting the poor. Amos unmercifully heaped rebuke upon reprimand and gives scolding after scolding, especially for the supercilious attitude of the rich women "who oppress[ed] the poor, who crush[ed] the needy, and [said] to [their] husbands, 'Bring us some drinks!'" (Amos 4:1). Instead of manifesting a generous hand, they "deprive[d] the poor of justice in the courts" (Amos 5:12; cf. Isa. 10:1–2). Greedily Israel "ruined [God's] vineyard; the spoil of the poor [was] in [their] houses" (Isa. 3:14). The Lord asked, "What do you mean by crushing my people, by grinding the faces of the poor?" (Isa. 3:15).

If the people wanted something "religious" to do, why, asked Isaiah, didn't they consider a new fast—one that God had ordered instead of all these concocted days of artificial grief? Isaiah called the people to "share [their] bread with the hungry," "provide the poor wanderer with shelter," "clothe [the naked]" and "do not turn away from [helping] your own flesh and blood" (Isa. 58:7). Probably there is no better chapter on a call for social justice in the Bible than Isaiah 58. It is a brilliant exposé of ceremonial religiosity with a stirring call for pure and undefiled religion which is to aid the helpless, poor, and the weak.

The proper model for godliness and holiness of life towards the poor and the needy is set forth in Job 29:12–16 and 31:16–22.

> I rescued the poor who cried for help,
>   and the fatherless who had none to assist him.
> The man who was dying blessed me;

> I made the widow's heart sing.
> I put on righteousness as my clothing;
>   justice was my robe and my turban.
> I was eyes to the blind
>   and feet to the lame.
> I was a father to the needy;
>   I took up the case of the stranger. (29:12–16)

> If I have denied the desires of the poor
>   or let the eyes of the widow grow weary,
> if I have kept my bread to myself,
>   not sharing it with the fatherless—
> but from my youth I reared him as would a father,
>   and from my birth I guided the widow—
> if I have seen anyone perish for lack of clothing,
>   or a needy man without a garment,
> and his heart did not bless me
>   for warming him with the fleece from my sheep,
> if I have raised my hand against the fatherless,
>   knowing that I had influence in court,
> then let my arm fall from the shoulder,
>   let it be broken off at the joint. (31:16–22)

Men and women cannot close their ears to the cries of the poor (Prov. 21:13). They must instead "share [their] food with the poor" (Prov. 22:9) and "care about justice for the poor" (Prov. 29:7). Happiness comes, in part, from being "kind to the needy" (Prov. 14:21) and from opening one's "hands to the needy" even as the woman of valor did (Prov. 31:20).

Social Responsibility to Widows and Orphans

Holiness also demanded that the cry of the widow[16] and orphan[17] be heeded. In no case were they to be taken advantage of or oppressed in any way (Exod. 22:22–23). Failure to observe this injunction would, as that text warned, excite the wrath of God against all offenders. These defenseless people had the special interest and protection of God: "The Lord . . . sustains the fatherless and the widow" (Ps. 146:9). He watches

---

[16]Beside the literature cited in footnote 14, see Harry Hoffner, "אַלְמָנָה," *Theological Dictionary of the Old Testament* 1:287–91; Roland DeVaux, *Ancient Israel: Its Life and Institutions*, trans. John McHugh (New York: McGraw-Hill, 1961), 39–40, 54–55, 149; Gustav Stählin, "The Widow in the Old Testament," *Theological Dictionary of the New Testament*, 9:444–48; and Jack B. Scott, "אַלְמָנָה," *Theological Wordbook of the Old Testament*, 1:47.

[17]Beside the literature in footnote 14, see John E. Hartley, "יָתוֹם," *Theological Wordbook of the Old Testament* 1:419; J. Pridmore, "Orphan," *New International Dictionary of New Testament Theology*, 2:737–38.

over the very edges of the widow's land, maintaining its boundaries (Prov. 15:25).

A "widow" (אַלְמָנָה) was a woman who had been divested of her male protector (husband, sons, brothers) and her source of financial support. Thus her needs were twofold when her husband died: protection from exploitation and help in time of distress. Society was put under obligation to this woman and she was to be protected from creditors of her deceased husband or predators who sought to seize her property as a spoil (Isa. 10:2). In all civil suits, she was to receive the benefit of doubt (Exod. 22:21; Deut. 10:18; 27:19; Isa. 1:17, 23; Jer. 7:6; 22:3; Zech. 7:10; Mal. 3:5). As a type of social security, once every three years a tithe of the harvest was shared with the widows, orphans, Levites, and immigrants (Deut. 14:28–29; 26:12–13). Widows along with other poverty-stricken people, were invited to share the festive tables of those celebrating the Feast of Weeks (Deut. 16:11) and the Feast of Booths (Deut. 16:14).

Thus the people were blessed when they aided the widows (Deut. 14:29) and the leaders were fulfilling their duty of seeing that justice was done when they gave special attention to the needs of widows (Isa. 1:17, 23).

The plight of the "orphan" (יָתוֹם) in the Old Testament, whether the mother is living or not, is that the father has died (Job 24:9). Forty-one times orphans are mentioned and God himself is called the "Father of the fatherless" (Ps. 68:5; cf. Ps. 10:14). Justice is owed these defenseless ones, just as the widows, the poor, and needy deserved it. Only a corrupt society would dare extort and cheat these little ones (Isa. 10:2; Ezek. 22:7). On the other hand, the quality of one's holy living could be quickly gauged by the way that person treated the orphan and the widow. In the meantime, the helplessness of the orphan's situation can be seen in the fact that they were "wandering beggars" (Ps. 109:9–10). Time and again the Old Testament warned against all evil dealings and exploitation of these special objects of the Lord's care (Deut. 27:19; Job 6:27; 22:9; 24:3, 9; Jer. 5:28), for Yahweh himself "executes justice for the fatherless" (Deut. 10:18; cf. Ps. 146:9; Prov. 23:10–11; Hos. 14:3).

Social Responsibility to the Oppressed and Oppression

Israel was specifically enjoined not to oppress foreigners and strangers[18] (Exod. 22:21; 23:9) since they knew what such treatment was like from their years in Egypt. Whole waves of oppressors followed the pattern of the affliction they had received in Egypt (Exod. 1:11–13; 3:8–9)

---

[18]Leonard J. Coppes, "עָנָה," *Theological Wordbook of the Old Testament* 2:682–84; and Walter C. Kaiser, Jr., "לָחַץ," *Theological Wordbook of the Old Testament* 1:478.

and during the period of the judges (Judg. 1:34; 2:18; 4:3; 6:9; 10:12; 1 Sam. 10:18). But in each case God sent a deliverer. In like manner, God will send deliverance when the nations also face oppressors (Isa. 19:20).

Such institution of oppression and bondage is strongly opposed by God. In all such physical, economic, or political bondage, his divine order is the same, "Let my people go."

When a government (or ruler) orders its subjects to do something that violates the direct commands of God, such as murdering children (Exod. 1:16–17) or worshiping an idol (Dan. 3) or ceasing to pray (Dan. 6), then the government and its rulers must be disobeyed. Obedience to God takes precedence over all other edicts even as Peter and John argued in their refusal to stop preaching as ordered by the authorities (Acts 4:19, "Judge for yourselves whether it is right in God's sight to obey you rather than God").

Oppression which is directed against spiritual obligations or personal rights is condemned by God. Magistrates, rulers, judges, employers, and individuals are all challenged to desist in perpetuating such practices or else they will face the judgment of God. As God's ministers and servants of his people, government officials are particularly liable to his wrath for failure to observe this warning.

Chapter 11

Holiness in a Regard for Life

God alone is the giver and maintainer of life, therefore he alone has the right to take it away. The sixth commandment makes plain the fact that anyone who snuffs out someone else's life without possessing the authority of God to do so, is a murderer.

THE SANCTITY OF LIFE

We have already discussed the meaning of the word רָצַח under our discussion on the Decalogue in chapter 5, but we must further develop here the meaning and extent of that prohibition. God's law could and did distinguish between deliberate premeditated murder and accidental manslaughter[1] (Exod. 21:13–14; Num. 35:11; Deut. 19:4–13). So the focus of the sixth commandment fell on the deliberate, premeditated taking of another person's life.

But that destruction of life could and did take other forms. All forms of self-murder or suicide were included. Murder could be self-induced, as Adam Clarke[2] informs us "by immoderate and superstitious fastings";

---

[1]See the numerous Hebrew expressions for unintentionality in chapter 6, under Exodus 21:12–17.

[2]Adam Clarke, *Discourses on Various Subjects Relating to the Being and Attributes of God and His Works* (New York: McElrath & Bangs, 1830), 2:31 as cited by Rousas J. Rushdoony, *The Institutes of Biblical Law* (Nutley, N.J.: Craig, 1973), 222.

"willful neglect of health"; an addiction "to riot and excess, to drunkenness and gluttony; to extravagant pleasures, to inactivity and slothfulness"; or even as a result of fierce and furious passions.

This commandment, like the others; was heeded not only when the negative precept was observed; it could only be said to have been truly fulfilled when its opposite affirmations were heeded as well. Accordingly, the sanctity of life is preserved not only when I refrain from all acts of suicide or premeditated murder; I must also:

> . . . study faithfully to defend the life of [my] neighbor, and prac-
> tically to declare that it is dear to [me]; for in that summary no
> mere negative phrase is used, but the words expressly set forth
> that [my] neighbors are to be loved. It is unquestionable, then,
> that those whom God there commands to be loved, He here com-
> mends the lives to our care. There are, consequently, two parts in
> the commandment,—*first*, that we should not vex, or oppress, or
> be at enmity with any; and, *secondly*, that we should not only live
> at peace with men, without exciting quarrels, but also should aid,
> as far as we can, the miserable who are unjustly oppressed, and
> should endeavor to resist the wicked, lest they should injure men
> as they list.[3]

Respect for life is not the same thing as Albert Schweitzer's rever-ence for life, insists R. J. Rushdoony.[4] To elevate anything, including life, above God was to violate the first commandment. It is wrong to place any life, including ours before our commitment to God himself. "To view death as the ultimate evil is thus morally wrong. Rather, death is a conse-quence of the real evil, sin; it was sin which brought death into the world, and it is sin rather than death that man must reckon with."[5]

THE NECESSITY OF CAPITAL PUNISHMENT

The life of an individual made in the image of God was so valued that all violent forms of snatching life away had to be requited on God's terms, not on human terms. While there apparently was a "ransom" or "substitute" payment available for all other crimes that demanded a capital punishment in the Old Testament, Numbers 35:31 explicitly denied this option in the case of first degree murder.

The key passage in this discussion is Genesis 9:5–6: ". . . I will demand an accounting for the life of his fellow man. Whoever sheds the

---

[3]John Calvin, *Commentaries on the Four Last Books of Moses* (Grand Rapids: Eerdmans, 1950), 3:21.

[4]Rushdoony, *Biblical Law*, 222.

[5]Rushdoony, *Biblical Law*, 222.

blood of man, by man shall his blood be shed. . . ." The verb, יִשָּׁפֵךְ, "he shall or may be shed," can be understood by its Hebrew form to be either giving merely a suggestion, permission, or order that that life must be surrendered.

The context makes plain that the verb יִשָּׁפֵךְ, "he shall shed," must be a command. Verse 5 states that God demands it: "I [=God] will demand an accounting for the life of his fellow man." The fact that God requires this retribution "by man," also makes it clear that this requital is an earthly retribution and not an ultimate or final time of reckoning. Though this ordinance does not specify any details on how it is to be carried out, it requires that the work be done "by man" (בָּאָדָם).[6]

While this ordinance is deliberately broad enough to cover all conditions, it does not contemplate or include the custom of blood revenge. H. C. Leupold remarks:

> . . . Blood revenge, unfortunately, substitutes revenge for the purposes of fair justice, and frequently it degenerated into the most cruel of feuds. When, therefore, the Scriptures do speak of blood revenge, it is merely for the purpose of mitigating its cruelty, Exod. 21:13; Deut. 4:41f.; 19:2–10; Num. 35:6ff. However, words like Deut. 19:12 are in entire harmony with our passage.[7]

Nor should we wonder why so harsh a penalty as capital punishment is required for all murderers. Verse 6 adds this final clause, "for [because] (כִּי) in the image of God has God made man." Some, like the Belgic commentator, Venema,[8] interpreted the word כִּי as "although" (as it can be rendered in Gen. 8:21 and Josh. 17:13) meaning that the murderer's being in the image of God should be no impediment to his sentence of death. But this scruple had already been met in the divine requirement that the murderer should be put to death by human hands. Bush[9] argued that the "because" clause referred to the fact that people represented their maker in their exercise of authority and the administration of justice. But the most natural interpretation is the one that states the reason why the death penalty had been required in verses 5–6: "The murderer is to suffer that which he has inflicted; for murder is not only the extreme of unbrotherliness, but also a crime against the inviolable majesty of the Divine image, which even after the Fall is fundamentally the *character indelebilis*

---

[6]The preposition בְּ with "man" is known as the *beth instrumentalis*. בְּ also is combined with the article thus making the reference to *generic* man.

[7]H. C. Leupold, *Exposition of Genesis* (Grand Rapids: Baker, 1953), 1:334–35.

[8]As cited by George Bush, *Notes on Genesis* (1860; reprint, Minneapolis, Minn.: James and Klock, 1976), 1:155.

[9]Bush, *Notes*, 1:155–56.

of mankind and of each individual."[10] The person who destroys another person, who bears the image of God, does violence to God himself—as if he had killed God in effigy.

While the concept of the *imago Dei* is notoriously difficult to define in its entirety, certainly most can agree with Nahum Sarna's comment:

> The idea of man "in the image of God" must inevitably include within the scope of its meaning all those faculties and gifts of character that distinguish man from the beast and that are needed for the fulfillment of his task on earth, namely, intellect, free will, self-awareness, consciousness of the existence of others, conscience, responsibility and self-control. Moreover, being created "in the image of God" implies that human life is infinitely precious.[11]

Since all persons continue to bear the image of God, it is fair to say that this ordinance has permanent relevance and validity. "No crime is as extreme and, as concerns the person who is victim, none is as irremediable, as the crime of taking life itself. Furthermore, in no other instance of biblical jurisprudence is the reason for the infliction of a penalty stated to be that man is made in the image of God.[12]

There are several objections to this ordinance. Derek Kidner argues that "one cannot simply transfer verse 6 to the statute book unless one is prepared to include verses 4 ("You shall not eat flesh with . . . its blood") and 5 ("of every beast I will require it") with it. Capital punishment has to be defended on wider grounds."[13] But is it not true that the New Testament specifically forbade Gentiles from eating blood or things strangled that had not been properly bled (Acts 15:20, 29; cf. Lev. 3:17; 17:14; Deut. 12:16, 23)? Thus the Jerusalem Council removed the demand for circumcision (Acts 15:5, 24) and urged that Gentiles keep three food laws of which one dealt with this proscription of blood. The reason appears to be that life and blood were connected, therefore, no life could be taken except as permitted by God. Likewise on verse 5, there was the principle of animal liability in the law (Exod. 21:28–36).

Others will point to God's apparent merciful treatment of Cain (Gen. 4:10–16). Did not God protect Cain, they will argue, by merely

---

[10]Franz Delitzsch, *A New Commentary on Genesis*, tr. Sophia Taylor (1888; reprint, Minneapolis, Minn.: Klock and Klock, 1978), 1:287.

[11]Nahum M. Sarna, *Understanding Genesis* (New York: McGraw-Hill, 1966), 15–16.

[12]John Murray, *Principles of Conduct* (Grand Rapids: Eerdmans, 1957), 112.

[13]Derek Kidner, *Genesis: An Introduction and Commentary* (London: Tyndale, 1967), 101. Norman Anderson, *Issues of Life and Death* (Downers Grove, Ill.: InterVarsity, 1978), 112 is of the same opinion.

putting a mark on his forehead? But even the question contains a false assumption, for Leupold carefully noted:

> . . . That the text [Gen. 4:16] does not say that God set a mark *in* or *on* Cain (Hebrew, *be*) but *for* Cain (Hebrew, *le*), marking a dative of interest or advantage. Consequently, we are rather to think of some sign that God allowed to appear for Cain's reassurance, "a sign of guaranty" or a "pledge or token". . . . There is therefore, no ground for supposing that Cain went about as a marked man all the rest of his life. Anyhow, *'oth* does not mean mark![14]

The key to answering the question of what God's purpose was in protecting Cain is to note the importance and significance of family law. The family was barred from acting as prosecutor, jury, witness, judge, and executor. Since we assume that only the family was available at this early stage in the history of civilization, the principles institutionalized in the law of juvenile delinquents in Deuteronomy 21:18–21 must have been in vogue restraining the family by virtue of blood ties from assisting in the prosecution of their own child. Therefore, the family was so important, that it could not kill any part of itself.[15] Thus God was not protecting Cain so much as the life and ties of the family. The death penalty belongs only to God and the state, it is not available to individuals, groups of vigilantees, or the family.

THE SANCTITY OF THE LIFE OF THE UNBORN

The key passage in the hotly contested debate over the destruction of the human embryo or fetus[16] is Exodus 21:22–25 (see my discussion of that passage in chapter 6). Even in the early church it is possible to cite contrary opinions on the issue of abortion. Thus Norman Anderson will appeal to Gregory of Nyssa, a fourth-century church father, who remarked, "It would not be possible to style the unformed embryo a human

---

[14]Leupold, *Genesis*, 1:211.

[15]See the fascinating and convincing discussion of Rushdoony, *Biblical Law*, 358–62. Sarna, in *Understanding Genesis*, remarks, "It is of interest that the culpability of Cain rests upon an unexpressed assumption of the existence of a moral law operative from the beginning of time," p. 31.

[16]The literature on this question is massive. Some of the more prominent articles have been: Bruce K. Waltke, "Old Testament Texts Bearing on Abortion," *Christianity Today* 13 (1968–69): 99–105; *idem*, "Old Testament Texts Bearing on the Problem of the Control of Human Reproduction" in *Birth Control and the Christian*, ed. W. O. Spitzer and C. L. Saylor (Wheaton, Ill.: Tyndale, 1969), 7–23; *idem*, "Reflections From the Old Testament on Abortion," *Journal of the Evangelical Theological Society* 19 (1976): 3–13; Jack W. Cottrell, "Abortion and the Mosaic Law," *Christianity Today* 17 (1972–73): 602–5; Meredith Kline, "*Lex Talionis* and the Human Fetus," *Journal of the Evangelical Theological Society* 20 (1977):193–201.

being, but only a potential one—assuming that it is completed so as to come forth to human birth, while as long as it is in this unformed state it is something other than a human being."[17] On the other hand, the church condemned abortion in the first part of the second century in the *Didache* (ii.2). The Apostolic Constitutions warned, "Thou shalt not slay the child by causing abortion, nor kill that which is begotten; for everything that is shaped, and has received a soul from God, if it be slain shall be avenged as being unjustly destroyed, Ex. 21:23" (8, 3). Tertullian in his *Apologeticum* (9) concurred: "To hinder a birth is merely a speedier man-killing; nor does it matter whether you take away a life that is born, or destroy one that is coming to birth. That is a man which is going to be one; you have the fruit already in its seed."[18]

Is the fetus a human being or is it not? There is the key question—and there are not a great many biblical texts to help us. Traditionally, biblical scholars have pointed to such evidences as both Jeremiah and Paul being known and called by God for their life's work while they were still in the womb (Jer. 1:4–6; Gal. 1:15); and God personally fashioning each individual in the womb as Job and the psalmist contend.

> "Your hands shaped me and made me.
>   Will you now turn and destroy me?
> Remember that you molded me like clay.
>   Will you now turn me to dust again?
> Did you not pour me out like milk
>   and curdle me like cheese,
> clothe me with skin and flesh
>   and knit me together with bones and sinews?
> You gave me life and showed me kindness,
>   and in your providence watched over my spirit." (Job 10:8–12)

David, in agreement with Job, sang:

> For you created my inmost being;
>   you knit me together in my mother's womb.
> I praise you because I am fearfully and wonderfully made;
>   your works are wonderful,
>   I know that full well.
> My frame was not hidden from you
>   when I was made in the secret place.

---

[17]Anderson, *Issues of Life*, 76–77, citing from "Adversus Macedonianos," trans. from *Library of Nicene and Post Nicene Fathers*, Series 2, ed. H. Wace and P. Schaff (Oxford, 1839) 5:320.

[18]All three of these quotes were cited by Rushdoony, *Biblical Law*, 265. See his footnote 6 on p. 265 for six other church fathers on this same question who concur with the judgments expressed in these three.

> When I was woven together in the depths of the earth,
>   your eyes saw my unformed body.
> All the days ordained for me
>   were written in your book before one of them came to be.
>   (Ps. 139:13–16)[19]

These texts, along with Job 3:11 and Luke 1:39–44 may be cited to indicate that God considers the fetus fully human. But Exodus 21:22–25 is even more definitive in its regard for the sanctity of unborn life.

How is the fetus regarded in the covenant code law? In the two cases presented in the Exodus 21:22–25 law, Case A in verse 22 has been widely held as being nothing more than a miscarriage for which an appropriate compensation is sought. Case B in verses 22 and 23, on the other hand, involves not only the loss of the fetus, but of the mother also and is therefore a capital case with the *talion* formula of "life for life."

But this construction of the law will not stand up to the scrutiny of the text. In the first place, "there is absolutely no linguistic justification for translating verse 22 to refer to a miscarriage."[20] The Revised Standard Version, Berkeley Version, New American Bible, Jerusalem Bible, Amplified Bible, Douay-Rheims, Moffatt, and Goodspeed translations and numerous commentaries such as the *Broadman, Wesleyan, Wycliffe, New Bible Commentary, Beacon Bible Commentary,* and *Interpreter's Bible Commentary* are all in gross error in referring to a miscarriage here.[21] The text literally reads "so that her children go [or come] out." The King James Version says "so that her fruit depart." The verb is יָצָא, meaning "to go (or) come out" and the noun is the regular word for "child" (יֶלֶד) with the only irregularity being that the noun (and hence, by agreement, the verb) is in the plural. The use of the term "child" makes it clear that a human being is in view here; the plural is generic to cover the contingency of multiple births or either sex.[22] In fact, Hebrew does have a word for miscarriage that is not used in Exodus 21:22–25, namely שׁכל, "to be bereaved [of children], or to be childless." This root in the *piel* participle is used as a substantive meaning "abortion" (מְשַׁכֶּלֶת, 2 Kings 2:21). Not only is this verb used of the sterile land and vines (2 Kings 2:19; Mal. 3:11)

---

[19]On these verses, see Donald R. Glenn, "An Exegetical and Theological Exposition of Psalm 139," in *Tradition and Testament: Essays in Honor of Charles Lee Feinberg,* ed. John S. and Paul D. Feinberg (Chicago: Moody, 1981), 170, 174–78.

[20]Cottrell, "Abortion," 604.

[21]Cottrell, "Abortion," 603.

[22]Kline, "Lex Talionis," 198–99 does not agree that the plural is used to allow for multiple births. He feels it is used to cover either contingency: a premature, but live birth (v. 22) or a miscarriage (vv. 23–25). But why was שָׁכֹל not used then along with יֶלֶד?

and animals which are caused to abort or experience an abortion (Gen. 31:38; Job 21:10), but it is also used of women who miscarry in Exodus 23:26: "And none will miscarry or be barren in your land"; and Hosea 9:14:

> Give them, O Lord —
> what will you give them?
> Give them wombs that miscarry
> and breasts that are dry.

Moreover, the verb "to come out" is used in every case except one (Num. 12:12, it is used for a stillborn child) for the birth of an ordinary child.[23]

Most of this evidence is now being conceded by those who previously had adopted the case for miscarriage.[24] But the penalty clause is another source of misunderstanding, for some interpret Case A as necessitating only a pecuniary penalty while Case B calls for the *talion* principle. This would seem, then, to suggest to some that the fetus of Case A is less than human!

Meredith Kline, however, has argued that בִּפְלִלִים does not denote a process of assessment[25] based, as in extrabiblical legislation, on the age of the fetus. Rather, he notes that in every context[26] where, what he takes to be an adjectival form (פְּלִילִי with an enclitic ם), פְּלִילִים is used, it deals with "an offense of a most serious nature. In fact, the meaning could well be liability to death."[27] The preposition בְּ is the *bêth* of equivalence that, interestingly enough, is also used in the *talion* formula in Deuteronomy 19:21 to replace the more usual תַּחַת: "a life as an equivalent of a life." Kline concludes, "Hence, *bpllym* in Exod. 21:22 may be regarded as an archaic legal formula expressing the same principle of ransoming a forfeited life that is more fully expressed in Exod. 21:30."[28] The suggested translation for verse 22 according to Kline would be "he must pay for his forfeited life" or "he must pay as one deserving of death (or retribution)."

---

[23]Cottrell, "Abortion," 604.

[24]For example, see Bruce Waltke's modifications in "Reflections on Abortion," *Journal of the Evangelical Theological Society* 19 (1976): 3, n. 3. "[It was] . . . the illogical conclusion I drew from it."

[25]As E. A. Speiser had argued, "The Stem PLL in Hebrew," *Journal of Biblical Literature* 82 (1963): 301–6.

[26]See besides Exod. 21:22; Job 31:11, 28; Deut. 32:31.

[27]Kline, "Lex Talionis," 195.

[28]Kline, "Lex Talionis," 195–96. Kline does argue that Case A involved death to the woman, rather than the fetus, because the verb נָגַף does not simply mean "push" or "shove," but it is normally used of fatal divine judgments in other contexts. Only in Case B is the harm directed to the aborted fetus as well as the mother in Kline's view. This order of victims is in proper sequence of victims as preserved in other laws asserts Kline.

Feticide,[29] we conclude, is indeed murder, and only when the fetus presents a danger to the life of the mother should abortion be considered at all.[30] The *lex talionis* refers to both cases: when harm (אָסוֹן) is done to either the child or the mother. But, in spite of Kline's moving discussion of בִּפְלִלִים, the contrast in verses 22–23 would appear to be between those instances when no damage has come to either mother or child (v. 22) and where damage has come to mother, child, or both (v. 23). The contrast is:

וְלֹא יִהְיֶה אָסוֹן "And no harm occurs" (v. 22)

and

וְאִם־אָסוֹן יִהְיֶה "And if harm occurs" (v. 23).

The value that God sets on the fetus can be seen from the text we quoted earlier from Psalm 139:16. The clause is "your eyes saw my un-formed body (i.e., my embryo)" גָּלְמִי.[31] God, it was then, who "knit me together in my mother's womb" (Ps. 139:13; cf. Job 10:18) and knew me in my prenatal state (Jer. 1:4–5). The value and worth of the forming child is clearly established.

THE PEACE OF GOD AND YAHWEH WARS

After the Lord's celebrated victory at the Red Sea, he was known as a "Man of War" (Exod. 15:3). Gerhard von Rad[32] named the wars that Yahweh commanded "holy wars," but in actuality the Old Testament called them "Yahweh wars" (1 Sam. 18:17; 25:28).[33] But therein lies our

---

[29]We have left out of our discussion infanticide, but such was practiced to the disgrace of Israel. See Morton Smith, "A Note on Burning Babies," *Journal of the American Oriental Society* 95 (1978): 477–79 as he disputes Moshe Weinfeld's explaining away of the Old Testament practice in "The Worship of Molech and of the Queen of Heaven and Its Background," *Ugarit-Forschungen* 4 (1972): 133–54. For the Carthagian cult, see Diodorus 20.14:4ff. and Tertullian, *Apologeticum* 9:2.

[30]See Waltke, *Journal of the Evangelical Theological Society* (1976):13 appealing to Charles Ryrie, *You Mean the Bible Teaches That* (Chicago: Moody, 1974), 91.

[31]Cf. the Aramaic word גּוֹלֶם, "shapeless mass." See Glenn, "Exposition of Psalm 139," 186, n. 99.

[32]Gerhard von Rad, *Studies in Deuteronomy* (Chicago: Regnery, 1953), 38–44; *idem, Der heilige Krieg im alten Israel* (Zurich: Zwingli Verlag, 1951).

[33]The literature is once again massive. We will cite: A Gelston, "Wars of Israel," *Scottish Journal of Theology* 17 (1964): 325–31; Norman K. Gottwold, "Holy War in Deuteronomy: Analysis and Critique," *Review and Expositor* 61 (1964): 296–310; Peter C. Craigie, "Yahweh is a Man of Wars," *Scottish Journal of Theology* 22 (1969): 183–88; Millard C. Lind, "Paradigm of Holy War in the Old Testament," *Biblical Research* 16 (1971): 16–31; W. Janzen, "War in the Old Testament," *Mennonite Quarterly Review* 46 (1972): 155–66; Gwilym H. Jones, "'Holy War' or 'Yahweh War'?" *Vetus Testamentum* 25 (1975): 642–58.

problem: the Old Testament seems to expect wars to take place. How can we reconcile God commanding his people to fight—given his call to holiness?

The commandment, "You shall not murder" (Exod. 20:13) was never applied by Israel to killing in war, for they understood this command to apply to what is classified as murder.[34] Moreover, war and war terminology enter into some of the central themes of Old Testament theology; therefore, war must be viewed as a theological as well as an ethical problem. But it is in the wars of conquest where the problem becomes most acute. There Yahweh uses war negatively as a means of judgment and positively as a means of fulfilling the patriarchal promises.

Interestingly enough it was not the sixth commandment but Exodus 32 that became the key text for many who wondered if and when Christians, or even the state, could go to war.[35] Exodus 32:25–29 reads:

> Moses saw that the people were running wild and that Aaron had let them get out of control and so become a laughingstock to their enemies. So he stood at the entrance to the camp and said, "Whoever is for the LORD, come to me." And all the Levites rallied to him.
>
> Then he said to them, "This is what the LORD, the God of Israel, says: 'Each man strap a sword to his side. Go back and forth through the camp from one end to the other, each killing his brother and friend and neighbor.'" The Levites did as Moses commanded, and that day about three thousand of the people died. Then Moses said, "You have been set apart to the LORD today, for you were against your own sons and brothers, and he has blessed you this day."

The approaches of Augustine, Aquinas, and Calvin to this text illustrate three answers to the problem of war. Augustine defended the persecution of heretical Christians (such as the Donatists) by the Roman state on the basis of Exodus 34. It was only after a long period of hesitation, during which he declared that spiritual men should fight heresy only with the Word of God, that Augustine finally concluded that wars with the sword could be aimed at heretics. "Thus," Augustine concluded, "we have two wars, that of the wicked at war with the wicked and that of the wicked at war with the good."[36] Just as Pharaoh oppressed the good, so Moses

---

[34]J. J. Stamm and M. E. Andrew, *The Ten Commandments in Recent Research* (Naperville, Ill.: SCM, 1967), 98–99. "Killing" involved all "illegal, impermissible violence" along with some aspects of "manslaughter" (see chapter 5 of this book).

[35]I am heavily indebted to Michael Walzer for the following discussion ideas, "Exodus 32 and the Theory of Holy War: The History of a Citation," *Harvard Theological Review* 66 (1968): 1–14.

[36]Augustine, *City of God XV*, 5.

oppressed the bad: both used the same weapons. The Bishop of Hippo could justify this action in this way:

> When good and bad do the same actions and suffer the same afflictions, they are to be distinguished not by what they do or suffer but by the causes of each: for example, Pharaoh oppressed the people of God by hard bondage; Moses afflicted the same people by severe correction when they were guilty of impiety [Exod. 32:27]: Their actions were alike; but they were not alike in the motive of regard to the people's welfare—the one inflated by a lust for power, the other inflamed by love.[37]

The war between the City of God and the City of Man is perpetual. Civil wars are marked by a "lust for power" by a tyrant, while the concern of the righteous is for the welfare of the people. Therefore, in defense of the peace of the earthly city, righteous men might enter into what Augustine called a "just" war.[38] Since the City of God represents only limited goodness, its members must fight a limited war. Such war begins when the peace on earth is directly violated and it ends when that peace is restored (not improved upon). "The theories of the just war and the holy war (or crusade) represent two radically different Christian defenses of the use of violence. Both have their origins in Augustine and a long history thereafter."[39] It should be noted that Augustine permitted the godly to wage war on heretics only if they held power in the state, otherwise they could not do so. Thus the sword belongs to the secular magistrate even when the purposes, in Augustine's view, exceed purely secular affairs. Augustine had stressed Moses' role in the Exodus 32 purge; he made no practical use of the Levites' role: that was to come later. His emphasis was on *Moses'* concern for "the people's welfare."

Thomas Aquinas's interpretation of Exodus 32 avoided reproducing Augustine's emphasis on Moses' role and concentrated instead on God and the Levites as the key actors. Aquinas made no mention of the Crusades fought in the century and a half before he lived. Against the radicals of his day who insisted on the private right of individuals to put sinners to death ("*Each* man strap a sword to his side" [v. 27]), Aquinas replied that this act was directly revealed by God ("This is what the LORD, the God of Israel says," Exod. 34:27). And when the radicals argued that priests and clerics might legitimately slay evildoers, Aquinas refused to equate Levites with modern Christian priests. Instead, this event had nothing to teach Chris-

---

[37]Augustine, *Letter to Vincentius*, Letter XCIII, paragraph 6.

[38]Augustine, *City of God*, XIX, 7.

[39]Walzer, "Exodus 32," 6. For a discussion of these two theories in later history, Walzer refers us to Roland Bainton, "Congregationalism: From the Just War to the Crusade in the Puritan Revolution," *Andover Newton Theological School Bulletin*, 35 (1943): 1–20.

tians since it was a unique case and God no longer gave instructions such as these. This Thomist analysis set in motion subsequent works that repeated Aquinas's two arguments[40] against the relevance of Exodus 32 as precedent for latter-day Christians.

John Calvin took the opposite point of view and found in the Levitical attack a precedent for the Protestant elect, the symbol of a coming generation of holy warriors, to kill their idolatrous brethren. Calvin, in Walzer's view, is not as radical as John Knox[41] and the English Puritans were on this question. Calvin, in his *Institutes*,[42] merely reaffirms Augustine's emphasis on the right of the magistrate to wage war—thus the role of Moses in Exodus 32.

Some of the seeds of contemporary Liberation Theology can almost be seen in the dramatic debate that took place over Exodus 32 in the seventeenth-century English Revolution. The Levitical wielding of the sword became a revolutionary purge, but men were still divided over whether it was conducted by magistrates or private individuals. Nor was it absolutely clear whether this passage offered a precedent for the Christian era and if it did, how far that authority extended: Did it extend to recover the doctrinal peace of the church? Was the earthly peace of the kingdom also to be included? Nor was it clear who was to be the instrument of effecting that peace if it were permitted: a godly man who also was a magistrate? the Christian clergy? the believing community of individuals at large? or a combination of the righteous and ungodly joined together for a righteous cause?

It would appear that Augustine and Calvin went beyond the hermeneutical boundaries of this text in trying to equate the situation of Exodus 32 with modern situations. In that aspect, Aquinas was closer to the truth-intention of the author. The text can be made universal, but one must always be hesitant in the area of carrying over sanctions on a one to one basis. The permanent principles appeal to the morality, theology, and ethics for their normativeness; rarely does this include the sanctions as well (except, of course, in the case of capital punishment for first degree murder, as argued above). Did not the apostle Paul recommend church discipline rather than the Old Testament sanction of stoning for the permanent injunction against incest in both testaments (1 Cor. 5:5; cf. Lev. 18:8,

---

[40]Michael Walzer shows this extension in a seventeenth-century treatise on the just war by Hugo Grotius, *De Jure Belli ac Pacis,* Book 2, 20, 24 for Thomas's first argument and Book 2, 20, 9 and 14 for the second.

[41]John Knox, *Works*, ed. D. Laing (Edinburgh, 1846–48), 3:311–12; and *Works*, ed. W. H. Goold (Edinburgh, 1862), 7:127ff.

[42]John Calvin, *The Institutes of the Christian Religion*, Book 4, 10:10.

29; Deut. 22:30; 27:20)? Therefore, Exodus 32 cannot help us with the ethics of war and peace for our day.

Nevertheless, it is clear that Yahweh was directly involved in a war on ungodliness that involved the use of the sword in Exodus 32. Whereas Moses was joined by the Levites in Exodus 32, Elijah appears to act on his own against the four hundred and fifty prophets of Baal at the Brook Kishon (1 Kings 18:40). Still, it is Yahweh's involvement with war in the Old Testament that poses the key problem for modern readers.

Several methods of extraditing the honor and character of God have been devised. One was to connect so-called Israel's holy wars with the miraculous intervention of God in a magical way so that the sword would not need to be used. The trumpet blast and the shout were better than the sword, spear, and shield.[43] Von Rad basically agreed, saying that it was a theological reinterpretation of Israel's ancient wars. While for him, holy wars began in the time of the judges, they were spiritualized into an absolute miracle beginning with the eighth-century prophets and finally institutionalized in the time of King Josiah.[44]

But what was the nature of human participation in war if holy war is so intimately to be equated with faith in a miraculous intervention that superseded the need for actual warfare? The answer is found in another contrast: warfare as Yahweh's action alone and warfare as a cooperative action. The former reflects the Sinai covenant and "The Song of the Sea" (Exod. 15) while the latter is linked with the Shechem covenant and "The Song of Deborah" (Judg. 5) in the phrase that only appears in Judges 5:23, "to help the LORD" (לְעֶזְרַת יְהוָה). While there are some helpful insights in these constructions, the contrast is too contrived and artificially imposed over the materials to reflect either the historical situation or give any aid in answering our ethical dilemmas.[45]

Norman K. Gottwald's estimate was that:

> Holy war was one of the vestiges of ancient Semitic religion that remained chaff amidst the wheat of ancient Israelite faith. It did Israel no credit and construed as a direct command from God was positively misleading to the religious perspective of Israel. . . . Exegesis of several prophetic passages would show that rejection of holy war concepts was in fact the mature view of Israel's own representatives (e.g. Isaiah 2:1–4; 19:18–25).
>
> Jesus Christ has emphatically put an end to the idea that war can be the choice instrument of God. But Christians have

---

[43]Friederich Schwally, *Der Heilige Krieg im alten Israel* (1901), 27f. as cited by Millard C. Lind, "Paradigm of Holy War in the Old Testament," *Biblical Research* 16 (1971): 17. So also essentially Johanas Pedersen, *Israel, Its Life and Culture* (1940), 3–4:18.

[44]Gerhard von Rad, *Der Heilige Krieg im Alten Israel* (1952), 43–70.

[45]See my brief theological analysis of "Yahweh wars" in W. C. Kaiser, Jr., *Toward an Old Testament Theology* (Grand Rapids: Zondervan, 1978), 134–36.

subtle ways of circumventing the New Testament witness. What they would not do in Christ's name they have done in the name of the state.[46]

But it is that easy to separate the direct command of God from Israel's wars of conquest? Only a literary and historical criticism that makes the wish parent to the thought can effect this move successfully. Furthermore, the prophetic rejection in Isaiah 2 and 19 is located in an eschatological setting rather than in the present.

Peter C. Craigie comes closer to a solution, but he must rely on a type of interim ethic. In his view, it is clear that:

> If God is to meet man in history and act on his behalf, it must be in the world as it is. But the world which is, is a world which is sinful, for God has given to man a certain freedom. Therefore, if God is to work on behalf of man in the world, He must give the appearance to man of using sinful means—He must seem to be unethical in His behaviour. . . . War cannot be looked at apart from man . . . . To say that God uses war is to say in effect that God uses sinful man in His purposes. In the Old Testament, if we were to expect to see God working only in what we might call an absolutely "ethical" manner, we would in effect be denying the possibility of seeing His work at all. . . ."[47]

But more must be said than to point to the realistic accounting for the presence of sin in the world, the inadequacy of language to describe God, and the nature of revelation. It must be stated forthrightly that God is never presented as the author of evil or involved in what is unethical: he remains the "Holy One of Israel."

The ethics of war in the Old Testament are never approved in a blanket manner, for many wars and methods of carrying them out receive the stern rebuke and threat of judgment from God because of their violent disregard for the all-seeing eye of God even in warfare (cf. Isa. 10:15–19 and Hab. 2:6–19). Amos strongly protested and firmly denounced a ruthless, pitiless, scorched earth policy in warfare (Amos 1:3, 6, 9, 11, 13; 2:1).

But the question of war is linked with the question of human government and law.[48] Coexistence with evil that results in religious compro-

---

[46]Norman K. Gottwald, "'Holy War' in Deuteronomy: Analysis and Critique," *Review and Expositor* 61 (1964): 308.

[47]Craigie, "Man of Wars," p. 186; also see Peter Craigie, *The Problem of War in the Old Testament* (Grand Rapids: Eerdmans, 1978), 93–112.

[48]See the compassionate, but well argued, treatment of Oliver O'Donovan, *In Pursuit of a Christian View of War* (Brameotte: Grove, 1977). Also compare *War: Four Christian Views*, ed. Robert G. Clouse, (Downers Grove: InterVarsity, 1981); and the anthology of primary source readings in *War and Christian Ethics*, ed. Arthur F. Holmes, (Grand Rapids: Baker, 1975). A less helpful book, because of its literary critical views is Marion J. Benedict, *The God of the Old Testament in Relation to War* (New York: Teacher's College, Columbia University, 1927).

mise is a barrier to peace *with God*, therefore the law declares of the Ammonites and Moabites, "Do not seek peace or good relations with them as long as you live" (Deut. 23:6). Thus the believer is trapped: if he makes peace in one area he thereby declares war in another (cf. Deut. 7:12–16). This, however, cannot be used as a vindication for holy war or new crusades. Israel only acted on the basis of a direct revelation from God and such authorization is most unlikely in our day since God has already completed his revelation in his Son (Heb. 1:1–2).

But principles do exist for the defense of an attacked home or city (either by the lawless criminal or an invading enemy). Resistance begins when the unprovoked intrusion of the home, city, or nation commences and it ends when the original peace has been restored. One other situation calls for "the Just War demand." When a weaker nation or neighbor is invaded and brutalized beyond being able to resist the intrusion, then the stronger neighbor is obligated to come to the armed rescue of this violated brother. Certainly Russia's invasion of Hungary during the Eisenhower years (when the United States shamefully stood by doing nothing) or her more recent take over of Afghanistan and threatened invasion of Poland provide examples of a call to arms in the name of a holy and righteous God who demands no less of nations and neighbors.

Oftentimes, without approving of the morality of the instrument or the method of her warfare, God will use more wicked nations to judge less wicked peoples in armed conflict. Assyria was such an "ax" in God's hands (Isa. 10:15) and so was Babylon (Hab. 1:6). But *permission* for conducting warfare must be sharply distinguished from *requirement* and primarily responsible for all that goes on. Sometimes God allows the wrath of men to praise him and this is one such instance. The distinction between the *permissive will* and the *directive will* of God can be seen in how frequently Old Testament writers attribute to secondary causes (such as the Red Sea being opened up by a "strong east wind," Exod. 14:21) that which could be charged directly ("blast of thy nostrils," Exod. 15:8) to God (since ultimately he was in charge of everything anyway.)[49]

War, then we conclude, is God's ultimate, but reluctant, method of treating gross evil that resists every other patient and loving rebuke of God. Christians may only be involved in a "just war," but often these become notoriously difficult to define. It is not as though no one can know for sure whether such are just or not, for certainly the "Judge of all the earth" will know and will confront men and nations in that final day for failing to answer some calls for help and for alleging in other cases that

---

[49]See Kaiser, *Old Testament Theology*, 260, n. 3.

their cause was just when they were doing no more than justifying their own economic or political opportunism and self-aggrandizements.

What then of "peace"?[50] In the biblical sense, peace begins in that security, order, and prosperity that comes from reconciliation to God and from being restored to living under God once again. *Shalom* occurs over 250 times in 213 separate verses.[51] In its basic meaning, שָׁלוֹם is more than just "peace"; it comes from the root meaning "to be whole" and hence speaks of "wholeness," "soundness," "health," and "well-being." It is peace as opposed to war, concord as opposed to strife.

Peace is a gift from the Lord. When Gideon built an altar, he named it יְהֹוָה שָׁלוֹם, "Yahweh is Peace" (Judg. 6:24). Peace, then, is a blessing from above. Jeremiah instructed the exiles in a letter, "seek the *shalom* and prosperity of the city to which I have carried you into exile. Pray to the LORD for it, because if it [has] *shalom,* you too will [have] *shalom*" (Jer. 29:7). God's plans for us are "plans [for] *shalom* and not to harm [us], plans to give [us] hope and a future" (Jer. 29:11). God wills (חָפֵץ) the prosperity (*shalom*) of his servants (Ps. 35:27; cf. Ps. 147:14).

The peace offered is an inner condition of contentedness, harmony, and quietness of spirit: "Great peace," promises the psalmist, "have they who love your law" (Ps. 119:165). Even the soul of the community can have its peace ripped away as Lamentations 3:17 says, "I have been deprived of peace."

War, as much as anything else, robs us of *shalom.* Some biblical instances chronicling such a loss are: Isaac's conflict with Abimelech's servant (Gen. 26:29, 31), Jacob's conflict and escape from his brother Esau in which he prays to return to his father's house in peace (Gen. 28:21), the mistaken opinion of the men of Shechem that Jacob's sons were peaceable (Gen. 34:21), Israel's offer of peace to Sihon (Deut. 2:26), Jael's act of violating the peace (Judg. 4:17), David's desire to make peace with Abner (2 Sam. 3:21–23), and David's inquiry about the peace of Joab, the peace of the people, and the peace of the war (2 Sam. 11:7). *Shalom* means the "absence of strife" in some forty to fifty passages in the Old Testament.[52]

---

[50]For some of the great literature on this question see Gerhard von Rad, "*Shalom* in the Old Testament," *Theological Dictionary of the New Testament,* 2:402–6; G. Lloyd Carr, "שָׁלוֹם," *Theological Wordbook of the Old Testament* 2:931–32; or Peter Craigie, "Peace in the Old Testament," *The Problem of War in the Old Testament,* 83–91; or a more popular treatment in Douglas J. Harris, *The Biblical Concept of Peace: Shalom* (Grand Rapids: Baker, 1970).

[51]G. Lloyd Carr, 931, citing John Durham, "Shalom and the Presence of God," in *Proclamation and Presence: Old Testament Essays in Honor of G. H. Davies* (Atlanta: John Knox, 1970), 272–93; especially p. 275.

[52]See the coded index of all instances in Harris, *Shalom,* 75–78.

Peace does not come merely with the cessation of hostilities; it aims instead at wholeness and a state of unimpaired relationships with others at all levels beginning with God. There can be the absence of overt strife while deep down the soul and body are constantly agitated and rankled because there is no wholeness and health there. Only with holiness can there come wholeness in this area as well.

Chapter 12

Holiness in Marriage and Sex

The first order of creation was for human procreation (Gen. 1:28). Closely aligned to it, and not from it in text and time, was the institution of marriage (Gen. 2:23–24). Marriage was God's gift to men and women. Its purpose was to satisfy the social nature of mankind, for Adam found out by experience that he was lonely without human companionship. God agreed with Adam's estimate, adding "it is not good for the man to be alone" (Gen. 2:18). The relationship that this marriage initiated was regarded in the Old Testament, contrary to many popular exaggerations, as indissoluble. That is the point of view expressed in Genesis 2:24; Deuteronomy 22:19, 29; Jeremiah 3:1; Hosea 3:1–3; and Malachi 2:10–16.

THE INSTITUTION OF MARRIAGE

The meaning of human sexuality is given in the narrative of God's creation of woman (Gen. 2:4–24). There the text pointedly emphasizes the value and worth of man and woman in mutual relationship. As early as Genesis 1:27 man and woman were equally declared to be made in the image of God. The theological perspective of Genesis 2 is that God has created a garden for man's pleasure, animals to serve him, and a woman for companionship. Man's solitude and loneliness were declared to be a condition that was "not good"; man had been made to be a social being. Therefore, God made a "helper suited to him" (עֵזֶר כְּנֶגְדּוֹ, "a helper corresponding to him" or "helper alongside him" [Gen. 2:20]). Such a

181

correspondence could not be found in the animals that were named by Adam and were subservient to him.

As if to stress this closeness and family propinquity even more, the text added two more phrases to the concepts of the *imago Dei* and כְּנֶגְדּוֹ עֵזֶר: Eve was formed from "one of his ribs" (אַחַת מִצַּלְעֹתָיו [Gen. 2:21]) and the second is that they "became one flesh" (וְהָיוּ לְבָשָׂר אֶחָד) when they came together. The detail about Adam's "rib"[1] stresses the singleness of a shared life. In the Sumerian mythology of the third millennium B.C., there may be a garbled remembrance of this event in the story of Enki for whose healing *Nin-ti,* "lady of the *rib*" or "lady who makes *alive*," was made. The Sumerian *ti* means both "rib" and "life". The only comparison with the biblical account is that "Eve" (who was made from a "rib") was so named because "she would become the mother of all the living" (Gen. 3:20). While the two themes may be verbally linked in Sumerian, they are not linked in Hebrew.

Man's joyful shout when he was shown Eve will never be forgotten: "This (זֹאת) is now (הַפַּעַם) bone of my bones and flesh of my flesh; she shall be called 'woman' for she was taken out of man" (Gen. 2:23).

Originally what had been the "one flesh" of Adam must now come together again and once more be "one flesh" in husband and wife. The bond was to be permanent (a man is to "leave" and to "cleave" to his wife, Gen. 2:24). It was also divinely inaugurated ("God . . . brought her to the man," 2:22), for ". . . God himself, like the father of the bride, leads the woman to the man."[2]

The Issue of Polygamy

Genesis 2:21–24 presents the creation of the first two human beings and their monogamous marriage as the will of God. Indeed, all the fathers from Adam to Noah in Seth's line of descent are said to be monogamous. Polygamy[3] appears for the first time in the reprobate line of Cain, for

---

[1]The Hebrew word translated "rib" nowhere else in the OT has this meaning. Elsewhere it means "side" of the ark (Exod. 25:12, 14), or "side" of the tabernacle (Exod. 26:20), etc. On the words "helper corresponding to him," I would render it now "a power (or strength) equal to him." See Chapter 10, n. 6 and the reference to R. David Freedman's article, "Woman, a Power Equal to Man," *Biblical Archaeology Review* 9 (1983): 56–58.

[2]Gerhard von Rad, *Genesis: A Commentary,* trans. John H. Marks (Philadelphia: Westminster, 1961), 82. "Bone of my bones" with the idea of becoming part of the family, one's blood relatives is also found in Gen. 29:14; 37:27; Judg. 9:2; 2 Sam. 5:1; 19:12–13 and 1 Chron. 11:1.

[3]Polygamy is that state in which a man has two or more wives at the same time; consider these representatives of a huge bibliography: E. G. Parrinder, *The Bible and Polygamy* (London: SPCK, 1958); Willard Burce, "Polygamy and the Church," *Concordice Theological Monthly* 34 (1963): 223–32; Robert Holst, "Polygamy and the Bible," *International Review of Missions* 56 (1967): 205–13; Eugene Hillman, "Polygamy Reconsidered,"

Lamech becomes the first bigamist when he marries Adah and Zillah in Genesis 4:19. Nor is there an instance of polygamy from Shem to Terah, father of Abraham.

Was polygamy ever lawful for the patriarchs or under the Levitical laws? Clearly, there never existed an express biblical permission for polygamy. The law governing marriage had always looked to Genesis 2:24 as normative. But some argue that the *practice* of the Hebrews proves otherwise. What is more, there are at least four passages that could be construed as giving temporary permission from God to override the general law on marriage found in Genesis 2:24. Each of these cases must be examined.

Notice first that, in addition to Lamech, only one other passage before the Deluge gives evidence of polygamy during this long period of time, namely, Genesis 6:1–7. But it was precisely because of man's autocratic and polygamous ways that God destroyed the earth with a flood. That could hardly be construed as tacit divine approval of polygamy—it is the reverse! Abraham's brother Nahor had a concubine and Abraham was talked into having temporary sexual relations with Sarah's handmaiden, Hagar. Esau was a profane person and took three wives, and Jacob married two sisters (even if he was deceived and lived among idolaters). At best then, during these thousands of years since the beginning we have only six examples of polygamy. In the next period, moving through the divided monarchy, there are only thirteen single instances[4] besides the children of Uzzi. ". . . Of these thirteen instances, twelve [are] . . . of persons possessed of absolute power."[5]

Some will wonder: why was no punishment inflicted on these polygamists by the government? "Nine of the thirteen were Absolute Monarchs, whom no earthly tribunal could call to an account, or punish, for their conduct; and three of the remaining four were those of Judges, . . . men equally absolute with the Monarchs of Israel."[6] On the contrary, there was censure for this type of adulterous action in the Deluge and in the law of Moses. In addition to this, the narratives of Scripture imply that this state of affairs is the major reason for much of the misfortune that comes into the

---

Practical Anthropology 17 (1970): 60–74; Nathaniel G. N. Inyamah, "Polygamy and the Christian Church," *Concordice Theological Monthly* 43 (1972): 138–43; Oswald C. Fountain, "Polygamy and the Church," *Missiology: An International Review* 11 (1974): 111–19; Thomas S. Piper, "Did God Condone Polygamy?" *Good News Broadcaster* 35 (1977): 28.

[4]These are Gideon, Jair, Ibzan, Abdon, Samson, Elhanah (Sons of Uzzi), Saul, David, Solomon, Rehoboam, Abijah, Ahab, and Jehoram. The case of Joash (2 Chron. 24:2–3) depends on the interpretation of לֹו, "for him" or "for himself" and whether he married these two wives in succession or simultaneously. These statistics are according to S. E. Dwight, *The Hebrew Wife* (New York: Leavitt, 1836), 24–29.

[5]Dwight, *Hebrew Wife*, 29.

[6]Dwight, *Hebrew Wife*, 30.

domestic lives of these polygamists. Scripture does not always pause to state the obvious; for example, even though Israel had been ordered to observe the Feast of Tabernacles seven days each year (Lev. 23:33–34), yet Nehemiah complains (Neh. 8:17) that from Joshua's day to his own day, well over one thousand years, the festival had never been celebrated—but never a word of censure appears for this neglect during that whole millennium of active revelation from God! Thus, the silence of Scripture must not be counted as acquiescence.

Those who believe there was direct or implied permission for polygamy in the Old Testament usually point to these four passages: Exodus 21:7–11; Leviticus 18:18; Deuteronomy 21:15–17; and 2 Samuel 12:7–8.

Exodus 21:7–11. The first of these passages deals with selling a daughter to be a maid-servant.

> If a man sells his daughter as a servant, she is not to go free as menservants do. If she does not please the master who has selected her for himself [footnote: "Or *master so that he does not choose her*"], he must let her be redeemed. He has no right to sell her to foreigners, because he has broken faith with her. If he selects her for his son, he must grant her the rights of a daughter. If he marries another woman, he must not deprive the first one of her food, clothing and marital rights. If he does not provide her with these three things, she is to go free, without any payment of money. (Exod. 21:7–11).

There are three mistakes made in this translation that are commonly repeated in other translations. The first is in verse 8 where the translators follow the Septuagint rather than the Hebrew text and substitute for the small but extremely significant "not" (לֹא), the reading לוֹ, "for himself." The preferred and majority reading is "not" in most Hebrew manuscripts; all manuscripts and editions of the Samaritan Pentateuch; and the versions of the Syriac, Persian, and Arabic.[7] Only in six Hebrew manuscripts does the *qerē*, codex Vaticanus of the Septuagint, the Lagardiana edition of the Septuagint, the Targum, and Vulgate suggest "for himself."[8] Verse 8 should read then:

> If she displease her master,
> so that he does not betroth her to himself,
> he shall not allow her to be redeemed.

The second mistake comes in the tenth verse, "if he marries (יִקַּח־לוֹ) another wife [or woman] (אַחֶרֶת)." It implies that he therefore has two

---

[7]Dwight, *Hebrew Wife*, 15.
[8]Critical apparatus of *Biblia Hebraica* (seventh edition).

wives at the same time; but verse 8 had already noted that the "other woman" had been rejected for marriage. The true meaning is: "if he marry another woman instead of her."

The third mistake is also located in verse 10. The word translated "marital rights" (עֹנָתָה), the third element that is owed to the first woman is almost certainly an improper guess at what this *hapax legomenon* means. S. M. Paul[9] suggests that it be translated "oil" or "ointments" since many Sumerian and Akkadian texts list the three items of "food, clothing, and oil" as the basic necessities of life. Once again the translators have been unduly influenced by the Septuagint (τὴν ὁμιλίαν αὐτῆς, "her cohabitation").[10] Others have conjectured "the conditions of her abode" deriving the word from the root עוּן.[11]

Leviticus 18:18. The second passage, allegedly permitting or tolerating polygamy, reads:

> Do not take your wife's sister as a rival wife and have sexual relations with her while your wife is living.

Two interpretations have been followed:

(1) Do not marry your wife's sister during the lifetime of your wife, because that will vex her; or

(2) Do not marry another wife who is the sister of your first wife, although you may take one who is not her sister, or even her sister after your wife's death, because that will not vex her.

The second view permits polygamy and the marriage of the sister of a deceased wife. The problem phrase is אִשָּׁה אֶל־אֲחֹתָה, "a woman to her sister," that everywhere else is rendered idiomatically "one woman to another" or "one wife to another." This phrase has both a masculine ("a man to his brother")[12] and a feminine form.[13] In twenty-five cases it is masculine and in ten it is feminine. In thirty-four cases out of the thirty-

---

[9]S. M. Paul, "Exodus 21:10: A Threefold Maintenance Clause," *Journal of Near Eastern Studies* 28 (1969): 48–53.

[10]Those who connect it with "marital rights" take it from the verb עָנָה, "to humble by ravishing [in illicit intercourse]." Hence, unlawful intercourse could not be used for lawful wedlock.

[11]Note Paul's use in 1 Corinthians 7:3, "due benevolence."

[12]The phrase אִישׁ אֶל־אָחִיו, "a man to his brother" or slight variations thereof occur in Gen. 13:11; 26:31; 37:19; 42:21, 28; Exod. 10:23; 16:15; 25:20; 37:9; Lev. 7:10; 25:14, 46; 26:37; Num. 14:4; Deut. 25:11; Neh. 4:19; Job 41:17; Jer. 13:14; 25:26; 34:14; Ezek. 4:17; 24:23; 33:30; 47:14; Joel 2:8 (twenty-five examples of "one to another"). Also add four other closely connected instances אִישׁ־רֵעֵהוּ, "a man, his companion" in Exod. 32:27; Isa. 19:2; Jer. 31:34; 34:17.

[13]The phrase אִשָּׁה אֶל־אֲחֹתָה, "a woman to her sister" is found ten times in Exod. 26:3 (twice), 5, 6, 17; Lev. 18:18; Ezek. 1:9, 11, 23; 3:13. Four more instances of אִשָּׁה רְעוּתָה should be mentioned in Isa. 34:15, 16; Jer. 9:20; Zech. 11:9.

five, (Lev. 18:18 purposely being set to one side), this phrase means "one to another" in an idiomatic sense.

Can we render it any differently, then, in Leviticus 18:18? Ordinarily, the answer would be a definite "no," but there is one large difference. There is no reference to a *relationship by blood* in the other thirty-four instances. Moreover, polygamy is expressly prohibited by God in his ordination of the institution of marriage in Genesis 2:24. The law of incest in Leviticus 18 expressly forbids marriage between a woman and her brother-in-law (husband's brother), or marriage between a nephew and an aunt, a mother and a son, an uncle and a niece, or a father and a daughter. The closeness of relationships given in the text would seem to force us to say that the text prohibits just as surely marriage between a man and his sister-in-law (wife's sister). Leviticus 18:18, then, is a single prohibition against polygamy and abides by the law of incest stated in the same context.

Deuteronomy 21:15–17. There is a third passage that may appear to authorize polygamy. The text reads:

> [15]If a man has two wives, and he loves one but not the other, and both bear him sons but the firstborn is the son of the wife he does not love, [16]when he wills his property to his sons, he must not give the rights of the firstborn to the son of the wife he loves in preference to his actual firstborn, the son of the wife he does not love. [17]He must acknowledge the son of his unloved wife as the firstborn by giving him a double share of all he has. The son is the first sign of his father's strength. The right of the firstborn belongs to him.

S. E. Dwight spells out the syllogism that those who contend that the Old Testament tacitly approves of polygamy use:

Major premise: "Moses here legislates on the case of a man who *has* two wives at the same time:

Minor premise: But he could not lawfully legislate upon that which might not lawfully exist:

Conclusion: To have two wives at the same time, was therefore lawful."[14]

Dwight's rejoinder to the minor premise is convincing:

> In Deut xxiii.18, it is said, "Thou shalt not bring *the hire of a harlot* into the house of the Lord thy God for any vow." Taught then by the schoolmen, we thus argue—Moses here legislates upon the wages of a harlot, and therefore supposes that harlots will receive the wages of prostitution: But he could not legislate upon

---

[14]Dwight, *Hebrew Wife*, 20.

that which might not lawfully exist: To be a harlot and earn the wages of prostitution, were therefore lawful. This conclusion sounds oddly, when we read the remainder of the verse, "for this is an abomination to the Lord;" or the preceding verse, "There shall be no harlot of the daughters of Israel."[15]

Consequently, as the legislation on harlots in no way authorizes harlotry, so the law on bigamy or polygamy is likewise not a case for its recognition, even if it be sort of *sub rosa*. But another problem must be identified: is Moses legislating for a man who *has* two wives or who *has had* two wives in succession, the second after the first one died? The versions adopt the second opinion.

Septuagint: Ἐὰν δὲ γένωνται (not γίνωνται). . . .
"If there *have been*. . . ."

Vulgate: *Si habuerit homo*. . . .
"If a man have had. . . ."

Samaritan
Version: "When a man has had. . . ."

Targum: (Same)

The Hebrew verb is not so easily translated. Verse 15 begins with כִּי־תִהְיֶין, "if there will be a man," or more smoothly "if a man have two wives." Hebrew is notoriously disinterested in our Western preoccupation with the tense of the verb and time in general. The fact that a man has *children* who were born of two wives is enough to think about without making the point that one wife has now been deceased and another, perhaps the favored one, is living. But it definitely is wrong to insist that both wives are living, for that would be asking the imperfect verb form (future or continuous action of the verb) to bear a load it was not meant to carry. The understanding of this passage is to be established from the concern of this law (inheritance rights, not polygamy), the history of exegesis (as indicated in the major translations), and the refutation of the alleged syllogism for tacit approval of polygamy; the understanding cannot be based solely on the grammar, which is imprecise. When these factors are taken into consideration, we conclude that the sense of the verse is, "If a man has had two wives."

2 Samuel 12:7–8.   The final passage usually cited to support God's approval of polygamy is 2 Samuel 12:7–8.

This is what the LORD, the God of Israel, says: "I anointed you king over Israel and I delivered you from the hand of Saul. [8]I gave

---

[15]Dwight, *Hebrew Wife*, 20.

your master's house to you, and your master's wives into your arms. I gave you the house of Israel and Judah. And if all this had been too little, I would have given you even more."

There were only two wives that Saul is said to have had: Ahinoam, the mother of David's wife Michal (1 Sam. 14:50), and Rizpah, Saul's concubine (2 Sam. 3:7). If this statement in 2 Samuel 12:8 be taken as divinely authorized marriage of Saul's wives, then more is involved than polygamy: David was authorized, on this supposition, to marry his wife's mother—a form of incest already condemned in the Levitical law, carrying the sanction of being burnt alive (Lev. 18:17). David also married Michal, Ahinoam's daughter when he was quite young, so this also precludes the thought that he may have married the mother much later.

Interestingly enough, even though David's wives are enumerated frequently after Saul's death, never once are Saul's two wives included. What then can the phraseology "I gave . . . your master's wives into your arms" mean? The expression is a stereotype formula which signified that everything that had belonged to his predecessor technically was his—all other [laws] being equal, which, of course, they were not! God had handed over to David "the house of Israel and Judah," in other words, the whole kingdom so that he could have chosen a young maiden from any of the eligible virgins as his wife. "And if [all that] was too little, I would have added to you this and that." No doubt the chief problem here is in translating the word "wives." That word should have been translated as "women," not "wives." Thus Saul's "house" and "women" were delivered by God into his "lap" (cf. Prov. 16:33, which is better than "bosom"). We can understand the phrase as everything that was Saul's, including all his female domestics and courtesans passed over into David's possession.

The word translated "bosom" (our "lap") or as the NIV has it "into your arms" is rendered freely by the New American Standard translation as "care." Surely something like this is appropriate here since Deuteronomy 17:17 had prohibited the king from multiplying wives for himself "or his heart will be led astray." We conclude that the expression of the divine donation of all that was Saul's means nothing more than the fact that everything was placed under the control and supervision of David much as a conquering king exhibited his full victory over a subjugated nation by taking control of the defeated king's household.

It is all too common to see statements by Christian anthropologists, sociologists, and theologians to the effect that the prohibition of polygamy based on Scripture is on extremely shaky grounds. Karl Barth, for example, intoned, "We can hardly point with certainty to a single text in which polygamy is expressly forbidden and monogamy is universally decreed. If, then, we approach the Bible legalistically, we cannot honestly conclude that in this matter we are dealing with an unconditional law of God."[16] Likewise, Oswald Fountain declared that the Church's case against polygamy "on the basis of Scripture is a flimsy one."[17]

Such complaints may be sustained by including numerous qualifying words that overload the proof required (e.g., notice Barth's "hardly," "with certainty," "expressly," and "universally") and by demoting the impact of the teaching of the law for regulating the morality of Christians during the New Testament era. Oftentimes the institution of marriage in Genesis 2:24 is viewed only as implying, but not enforcing monogamy! But that is not what our Lord felt was a legitimate minimum to be derived from the Genesis passage. His affirmations dealt with the monogamous nature of it. And that is what the laws of affinity stressed in Leviticus 18 when they took up the same subject—Leviticus 18:18 explicitly and expressly prohibits polygamy. In effect it says, "Neither shall you take one wife to another in her lifetime, to vex her." Similarly, the five New Testament passages built on the original decree of marriage in the Old Testament (Matt. 5:31–32; 19:3–9; Mark 10:2–12; Luke 16:18) forbid polygamy just as much as the Genesis teaching does. Other New Testament passages are explicit on this same matter. First Corinthians 7:1–2, "each man should have his own wife, and each woman her own husband" and 1 Timothy 3:2 and 12 required that at least the bishop and deacons be "the husband of but one wife." These last two texts would seem to imply that there were converted heathen in the church who still were polygamous, but who should be disqualified from the office of bishop or deacon. Nevertheless, polygamy was no more "lawful" or "normative" for the Christian church than it was for the patriarchs or the kings of Israel and Judah.

Too many Old Testament texts continue to represent the norm as a monogamous relationship to be dismissed out of hand.

In the curses of Deuteronomy 28, verses 54 and 56 describe marriage as it was then and as it was to be in every age: "the wife he loves" and "the husband she loves." The law does not specify which one of his wives or threaten all the wives of his harem should he disobey God; it presumes that there is only *one* wife and *one* husband. Again in Psalm 128:3 the promise is "Your wife [not wives] will be like a fruitful vine. . . ." Only one is to be blessed. But what of the other nineteen, if he had that many—were they not to be fruitful and blessed? But the best statement on the monogamous marriage is Proverbs 5:15–21.

> Drink water from your own cistern,
> running water from your own well.

---

[16]Karl Barth, *Church Dogmatics* (Edinburgh: T. & T. Clark, 1957) 3–4:199.
[17]Fountain, "Polygamy and the Church," 111.

Should your springs overflow in the streets,
your streams of water in the public squares?
Let them be yours alone,
never to be shared with strangers.
May your fountain be blessed,
and may you rejoice in the wife of your youth.
A loving doe, a graceful deer—
may her breasts satisfy you always,
may you ever be captivated by her love.
Why be captivated, my son, by an adulteress?
Why embrace the bosom of another man's wife?
For a man's ways are in full view of the LORD,
and he examines all his paths.

Could these instructions possibly be obeyed by a man who had many additional wives beside "the wife of [his] youth?" Could "her breasts satisfy [him] always" when he devoted himself to the other women of the harem? Could he "always be captivated by her love" when she was supplanted by others?[18] Malachi 2:14 insists that the Lord was a witness at the wedding between this same "wife of your youth" who has now been left in tears at the altar of God while her husband shares his affection with others. This same monogamous state of affairs is assumed in Jeremiah 5:8 where every man was "neighing for another man's wife." Had polygamy been customary, or tacitly approved, the text would have innocently read, "every one neighed after his neighbor's *wives*" or "*harem*." Instead, the judgment of God will fall upon Israel, according to Jeremiah 6:11, "both husband and wife will be caught in it." Again, the text did not intimate that polygamy was in vogue, for had it been this Scripture would have said, "the husband with his wives." Polygamy never was God's order of things for marriage even though it is present in the society of the Old Testament and New Testament.

The Issue of the Levirate

The institution called levirate,[19] from the Latin *levir* that translates the Hebrew יָבָם, "brother-in-law," is legislated in Deuteronomy 25:5–10 and illustrated in only two Old Testament examples: the stories of Tamar (Gen. 38) and Ruth (Ruth 2:20; 3:13; 4:5, 6, 10, 17).

Since the Old Testament law forbade the marriage of those related by blood or by marriage, marriage and sexual union by a widow or a widower to in-laws was considered incest—except in this one instance.

---

[18]Dwight, *Hebrew Wife*, 46.

[19]See Millard Burrows, "Levirate Marriage in Israel," *Journal of Biblical Literature* 59 (1940): 23–33; *idem*, "The Ancient Oriental Background of Hebrew Levirate Marriage," *Bulletin of the American Schools of Oriental Research* 77 (1940): 2–15.

The law (Deut. 25:5–10) did permit a widow, if her deceased husband died childless, to marry her next of kin in order to raise up a family to bear the name of the dead man.

In the case of Tamar, Judah's firstborn son, Er, died and left his wife Tamar without having a child (Gen. 38:6–7). It fell then to Er's brother, Onan, to marry Tamar and to raise up a family to Er's memory and property. Onan, while outwardly pretending that he was fulfilling this law, regularly spilled his seed and thereby prevented the conception from taking place (Gen. 38:8–10). He too died and Tamar expected that Judah would give Tamar his youngest son, Shelah, but he hesitated to do so (v. 11), so Tamar tricked her father-in-law into having intercourse with her (vv. 15–19) and thus bore twins. Tamar's act was not a levirate relationship; rather, it was a desperate act of a woman who desired children from the same stock as her husband.

For Ruth, the levirate did not directly apply since she had no more brother-in-laws (Ruth 1:11–12).[20] The duty of redemption fell on the "kinsman-redeemer" (גֹּאֵל).[21] In her case it was a near relative who must marry her to redeem the property and raise up a name to the deceased. The aim and effects of kinsman-redeemer marriages were the same as those of the levirate marriage and so may be joined here.

A number of exegetical issues are not so easily settled. The deceptively simple "when brothers dwell together" of Deuteronomy 25:5f. has been interpreted to mean: (1) alive at the same time, (2) living in the same town, and (3) brothers who dwell in a consortium on a family estate.[22] David Daube has argued well for the third alternative,[23] but the first explanation may be (on the grounds of parsimony) the best explanation.

The purposes of the Levirate were: (a) "that his name may not be blotted out of Israel"[24] (וְלֹא־יִמָּחֶה שְׁמוֹ מִיִּשְׂרָאֵל, Deut. 25:6, cf. v. 7), and (b) to prevent the dissipation of the family property. Perhaps this is why Deuteronomy 25:5 makes it a condition that the brothers be living together and this may move us more to Daube's consortium idea. Notice in Ruth the idea of redeeming the land is linked with marrying the widow as

---

[20]The case cited by the Sadducees of seven childless brothers (Matt. 22:23–33) seems to accept the lawfulness of the levirate marriages of real "brothers" instead of just near relatives.

[21]See Donald A. Leggett, *The Levirate and Goel Institutions in the Old Testament with Special Attention to the Book of Ruth* (Cherry Hill, N.J.: Mack, 1974): cf. the review of Etan Levine, "On Intra-familial Institutions of the Bible," *Biblica* 57 (1976): 554–59.

[22]These alternatives are given by Levine, "Intra-familial Institutions," 556.

[23]David Daube, "Consortium in Roman and Hebrew Law," *Juridical Review* 42 (1950): 71–91 as cited by Levine, "Intra-familial Institutions," 556.

[24]The connection between having sons and continuing the name is strong in the OT: 1 Sam. 24:22; 2 Sam. 14:7; 18:18; Pss. 45:16–17; 109:13; Isa. 56:5; 66:22; Jer. 11:19.

is the law about the daughters who became heiresses (Num. 36:2–9).[25] Perhaps this law also had the welfare of widows at heart as well.

What then of the moral issue? Since illegitimate sons and children of marriages forbidden by the Old Testament (because of previous relation by blood or marriage) could not be recognized as legitimate heirs, could offspring from levirate relationships be any more acceptable? The answer is that this is the single exception since it aids in fostering the goal of godly families. God can, and did permit and bless such exceptions. Only he can modify his own directives for his good purposes.

THE PURPOSE OF SEX

Human sexuality is not some awesome force over which men and women have no control. Nor is it some drive that is earthy and outside the boundaries and interest of morality or religion. Instead, Scripture calls it "good" from the very beginning and credits it as being a gift from God.

Its Enjoyment

An all too popular perversion of the biblical picture of sexuality is that it is somehow connected with the fall of man in Genesis 3. But the idea is absurd and unwarranted. The shame that Adam and Eve felt was first of all towards God, from whom they hid (Gen. 3:8), and then to one another.

In fact, there is a strange combination of frankness and reticence in the Bible's discussion of sex. A number of euphemisms were used such as "nakedness"[26] (עֶרְוָה) to refer especially to a woman's sex organs (Lev. 18:6, 7 [*twice*], 8, 9, 10 [*twice*], 11, 12, 13, 14, 15, 16, 17 [*twice*], 18, 19; 20:17 [*twice*], 18 [*twice*], 19, 20, 21; 1 Sam. 20:30; Lam. 1:8; Ezek. 16:37; 23:10, 29); or the word "feet" (רֶגֶל) may refer to male genitals (Exod. 4:25; Isa. 7:20) or of women with a similar connotation (Deut. 28:57; Ezek. 16:25). The word sometimes translated "thigh," especially in the expression "offspring," or literally "the ones coming or going out of his יָרֵךְ" (Gen. 46:26; Exod. 1:5; Judg. 8:30) is another euphemism for the male reproductive organ (compare the same word used in making an agreement

---

[25]Roland DeVaux, *Ancient Israel: Its Life and Institutions* (New York: McGraw-Hill, 1961), 37–38; Leggett, *Levirate and Goel*, 48–54.

[26]The Bible has no legislation on nakedness as such. More frequently it is used figuratively of being "discovered" (Job 26:6) or being "disarmed" (Jer. 49:10) or literally of a person who is shamed when he or she is taken into captivity by a conqueror. The man and his wife were עֲרוּמִים, "naked" without shame (Gen. 2:25) while the Serpent was עָרוּם, "crafty." Obviously, there is a kind of pun being made on these two terms: perhaps the guileless simplicity of their nakedness is being contrasted with the subtle wiles and entrapments of the evil one.

and placing one's hand on the "thigh" [יָרֵךְ] of the person to whom the oath was made [Gen. 24:2, 9; 47:29]).

On the other hand, there was no prudery or apparent hesitancy and embarrassment in referring openly to certain parts of the body that Western sensitivities would not speak of openly; for example, the frequent references to the "breast," שַׁד, in Song of Solomon (1:13; 4:5; 7:3, 7–8; 8:8, 10) or the "foreskin," עָרְלָה (1 Sam. 18:25, 27).

Sex was meant for enjoyment as the brief, but joyful allegory of Proverbs 5:15–21 demonstrates. "Rejoice," urges Solomon, "in the wife of your youth" and "may you ever be captivated by her love." Few statements in the Bible are filled with more excitement and wholesome appreciation of anticipated joy than the one Adam blurts forth when the Lord introduces Eve to him. "There she is," he practically sings, "Miss Universe. Now at last here is what I have been waiting for." True, this paraphrase attempts to give more of the emotion than all of the exact words, but we might call these Kaiser marginal readings!

In our view, there is one Old Testament book that is devoted to enlarging on this theme. "Why," asks Meredith Kline,

> should the Church stumble at the presence in her inspired canon of a song extolling the dignity and beauty of human love and marriage? Considering how large the subject looms in the attention of men, had it not been remarkable if there were not such an extended treatment of it in the volume God has given us for "reproof, for correction, for instruction in righteousness"?[27]

The portrayal of love is that of prospective marriage and anticipated wedded love. "The representation is in no respect that of illicit passion. It is doubtless due to oriental taste that so much is said of personal attractions, and that such a standard of personal beauty is assumed."[28]

This book stands opposed to some of the early Christian church fathers who spoke against connubial love, even in its purest form, and argued instead that such love necessarily involved to a greater or lesser degree sin. But how can interpreters of this, the best of songs, denounce in such scathing terms any construction that finds connubial love in this song? Surely, the parties in Song of Songs find themselves longing for and thoroughly fascinated in each other's company. We would rather affirm with Cowles that:

> In so far as this song commends conjugal fidelity; points attractively the pure devotion of husband and wife to each other ["my

---

[27]Meredith Kline, "The Song of Songs, *Christianity Today* April 27 (1959), 39.
[28]Henry Cowles, *Proverbs, Ecclesiastes and Song of Solomon with Notes* (New York: Appleton, 1871), 323.

beloved is mine and I am his,"]; sets forth the beautiful blending of the love of nature and the charms of rural life with the social endearments of the connubial relation, it has done a noble work for the purity and elevation of our common humanity.[29]

The real interpretive clue and entrée into the book is supplied by the allegory on marital and conjugal fidelity in Proverbs 5:15–21. The frankness of portraying the parts of the body involved in lovemaking, the frank, but sensitively cushioned reference to coition under the figure of a fountain and garden are already present in Solomon's proverb. Thus we are not surprised by the garden-motif in the poem in Song of Songs 5:2–6:3. The prospect of marital love and conjugal erotic play is veiled by circumlocution, by metaphor, and other round about ways that preserve the privacy and beauty of something that is very delicate and personal while still necessarily providing "instruction in righteousness."

The bearing this song has on human sexuality can be seen in these themes:[30]

(1) Presence/absence. The longing of the Shulamite maiden for her shepherd boyfriend, to whom she is engaged, dominates her thoughts and dreams. It is the presence of the lovers with each other that is so highly valued and when they are absent from one another the longing to be back together is all the more intensified. Here the essence of human love is epitomized in the yearning of these lovers for each other. The Bible dwells on this call for presence with a wholesome joy.

(2) Mutuality. There is a strong desire to share the depth of feelings. When she is described as a "garden," she invites him into "his garden" to taste its choicest fruit (4:12–5:1). The "garden," however, was "locked"; a "sealed fountain" (4:12); and reserved for its sole owner.

---

[29]Cowles, *Song of Solomon*, 323. Other bibliography on the Song of Songs includes: F. Godet, "The Interpretation of the Song of Songs," in *Studies in the Old Testament*, 9th ed. (New York: Hodder and Stoughton, 1894), 241–90 or in W. C. Kaiser, Jr. (ed.), *Classical Evangelical Essays in Old Testament Interpretation* (Grand Rapids: Baker, 1972), 151–75; Arthur G. Clarke, *The Song of Songs* (Kansas City: Walterick, n.d.); Roland Murphy, "Interpreting the Song of Songs," *Biblical Theology Bulletin* 9 (1979): 99–105; J. Bowman, "Thoughts on the Song of Solomon," *Abr-Naharain*, ed. J. Bowman (Leiden: Brill, 1961), 1: 11–36; J. Cheryl Exam, "A Literary and Structural Analysis of the Song of Songs," *Zeitschrift für die alttestamentliche Wissenschaft* 85 (1973): 47–79; and Weston W. Fields, "Early and Medieval Jewish Interpretation of the Song of Songs," *Grace Theological Journal* 1 (1980): 221–31.

[30]As suggested by Murphy, "Interpreting the Song," 104; although his emphasis is different at several points.

(3) Pleasure. The pleasant sensation of his embrace is remembered (2:6; 8:3) while the delicateness of her lips (4:11) and the sweetness of his mouth (5:16) are all set in the sights and smells of nature radiant with the blooms of spring. The perfume of her garment is like "that of Lebanon" (4:11) while he smells of myrrh and henna (1:13–14) in the vineyards of En Gedi.

This love is a gift from God: "the very flame of the LORD" (8:6). It is impossible to drown it, buy it, or distract it. All such attempts would only be totally scorned (8:7). This girl, the shepherd's "fountain," "garden," and "vineyard" is his very own (6:8–9; 8:12). Solomon may own his thousand, but the shepherd is wealthier still with his single bride. If all this is not a theology for human sexuality and a joyful celebration of connubial love, what is it?

Sex is God's gift reserved for the marriage bed. He declared it "good" from the very beginning. Thus the Song does for marriage and connubial love what the living Word did by his presence at the marriage feast of Cana.

Its Distortions

Beside the perversion of human sexuality already covered in our discussion of incest and adultery, which we will treat under the topic of divorce, there are five other sexual abnormalities faced by the Old Testament: bestiality, homosexuality, fornication, transvestitism, and "uncovering the springs."

Bestiality. Four times the Old Testament takes up this topic; three times in the law and once in the curses of the law. The texts are: Exodus 22:19; Leviticus 18:23–30; 20:15–16; and Deuteronomy 27:21. Sexual commerce with an animal was contrary to God's purpose and provision, and this can be seen in Adam's realization that no animal could ever be a helper fit for him or a companion to relieve his loneliness (Gen. 2:20). Moreover, bestiality was all too common a practice attested in the Canaanite, Egyptian, Babylonian, and Hittite sources. For example, in the Eastern delta of the Nile there was a cult that involved the cohabitation of women and goats.[31] The Hittite Laws (c. 1500 B.C.) prohibit some forms of bestiality (Laws 187–88) while allowing others (Laws 199–200). The gods of Ugarit also freely copulated with animals.[32]

No wonder, then, that Leviticus 18:23–30 warns against this Ca-

---

[31]Gordon J. Wenham, *The Book of Leviticus* (Grand Rapids: Eerdmans, 1979), 252.
[32]A. van Selms, *Marriage and Family Life in Ugaritic Literature* (London: Luzac, 1954), 81–82; as cited by Wenham, *Leviticus.*

naanite practice. It was such an "abomination" that the physical condition of the land was affected by it: "the land was defiled" (Lev. 18:25). Rushdoony offers this further explanation: "Pagan religions, with their belief in an evolution out of chaos, looked downward to chaos for religious vigor, power and vitality, not upward. Strength was believed to lie downward, in contact with the 'earth,' with man's primitive past. As a result, religious renewal required acts of bestiality. . . ."[33]

Bestiality is also condemned because it is a "confusion" (תֶּבֶל; used only in Lev. 18:23 and 20:12). It comes from the verb בָּלַל, "to mix," and thus it crosses or mixes the boundaries between man and animal set by God. It is another one of God's laws dealing with unnatural mixtures (cf. Lev. 19:19; Deut. 22:5, 9–11).

Homosexuality. Current exegetical fashion would like to avoid identifying the crime committed by the citizens of Sodom as homosexuality (Gen. 19); many would prefer to call it a lack of hospitality or even rape.

Besides the two narratives of Genesis 19:4–7 and Judges 19:22 involving contemplated acts of homosexuality, three passages in the Old Testament specifically proscribe all such acts, namely, Leviticus 18:22; 20:13; and Deuteronomy 23:17. This would include male homosexuality, female homosexuality or lesbianism, and pederasty, the "love of boys." Thus, when members of the same (*homo*) sex practice intercourse with each other (or in the biblical idiom "to lie with," שָׁכַב אֵת), they violate the basic order that God has intended for creation and bring defilement on the nation and do that which God declares is an "abomination" (תּוֹעֵבָה). The word "abomination" is used five times in Leviticus 18 (vv. 22, 26, 27, 29, 30) and once in Leviticus 20:13. It comes from the root meaning "to hate" or "abhor" and hence it is something that is hated by God and is detestable (e.g., Prov. 6:16; 11:1).[34]

For those who would once again attempt to dismiss these three passages in the law as being merely ceremonial and temporary in their authority must come to terms with the context of these prohibitions in the holiness law. Encased and framed as they are in the statements of aseity ("I am the LORD your God," Lev. 18:4, 30) and continued with a call to general holiness ("Be holy because I, the LORD your God, am holy," Lev. 19:2; 20:26), such a case for ceremonialism is hopeless from the very start.

---

[33]R. J. Rushdoony, *The Institutes of Biblical Law* (Nutley, N.J.: Craig, 1973), 439.

[34]Wenham, *Leviticus,* 259 notes that תּוֹעֵבָה is more common in Deuteronomy (17 times), Proverbs (21 times) and Ezekiel (43 times). Note these somewhat disappointing articles: Wolfgang Roth, "What of Sodom and Gomorrah? Homosexual Acts in the Old Testament," *Explor* 1 (1975): 7–14; Robert L. Sample and Randy Akers, "Homosexuality in Ancient Greece and in the Christian Middle Ages," *Explor* 1 (1975): 15–19. Note also the discussion in the Holiness Law in chapter 7 of this book and the bibliography there.

The overwhelming character of the injunctions in Leviticus 18–20 (as we have argued in chapter 7) is moral with only a few ceremonial instructions (Lev. 19:5–8, 21, 22). Even Christ himself appealed to one of these laws (Lev. 19:18) as still having force in his own time (Matt. 22:39–40).

Homosexuality must be listed as a sexual perversion, a defilement of a country in which it is practiced, and an abomination in God's eyes. Anything less than this is a form of specious reasoning. It is a sin that must be dealt with as any other sin even though the gospel also offers freedom, forgiveness, and healing from this sin as from any other—or it is no gospel at all.

Fornication. The Old Testament contains no straightforward condemnation of what people today call fornication, but that is due in part to the artificial distinctions that are sometimes made between the privileges of married men and women. S. E. Dwight exposed this distinction which was mainly made in the past:

> According to the law of some of the states, unlawful intercourse, between a married woman and a married or single man is adultery; whereas unlawful fornication, between a married man and a single woman is merely fornication.
> . . . We will suppose a Legislature of Married Women assembled to make laws for one of the States, and actually enacting that unlawful intercourse, between a married man and woman whether single or married, should be punished as adultery: but that such intercourse, between a married woman and a single man should be mere fornication. What words could express the abhorrence of our existing legislators, at such shameless profligacy? Would they not pronounce such a body of females just fit for the purlieus of a brothel?[35]

More accurately, fornication is usually described as heterosexual activity between unmarried persons. Apparently this was such a rare phenomena that it is not considered separately in the Old Testament. There were laws against rape (Deut. 22:23–29) and seduction of a girl who was not yet engaged (Exod. 22:16–17) or the seduction of a betrothed girl (Deut. 22:23).

The existence of male prostitutes (קָדֵשׁ) or female prostitutes (קְדֵשָׁה; Deut. 23:18) was commonplace with the Canaanites, thus Israel had to be warned against prostituting their daughters (Lev. 19:29) as harlots (זוֹנָה). So despicable were these practices that a male prostitute was referred to as a "dog" (כֶּלֶב) or a "sodomite."

The truth of the matter is that Proverbs, especially chapters 1–9,

---

[35]S. E. Dwight, *The Hebrew Wife* (New York: Leavitt, 1836), 12–13.

warns against all illicit sex with the seductress including premarital and extramarital. Furthermore, when sex included a ritual connotation, as it did for those who celebrated on behalf of the dead and in honor of Baal of Peor (Num. 25:6–9), it was doubly condemned. The case cited in Numbers called for the prompt sanction delivered by the duly authorized official, Phineas, the heir-apparent to the high priesthood.[36]

The outstanding New Testament prohibition on fornication is the passage in 1 Thessalonians 4:1–8, which reaffirms the immorality of fornication.

Transvestitism. Deuteronomy 22:5 enjoins "a woman must not wear men's clothing, nor a man wear women's clothing, for the LORD your God detests (תּוֹעֵבָה) anyone who does this."

The maintenance of the sanctity of the sexes established by God in the created order is the foundation of this legislation, and not opposition to idolatrous practices of the heathen. The tendency to obliterate all sexual distinctions often leads to licentiousness and promotes an unnaturalness opposed to God's created order. Such a problem can arise in contemporary culture when unisex fashions are aimed at producing the bland person in a progressive desexualization of men and women.[37]

Thus, this provision aims mainly at one's clothes as an indication of one's sex. Whether this principle may also be extended to all that pertains (כְּלִי) to a man, namely, the implements, tools, weapons, and utensils, as W. L. Alexander[38] argues, is more doubtful. It would appear that this is pressing too hard and extrapolating the principle beyond the institution of sexual differences to also embrace cultural freight that the sexes carry.

Uncovering the Springs. What is the moral connection, if any, between the repeated warning in the Old Testament about having sexual relations with one's wife during her menstrual cycle or just after childbirth, and connubial love today? The law, given in Leviticus 15:24; 18:19; 20:18 and enlarged on in Ezekiel 18:5–9, requires seven days abstinence from sexual intercourse during menstruation, forty days after the birth of a son (Lev. 12:2–4) and eighty days after the birth of a daughter (Lev. 12:5).

This act is faulted because of its aggressiveness and because it pollutes the land. R. J. Rushdoony places great emphasis on Leviticus 20:18: "he has exposed the source of her flow [fountain]." In his view, two words for "fountain" (עַיִן and מָקוֹר) are used both figuratively (of God in Ps.

---

[36]See the discussion by George E. Mendenhall, "The Incident at Baal Peor," in *The Tenth Generation* (Baltimore: Johns Hopkins Press, 1973), 105–21.

[37]Rushdoony, *Biblical Law*, 436.

[38]W. L. Alexander, *Deuteronomy: The Pulpit Commentary*, ed. H. D. M. Spence and Joseph Exell (London: Kegan Paul, Trench, 1882), 355.

36:10; Jer. 17:13; of the source of grace in Ps. 87:7; of Israel as the source and father of a great nation in Deut. 33:28); and naturally (of a wife intimately in Prov. 5:18; Song of Sol. 4:12, 15). Therefore, just as a fountain is the source from which water comes, so there is an "obvious analogy to the woman's ovulation."[39] For Rushdoony

> Our fountains are in God; He alone therefore has the total right and power to unrestricted knowledge of us, and jurisdiction over us. . . . Man cannot transgress on any area. . . . and . . . exercise an unreserved lordship over anyone or anything. There is thus in all things a private domain which man cannot transgress, . . . No man can thus make a woman his creature.[40]

In other words, in order to show that no husband has sovereignty over his wife or her body, but that ultimately all is owed to God, married men are required to refrain from relations during these times. That would avoid a domineering and aggressive offense against the living God. Ezekiel 22:9–10 calls this act "perversity" or "lewdness" and an attempt "to humble" women.

The violation of a woman during the times of "her uncleanness" leads to an uncleanness or pollution of the land. H. L. Ellison reflected on this point saying:

> The fact is that the popular conception of the individual is derived from Greek thought rather than from the Bible, and may even be regarded as anti-Biblical. We tend to think of our bodies giving us individuality and separating us, one from the other. In the Old Testament it is our flesh—a word for body hardly exists in Hebrew—that binds us to our fellow-men; it is our personal responsibility to God that gives us our individuality. Since man (*'adam*) is bound to the ground (*'adamah*) from where he has been taken, and through it all who live on the same ground, he cannot help influence them by his actions. Abominable conduct causes "the land to sin" (Deut. 24:4; cf. Jer. 3:1, 9). That is why drought, pestilence, earthquake, etc., are for the Old Testament the entirely natural punishment of wickedness (cf. Psa. 107:33f.). If a man dwelt in a polluted land, he could not help sharing in its pollution. The chief terror of exile was not that the land of exile was outside the control of Jehovah—a view that was probably held by very few—but rather that it was an unclean land (Amos 7:17).[41]

---

[39]Rushdoony, *Biblical Law*, 429.
[40]Rushdoony, *Biblical Law*, 429.
[41]H. L. Ellison, *Ezekiel: The Man and His Message* (Grand Rapids: Eerdmans, 1956), 72 as cited by Rushdoony, *Biblical Law*, 428.

THE PERMISSION FOR DIVORCE

The most significant passage in the Old Testament dealing with divorce is Deuteronomy 24:1–4. This text is usually understood as giving permission for a husband to divorce his wife on grounds such as infidelity.

Its Grammatical Construction

Unfortunately, the Authorized Version (AV, King James), the American Standard Version of 1901 (ASV), and the English Revised Version (RV) contribute to the problems associated with this passage by giving verses 1–3 a jussive force. It is the presence of the word "shall" in "then it *shall* be . . . that he *shall* write a bill of divorcement." But an even more crucial point is the way the apodosis is attached already in verse 1 to the protasis. The effect is this: "When a man takes a wife and marries her and it come to pass that she finds no favor in his eyes because he has found some uncleanness in her; *then* let him write her a bill of divorce. . ." (italics added). On this rendering, divorce would not only be permitted or tolerated, but commanded when the uncleanness described in the protasis occurs.

It is now almost universally accepted that the first three verses form the protasis and that the apodosis only comes in verse 4.[42] That is the way the Septuagint also understands the passage. The importance of this observation is that this construction does not make divorce mandatory, encourage and advise men to put wives away, or even authorize or sanction divorce. Instead, it simply disallows a husband to return to the wife whom he had previously divorced and married another in the meantime. He cannot, under any circumstances, take her again as his wife. That is the only regulative statement in this passage.

Therefore, it would be wrong to speak of divorce in the Old Testament as a "right"[43] (i.e., an intrinsic right or prerogative) or as something that has divine approval and legitimation. The practice of divorce was, of course, well known in the Old Testament (e.g., Lev. 21:7, 14; 22:13; Num.

---

[42]See, for example, C. F. Keil and Franz Delitzsch, *Biblical Commentary on the Old Testament*, trans. James Martin (Grand Rapids: Eerdmans, 1956), 3:417; S. R. Driver, *The International Critical Commentary, A Critical Exegetical Commentary on Deuteronomy* (Edinburgh: T. & T. Clark, 1895), 269; Robert C. Campbell, "Teachings of the Old Testament Concerning Divorce," *Foundations* 6 (1963):174–78.

[43]Joseph Reider, *Deuteronomy with Commentary* (Philadelphia: Jewish Publication Society of America, 1937), 220. He said, "Here, as elsewhere (Lev. 21:7, 14; 22:13; Num. 30:10), the right of divorce is taken for granted. . ." as cited by John Murray, *Divorce* (Philadelphia: Presbyterian and Reformed Publishing Co., 1961), 7; and Driver, *Deuteronomy*: ". . . the right of divorce is assumed, as established by custom (comp [Deut.] 22:19.29. . .)," 269. Driver does clarify his use of "right" saying, "Hebrew law, as remarked above, does not institute divorce, but tolerates it, in view of the imperfections of human nature . . . , and lays down regulations tending to limit it, and preclude its abuses," p. 272.

30:9; Deut. 22:19, 29; cf. Isa. 50:1; Jer. 3:1; Ezek. 44:22), but this is different from establishing it as right and divinely approved. There are two cases in Deuteronomy 22:19–29 that record that divorce was denied on the basis of whim with attempted false slander or in the case of a rape of a virgin for whom the man then gave the bride-price. The implication is that there might be permission in other circumstances than these two. But it must not be forgotten that permission or toleration is different from divine approval or sanction. Permission and toleration may exist for something that is basically evil and wrong.

Its Grounds

The most precarious part of Deuteronomy 24:1–4 to explain is the "unseemly thing" (עֶרְוַת דָּבָר) of verse 1. Literally it means "nakedness of a thing." John Murray[44] argues that it cannot refer to adultery[45] for the following reasons:

(1) The Pentateuch prescribed death for adultery (Lev. 20:10; Deut. 22:22; cf. 22:23–27);

(2) Numbers 5:11–31 even cared for cases of suspected but unproven adultery, so that could not be the intent of this provision;

(3) Deuteronomy 22:13–21 also covered the case of a bride who was charged with previous sexual promiscuity and who vindicated herself; so that could not be the alternative meant here;

(4) Deuteronomy 22:23–24 treats the case of a betrothed virgin and another man who voluntarily defiled themselves and hence the sanction was death for both;

(5) Nor can the "unseemly thing" of Deuteronomy 24:1 be a matter of coercing a bride-to-be to have sexual relations for Deuteronomy 22:25–27 exonerated the virgin and put the man to death;

(6) Nor was it a matter of premarital sex between unbetrothed man and woman, for in that case the man must marry her and never divorce her (Deut. 22:28–29).

In none of these cases does our phrase עֶרְוַת דָּבָר or even עֶרְוָה by itself appear and in none of them does the proper action of recompense involve divorce. The full expression does occur once more in Deuteronomy 23:14 [15] of excrement while the word עֶרְוָה, "nakedness" appears frequently in Leviticus 18 and in Genesis 9:22–23; Exodus 20:26; Lamen-

---

[44]Murray, *Divorce*, 10–12.

[45]Peter Craigie, *The Book of Deuteronomy* (Grand Rapids: Eerdmans, 1976), 305 also rejects the adultery explanation but suggests tentatively that "a physical deficiency such as the inability to bear children may be implied."

tations 1:8; Ezekiel 16:36–37. The conclusion we are left with is that it must refer to "some indecency or impropriety of behavior; . . . while falling short of illicit sexual intercourse it may well be that the indecency consisted in some kind of shameful conduct connected with sex life."[46] Thus we cannot interpret it as strictly as the school of Shammai (allowing divorce only for adultery) or as loosely as the school of Hillel (allowing divorce for marital incompatibility), to state our conclusion in terms of the two reigning opinions in the time of our Lord's sojourn on earth. The issue must be something so shameful and repulsive as to arouse the husband's disgrace and revulsion.

This divorced woman may never return to her former husband who subsequently has been the husband of another woman. His and her second marriage has brought defilement. The word for "defile" is a *Hothpaʿel* (הֻטַּמָּאָה), the more uncommon reflexive passive conjugation (v. 4). The second marriage put the wife forever beyond the reach of her first husband and that is probably the impact of this verb to "defile."

In 1966, R. Yaron, offered a new explanation of this passage. He explained it not by the rules of incest, not some "unseemly thing," or even adultery. Said he:

> We wish therefore to submit that the prohibition expressed in verse 4 aims at the protection of the second marriage. When the divorcee has married another man, we have before us the possibility of tension within the "triangle" which has come into being. The first husband may wish to get back his wife, having repented of dismissing her, the wife may draw comparison between her two husbands unfavorable to the second one, and may indulge in overtures disruptive of the second marriage.[47]

But why, challenged C. M. Carmichael,[48] does this rule apply after the death of the second husband (Deut. 24:3)?

Its Connection with Incest Rules

More recently, Gordon Wenham[49] has noted along with many others that verse 4 gives three reasons why the first husband may not take back his first wife.

---

[46]Murray, *Divorce*, 12.

[47]R. Yaron, "The Restoration of Marriage," *Journal of Jewish Studies* 17 (1966): 8–9; This view was adopted by J. A. Thompson, *Deuteronomy* (London: Inter-Varsity, 1974): 244.

[48]C. M. Carmichael, *The Laws of Deuteronomy* (Ithaca: Cornell University Press, 1974): 205.

[49]Gordon J. Wenham, "The Restoration of Marriage Reconsidered," *Journal of Jewish Studies* 30 (1979): 36–40.

(1) "She has been defiled,"
(2) it is "an abomination to the Lord," and
(3) it "causes the land to sin."

These same three reasons, defilement, abomination, and pollution, are constantly repeated in connection with the sexual offenses of Leviticus 18 and 20. The concern in the holiness law, Wenham observes, is not only to outlaw incest, but also to outlaw sexual relations with affines (i.e., in-laws and step-relatives) after the death of their original partner and consanguines of the first and second degree (mother, sister—first-degree; or aunt, grand-daughter—second-degree).

Wenham's insight is that marriage and marital intercourse make a man and woman as closely related as parents and children—"one flesh." Marriage results in vertical blood relationships in the form of children, but it also creates a horizontal "blood" relationship between spouses.[50]

Therefore, just as the holiness law prohibited sexual relations with relatives by marriage, not during the lifetime of the affected blood relative (e.g., brother or uncle) since that was covered by the prohibition of adultery, but marriage with an in-law after the death of the first husband or after divorce by him; so remarriage to a previous horizontal blood relation is prohibited on the same grounds. That is why the motive clause about "nakedness" joins Leviticus 18, 20, and Deuteronomy 24. Furthermore, "the wife who marries into a family becomes an integral and permanent part of that family in the same way that children born into the family do. Even if her husband dies or divorces her, she still has this horizontal 'blood'-relationship with the family. In Hebrew thinking marriage made a girl not just a daughter-in-law, but a daughter of her husband's parents (Ruth 1:11; 3:1). She became a sister to her husband's brother. That is why if her husband dies or divorces her, her brother-in-law may not marry her (Lev. 18:16; 20:21)."[51]

Deuteronomy 24 uses the logic of the incest laws in denying a woman to reenter into marriage with her previous husband who has remarried in the meantime. "The result is paradoxical. A man may not remarry his former wife, because his first marriage to her made her into one of his closest relatives."[52] The restoration of such a marriage would be a type of incest.

Beside this central ethical concern there were three checks or guarantees made against rash or arbitrary divorce in this legislation: (1) definite grounds had to be alleged, (2) a proper legal instrument had to be prepared

---

[50]Wenham, "Marriage Reconsidered," 39.
[51]Wenham, "Marriage Reconsidered," 39.
[52]Wenham, "Marriage Reconsidered," 40.

and put in writing, and (3) the case (by implication) had to be brought before a public servant or official.

But should any doubt remain as to what the Old Testament thought about divorce, Malachi dispels it quickly. Divorce was pronounced as hateful to Yahweh in Malachi 2:16: "'I hate divorce,' says the LORD God of Israel."

THE STATUS OF WOMEN IN THE OLD TESTAMENT

The Old Testament defines Eve as a "counterpart" and companion suited or fitted especially to help man (Gen. 2:18). This "helpmeet" (not "helpmate") was made a joint heir with man of the mysteries of the kingdom and given the ability to "increase and multiply" through procreation.

Her "Desire" (Gen. 3:16)

A false translation of Genesis 3:16 has reduced women from the high station God gave them, being made in the image of God, to creatures now afflicted with some morbid type of intense sensuality. Keil and Delitzsch subscribe to such an interpretation of woman's punishment: "She was punished with a *desire* bordering upon disease."[53] Likewise, Driver assures us that "woman is to be dependent in two respects upon her husband: (1) she will desire his cohabitation, thereby at the same time increasing her liability to the pain of child-bearing; (2) he will *rule over her*, with allusion to the oppressed condition of woman in antiquity, when she was often treated not more than the slave of her husband. . . ."[54] All of this (except Driver's second observation) is quite unnecessary if we examine the text closely.

The word תְּשׁוּקָה, translated "desire," appears only three times in all of Scripture:

Genesis 3:16 to Adam,	Eve's תְּשׁוּקָה ("desire")
Genesis 4:7 to Cain,	Abel's תְּשׁוּקָה ("desire")
Song of Solomon 7:10[11] to the bride	Man's תְּשׁוּקָה ("desire")

Moreover, in not one of the three sentences is a verb expressed in the relationships listed here; there is simply a preposition before Adam, Cain, or the Beloved. Usually the translators supply the verb "shall be" with the force of some mandatory teaching.

The truth of the matter is that תְּשׁוּקָה does not mean sensual desire or libido. The word is from the verb שׁוּק, "to run" with the תְּ prefix

---

[53]C. F. Keil and Franz Delitzsch, *Biblical Commentary on the Old Testament*, trans. James Martin (Grand Rapids: Eerdmans, 1956), 103.
[54]S. R. Driver, *The Book of Genesis*, 11th ed., (London: Methuen, 1920), 49.

indicating an abstract noun formation corresponding to our suffix -*ness* on a word like good*ness*. The הָ֫ ending shows it is a feminine noun that normally is used with Hebrew abstract nouns. The literal meaning then is a "running back and forth" (in the intensive form) or a "turning" (toward her husband). Consistently, the Septuagint, Syriac Peshitta, Samaritan, Old Latin, Ethiopic, Sahidic, and Arabic versions each translated all three texts as "turning." The word "desire" appeared in English versions for the first time in A.D. 1380 by Wycliffe. After Wycliffe's version, an Italian Dominican monk, named Pagnino, translated the Hebrew Bible that became the main stimulus for every English version almost up to our own day. Most versions used the word "lust" that was later softened to "desire"[55] to translate תְּשׁוּקָה.

There is a further question connected with Genesis 3:16. So far we have, "You are turning away to your husband." Now we must decide whether the text says "he *shall* rule over you" or "he *will* rule over you," that is, whether this "rule" is a God ordained injunction for the proper ordering of domestic relations and the family or is it a prediction about what will ensue as a result of the woman's overdependence on man and her "turning" away from God?

We believe it is the latter and not the former. The Hebrew is an imperfect verb form, יִמְשָׁל, "he will rule" with the preposition and pronominal suffix בָּךְ, "over you." Katherine Bushnell quoting J. H. Moulton in his *Grammar of New Testament Greek* says:

> The use of *shall* where prophecy is dealing with future time is often particularly unfortunate. I have heard of an intelligent child who struggled for years under perplexity because of the words, "thou shalt deny me thrice!" It could not therefore be Peter's fault, if Jesus had commanded him![56]

In order to establish the mandatory nature of this verb, one would expect an imperative verb just ahead or following the clause containing the יִמְשָׁל. But that obligatory note is missing. Therefore we simply translate it

---

[55]This argument is found in Katherine C. Bushnell, *God's Word to Women* (1923; reprint, Ray B. Munson, Jacksonville, Fla., n.d.), lessons 16, 17, 18, paragraphs 126, 128, 129, 130, 138–45. Richard Simon complained, according to Bushnell, paragraph 142, "Pagnino has too much neglected the ancient versions of Scripture to attach himself to the teachings of the Rabbis." (*Biographie Universelle*). Susan T. Foh ("What is the Woman's Desire?" (*Westminster Journal of Theology* 37 [1975]: 376–83) argues, instead, that Eve will have the same type of "desire for her husband that sin has for Cain; a desire to possess or control him. This desire disputes the headship of the husband" (pp. 381–82). Therefore, just as Cain was instructed to rule over and master sin, so the husband must rule over his wife, argued Foh.

[56]Bushnell, *God's Word*, paragraph 274. She does not identify the page number or edition of Moulton's work.

"and he *will* rule over you" as a result of your "turning" to your husband and away from your dependence on God.

Her Worth (Lev. 12 and 27)

Many argue from passages like Leviticus 12:1–8 and Leviticus 27:1–8 that the value or worth of women in the Old Testament was greatly reduced over what it is now in the enlightened age of the New Testament church.

The argument is false from an exegetical viewpoint. While it is true that Leviticus 12 only required forty days isolation for the birth of a son, but eighty days for a new-born daughter (including seven and fourteen days "uncleanness" respectively), it must be remembered that circumcision of the son on the eighth day (Gen. 17:12) cut short the period of "uncleanness" for a male child and thus a second purification ceremony reduced by half the normal time of "uncleanness." The "purification" belonged to both mother and child (cf. Luke 2:22 "*their* purification" as used of both the holy child Jesus and the Virgin). But it is wrong to read from this that female children are attached to greater sinfulness, as some commentators argue, for the offerings at the end of the period of purification are the same for males and females. Moreover, childbirth involved no sin offering, else it would have been necessary to put it first before the mother could have access to God to dedicate herself and her child to him. Only after she had had access to God, in some exceptional cases, was a sin offering made as a formal restoration of fellowship since she had been separated from the privileges of the sanctuary during her days of confinement.[57]

No less significant is Leviticus 27:1–8. The basis for the difference in the valuation of men as over against women in the special vows in this chapter is simply the value of their services in the tabernacle. These persons who had been "vowed" to serve in the tabernacle could be "redeemed" from fulfilling this vow at the following rates:

men (20 to 60 years old) — 50 shekels
women (presumably same age) — 30 shekels
males (5 to 20 years old) — 20 shekels
females (presumably the same age) — 10 shekels
males (1 month up to 5 years old) — 5 shekels
females (presumably the same age) — 3 shekels
males (over 60 years old) — 15 shekels
females (presumably the same age) — 10 shekels

This can hardly be an explicit or even a tacit statement of intrinsic worth.

---

[57]This argument closely follows Bushnell, *God's Word*, paragraph 573.

Since one of the chief occupations of the sanctuary was the slaughtering and offering of animals and in the wilderness of disassembling and transporting the tabernacle around, it is easy to see that the service involving heavy manual work made the value of the service of men in the prime of their life much more costly to replace once they had been vowed to this work. This principle of "ability" to perform work is clearly stated in verse 8, but there is no breach of God's justice and the fact that he is "no respecter of persons."[58]

Her Worship (Deut. 16:11)

Of the three great festivals divinely appointed for Israel—Passover, Pentecost, and Tabernacles—Deuteronomy 16:11 specifically directed that women should be included in this festival. Providential it was, for on the Day of Pentecost in Acts when the Holy Spirit descended on the believers, he came with power on women as well as men!

Women also participated in the temple worship, for Ezra 2:65 and Nehemiah 7:67 mention the "women singers." And along with Heman's fourteen sons were three daughters who also appear to have joined in the temple service with this divinely gifted musical family (1 Chron. 25). Thus in the tradition of "Miriam the prophetess" (Exod. 15:20), they sang to God in public. In a similar way, Hannah's prayer (1 Sam. 2:1) became public property for worship and subsequently was used by Mary, the mother of our Lord.

Along with Miriam were other prophetesses such as Isaiah's wife, who apparently ministered along with him, and that most remarkable of all, Huldah (2 Chron. 34:22; 2 Kings 22:14). There also were false women prophets, such as Noadiah in Nehemiah 6:14 and those prophetesses in Ezekiel 13:17, but they were rebuked not because they were women or because they prophesied; instead, they were rebuked because what they said was false and not a revelation from God.

Women[59] were not chattel to be ordered about and used as men

---

[58]This argument also follows Bushnell, *God's Word*, paragraph 579.

[59]For further, and sometimes, contrasting studies on women, see: Ismar Peritz, "Women in the Ancient Hebrew Cult, *Journal of Biblical Literature* 17 (1898): 111–48; Caroline M. Breyfogle, "The Religious Status of Women in the Old Testament," *Biblical World* 35 (1910): 405–19; Isaac Mendelsohn, "The Family in the Ancient Near East," *Biblical Archaeologist* 11 (1948): 24–40; M. B. Crook, "The Marriageable Maiden of Proverbs 31:10–31," *Journal of Near Eastern Studies* 13 (1954): 137–40; O. J. Baab, "Woman," *Interpreter's Dictionary of the Bible* (Nashville: Abingdon, 1962) 4:864–67; Samuel Terrien, "Toward a Biblical Theology of Womanhood," *Religion in Life* 42 (1973): 322–33; Phyllis Bird, "Images of Women in the Old Testament," in *Religion and Sexism*, ed. Rosemary R. Ruether (New York: Simon and Schuster, 1974), 41–88; Phyllis Trible, "Women in the Old Testament," *Interpreter's Dictionary of the Bible*, Supplementary volume (Nashville: Abingdon, 1976), 962–66.

pleased in the Old Testament, ranking slightly above a man's ox or donkey! They were fellow heirs of the image of God, charged with tasks that exhibited the originality, independence, and management ability of the "woman of valor" in Proverbs 31 and were called to enter holistically into sharing all of the joys and labors of life.

Chapter 13

Holiness in Wealth and Possessions

When the eighth commandment enjoined, "You shall not steal," it covered a wide gamut of topics including the accumulating of wealth, the earning, saving, spending, and the inheriting of money, possessions, and property.[1] Probably no book in the Old Testament deals more frequently with the problems and blessings of wealth, affluence, and possessions than Deuteronomy. Typical of its concerns is Deuteronomy 8:17–18:

> You may say to yourself, "My power and the strength of my hands have produced this wealth for me." But remember the LORD your God, for it is he who gives you the ability to produce wealth, and so confirms his covenant, which he swore to your forefathers, as it is today.

People have nothing to boast about; what they have is a gift from above; and no Old Testament book stresses this fact more than Ecclesiastes. Repeatedly the "preacher" acknowledges that even his food, drink, and paycheck are the gifts of God (Eccles. 2:24–26; 5:18–20; 8:16).

---

[1]On the eighth commandment, see Walter Eichrodt, "The Question of Property in Light of the Old Testament," in *Biblical Authority for Today*, ed. Alan Richardson and Wolfgang Schweitzer (London: SCM, 1951), 257–74; A. Troost, "Property Rights and the Eighth Commandment," *International Reformed Bulletin* 24/25 (1966): 23–41; Gerhard Wehmeier, "The Prohibition of Theft in the Decalogue," *Indian Journal of Theology* 26(1977): 181–91; Christopher Joseph Herbert Wright, "Family, Land and Property in Ancient Israel" (Ph.D. diss., University of Cambridge, 1976).

THE POSSESSION AND USE OF WEALTH

Material things, goods, and natural resources are in and of themselves "good," for they are all made by God: that is the constant refrain in the creation narrative of Genesis 1—"and God saw that it was good."[2] In addition to this, no one who possesses goods may say, "I did it by myself; I worked and slaved and my power and my sweat produced all the wealth that you see." Deuteronomy 8:17–18 gives the lie to that boast as we saw above. So the problem with goods is not an inherent evil in the possessions themselves: the problem rests elsewhere.

The misuse of goods comes from unholy people. Forgetting that: (1) these are creations by God, (2) God gave men and women the ability to earn these possessions, and (3) goods must not be exalted to the level of ultimate or absolute concern and worth; people begin to worship the created realm rather than the Creator himself. Such idolizing of the things of this world violates the first commandment and leads to an inversion of values in life.

Others in protest of this new type of Baalism turn in revulsion from such greedy and unthankful souls to asceticism. Neither the idolatry of things nor asceticism are the biblically approved response to wealth and possessions.

The biblical pattern of the holy life can never lead us to make the aim of our lives the securing of material possessions and wealth; pleasing God and enjoying him is to be the goal. Yet the Old Testament is not embarrassed by affluence. Affluence, when God is pleased to bestow it, is a gift of God—never in itself an evil. Affluence is also always a tool by which people can carry out the work of God in this world. The only concern that the Old Testament continually repeats is that men and women will be tempted with the gift of affluence to forget God. Hence Deuteronomy 8:11–14 warns:

> Be careful that you do not forget the LORD your God, . . . Otherwise, when you eat and are satisfied, when you build fine houses and settle down, and when your herds and flocks grow large and your silver and gold increase and all you have is multiplied, then your heart will become proud and you will forget the LORD your God. . . .

---

[2]On the discussion of wealth and poverty in the Old Testament see: Reginald H. Fuller, "The Old Testament Background," in *Christianity and the Affluent Society,* ed. Reginald H. Fuller and Brian K. Rice (Grand Rapids: Eerdmans, 1966), 11–22; James Kelly, "The Biblical Meaning of Poverty and Riches," *Bible Today* 33 (1967): 2282–91; Jon D. Levenson, "Poverty and the State in Biblical Thought," *Judaism* 25 (1976): 230–41. Also note Friedrich Hauck and Wilhelm Kasch, "Riches and the Rich in the Old Testament," *Theological Dictionary of the New Testament* 6:323–25. Cf. also David Murchie, "The New Testament View of Wealth Accumulation," *Journal of Theological Studies* 21 (1978): 335–44.

Possessions, wealth, and affluence bring with them responsibilities. There is a constant reminder that ownership is not an absolute good—it is a relative good. The temptation is ever present to make these goods, instead of God, our lasting companions. Then there is the responsibility of the right use of wealth to aid our neighbor. Said Deuteronomy 15:7–8:

> If there is a poor man among your brothers in any of the towns of the land that the LORD your God is giving you, do not be hard-hearted or tightfisted toward your poor brother. Rather be openhanded and freely lend him whatever he needs.

Wealth, finally, should breed a spirit of thankfulness to God for all that he has loaned, for all the earth belongs to the Lord and everything that is in it (Ps. 24:1). Therefore, Deuteronomy 26:1–11 urges:

> When you have entered the land the LORD your God is giving you as an inheritance and have taken possession of it and settled in it, take some of the firstfruits of all that you produce from the soil of the land the LORD your God is giving you and put them in a basket. Then go to the place the LORD your God will choose as a dwelling for his Name and say to the priest in office at that time, . . . "I have come to the land the LORD swore to our fore-fathers to give us. . . . And now I bring the firstfruits of the soil that you, O LORD, have given me!" Place the basket before the LORD your God and bow down before him. And you and the Levites and the aliens among you shall rejoice in all the good things the LORD your God has given you and your household.

The dangers of trusting in one's wealth came to be legendary in the time of the prophets. The idolatry of the *nouveau riche* who forgot God can be seen in Amos' castigations. The rich, he thundered, "sell the righteous for silver, and the needy for a pair of sandals" (Amos 2:6). They "trample on the poor and force him to give . . . gifts of wheat . . . [while] [they] have built stone mansions . . . [and plant] lush vineyards" (Amos 5:11). The disgusting contrast between the lush affluence of the women of Samaria in Amos 6:4–6 is contrasted with the crying needs of the people of that nation. Like the stuffy women Isaiah mentions, they too are "haughty, walking along with outstretched necks, flirting with their eyes, tripping along with mincing steps, with ornaments jingling on their ankles" (Isa. 3:16).

Moreover, wealth is not an unmixed blessing. It can: (1) make a person blind to his or her own faults (Prov. 28:11, "a rich man may be wise in his own eyes"); (2) lead to pride that goes before a fall (Prov. 18:10–12; 11:28); (3) lead to cares and anxieties (Eccles. 5:12, "The abundance of a rich man permits him no sleep"); and (4) lead to a distortion of values and priorities (Prov. 22:1, "a good name is more desirable than great riches").[3]

On the other hand, neither was poverty a state to be sought for its own sake. Some people are poor and proud of it! The problem once again is not located in things, but in people. Thus, we may affirm that God loves the poor but hates poverty. Deuteronomy 15:4 emphasizes, "There shall be among you no needy for the Lord will bless you in the land." Yet the realities of life also dictate, *in that same context*, that "there will always be poor people in the land" (Deut. 15:11). Poverty is systemic and continues in the face of the best efforts of the best government to eradicate it. This can be no reason for a people or a government to excuse itself, but it does call for a constant "open hand" (Deut. 15:11) on the part of those who have been provided with more than the needy.

Poverty will dispose us to do what affluence will not—trust God and observe his ways and instruction. But poverty will not automatically make one virtuous, for some will harden their hearts under the weight of this type of suffering (Prov. 29:1), and others will be tempted to envy the proud and affluent (Ps. 73:3–9).

No wonder, then that the wise man prays:

> Give me neither poverty nor riches,
>   but give me only my daily bread.
> Otherwise, I may have too much and disown you
>   and say, "Who is the LORD?"
> Or I may become poor and steal,
>   and so dishonor the name of my God   (Prov. 30:8–9).

While part of the means to gaining wealth is indeed labor (Prov. 13:11, "he who gathers money little by little makes it grow") and the result is the blessing of God, it still raises the difficult problem of theodicy: many of the ungodly appear to be rich and prosperous while many of the righteous are left in poverty (Job 21:7; Ps. 73). But the answer, in part, is the reminder of the psalmist (49:17–18) that no man can carry his wealth with him in death. Wealth and fortune are all impermanent and relative to the changing times, but "those who seek the LORD lack no good thing," promises the psalmist (Ps. 34:10).[4]

THE QUESTION OF INTEREST AND USURY

Righteousness, justice, and holiness must be carried into the marketplace as well as the sanctuary and altar. The same Lord who exacted justice from the Egyptians when he delivered Israel will likewise govern

---

[3]This discussion follows the lead of Fuller, "Background," 18–21.
[4]See the discussion of the problem of eudaemonism in part IV of this volume.

all others by the same standard; therefore looseness in weights and measurements (i.e., fiscal policies, currencies, and merchandizing techniques) will earn the quick rebuke of God (cf. Lev. 19:35–37). The whole matter of a concern for a right or proper measure comes from God himself.[5]

Honesty in Merchandising

It is dishonest merchandising of the worst sort, branded "an abomination to the Lord" (Prov. 20:10–23), to foist off on the public something less than they think they are buying, or to cheat the seller by weighing out less than the proper amount of value for those goods. In this connection, "the old Latin and modern laissez-faire principle, *caveat emptor*, 'let the buyer beware,' is not Biblical."[6] Neither, adds Rushdoony, is the liberal principle, "let the seller beware," biblical either. God's call to holiness demands that both buyer and seller be fair and responsible. Thus all imitations, adulterations, changes, false claims in advertisements, and failures to notify the buyer about defects are plainly forbidden by this commandment.

Loaning and Interest

But what about loaning money at "interest" or "usury,"[7] as some translations render it? There are three texts that take up this matter. They read:

> If you lend money to one of my people among you who is needy, do not be like a moneylender; charge him no interest. (Exod. 22:25 [24])

> If one of your countrymen becomes poor and is unable to support himself among you, help him as you would an alien or a temporary resident, so he can continue to live among you. Do not take interest of any kind from him, but fear your God, so that your countryman may continue to live among you. You must not lend him money at interest or sell him food at a profit. (Lev. 25:35–37)

---

[5]See Deut. 25:13–15; Ezek. 45:10, 12; Hos. 12:7; Amos 8:5; Mic. 6:10–11.

[6]R. J. Rushdoony, *Institutes of Biblical Law* (Nutley, N.J.: Craig, 1973), 469.

[7]The literature can be represented by: Benjamin Nelson, *The Idea of Usury From Tribal Brotherhood to Universal Otherhood* (Princeton: Princeton University Press, 1944); S. Stein, "The Laws on Interest in the Old Testament," *Journal of Theological Studies* 4 (1953): 161–70; Edward Neufeld, "The Prohibitions Against Loans at Interest in Ancient Hebrew Laws," *Hebrew Union College Annual* 26 (1955): 78–80; S. Stein, "Interest Taken From Gentiles," *Journal of Semitic Studies* 1 (1956): 141–64; Hillel Gamoran, "Biblical Law Against Loans on Interest," *Journal of Near Eastern Studies* 30 (1971): 127–34; Robert P. Maloney, "Usury and Restrictions on Interest-taking in the Ancient Near East," *Catholic Biblical Quarterly* 36 (1974): 1–20; Rushdoony, *Biblical Law*, 473–81.

> Do not charge your brother interest, whether on money or food or anything else that may earn interest. You may charge a foreigner interest, but not a brother Israelite, so that the LORD your God may bless you in everything you put your hand to in the land you are entering to possess. (Deut. 23:19–20 [20–21])

Besides these three passages, three other books condemn the practice of charging interest, namely, Psalm 15:5; Proverbs 28:8; and Ezekiel 18:8, 13, 17; 22:12.

Terms for Interest

There are two Hebrew words used for "interest" in the Old Testament: נֶשֶׁךְ and תַּרְבִּית are used in Leviticus (25:36–37), four times in Ezekiel (18:8, 13, 17; 22:12), and once in Proverbs (28:8).

It would appear that נֶשֶׁךְ is the dominant word since it always appears first when used with תַּרְבִּית and is also found alone whereas תַּרְבִּית is never found by itself. The relationship that the noun נֶשֶׁךְ has to the verb "bite" is now also attested in Ugarit where *ntk*, "bite" is also used with "serpent" as its subject, which is also true of Hebrew. Hence, scholars like Speiser[8] and Neufeld[9] argue that נֶשֶׁךְ refers to those loans that had the interest "bitten off" or deducted before the loan was made, thus a debtor might get only 80 shekels on a 100 shekel loan as parallels in Alalakh or Nuzi tablets show. But Samuel E. Loewenstamm[10] has challenged the view of Speiser and Neufeld (that has been recently incorporated into the new Jewish Publication Society translation of the Torah). He suggests that נֶשֶׁךְ refers to interest on a loan of money and תַּרְבִּית on a food loan. It is true that in Exodus and Psalms only money is mentioned and Leviticus explicitly makes this division: ". . . your money at נֶשֶׁךְ". . . . "Your food for מַרְבִּית." One problem with this view is that Deuteronomy speaks of both נֶשֶׁךְ on money and נֶשֶׁךְ on food. Loewenstamm answers, "Deut. 23:20 is the only scripture recording *the loan of anything which bears interest*, following the loans of money and victuals. The tendency to an abstract and comprehensive formulation is evident."[11]

---

[8]Ephraim A. Speiser in *Oriental and Biblical Studies, Collected Writings of E. A. Speiser*, ed. Finkelstein and M. Greenberg (Philadelphia: University of Pennsylvania Press, 1967), 131–35; 40–41.

[9]Neufeld, "Prohibitions Against Loans," 355–57.

[10]Samuel E. Loewenstamm, "נשך and תרבית/מ," *Journal of Biblical Literature* 88 (1969): 78–80. He even discounts the Ugaritic *ntk* as reflecting a proto-Semitic stem. He thinks the Ugaritic form may derive from metathesis of proto-Semitic *nkt* as in Arabic and Aramaic.

[11]Loewenstamm, "תרבית/מ," 79. He sees this same abstract or generalizing tendency in Deut. 17:6–7; 19:15 as against Num. 35:30; or Deut. 22:1–3 as against Exod. 23:4.

If the two terms are not a simple case of hendiadys, as was previously argued,[12] there are two schools of thought concerning the distinction made between them. For some the distinction lies in the *substance* of the thing loaned (money or food as argued by Loewenstamm); for others it lies in the *method* by which the loan was computed. S. Stein, citing Nachmanides and David Hoffmann, argues that נֶשֶׁךְ was a "long-term yearly recurring form of interest" whereas תַּרְבִּית "would constitute a fixed rate of interest for a small loan of money or grain to be paid together with the capital after the harvest."[13] No one can say for sure which of these views is correct. For our purposes, it is only significant to note that both words are dealing with some type of compensation for a loan, and that neither word can be shown to mean an exorbitant or excessive increase beyond some commonly received fixed rate. That emphasis and interpretation did not come until the Christian era, but many interpreters still insist on explaining it that way without presenting any documentation for their preferences.[14]

Nationality and Condition of the Borrower

The law on interest applied only to the Israelite. Exodus uses "my people" while Leviticus applies this prohibition to "your brother." However, Deuteronomy makes explicit what Exodus and Leviticus had only implied, "you may charge a foreigner (נָכְרִי) interest, but not a brother Israelite. . ." (23:20). The foreigner fell into a separate category from the גֵּר ("resident alien") who had taken up permanent residence among the Israelites. Since the law protected the גֵּר and gave him many of the same privileges as the native Israelite, we may expect that the same prohibition on loaning at interest extended to him as it did to the loaner's own "brothers"—and that is what Leviticus 25:35 explicitly spells out.

The key feature of this legislation on interest was not to stifle business or the practice of corporate laws as we know them today. Its aim was mainly to protect the poor. The would-be creditor should not take advantage of the economic hardship that had forced his "brother" (i.e., fellow member of the Hebrew commonwealth) to seek a loan. Instead, righteous and holy living would dictate that a loan be given at no interest whatsoever.

Edward Neufeld and S. R. Driver felt this prohibition was made for

---

[12]D. H. Mueller, *Semitica* 1 (1906): 13–19 as cited by Loewenstamm, "מ/תרבית," 78, n. 3.

[13]S. Stein, "The Laws on Interest in the Old Testament," *Journal of Theological Studies* 4 (1953): 163. See Milton C. Fisher, "נֶשֶׁךְ," *Theological Wordbook of the Old Testament* 2:604–5.

[14]See Fisher, "נֶשֶׁךְ," 604–5.

the specific relief of the poor and needy, but it was never intended to be permanent.[15] Yet, Hillel Gamoran counters by saying that out of the sixteen biblical passages dealing with loans, not one deals with the commercial loans Neufeld and Driver are arguing for, and Deuteronomy lays down a blanket prohibition without specific reference to the poor.[16] Yet, as Gamoran himself acknowledges, "even though the Deuteronomic version doesn't mentioned the poor, it was nevertheless written for their protection as were its sister statements in Exodus and Leviticus."[17]

Driver makes this summary:

> In condemning the practice of taking interest on money, Hebrew legislation agreed with the thinkers of Greece and Rome (Plato, *Legg*, v. 742; Arist. *Pol.* i. 10.5; Cato *ap. Cic de Off.* ii. 25;—Arist. for instance arguing, in view of its Greek name *tokos*, to extract *offspring* from it must be *contrary to nature*); and the same opinion was shared largely in the early Christian Church. The change of sentiment which has supervened in modern times is due partly to a clearer perception of the nature and use of money, partly to the fact that the purposes for which loans are now required, are (as a rule) different from those for which they were needed in ancient societies. In modern times, loans are required principally by merchants and other traders, for the purpose of developing an industry by increasing the capital with which it is worked; and the increased capital bringing with it an increased income it is both natural and proper that a reasonable payment done for the loan (i.e. the hire) of a house, or of any other commodity. In ancient times, however, commercial relations were comparatively undeveloped, and loans were commonly needed for the purpose of relieving distress (cf. Ex. 22:24, 25). . . . The loans on which interest was prohibited, were thus originally not advances of money needed for the development of a commercial industry, but advances intended for the relief of destitution.[18]

The Permanence of the Law Prohibiting Interest

A distinction may be made, therefore, between using another person's distress (especially, one to whom I owe brotherly love) as an opportunity for profit and extending loans for the purpose of international commerce. Thus Proverbs 28:8 rebuked the employer who refuses to take pity on his poor employees and uses their grief as an opportunity to in-

---

[15]Neufeld, "Prohibitions Against Loans," 400–401; S. R. Driver, *A Critical and Exegetical Commentary on Deuteronomy*, 3rd ed. (Edinburgh: T. & T. Clark, 1895), 266–67.

[16]Gamoran, "Law Against Interest," 131.

[17]Gamoran, "Law Against Interest," 131.

[18]Driver, *Commentary on Deuteronomy*, 266–67.

crease his wealth. Jeremiah (15:10), Ezekiel (18:13; 22:12), and Nehemiah (5:1–13) all required that this abuse cease.

The fact that interest was approved for ventures that did not try to circumvent one's obligation to the poor is reinforced by Jesus' allusion and apparent approval of taking interest on commercial loans in Luke 19:23 and Matthew 25:27. Thus, the use of money for commercial or international ventures, and the security of a reasonable rate of interest, was a different matter from the requirement of aiding one's destitute brother. No one could hold another person's life for ransom, for God was the only owner of mortals. Accordingly, any pawn or security that involved anything necessary to a person's living or work, for example, his clothes or his plow, could not be seized; it was tantamount to an attack on his life.

THE YEAR OF JUBILEE

Leviticus 25 has been the occasion for an extended discussion recently, especially in the reformed community of the Netherlands. This discussion is summarized well in the work of Marten H. Woudstra.[19]

The structure of Leviticus 25, using the key rhetorical device of the phrase "I am the LORD your God" (vv. 17, 38, 55) in order to locate the divisions in the text, falls into three sections, not counting the introduction in verse 1.

Introduction 25:1
A Sabbath for the Land 25:2–22
The Redemption of Property 25:23–38
The Redemption of a Slave 25:39–55
Each section has a closing theological exhortation:
25:17–22
25:35–38
25:55

In the past, it has been traditional to see a combined typological and eschatological picture in this chapter. Keil and Delitzsch were fairly typical of this major view when they argued that the Jubilee law was given to show the "sanctification of the whole land by the appointment of the Sabbatical and the Jubilee years."[20] Thus as the full enjoyment of the blessings of God were realized on the land and by its people Israel, the land was transformed into a kingdom of peace and liberty. Moreover, it prefigured a time

---

[19]Marten H. Woudstra, "The Year of Jubilee and Related Old Testament Laws— Can They be 'Translated' For Today?" *Theological Forum* 5 (December 1977): 1–21.

[20]C. F. Keil and Franz Delitzsch, *A Biblical Commentary: The Pentateuch* (Grand Rapids: Eerdmans, 1951), 2:263.

of the completion of the kingdom of God when the glorious liberty of the kingdom of God would dawn and the bondage of sin and death would be abolished forever. Since the Jubilee was proclaimed on the Day of Atonement (Lev. 25:9), the removal of sin on *Yom Kippur* made possible the restored relationship between God and his people, and looked forward to the kingdom of peace and liberty in the *eschaton* as pictured in the Jubilee.

More recently, John Bright[21] made a distinction between the law (which for him, "as law, is ancient, irrelevant, and without authority") and the "theology of the law" (which we "are enjoined in all our dealings ever to strive to make . . . actual").[22] Leviticus 25, for Bright:

> . . . Seeks to tell us that the land is God's and that we live on this earth as aliens and sojourners, holding all that we have as it were on loan from him (vs. 23); that God narrowly superintends every business transaction and expects that we conduct our affairs in the fear of him (vss. 17, 36, 43) dealing graciously with the less fortunate brother in the recollection that we have all been recipients of grace (vss. 38, 42). And that is normative ethics![23]

A third approach to the law of Jubilee is represented by B. Maarsingh in a Dutch work entitled *Maatschappijcritiek in Het Oude Testament—Het Jubeljaar*.[24] Maarsingh finds three principles of the Jubilee that can be "translated" for modern society in this way: "Each person receives the possibility of living independently by means of that which is his; each man is a free man, free from whatever dictatorship; each man is personally united with and bound in obedience to that God who in Christ has given complete deliverance."[25]

The purpose of the Year of Jubilee is this: "Each Israelite lives as a free man on his own land, dependent upon and obedient to the God of whom the land is and whose slave he is."[26] We may list three principles in the Jubilee law as follows:

(1) Each person is to live as a free man.
(2) Each person is to own his own land.
(3) Each person is to be personally united with and bound in obedience to the Lord who has delivered us.

---

[21]John Bright, *The Authority of the Old Testament* (Nashville: Abingdon Press, 1967).

[22]Bright, *Authority of Old Testament*, 153.

[23]Bright, *Authority of Old Testament*, 153.

[24]B. Maarsingh, *Maatschappijcritiek in Het Oude Testament—Het Jubeljaar* (Kampen: J. H. Kok, 1976).

[25]Maarsingh, *Maatschappijcritiek*, 67 as cited and translated by Woudstra, "Year of Jubilee," 6.

[26]Maarsingh, *Maatschappijcritiek*, 67 as cited and translated by Woudstra, "Year of Jubilee," 6.

When one of these three is neglected, says Maarsingh, or the system under which one lives makes it impossible to receive one or more of these principles and the benefits of the Year of Jubilee, then God will intervene.

But can one so facilely, Woudstra complains, draw a line from the covenant promise of the land of Canaan given over to Israel (Lev. 25:23; cf. Gen. 12:7; 15:18; 17:6–8) to the "soil" today or even to nations and king-doms of the present? This is not to say that elsewhere the Bible overlooks the worldwide "earth" and its possessors (Pss. 24:1; 37:11), for it does not, but is not this chapter addressed immediately to Israel? Note the themes of redemption from Egypt (Lev. 25:38, 42) and the frequent references to the "fear" of God (Lev. 25:17, 36, 43).

In yet another viewpoint, John Howard Yoder[27] connected the Jubilee Year with Isaiah 61:1–2 and Luke 4:16–21. The Jubilee event, Yoder judged, "is a visible socio-political, economic structuring of relations among the people of God, achieved by his intervention in the person of Jesus as the one Anointed and endued with the Spirit."[28] Woudstra notes that, while Yoder goes beyond the others surveyed here, he does not go beyond a restructuring of *relations*.[29]

How then may we today appeal to Leviticus 25? Is it not, as Woudstra so accurately observes,[30] for the social, economic, and territorial aspects of the Jubilee law that we go to this chapter in hopes that we may find some of the same guidance applicable to our day? Yet, to abstract from it those aspects would leave the text denuded and robbed of one part of its message while the redemptive significance of the land, the Sabbath, and the "rest" of God would be put in jeopardy. One loses immediately the wholeness of God's law when we subtract the civil part and attempt to make it normative for today while leaving the spiritual or ceremonial ele-ment as worthless and remaining in the mined text. The tragic near-sightedness of "liberation theology," which loves to focus on the Exodus and laws like Leviticus 25, is that it overlooks the redemptive themes of the Lamb's blood, the atonement, and the conditions of the covenant and thus it is left with merely a humanistic leftover from the passage. Likewise, it is unfair to go the other way and so spiritualize Leviticus 25 that nothing is left except a personal biographical note on individual redemption, deliv-erance, and rest in the Savior.

It may be possible to separate out as a significance (as opposed to its meaning or sense) that all peoples and lands need a periodic rest or sab-batical, not just university and seminary professors. But that could hardly

---

[27]John Howard Yoder, *The Politics of Jesus* (Grand Rapids: Eerdmans, 1972), 39.
[28]Yoder, *Politics of Jesus*, 39.
[29]Woudstra, "Year of Jubilee," 9.
[30]Woudstra, "Year of Jubilee," 10.

ever be the direct ethical teaching of this passage. Neither could we press the point that the land is to be the means of production and so every person ought to be able to provide his livelihood from it (Lev. 25:16, 30, 31; note the contrast between houses in cities and farm properties). Nor can we go from a limited time for slavery to a whole statement on freedom as a desired goal for all people. These are all worthy issues, but this exercise illustrates how not to use a legal text.

If we were to settle down on an approach to this text, it should be a combination of Keil and Delitzsch along with John Bright. In that combination, the unity of the law along with the universal concepts from the theology of the law are brought together as they ought to be in every text.

The possession and careful use of private property is not against God's order of things. Scripture is more concerned about the forgetting of God in the midst of our wealth than about the fact of possessions or wealth per se (Deut. 8:17–18). Only the arrogance, idolatry, and selfish use of wealth are condemned in the Scriptures. Wealth, when it comes, must be received as an aspect of God's blessing. As Proverbs 10:22 said, "The blessing of the LORD brings wealth, and he adds no trouble to it."

Before we conclude this chapter, we should mention the view of Albrecht Alt who reinterpreted the eighth commandment to refer only to the kidnapping of a free Israelite man in its original form[31] while the tenth commandment dealt with waylaying women, children, and slaves, in short, all who were not free. Based on analogy with the sixth and seventh commandment, Alt makes the eighth into a capital offense (i.e., kidnapping or stealing a freeman) and then uses form criticism not only to judge on the originality of a text, but also to restore and reconstruct it for the eighth commandment and Exodus 21:16. But why must an analogy be posed, and how can form critical methods triumph over the common meaning of a term in reconstructing texts?

Moreover, the verb גָּנַב "to steal" can mean "to kidnap" when it has persons as the direct object of the verb; but, as Jackson points out, nowhere does it have the meaning "to kidnap" when it stands alone without an object.[32] Therefore, Alt cannot have it both ways. If גָּנַב originally had a direct object, it meant "to kidnap"—a fact unattested as yet; but once it

---

[31]Albrecht Alt, "Das Verbot des Diebstahls im Dekalog," *Kleine schriften zur Geschichte des Volkes Israel* (Munich, 1953), 1:333–40. For a slightly different view, "You shall not steal a man *or a woman*," see K. Rabast, *Das apodiktische Recht in Deuteronomuim und in Heiligkeitsgesetz* (Berlin, 1949), 35ff. or H. Schulz, *Das Todesrecht im Alten Testament* (Berlin, 1969), 36ff. Schulz sees it as a prohibition on kidnapping a member of one's kin—all cited by Bernard S. Jackson, "Liability for Mere Intention in Early Jewish Law" (*Hebrew Union College Annual* 42 (1971): 202, n. 19.

[32]Jackson, "Liability," 203.

lost that object, in what Alt views as its shortened form, it *radically* altered its meaning to that of stealing property.

It is best to reject Alt's thesis as being too speculative until harder textual evidence supports it. Not even the paraphrase on Deuteronomy 5:21 found at Qumran (4 Q Deut. 158.7–8) begins to suggest anything like this elaborate thesis.[33] The prohibition remains on misappropriating and stealing anything that does not belong to us.

---

[33]Jackson, "Liability," 202, n. 19[b].

Chapter 14

Holiness in Obtaining and Using Truth

The ninth commandment has been the subject of wide disagreement. It simply states: "You shall not give false testimony against your neighbor" (Exod. 20:16). The main point that is usually contested is this: Must all persons, at all times, under all circumstances tell the truth to all persons, in word and deed, when asked and when not asked?[1]

THE STANDARD OF TRUTH

The basic Old Testment word for truth is אֱמֶת and its kindred word אֱמוּנָה. Both are derived from the verb אָמַן (cf. English "Amen"), which means in its basic stem "to be steady or firm" and in its derived stems "to make firm, to support, sustain, or last." Our word "truth" in the English versions almost always corresponds to Hebrew אֱמֶת even though it is not always translated that way. It often is rendered "faithfulness." That meaning more properly and frequently belongs to אֱמוּנָה, for אֱמֶת is that which is opposed to falsity or falsehood. Luther consistently distinguished be-

---

[1]On this topic, see Edward Thomas Ramsdell, "The Old Testament Understanding of Truth," *The Journal of Religion* 31 (1951): 264–73; Henri Blocher, "La Notion Biblique de Verite," *Themelios* 4 (1968): 8–20; and *idem*, "The Biblical Concept of Truth," trans. H. O. J. Brown *Themelios* 5 (1969): 47–61; H. McKeating, "Justice and Truth in Israel's Legal Practice: An Inquiry," *The Church Quarterly* 3 (1970): 51–56; Alfred Jepsen, "אֱמֶת, אֱמוּנָה, אָמַן," *Theological Dictionary of the Old Testament* 1:309–23. Also see the long bibliography of moralists on this topic in John Murray, *Principles of Conduct* (Grand Rapids: Eerdmans, 1957), 131–32, n. 3. M. E. Andrew, "Falsehood and Truth," *Interpretation* 17 (1963): 425–38.

tween these two nouns in his German translation rendering "fidelity" or "faithfulness" by *Treue* and "truth" by *Wahrheit*.

Truth

Does אֱמֶת mean "faithfulness" or is the fact of the matter as Quell argues: "The translation 'faithfulness' nowhere commends itself."[2] But Quell wants to avoid using "faithfulness" here in order to differentiate it from חֶסֶד ("loving kindness") which he feels is the proper legal term for faithfulness to a compact. God confirms his חֶסֶד by acting according to the norm of אֱמֶת. "Truthfulness is thus the presupposition of faithfulness. Hence to use the latter term for אֱמֶת always implies a measure of refining and retouching, and ought to be avoided."[3]

Jepsen concluded that the word, "reliability" was the best comprehensive word in English for אֱמֶת.[4] This is in keeping with the overall concepts of stability, solidity, and firmness found in this word and its kindred words. For example, the columns of the temple (2 Kings 18:16) were אֹמְנוֹת (from the same root אמן); hence that which one could rest on, rely upon, and thus believe. When connected with דָּבָר "word" (as it often is in the Old Testament), those were words a person could rely on. "Speak אֱמֶת one to another," urged Zechariah (8:16).

While truth in one's words usually is the primary focus in discussions on this subject, the Old Testament relates such truth telling to the *character* of men ("men of truth," i.e., of integrity, and reliability; Exod. 18:21; Deut. 1:13; Neh. 7:2) and to the *behavior* of men ("to do" the truth, or to "walk" in it; Ps. 86:11; cf. Pss. 25:5; 43:3). Henri Blocher summarizes truth in the Old Testament as follows:

> When a word communicates a knowledge of facts—facts to come, facts in the present, facts in the past it is not sure (reliable) unless it corresponds to these facts, unless there is a permanent correspondence which is valid for the other person as well as for me if he trusts my word and therefore commits himself.[5]

The standard for truth is first of God himself. The "God of Truth" in Isaiah 65:16 is literally the "God of Amen." The attribute of אֱמֶת is his, because he is the "God of truth" (Ps. 146:6; Jer. 10:10). He "keeps אֱמֶת" "forever" (Ps. 146:6). חֶסֶד and אֱמֶת go before him (Ps. 89:14[15]). He is great in חֶסֶד and אֱמֶת (Exod. 34:6; Ps. 89:14[15]). Above all, God's speech is אֱמֶת, even as David praises God: "O Sovereign LORD, you are God! Your words are trustworthy" (2 Sam. 7:28). Thus, more than any other words, "The

---

[2]Gottfried Quell, "The OT Term אֱמֶת," *Theological Dictionary of the New Testament* 1:233, n. 2; also 236, n. 12.

[3]Quell, "אֱמֶת," n. 12.

[4]Jespen, "אֱמֶת," 313.

[5]Blocher, "Biblical Concept," 50.

essence (*ro'š*; the foundation sum, totality, or principle)[6] of your word is truth" (Ps. 119:160).

Unlike Greek ἀλήθεια (privative prefix *a*-, "not" and λανθάνω "to see"; cf. the river *Lethe*, the river of forgetting),[7] the Old Testament אֱמֶת is interested in *more than* just bringing to light knowledge; it is also the basis for life.[8] 'Αλήθεια is impersonal, while Old Testament "truth" is internalized in the speaker or actor as well as it is shared in a relationship between persons.[9] Accordingly, Joseph demanded that his brothers produce Benjamin so that he might know that there really was "truth" in them (Gen. 42:16; הַאֱמֶת אִתְּכֶם).

Old Testament "truth," then, ties together "personality and objectivity." It "claims an exclusive divine origin,"[10] yet on the basis of this norm all users of אֱמֶת may be tested for correspondence to what is real.

Moral integrity, both as it relates to facts and principles, is our concern in this investigation of truth. Scripture frequently condemns lying and labels it as hateful to God. Leviticus 19:11 clearly cautions: "Do not lie," while Proverbs 6:16–19 includes a "lying tongue" as one of the seven things God "hates." "The LORD detests lying lips" (Prov. 12:22), but "truthful lips endure forever" (Prov. 12:19). David's sad experience with Doeg the Edomite led him to dedicate one of the eight "fugitive Psalms" to this matter of the improper use of the tongue (Ps. 52).

Lying and Concealment

But what constitutes a lie? Ezekiel Hopkins, following St. Augustine's definition says, "A lie . . . is a voluntary speaking of an intent to deceive."[11] He went on to explain that a lie must have, then, three ingredients:

> [a] There must be the speaking of an untruth; [b] It must be known to us to be an untruth; and [c] it must be with a will and intent to deceive him to whom we speak it, and to lead him into error.[12]

Asa Mahan's definition sharpens the focus even more: a lie is "the intentional deception of an individual who has a right to know the truth of us, and under circumstances in which he has a claim to such knowledge."[13]

---

[6]Blocher, "Biblical Concept," 52.
[7]Blocher, "Biblical Concept," 53.
[8]Blocher, "Biblical Concept," 53.
[9]Blocher, "Biblical Concept," 53.
[10]Blocher, "Biblical Concept," 53.
[11]Ezekiel Hopkins, "Exposition of the Ten Commandments," *The Whole Works of Ezekiel Hopkins* (1701; reprint, Edinburgh: A. & C. Black, 1841), 134.
[12]Hopkins, "Ten Commandments," 134.
[13]Asa Mahan, *Abstract of a Course of Lectures on Mental and Moral Philosophy*

Mahan commented on this definition in the following manner:

> The deception must be intentional, else guilt does not attach to the agent, or the crime falls under some other denomination than lying. The person or persons deceived, must have a claim to know the truth, if anything is communicated, else no obligations are violated in the act of deception. Lying, should be carefully distinguished from concealing. It is proper to conceal facts from individuals whom we have no right to deceive. Concealment is a sin when and only when, an obligation exists to reveal the fact which is concealed.[14]

Thus lying is more than "a breach of promise" (for lying is a moral evil in that it violates an obligation that comes from the relations of the parties involved and which binds them independently of all pledges) and it is more than "intentional deception" (which may be a moral evil, but I cannot tell if it is such until I can determine if all men in all circumstances have a claim on me to know the truth if they receive anything from me).

The importance of this definition can be seen in those instances where concealment was present without it being a moral evil. Thus Mahan teaches that concealment is proper, or even a duty, when it does not violate a moral obligation. Several instances will illustrate what types of situations these are.[15]

Prophecy, almost regularly, involves the withholding of part of the truth while part of the truth is communicated. All that fairness and benevolence demands, however, has been disclosed and that is all that we have a right to ask for.

Sometimes there is concealment when a certain type of language is used that could be interpreted to infer something more than what is said. For example, our Lord was not practicing dissimulation with the two disciples on the road to Emmaus when he asked, "What things?" (Luke 24:13–34). He meant only to draw them out, but on the issue of whether he knew or did not know what had happened that weekend in Jerusalem, nothing is affirmed or denied. Likewise, our Lord's discussion with the Syrophoenician woman, the Jews in the temple, and the woman taken in adultery all point in the same direction.

Concealment is also demanded when the person from whom the truth is withheld has forfeited his or her right or has no legitimate claim to that truth. That was Saul's position in 1 Samuel 16:1–3. Having been

---

(Oberlin: James Steel, 1840), 285 as pointed out to me by Rick Heyn, a student at lectures given at Belhaven College in 1979.

[14]Mahan, *Moral Philosophy*, 285.

[15]Many of these examples and the line of reasoning I owe to Mahan whom I happily discovered agreed with my own prior conclusions on all these same matters.

instructed by God to " 'Fill your horn with oil and go on your way; I am sending you to Jesse of Bethlehem. I have chosen one of his sons to be king' " (v. 1). "But Samuel said, 'How can I go? Saul will hear about it and kill me.' The LORD said, 'Take a heifer with you and say, "I have come to sacrifice to the LORD" ' " (v. 2).

"Without question," opined John Murray, "here is divine authorization for concealment by means of a statement other than that which would have disclosed the main purpose of Samuel's visit to Jesse."[16] But, it is just as important to note that Samuel had no special prerogative to speak a falsehood either. The only point that may legitimately be made is that concealment, in some situations, is not lying. Only what was true was presented to Saul. As for Samuel's ultimate intentions, nothing is affirmed or denied, and nothing incited Saul's mind to probe concerning what may have been Samuel's ultimate motives for coming to Bethlehem at this time. Had such questions been raised, an altogether different problem would have confronted Samuel and he would have to avoid either affirming or denying what those purposes were or face the wrath of Saul in his disclosure.

Mahan faced the question whether an intentional deception was ever allowable. His answer was ". . . if there is any being who has no claims upon us to receive from us the truth if he receives anything, to deceive such a being is no sin. If a man was pursued by a tiger or boa-constrictor, and he should escape from it by deceiving it, all would say that he had not sinned. . . . To deceive human beings in a similar relation for self-preservation, would not be sin."[17]

Even though Mahan would restrict these legitimate cases of deception to cases where the deception was only *temporary*, where it involved a *mortal enemy* (not enemies in our everyday lives), and where it *excluded* the use of *conventional signs*, as a decoy (such as flags of truce or signals of distress); it is not clearly established that some of these instances he cited are not those where the individual did have a claim to the knowledge requested.

What then constitutes a "claim to knowledge"? Would Saul have had a right to know, had he asked, what Samuel was doing in Bethlehem beside offering a sacrifice (off his scheduled circuit) to the Lord? We believe he would have—had he asked. He was the king! Did Pharaoh have a

---

[16]Murray, *Principles of Conduct*, 139. A somewhat similar case may be cited in Jer. 38:24–28. Jeremiah is instructed by King Zedediah not to reveal the full subject of their conversation when the princes would hear that he had met with Jeremiah and would want to know what they talked about. Instead, he was to tell them he had petitioned the king not to be sent back to Jonathan's house (Jer. 38:27) which was not a falsehood, for such a petition is certainly implied in vv. 15–16.

[17]Mahan, *Moral Philosophy*, 289.

right to know what the midwives were doing with regard to his edict even though they had rightfully refused to carry it out? We believe he did, in one way, have that claim even though the substance of that claim was wrong. These men were rightly opposed at the level of their error (e.g., the sanctity of life for the midwives) rather than at the level of their right to pose such questions. No one has a right to lie; but then, neither does everyone have the right to know all the facts in a case when their evil actions have forfeited that right. So we make a distinction between the right of the king, for example, to ask the question and the right to receive all the information he might hope to get.

There are situations where one knows that the rules have been altered, by conventions peculiar to those unusual circumstances. But even in instances such as warfare or team sports, it does not mean that all bars are removed. Massive brutality, deliberate involvement of nonmilitary targets, and using as decoys the banner of the Red Cross or flags of truce and distress are reprehensible and usually demand punishment after the conflict has been settled. Just as surely, no ethical Christian has ever protested in a football huddle in this manner: "I'm sorry gentlemen; either I carry the ball or else: I refuse to deceive the opposition with a fake around the right end: that is unethical and an outright lie!" The very nature of warfare and team sports makes us alert to the fact that a type of deception will be naturally used to throw us off balance. We must learn to quickly recognize it for what it is and to concentrate on the authentic movement. But all of this is a separate issue from the intentional deception we are discussing under the definition of lying.

Perjury

Just as serious a matter is that of giving false testimony in a court of law. Honest testimony is at the heart of the judicial system and any deviation from this standard is an attack on the whole legal process.

The warning against false witnesses appears frequently. The fullest teaching passage is Deuteronomy 19:16–21. But there also are references to this same matter in Proverbs. In Proverbs 19:5 the false witness is promised punishment; "a false witness will not go unpunished"; indeed, he "will perish" (Prov. 19:9). A person, who would do so evil a deed against a neighbor, is like "a club or a sword or a sharp arrow" (Prov. 25:18).

Perjury is equated with blasphemy in Leviticus 19:12 because ultimately it is God's justice that is being offended and the witness's testimony is made before the Lord, his priests, and his judges (Deut. 19:17). Anyone who perjures himself is not to be pitied (Deut. 19:21). He or she is to receive the penalty tit for tat, in other words, according to the *lex talionis* (Deut. 19:19, "Then do to him as he intended to do to his brother. You must purge the evil from among you."

G. Ernest Wright comments on this principle as follows:

> The principle of an eye for an eye (vs. 21) is that on which Israelite law is based. It is one of the most misunderstood and misinterpreted principles in the O.T., owing to the fact that it is popularly thought to be a general command to take vengeance. Such an understanding is completely wrong. In neither the O.T. nor the N.T. is a man entitled to take vengeance. That is a matter which must be left to God. The principle of an eye for an eye is a legal one which limits vengeance. It is for the guidance of the judge in fixing a penalty which shall befit the crime committed. Hence it is the basic principle of all justice which is legally administered.[18]

If truth telling was valued so highly in the courts that the perjurer was to be punished without pity, could it be esteemed any less in situations outside of the courtroom? Since truth ultimately was grounded in no one less than the God who was truth, all interpretations that would raise caveats and equivocations of one sort or another, outside a proper definition for truth or lying, must come to terms not with a system of God, but with a personal accounting to the true and living Lord.

THE ISSUE OF SLANDER

Six times the Old Testament uses the rather obscure masculine noun, רָכִיל, to denote a "slanderer." Such a person traffics in ruining the character and lives of innocent people by failing to tell the truth about these persons.

The initial occurrence of these six instances is in Leviticus 19:16, "Do not go about spreading slander among your people." The translation "talebearer" or "gossip" is not strong enough to fit most of the six contexts, for the second half of this verse goes on to say, "Do not do anything that endangers your neighbor's life. I am the LORD." It is clear, therefore, that the conduct of the first part of Leviticus 19:16 could endanger a neighbor's life. The meaning, then, of the second half is not to encourage men to come forward to rescue someone whose life is in danger from robbers, drowning, or the like; it is, like Exodus 23:1, 7, emphasizing the devastation of slander.

The indictment God made of Judah to Jeremiah was that they were "going about to slander" (Jer. 6:28; 9:4[3]). The fact that slander did actually lead to bloodshed is witnessed by Ezekiel 22:9.

Slanderers are the opposite of being trustworthy. They divulge secrets and speak foolishly (Prov. 11:13; 20:19). Thus words are more than

---

[18]G. Ernest Wright, "Deuteronomy," *Interpreter's Bible*, ed. George A. Buttrick (Nashville: Abingdon), 2:454–55.

sticks and stones; they can and do hurt people. Our contemporary proverb, to the contrary, is (as Rushdoony observes) bravado. To put the matter as bluntly as the text does, "slander is a form of murder."[19]

Slander of a Marriage Partner

Deuteronomy 22:13–21 is a most unusual case law. It revolved around the fact that a "bad name" had been given to an "Israelite virgin." In this case, a married man suddenly decided he "disliked" his bride and so he began to talk about her in a slanderous way by alleging that she was not a virgin when he married her.

Such a charge is taken with utmost degree of seriousness in Israel. In this one case, the woman is presumed guilty until she proves her innocence.[20] But the husband also must prove evidence for his claim that unchastity was involved. The seriousness of these proceedings is underscored by the fact that slander was treated as a criminal, not a private offense. It carried with it a fine twice as heavy as that for rape or seduction (Deut. 22:29)—"fifty shekels of silver." This was a princely sum of money when one remembers that the annual poll tax was only a half shekel (Exod. 30:15) in Moses' day and one-third of a shekel in Nehemiah's day (Neh. 10:32).

> . . . Biblical law requires a high degree of care and thoughtfulness of speech between husband and wife. . . . A husband can defame his wife not only by speech but by distrust. If he refuses to allow her those duties and privileges which she is competent to administer, he has defamed her.[21]

When the husband, instead of loving and protecting his wife, proceeds to defame her, he introduces instability not only into his own domestic life, but also into the whole nation. The evil name is on a virgin of *Israel*. Such an attack on the family is ultimately an attack on the very fiber of the nation.

Thus the commandment that demands that we not bear a false

---

[19]R. J. Rushdoony, *The Institutes of Biblical Law* (Nutley, N.J.: Craig, 1973), 596.

[20]Some regard this demand cruel in those cases where the hymen has already been broken prior to marriage through causes unrelated to intimate relations with a man. Josephus has a curious, but probably unhelpful, attempt to relieve this enigma. He commented in part: "These tokens . . . seem to be very different from what our later interpreters suppose. They appear to have been such close linen garments as were never put off virgins, after a certain age, till they were married, but before witnesses . . . 2 Sam. 13:18." *Antiquities* IV, viii, as quoted by Katherine Bushnell, *God's Word to Women*, (1923; reprint, Ray B. Munson, Jacksonville, Fla., n.d.), paragraph 585. His reference to 2 Sam. 13:18 is hardly convincing. The rest of the case is speculative, it would appear and does not seem to resolve the problem of how such garments could serve as proof.

[21]Rushdoony, *Biblical Law*, 592–93.

witness against our "neighbor" is illustrated by this case law that makes it clear that my closest "neighbor" may be my wife (or husband). The severity of the fine for a breach of domestic peace by slander indicates the importance that biblical law places on truth telling in all of society, but especially within marriage.

An even more curious case is the only instance of trial by "ordeal"[22] in the Old Testament, Numbers 5:11–31. In this case, either the wife had been unfaithful and there are no witnesses, leaving her husband indignantly jealous (Num. 5:12–14, 27, 29), or the woman is innocent and her husband is riled up for no good reason at all (vv. 14, 28, 30). What are they both to do in the absence of hard evidence? The jealousy itself, regardless of whether the woman is innocent or not, has brought harm into Israel.

This suspicion with its charge and counter charge is dealt with by first giving an offering to God. The sin is once again not just between the two parties involved, but against God (v. 15). Unlike the cereal offering in Leviticus 2, this one forbids oil and frankincense (usually symbols of the joy and Spirit of God, Ps. 45:7; 1 Sam. 10:1) and even substitutes relatively inexpensive barley meal for fine (wheat?) flour. Here then, is the lowliest of sacrifices being offered in a domestic situation where joy and the Spirit of God have been absent.

The test for guilt may now proceed (vv. 16–31). The unlikely ingredients of the potion that the woman must drink after she has: (1) appeared "before the LORD" (v. 16) in the court of the tabernacle; (2) unbound her hair (18); and (3) held the bitter water in her hand and said, "Amen, Amen" to the curses recited by the priest; are dust from the tabernacle floor and holy water. This episode may well repeat the drink made with the ashes of the golden calf (Exod. 32:20) and be behind the prophetic references, as Gordon Wenham points out,[23] to the "cup" of judgment which the Lord will make unfaithful Israel drink (Isa. 51:17, 22; Ezek. 23:30–34).

The penalty that would result from the woman's guilt (if she were found to be such) was serious ailments to her reproductive organs; but if she were innocent, then she would be favored with fertility (v. 28). The ingredients were innocuous enough and fairly harmless, but the test must have hung on two facts: (1) God's providential and miraculous interven-

---

[22]See T. S. Trymer, "Ordeal, Judicial," *Interpreter's Dictionary of the Bible*, Supplementary volume (Nashville: Abingdon, 1976), 638–40. Also see, J. Morgenstern, "Trial by Ordeal Among the Semites and in Ancient Israel," *Hebrew Union College Annual* (1925): 113–43; Moshe Weinfeld, "Ordeal of Jealousy," *Encyclopedia Judaica* 12:1449–50; M. Fishbane, "Accusations of Adultery: A Study of Law and Scribal Practice in Numbers 5:11–31," *Hebrew Union College Annual* 45 (1974): 25–45. One of the books of the Talmud, *Sotah* deals extensively with this trial for jealousy.

[23]Gordon Wenham, *Numbers* (Downers Grove, Ill.: InterVarsity, 1981), 80.

tion, and (2) the physical effects left by a damaged guilt-ridden psyche.[24] Thus, this was not an "ordeal" in the normal sense, for behind the ordeal lay the concept that nature, rather than God directly, was the source of law.[25]

Impugning a wife's sexual morality was not a matter to be treated lightly. Once again slander became the occasion for involvement of others outside the parties involved. It called for involvement of God himself and his ministers.

Slander and Stealing

Lying to one another is linked in Leviticus 19:11 with stealing and cheating. The three sins are made kindred sins. Colossians 3:9 will likewise affirm: "Do not lie to each other, since you have taken off your old self with its practices." In a similar vein, Ephesians 4:25 orders, "Therefore each of you must put off falsehood and speak truthfully to his neighbor, for we are all members of one body."

Slander is a type of verbal fraud. It robs reputations, honor, status, standing in the eyes of others, and peace of mind.

Speak evil of no man warns Proverbs 11:9, for he who indulges in slander "is a fool" (Prov. 10:18). To privately slander one's neighbor is to receive this divine judgment: "him will I put to silence" (Ps. 101:5). But slander goes beyond theft; it is also a form of character assassination and hence is murder (Prov. 11:9). Only the "wicked" truly love to destroy others with their slander (Ps. 52:4). Such deceit and slander can only spring from "hate" (Ps. 109:2–3) and the wicked are so brutal and unconscionable about it that they will even slander their own family (Ps. 50:19–20).

THE VERIFICATION OF TRUTH

The problem of testing what was true and what was false was nowhere more acute than with the writing prophets. The God who cannot lie (Num. 23:19; I Sam. 15:29) could not tolerate witnesses who spoke "falsehood" (שֶׁקֶר).

Evidences of Falsehood

Jeremiah uses the term שֶׁקֶר more frequently than any other prophet or Old Testament writer. Out of some 114 instances of this noun, Jeremiah

---

[24]See Alan MacRae, "Numbers" in *The New Bible Commentary*, 2d ed., ed. F. Davidson (Grand Rapids: Eerdmans, 1954), 169.

[25]Rushdoony, *Biblical Law*, 608.

has 36 references to it. This suggests that the concept of falsehood constituted a special area of concern for him.

T. W. Overholt[26] organized Jeremiah's concern over the wrong of falsehood in three key objectives in his preaching. They were guilty of:

(1) A *false* sense of security that obstructed the people from responding to Yahweh's call for repentance (Jer. 7:1–8),

(2) The *false* proclamation which opposed Jeremiah (Jer. 23:27–29), and

(3) The *falsehood* of idolatry.

It was sheer bravado to repeat, as if it were a talisman or rabbit's foot of good luck, "The temple of the LORD, the temple of the LORD" (Jer. 7:4). Such words were "deceptive" or "false" words (דִּבְרֵי הַשֶּׁקֶר). Why, Jeremiah reasoned, would it seem so unlikely a feat for God to bring destruction to the very city where his temple dwells? To hide behind the temple was to introduce "falsehood." Such a slogan was a hollow, empty lie (cf. another Hebrew word for falsehood כָּזָב) or sheer "vanity" and "nothingness" (שָׁוְא). The plain fact was that there was nothing in these words that could serve as a real basis for hope. It was all so utterly pointless and hopeless. In fact, those were the two most constant results of falsehood: pointlessness and hopelessness (cf. Ps. 27:12; Prov. 12:17; 17:14; 25:18; Isa. 32:7).

But the test for the veracity of one's claim, especially when pretending to be representing God, was most critical in Jeremiah's contest with the false prophets of his day. He condemned the prophets of his day on four grounds:[27]

(1) They were men of immoral character and lives (Jer. 23:14),

(2) They were popularity seekers (Jer. 23:17),

(3) They did not distinguish their own dreams from a true word from God (Jer. 23:28), and

(4) They were plagiarists (Jer. 23:30, 36).

John Skinner[28] reduced Jeremiah's declamations to three:

(1) The character of the prophets,

(2) The substance of their message, and

(3) The form in which they gave it out as the Word of Yahweh.

Underlying all was the fact that they were either deluded or dishonest. "They are prophesying to you false visions, divinations, idolatries and the

---

[26]Thomas W. Overholt, *The Threat of Falsehood* (London: SCM 1970), 1. Cf. also Andrew, "Falsehood and Truth," 429–33.

[27]This list was first pointed out to me by H. Wheeler Robinson, *Inspiration and Revelation in the Old Testament* (Oxford: Oxford University Press, 1946), 187.

[28]John Skinner, *Prophecy and Religion: Studies in the Life of Jeremiah* (Cambridge: Cambridge University Press, 1926), 120–200.

delusions of their own minds," moaned Jeremiah (14:14). They led people astray by their "reckless lies" (Jer. 23:32).[29] Jeremiah's denunciation of these false prophets was not alone; he had been anticipated by Isaiah (28:7–13) and Micah (3:5–12) and he would be followed by Ezekiel (13:1–16).

The use of the term שֶׁקֶר in these situations points up the fact that falsehood was first of all a legal matter. Anyone who gave a false witness received the same punishment as it would have brought on the person he witnessed against (Deut. 19:19, 21). More importantly, at the heart of falsehood lay a contradiction against the very nature of God who is truth.

Vindication of Truth

The contest between Jeremiah and Hananiah in Jeremiah 27–28 serves as the classic means of distinguishing between a true and false prophet. Hananiah's message (Jer. 28:2–4) was in direct contradiction with what Yahweh had said. But that set up one way to determine a true prophet (cf. Deut. 18:21–22), namely, if the predicted words were fulfilled.

When Hananiah precipitously broke the divinely ordered yoke that Jeremiah was symbolically wearing about his neck, it turned out to be his own undoing. Jeremiah was vindicated as the true prophet of God (Jer. 28:12–14) while Hananiah was condemned as a false prophet whom Yahweh had not sent and who had caused the people to trust in a "falsehood" (שֶׁקֶר; Jer. 28:15–17). He had, in fact, uttered "rebellion" (סָרָה). That same term, סָרָה, was the one that had been used in Deuteronomy 13:5[6] for the dreamer (false prophet) who had taught "rebellion" to Israel.[30]

According to Deuteronomy 18:20, to prophesy falsely in Yahweh's name was to commit a capital offense. Hananiah died two months later (Jer. 28:17) in fulfillment of the curse with which Jeremiah had threatened him.

The truth, then, was not to be treated in an offhand, haphazard manner. Investigations were to be made to verify the truthfulness of a word or deed (Deut. 13:14; 17:4). Material evidence was to be gathered

---

[29]John Bright, *Jeremiah*, vol. 21 of *The Anchor Bible Commentary* (Garden City, N.Y.: Doubleday, 1965), 153. "Their lies and their *paḥᵃzut*—which has the force of 'loose talk,' 'exaggerated, boastful tales,' or the like." Andrew, "Falsehood and Truth," 431, defines falsehood as having three meanings wrapped up in one concept: "that which is not true" as Jer. 23:32 exhibits: "Behold, I am against those who prophesy *lying dreams,* says the LORD, and who tell them and *lead my people astray* by their lies and their mendacious claptrap, when I did not send them or charge them; so they *do not profit* this people at all, says the LORD" (italics added to show the three parts to falsehood).

[30]I owe this observation to J. A. Thompson, *The Book of Jeremiah* (Grand Rapids: Eerdmans, 1980), 541.

(Deut. 22:14–17; Exod. 22:13) as well as the reliability of the verbal promises of people (cf. Joseph's testing of his brothers for the benefit of Pharaoh's court, Gen. 42:16).

Truth, according to Henri Blocher has four basic characteristics in the Old Testament: (1) it is personal, (2) it is objective, (3) it is exclusively divine in its origins, and (4) it has a historical fullness. Harvesting all these points, Blocher concludes that:

> *Truth is the Word of God* inasmuch as it is his word. It gives us his Name and the knowledge of him; it is the foundation of our life and of our assurance; finally it requires our obedience. As far as our words are concerned, their truth is their *conformity* to the Word of God. . . .[31]

---

[31]Blocher, "Biblical Concept," 60–61.

Chapter 15

Holiness in Motive and Heart

It is still the prevailing opinion that the tenth commandment deals with a covetous will and takes the whole matter of holiness of life explicitly into the offence that begins with a person's heart and mind. This understanding finds support in the Septuagint translation of both Exodus 20:17 and Deuteronomy 5:21, οὐκ ἐπιθυμήσεις (twice in Exodus and once in Deuteronomy). Luther also put his authority behind this interpretation in his Longer Catechism noting that this commandment was "directed particularly against envy and loathsome avarice."[1]

THE CASE FOR INCLUDING INTENTIONS

In spite of the fact that most interpreters find in this tenth commandment a reference to an offense of the mind and impulses of the heart, a significant number of scholars have recently challenged that conclusion since all the other commandments referred to actions and not to motives or interior promptings to those actions.

In chapter 1 I advocated, against B. D. Eerdmans's thesis of 1903 that Old Testament ethics did, as a matter of fact, "meddle with the inner

---

[1]As cited in Johann Jakob Stamm, *The Ten Commandments in Recent Research* (Naperville: Allenson, 1967), 101, n. 77.

thoughts of men."[2] There, following B. Gemser, I listed ten of his thirty-six texts in which the Old Testament clearly explored the inner thoughts, plans, intentions, and ruminations of a person's heart. It remains for us now to pick-up the discussion on the verb חָמַד.

Liability for Acts Expressing Intentions

The most significant writer after B. D. Eerdmans was Johannes Herrmann's 1927 article on the tenth commandment.[3] Herrmann's contribution was to show that the verb חָמַד is often followed in the Old Testament by verbs that mean "to take away" or "to rob" as in Deuteronomy 7:25 and Joshua 7:21. For example, Micah 2:2 joins the two verbs this way:

> "They covet (חָמְדוּ) fields and seize them, and houses, and take them."

חָמַד, then for Herrmann, meant "an emotion which, with a certain necessity, leads to corresponding actions."[4] Two additional passages are cited by Stamm and Andrew that do not have the supplementing verbs following the word for "desire," but nevertheless show that it was the *attainment* as much as the desiring that was involved in the idea of חָמַד. The first reads:

> "Why gaze in with envy, O rugged mountains, at the mountain where God chooses (חָמַד) to reign, where the LORD himself will dwell forever?" (Ps. 68:16 [17]).

To desire here, claim the scholars, already assumes that he has taken possession and so a second verb is unnecessary. Likewise, a second text says:

> For I will drive out nations before you and enlarge your territory, and no one will covet (יַחְמֹד) your land when you go up three times each year to appear before the LORD your God. (Exod. 34:24)

Presumably *included* in "desire" in this text was also the invasion of the nations that followed their coveting. Thus, all these passages demonstrate, "that *hāmad* does not only mean 'covet' as an impulse of the will, but that it also includes the intrigues which lead to the taking possession of that which was coveted."[5] Thus, חָמַד aims not only at the will, but also at all

---

[2]See n. 16. in chapter 1. Note some of the articles on this commandment: J. R. Coates, "Thou shalt not Covet," *Zeitschrift für die alttestamentliche Wissenschaft* 52 (1934): 238–39; Cyrus H. Gordon, "A Note on the Tenth Commandment," *Journal of Bible and Religion*, 31 (1963): 208–9; B. Jacob, "The Decalogue," *Jewish Quarterly Review* n.s. 14 (1923/24); 141–87.

[3]Johannes Herrmann, "Das zehnte Gebot," in *Festschrift für Sellin* (Leipzig, 1927), 69–82.

[4]J. Herrmann, p. 72, as cited by Johann J. Stamm and Maurice E. Andrew, *The Ten Commandments in Recent Research* (Naperville: Allenson, 1962), 102.

[5]Stamm and Andrew, *Ten Commandments*, 103.

those "violent intrigues which a person uses in order to attain to the property of his neighbor."[6]

It is also now fashionable to cite a Phoenician inscription from Karatepe where the same verb is used in Phoenician of a foreign ruler, Azitawadda, taking possession of a city: "Or if he [i.e., Azitawadda] covets this city and tears down this door."[7]

But can this new extension of the definition of חָמַד stand? How can the tenth commandment be distinguished from the eighth which also deals with theft? This problem alone has caused some to reject Herrmann's view.[8] Albrecht Alt tried to rescue the situation by showing that the eighth had in mind not stealing in general, but the kidnapping of free Israelite men only, while the tenth dealt with taking dependent people who were not free—women, children, and slaves.[9] This construction, however, is a tautology and artificial and conjectural at too many points. Bernard Jackson's assessment is to be preferred. He opined:

> The best that can be said of the interpretation of *ḥamad* as "to take" is that there is the possibility that the word can bear that meaning in some contexts. That this is the regular meaning of the verb completely fails of proof. Indeed, Nielsen *The Ten Commandments in New Perspective*, pp. 43, 105, 110, one of the latest supporters of the Hermann [sic] theory, concedes that the Deuteronomic version of the Decalogue *ḥamad* is given a psychologized interpretation, as is shown by the association with *tit'awweh*, "desire."[10]

Jackson discounts the parallelism between חָמַד "to covet" and לָקַח "to take" or "seize" in Deuteronomy 7:25 and Joshua 7:21 because parallel pairs of

---

[6]Stamm and Andrew, *Ten Commandments*, 103.

[7]Stamm and Andrews, *Ten Commandments*, 103, citing A. Alt, "Die phönikischen Inschriften von Karatepe," *Die Welt des Orients* 1, 1947–52, 274–75, 278–89. Also see *Ancient Near Eastern Texts* (2d ed.), p. 500 for a different translation—Note Gunther Wittenburg, "The Tenth Commandment," *Journal of Theology for Southern Africa*, 22 (1978): 3–17; and C. H. Gordon, "Phoenician Inscriptions from Karatepe," *Jewish Quarterly Review* n.s. 39 (1948): 48; *idem*, "Azitawadd's Phoenician Inscription," *Journal of Near Eastern Studies* 8 (1949): 111.

[8]Stamm and Andrew, *Ten Commandments*, 103–4. He cites Paul Volz and Georg Beer as examples.

[9]As cited by Stamm and Andrew, *Ten Commandments*, 104; Albrecht Alt, "Das Verbot des Diebstahls im Dekalog," *Kleine Schrift zur Geschichte des Volkes Israel* (Munich, 1953), 1:333–40.

[10]Bernard S. Jackson, "Liability For Mere Intention in Early Jewish Law," *Hebrew Union College Annual* 42 (1971): 201. Cf. however, Th. C. Vriezen, *An Outline of Old Testament Theology*, 2d ed. (Newton, Mass.: Branford, 1970), 392–93, who agrees in part with Herrmann: חָמַד means "to covet" and "to try to obtain," i.e. "to cast a look at something and attempt to obtain it."

words and Hebrew parallelism is more routinely found in prophetic writings and the poetry of Psalms and wisdom literature. There is no "certain necessity" that "desire" should culminate in action in contexts like Proverbs 1:22; Isaiah 53:2; and also in the derived noun and adjective usages in Genesis 2:9; Psalm 19:11; and Isaiah 44:9.[11] חָמַד often refers to a step prior to the action listed in the next verb associated with it.

G. Wallis also concurs in this decision:

> Whether or not Alt is right that the prohibition refers exclusively to the theft of persons, it is probably impossible to interpret "desire" in the tenth commandment as meaning the wish to steal. The only remaining possibility, then, is to interpret חָמַד within the framework of an ethics of pure intention. This is how Jesus interprets the commandment in Matt. 5:28.[12]

Liability for Mere Intention

Desire, then in and of itself, can be sinful for it makes us liable to move from a first step involving actions of the heart to those acts prohibited in the sixth, seventh, and eighth commandments. The list of things that are not to be coveted includes:

(1) a neighbor's wife,

(2) his male slave,

(3) his female slave,

(4) his ox,

(5) his ass, and

(6) anything that belongs to your neighbor.

While it was usually true that there was no liability for intention until it actually expressed itself in some concrete way (for example, the falsely accused Joseph of attempted rape of Potiphar's wife in Gen. 39:13, 15, 18; or the "strong cravings" of the "rabble" in Num. 11:4 for meat), there are other passages in the Old Testament that demonstrate that even the intention itself is culpable. Genesis 6:5 faults the people on the thoughts and evil imaginations of their hearts while the very intention of David to build a temple is worthy of a blessing in 1 Kings 8:18.[13] But it is most important to note that this standard is applied *by God* and not by man. He, it is, who knows the thoughts and desires of our heart. Herrmann and his followers wish to deny that this commandment refers to coveting and applies rather to actual misappropriation, but that was the very problem Jesus was attacking in the Sermon on the Mount in Matthew

---

[11]Jacob, "The Decalogue," 168–69.

[12]G. Wallis, "חָמַד," *Theological Dictionary of the Old Testament*, 4:457. One who does not follow Herrmann is Umberto Cassuto, *A Commentary on the Book of Exodus*, trans. Israel Abrahams (Jerusalem: Magnes Press, 1967), 248–49.

[13]These passages were pointed out to me by Jackson, "Liability," 205–7.

5:27–28, ". . . anyone who looks at a woman lustfully has already committed adultery with her in his heart." In so saying, Jesus was not adding to the written law of the Old Testament, but rather countering the narrower oral interpretation that had grown up around that written word. Surely Job understood this concept when he asserted:

> I made a covenant with my eyes
> not to look lustfully at a girl. . . .
> If my heart has been enticed by a woman,
> or if I have lurked at my neighbor's door,
> then may my wife grind another man's grain,
> and may other men sleep with her.
>
> (Job 31:1, 9–10)

Coveting pointed to the internal nature of all God's law. The movement of the heart, mind, and will did count with God. Evil desires that aroused greed, deceit, desire to own or control what never was, or ever could be, ours were clearly condemned. Both the desire itself *and* all conversions of that desire into forbidden acts were culpable and denounced in Old Testament ethics. It is no small wonder, then, that so much weight was attached to the meaning of the verbs in this tenth commandment.

THE CASE FOR INCLUDING MOTIVES

The first scholar who directed the biblical word of scholarship to the issue of motives was Berend Gemser.[14] He defined motive clauses as "grammatically subordinate sentences in which the motivation for the commandment is given. The German designation would be '*Begründungssätze*' or '*Bergründungsklauseln*.' They are by no means scarce in the Old Testament laws, although their frequency differs in the separate collections."[15] More recently Rifat Sonsino refined that definition to be "a dependent clause or phrase which expresses the motive behind the legal prescription or an incentive for obeying it."[16] R. W. Uitti[17] complained about Gemser's definition, but he did not chose to propose his own general definition and opted instead for spelling out formal characteristics of motive clauses. Henry John Postel did accept the challenge and proposed this

---

[14]Berend Gemser, "The Importance of the Motive Clause in Old Testament Law," *Vetus Testamentum*, Supplementary vol. 1 (1953): 50–66. Reprinted in *Adhuc Loquitur: Collected Essays by B. Gemser*, ed. A. van Selms and A. S. van der Woude: Pretoria Oriental Series, 7 (Leiden: Brill, 1968), 96–115.

[15]B. Gemser, *Adhuc loquitur*, 96.

[16]Rifat Sonsino, *Motive Clauses in Hebrew Law: Biblical Forms and Near Eastern Parallels* (Chico, Calif.: Scholar's Press, 1980), 65.

[17]R. W. Uitti, "The Motive Clause in Old Testament Law," (diss., Chicago Lutheran School of Theology, 1973), 6–8.

definition: "A motive clause is a grammatically subordinate clause, ordinarily located in a secondary position, the purpose of which is to offer motivation (promissory or dissuasive) for heeding the advice given. Such clauses frequently commence with a deictic word (e.g., *ki, pen,* etc.) but may also be asyndetic."[18]

The Contents of Motive Clauses

Gemser arranged the contents of these clauses thematically around four categories of motivation:

(1) Explanatory—appeals to common sense of the hearer.
"If anyone curses his father or his mother, he must be put to death. *He has cursed his father or his mother, and his blood will be put on his own head*" (Lev. 20:9; italics indicate motive clauses, cf. Deut. 20:19; 20:5–8).

(2) Ethical—appeals directly to ethical sentiments or to the conscience.
"When you build a new house, make a parapet around your roof so *that you may not bring the guilt of bloodshed on your house if someone falls from the roof*" (Deut. 22:8; cf. Lev. 23:22; Deut. 5:14–15).

(3) Religious and Theological—grounded in the nature and will of God.
"The priests must not desecrate the sacred offering the Israelites present to the LORD *by allowing them to eat the sacred offerings and so bring upon them guilt requiring payment. I am the LORD, who makes them holy*" (Lev. 22:15–16; cf. Deut. 18:9–12).

(4) Historico-religious—appeal is to Yahweh's acts in history.
"When you harvest the grapes in your vineyard, do not go over the vines again. Leave what remains for the alien, the fatherless and the widow. *Remember that you were slaves in Egypt. That is why I command you to do this*" (Deut. 24:21–22).

On formal grounds, the most frequent "motivating or causal conjunction is כִּי (e.g., Exod. 20:7; Deut. 24:6)." But there are many other words or phrases that also introduce motive clauses. They include: "*bᵉ* (Exod. 21:8), *taḥat ᵃšer* (Deut. 21:14), *ᶜal dᵉbar ᵃšer* (Deut. 22:24), *wᵉ* (Exod. 23:9), *ᶜal ken* (Exod. 20:11), *ᵃšer* (Deut. 16:22), *pen* (Deut. 19:6), and *lᵉmaᶜan* (Deut. 5:16)."[19] Sometimes the motive clauses are asyndetic,

---

[18]Henry John Postel, "The Form and Function of the Motive Clause in Proverbs 10–29," (dissertation, University of Iowa, 1976), 22.

[19]Postel, "Motive Clause," 17. See also Sonsino, *Motive Clauses,* 70–76, 118–19.

having no introductory particle or phrase (Lev. 18:6–8). In a few cases there may be a double motive clause (e.g., Exod. 22:25–27).

Basically there are two ways in which a motive clause is attached especially to Old Testament laws: (1) by repeating a key word or element in the law (e.g., the death penalty is imposed in Lev. 20:9 for *insulting* one's parents with the motive clause explaining he has *insulted* his father and his mother), and (2) by giving the law a new clause or phrase that spells out the reason or purpose for this legal proscription. The first method does not add anything new to the law. It is the second way, described here, that enlarges our understanding and provides new information beyond what the law expresses.

The Area to Which Motive Clauses Appeal

Gemser's fourfold classification of motive clauses has two basic problems.[20] His first category is hardly a distinct type since in a way all motive clauses are basically explanatory. Then his third and fourth categories are so similar (religious-theological and historico-religious) as to be confusing.

Uitti found it more convenient to distinguish between "the kind of motivation" and "the area appealed to" for a given motivation. For "the kind of motivation," he meant to differentiate those motive clauses that had as their major thrust the desire: (1) to warn, (2) to incite/encourage, or (3) to explain.[21] The areas appealed to, Uitti found, were: (1) the evidence of logic, reason, common sense; (2) the instinct or desire for blessing, well-being, self-preservation; (3) the dictates of conscience or concern for ethics and humanitarian or ecological causes. These were all used in a person's confrontation with the human world and its environment. But when the commandments led a person to deal with the world of Yahweh, then other areas came into play, according to Uitti, such as: (1) Yahweh's person, nature and will; (2) Yahweh's election and redemption.[22]

Sonsino reorganizes the various patterns and settles on a new arrangement of four different categories of motive clauses according to their general orientation. These are clauses which: (1) express God's authority, (2) allude to historical experiences of the people, (3) instill a fear of punishment, and (4) promise well-being. Each carries a measure of interest for our concern in Old Testament ethics.[23]

The first is concentrated in the Holiness Law where more than twenty times the appeal is simply "(for) I the LORD your God" or "I am the

---

[20]These criticisms were made by Sonsino, *Motive Clauses*, 105.
[21]Uitti, "Motive Clause," 92.
[22]Uitti, "Motive Clause," 92.
[23]Sonsino, *Motive Clauses*, 109–13.

LORD." The appeal here is indeed to authority, but that authority must be first recognized by an awakened heart and conscience. Only those who have Yahweh as their own God will be moved at all by this motivational postscript, "I am the LORD your God." Other forms of this type express the profanation of the name or person of God when those who claim a relationship with him run directly counter to that claim in their lifestyles (e.g., swearing falsely in his name, Lev. 19:12; offering children to Molech, Lev. 18:21; and the frequent formulas of abomination in Lev. 18:22 or 20:13).

The motivations based on historical experiences are related basically to attitudes of gratitude and faithfulness, and so are not directly related to promptings of human conscience, will, or desires. Nevertheless, the theology of "remembrance" (Deut. 15:15) and the experience not only of external deliverance, but also of interior holistic salvation is relevant to our topic.

The third area, fear of punishment, has both an external as well as internal motivating force. The graphic reality of being "cut-off" from one's people provided high motivation for those who otherwise did not possess the requisite internal disposition of reverential awe and respectful fear of offending a holy God. "Learn to revere the LORD your God" (Deut. 14:23; 17:19) is one of the key forms of this type of motive clause.

The clauses are found in other areas beside law, for example, in Proverbs.[24] But the bottom line in all these clauses, which are usually attached to some type of imperative, is to respond to this question: "Why should I heed the instruction or command given here?" They wish to set forth the reasonableness of this admonition, the consequences that will follow if it is not followed, and the emotions from or signals to the will that will aid the listener in responding to this commandment, precept, or proverb.

All of this tends to reinforce the argument that for Old Testament ethics obedience starts in the heart of one who hears a commandment. Rote performance without the attached affections of the will and the desires of the heart is hardly the standard by which Old Testament ethics wished men and women to be measured.

The Place of the "Heart" in Ethics

Study of motives and laws brings us full circle to face the question once again: what is morally judged in the Old Testament, the single act or the disposition and the act of the person? Gemser's list of thirty-six texts

---

[24]See Postel, "Motive Clause."

linking the Hebrew words for thought, plan, counsel, intent, and heart with ethical judgments is appropriate in this context.[25] Was not "the clear conscience" of Abimelech's heart relevant in the matter of the ethics of human sexuality? (Gen. 20:6). Why is it a matter of special note that "the LORD looks at the heart" (1 Sam. 16:7)? Surely, God's estimate of a person's character and deeds penetrates more deeply than the skin or the mere act itself in the Old Testament. In the postexilic periods, the chronicler reiterated the same theme: "Serve him [God] with wholehearted devotion and with a willing mind, for the LORD searches every heart and understands every motive behind the thoughts" (1 Chron. 28:9).

Proverbs is no stranger to this emphasis either. The problem with the sacrifice of some men is that they "bring it with evil" intent (בְּזִמָּה; Prov. 21:27). It is the "thoughts" (מַחְשְׁבוֹת) of the wicked that are an abomination to the Lord (Prov. 15:26; cf. Ps. 94:11; Isa. 59:7; Jer. 4:14; Ezek. 38:10).

The connection between the "heart" and the self in Proverbs is strong.[26] "Who can say, 'I have made my heart pure; I am clean and without sin'?" asks Proverbs 20:9. Thus the heart and the person are identified. But as Bouffier notes, the two are not the same for Proverbs 14:13 says, "even in laughter the heart may ache." We are taught to differentiate the external appearances from the internal state of the heart.

The heart is the deepest self, the very core of a person as difficult for others to comprehend as the abyss or nether world (see Prov. 15:11, "Death and Destruction lie open before the LORD—how much more the hearts of men"). So "the LORD tests the heart" (Prov. 17:3) for the "purposes of a man's heart" are stored there and known only to God and the individual.

The heart is the seat of wisdom, understanding, and the will (1 Kings 3:12; Prov. 16:23; also 2 Chron. 9:23; 12:14; Prov. 11:12). Moral rectitude begins when "you devote your heart to him [God]" (Job 11:13), for that is where sheer moral evil makes its first foothold (Jer. 17:9).

SUMMARY

Holiness in the ethical realm, then, begins with the "fear of the Lord" (יִרְאַת יְהוָה; Prov. 1:7; 9:10; 15:33). With the recognition of evil, the writer(s) of the Proverbs urged us to avoid evil.

---

[25]See chapter 1, n. 16.

[26]Robert J. Bouffier, "The 'Heart' in the Proverbs of Solomon," *The Bible Today* (1971): 249–51. Also Friedrich Baumgärtel, "לֵב, לֵבָב in the OT," *Theological Dictionary of the New Testament* 3:606–7; Andrew Bowling, "לֵב, לֵבָב," *Theological Wordbook of the Old Testament*, 1:466–67.

The frequent connecting motivational clauses with the admonitions in Proverbs have recently been studied by Philip Nel.[27] He concluded that:

> The very nature of the motivation embraces an effective appeal to reason and observation because the cosmic order and ethical order are not a contradiction to one's thought. The understanding of the cosmic order and ethical order is the imperative of wise thought within the frame of the *yir'at Jahweh*—the theological "setting in life" of the wisdom: the order of creation is comprehensible. Knowledge of this order is wisdom. It is understanding of one's life as part of the Order Jahweh created.[28]

We conclude by refusing to bifurcate a person's response in the ethical world of the Old Testament. Neither Pietism, which often emphasizes the *heart* and attitudes of a person while underrating the importance of ethical action, nor social activism, which places its emphasis on action in the marketplace and community while often underrating the priority of the heart and attitudes of man, will fit the Old Testament pattern. Both, in a balanced and biblically arranged set of priorities, must play their part. Both emphases, in abstraction from each other, are to be faulted as being subbiblical and clearly counter to the call for a holistic view of ethics as set forth not only in the summarizing texts of the Old Testament but also in the leading strains of Old Testament ethics as we have just seen in organizing them around the most extensive symbol of ethical teaching in the Old Testament: the Decalogue.

---

[27]Philip Nel, "Authority in Wisdom Admonitions," *Zeitschrift für die alttestamentliche Wissenschaft* 93 (1981): 418–26. Also see his earlier preparatory article, *idem,* "A Proposed Method for Determining the Context of Wisdom Admonitions," *Journal of Northwest Semitic Languages* 6 (1978): 33–39.

[28]Nel, "Authority," 425.

PART IV
MORAL DIFFICULTIES
IN THE OLD TESTAMENT

Chapter 16

The Morally Offensive Character
and Acts of God in the Old Testament

Probably very little impedes individual contemporary reader's appreciation and use of the Old Testament more than the frequent number of moral difficulties that have been encountered in the Old Testament. The roots to these objections go back to the first centuries of the Christian era, for they were already a difficulty at that time.

Usually the discussion conveniently begins with Marcion, a prominent heretic and wealthy ship owner who came to Rome just before A.D. 140. At first he was active in the orthodox community, but then was excommunicated c. 144. Marcion ran into grief when he pressed the Pauline contrast between gospel and law to such lengths that he ultimately rejected the whole Old Testament, whose God of law and righteousness he called a demiurge (a secondary deity who made the world). Thus, the Old Testament and its morality became a document of an alien religion and its god a dangerous power and reality.

In the dualistic system of the fourth century Manichaeism, the contrast between the God of the Old Testament and their brand of "Christianity" was similar to the sharp lines already drawn by Marcion. The Old Testament was ransacked for all the examples of offensive morality that could be found in order to justify their stance of regarding the Old Testament as an inferior and unchristian book. This same line was still being fostered in the twelfth-century Cartharists ("the pure ones").

247

Perhaps a more contemporary sample might illustrate the depth and seriousness of this position. Harry Emerson Fosdick in his *Guide to Understanding the Bible* devoted his third chapter to "The Idea of Right and Wrong."[1] Fosdick found three offensive characteristics in the Old Testament ethics: (1) its exclusivism, provincialism, and Jewish favoritism; (2) its inhumanity, class-consciousness (where women were treated as chattel along with the rest of a man's possessions), slavery, and polygamy; and (3) its externality of rites, ritual, bans on census, and religious calendar. In contrast with each of these features, the New Testament was the exact opposite: (1) universal, (2) humane, and (3) inward.

These are the challenges I wish to address in Part IV. The question remains about the organization of these long lists of moral difficulties. One of the few lists that attempts to bring some order in this whole field is an article by William Brenton Greene, Jr. He reduced the list of objections known to him into seven:[2]

a. God is represented sometimes in the Old Testament as partial, fickle, hateful, revengeful, and otherwise morally unworthy. . . .

b. [The Old Testament] often gives the divine endorsement to character not approved by our moral sense. . . .

c. The Old Testament . . . endorses, not only characters that we cannot justify, but even expressions of individual feelings towards one's fellows that are offensive to our moral judgments. . . .

d. . . . In addition to endorsing . . . expressions of individual feelings that offend our moral judgments, it [the Old Testament] represents God as explicitly requiring in some instances acts condemned by our moral sense. . . .

e. . . . The sanctions by which it [the Old Testament] commends and enforces what it requires, are mercenary and, therefore, inferior, if not immoral. . . .

f. . . . The principle of human brotherhood receives only very partial and inconsistent treatment. . . .

---

[1]Harry Emerson Fosdick, *Guide to Understanding the Bible* (New York: Harper, 1960), 8.

[2]William Brenton Green, Jr., "The Ethics of the Old Testament: The Objections to Old Testament Ethics," *Princeton Theological Review* 28 (1929): 313–66 reprinted in *Classical Evangelical Essays in Old Testament Interpretation*, compiled and edited by W. C. Kaiser, Jr. (Grand Rapids: Baker, 1972), 207–35, in particular p. 207 (e.g., repentance, jealousy, and deception by God); pp. 211–12 (e.g., lies of Abraham, adultery of David, the lives of the Judges); p. 213 (e.g., the imprecatory Psalms); p. 216 (e.g., the sacrifice of Isaac, deceiving Pharaoh, borrowing jewelry from the Egyptians); p. 222 (e.g., motivations of prudence, well-being, etc. rather than love); p. 224 (e.g., Hebrew particularism); p. 226 (e.g., loose divorce, polygamy, slavery, and retaliation).

> g. . . . The Old Testament . . . contains positive precepts and in-
> direct requirements and sanctions that are in conflict with the
> teachings and implications of the New Testament and so with
> high morality.

In our treatment of these same issues, we shall propose to handle them in three classes in the next three chapters:

16. The Morally Offensive Character and Acts of God in the Old Testament.
17. The Morally Offensive Character and Acts of Men and Women.
18. The Morally Offensive Precepts and Sanctions in the Law of God.

This approach is somewhat similar to W. S. Bruce's[3] approach. He listed them this way:

> a. Difficulties connected with the manner in which the character or action of God is presented.
> b. Difficulties arising from traces of an irreligious spirit in Old Testament saints.
> c. Difficulties arising from moral defects in some of the laws of Moses.

CHARGES AGAINST THE CHARACTER OF GOD

Marcion was offended, as many Christians often are, by the way Yahweh appears to be depicted in the Old Testament. Could it really be true that the God of the Old Testament was fickle, hateful, deceptive, and revengeful? Certainly, if this were true, it could not be harmonized or integrated into the picture that the New Testament paints of God.

Yahweh is Fickle

Many have taken offense because Genesis 6:6 said, "The LORD was grieved [repented] that he had made man on the earth." How could God appear to regret having made a decision once it was made? What does Genesis 6:6 mean when it describes him having "repented"?[4]

Interestingly enough, Numbers 23:19 represents repentance as an impossibility for God: "God is not a man, that he should lie, nor a son of man, that he should change his mind." But lest this be thought to be an obvious contradiction, we must call the reader's attention to another place in the Old Testament, where in the scope of one and the same chapter

---

[3]W. S. Bruce, *The Ethics of the Old Testament*, 2d ed. (Edinburgh: T. & T. Clark, 1909), 283.

[4]On the repentance of God, see Lester J. Kuyper, "The Suffering and the Repentance of God," *Scottish Journal of Theology* 22 (1969): 257–77.

both affirmations are made about God—God repented and God never repents. The chapter is 1 Samuel 15. In verse 11 it reads: "I am grieved that I have made Saul king, because he has turned away from me"; verse 29 just as strongly affirms, "He who is the Glory of Israel does not lie or change his mind; for he is not a man that he should change his mind." Yet, Exodus 32:14, which says that "Then the LORD relented and did not bring on his people the disaster he had threatened" must be weighed with Jonah 3:10, "When God saw what they did and how they turned from their evil ways, he had compassion and did not bring upon them the destruction he had threatened." The Ninevites, then, reaped the benefit of a deliverance from their repentance that led to God's repentance. Israel, too, was often the beneficiaries of this same repentance. But he took note of their distress when he heard their cry; for their sake he remembered his covenant and out of his great love he relented" (Ps. 106:11–45).

Almost as frequently as the Old Testament mentions the repentance[5] of God it argues that he is unchangeable.[6] Over and over again, Scripture stresses how patient, longsuffering, and slow to anger God is; however, never once does he evidence apathy or indifference.

The word to "repent," נָחַם,[7] is almost always used of God in its thirty-eight instances.[8] The basic idea then is that God can and does change in his actions and emotions towards men so as not to change in his basic character. God's repentance does not prove him to be fickle, mutable, and variable in his nature or purpose. Rather, as William Brenton Greene, Jr., commented, ". . . if God had willed to treat the Ninevites after their repentance as He had threatened to treat them before their repentance, this would have proved Him mutable. It would have revealed Him as displeased, at one time with impenitence and at another time with penitence."[9]

God's repentance, then, is a form of anthropomorphism that dares to picture the God-man relationship in terms of our everyday lives. While these anthropomorphisms (the description of God in human forms) and more particularly, in this case, anthropopathisms (the description of God

---

[5]E.g. in addition to the verses discussed above, see Judg. 2:18; 2 Sam. 24:16; 1 Chron. 21:15; Jer. 18:8, 10; 26:3, 13, 19; 42:10; Joel 2:13, 14; Amos 7:3, Jonah 4:2.

[6]E.g., Ps. 110:4; Jer. 4:28; 20:16; Ezek. 24:14; Zech. 8:14; Mal. 3:6.

[7]Robert Baker Girdlestone, *Synonyms of the Old Testament* (Grand Rapids: Eerdmans, 1956) 87–91; Marvin R. Wilson, "נָחַם," *Theological Wordbook of the Old Testament* (Chicago: Moody, 1981), 570–71.

[8]Jer. 8:6 and 31:19 are two exceptions which show נָחַם used of man. שׁוּב is the normal OT word for repentance of men.

[9]Greene, *Classical Evangelical Essays*, 209.

in human feelings) are valuable in communicating to us the emotions and feelings of God, they also pose limitations—especially when it comes to describing the justice of God whose qualities of justice exceed anything known or found in the justice of men.[10]

To deny any humaneness to God would be to *under*interpret these figures of speech; but to reduce God to the common failures and quirks of human inconsistency would be to *over*interpret these anthropopathisms.[11] The exalted state of God also embraces within himself a variety of emotions including regret, grief, and change in response (repentance) to mortals when they have changed against his divine purpose or nature.

This change in God takes place when there has been a clear change for the worse in the moral and ethical integrity of people with whom he is in covenant, in response to the intercessory prayer of his appointed prophet, or when people renounce their evil ways and deeds and turn back to him.[12] In these cases, God must be changeable, for if he did not relent in these instances, it would dramatically signal that he had had a reversal in his own nature, character, and being. Thus when Malachi 3:6 affirms, "I the LORD do not change," it is not declaring that Yahweh is frozen immobile and impassible; instead, it is only declaring that he may be counted on for consistency in his purposes, character, and being.

Yahweh is Hateful

"Jacob I loved, but Esau I hated" (שָׂנֵא, Mal. 1:2–3; Rom. 9:13) is the most notorious statement in this charge. The Old Testament concept of God includes the fact that God can and does hate.[13]

Most prominent among God's hates or dislikes is hypocritical worship (Isa. 1:14; Amos 5:21) and evil. Seven of these evils, which Yahweh "hates," are listed in Proverbs 6:16–19. The first three are mental, verbal, and actual (pride, lying, murder); the next four deal with the heart, the feet, or will; and the sixth and seventh evil are related to the mouth.

It must also be recognized that the incarnate Word of God, the sinless Jesus, was filled, on occasion with emotions of indignation and anger.[14] Thus hate was a proper emotion for differentiating, disavowing,

---

[10]Kuyper, "Repentance of God," 257–58.

[11]Kuyper, "Repentance of God," 257–58.

[12]Abraham J. Heschel, *The Prophets* (New York: Harper and Row, 1969), 1:194: "No word is God's final word. Judgment, far from being absolute, is conditional. A change in man's conduct brings about a change in God's judgment."

[13]O. Michel, "μισέω, the OT and LXX," *Theological Dictionary of the New Testament* 4:685–88, 691.

[14]Mark 3:5; 10:14; John 2:17; 11:33, 38. See also Marten H. Woudstra, "Edom and Israel in Ezekiel," *Calvin Theological Journal* (1968): 21–35.

and espousing its opposite, love. Only the one who truly loves can understand the need to hate with a burning hatred all wrong and evil.

But these antonyms, אַהֲבָה ("love") and שִׂנְאָה ("hatred"), are also used with a special flavor in Deuteronomy 21:15–17 as meaning the loved one and the hated, that is, the less-loved one. In Greek, the same Semitisms are carried over in the antonymic use of ἀγαπᾶν/μισεῖν with the same special flavor in Matthew 6:24 and Luke 16:13 "where, in dependence on Dt. 21:15–17 and Ex. r., 51(104) [footnote—on Ex. 38:21 'Why is the mount of the Law called Sinai? Because God disregarded (שָׂנֵא) the lofty and loved (אָהֵב) the lowly'] they mean 'to prefer' ('to be faithful to') and 'to slight' ('to despise'). We have here a Hebraism, as in the requirement for discipleship."[15] This last reference is to the two parallel lists of requirements for discipleship; Matthew 10:37 uses the formula ὁ φιλῶν ὑπὲρ ἐμὲ, "He who loves . . . more than me," while Luke 14:26 simply parallels it by saying καὶ οὐ μισεῖ "If any one comes to me and does not hate. . . ."

The reference to Esau, father, mother, wife, children, brothers, or sisters is not one of psychological hatred, but one of preference, temporary disregard for higher purposes, and exclusive separation.

In the case of Jacob and Esau, the love of God signaled an election and call for service ("To be a blessing to all the nations") that had not come to Esau. But Esau was not hated as God held evil in contempt, for Esau was the object of deliverance in the end times in Amos 9:12 and Obadiah 19–21.[16]

Another alleged evidence of God's hatred of persons is his treatment of Pharaoh. The passages dealing with the hardening of Pharaoh's heart in Exodus 4–14 have continued to trouble and perplex many readers of the Bible.

In order to graphically see the issue of the agent of hardening of Pharaoh's heart, this chart should present the problem quickly:

	Exodus	Pharaoh is the subject of the verb	Yahweh is the subject of the verb
Prediction	4:21		אֲחַזֵּק H; Piel Impf.
Prediction	7:3		אַקְשֶׁה Q; Hiphil impf.
Signs	7:13	וַיֶּחֱזַק H; Qal impf.	
Prelude	7:14	כָּבֵד K; Qal perf.	
1. Blood	7:22	וַיֶּחֱזַק H; Qal impf.	
2. Frogs	8:15	וַהַכְבֵּד K; Hiphil impf.	
	[11]		

---

[15]Michel, "μισέω," 690 and n. 23.

[16]Cf. however, Woudstra, "Edom and Israel," with reasons for God's hatred of Edom (Esau) in the other sense that this word has.

	Exodus	Pharaoh is the subject of the verb	Yahweh is the subject of the verb
3. Gnats	8:19 [15]	וַיֶּחֱזַק H; Qal impf.	
4. Flies	8:32 [28]	וַיַּכְבֵּד K; Hiphil impf.	
5. Cattle	9:7	וַיִּכְבַּד K; Qal impf.	
6. Boils	9:12		וַיְחַזֵּק H; Piel impf.
7. Hail	9:34	וַיַּכְבֵּד K; Hiphil impf.	
	9:35	וַיֶּחֱזַק H; Qal impf.	
8. Locusts	10:1		הִכְבַּדְתִּי K; Hiphil impf.
	10:20		וַיְחַזֵּק H; Piel impf.
9. Darkness	10:27		וַיְחַזֵּק H; Piel impf.
Summary	11:10		וַיְחַזֵּק H; Piel impf.
	13:15	הִקְשָׁה Q; Hiphil perf.	
Egyptian	14:4		וְחִזַּקְתִּי H; Piel perf.
chase	14:8		וַיְחַזֵּק H; Piel impf.
	14:17		מְחַזֵּק H; Piel ptcp.

Key:

K = כָּבֵד, "to be heavy, cause to be heavy, harden"
H = חָזַק, "to be firm, hard, strong, harden"
Q = קָשָׁה, "to be harsh, harden"

This motif of hardening appears twenty times in the passages between Exodus 4 to 14. The most troublesome aspect of the motif is the ten times when God himself is said to harden Pharaoh's heart. It is this fact which most theologians have found difficult to accept.[17]

Literary and form criticism have not made the analysis of this problem any less difficult; in fact, it has only laden the problem of the *function* of the hardening episodes in each layer and in what many refer to as the final version.

Since this motif only occurs in Exodus 4–14, most modern interpreters suggest that it was simply created by the authors or editors of these narratives and that it was not part of the original narrative. This argument

---

[17]For a sample of recent discussions on this issue, see Robert R. Wilson, "The Hardening of Pharaoh's Heart," *Catholic Biblical Quarterly* 41 (1979): 18–36; Gerhard von Rad, *Old Testament Theology* (New York: Harper and Row, 1962–65), 2:151–55; Walther Eichrodt, *Theology of the Old Testament* (London: SCM, 1967), 2:177–81; Umberto Cassuto, *A Commentary on the Book of Exodus* (Jerusalem: Magnes Press, 1967), 55–57; J. Plastaras, *The God of Exodus* (Milwaukee: Bruce, 1966), 133–37; H. Räisänen, *The Idea of Divine Hardening* (Publications of the Finnish Exegetical Society, 25; Helsinki: Finnish Exegetical Society, 1972); Brevard S. Childs, *The Book of Exodus: A Critical, Theological Commentary* (Philadelphia: Westminster, 1974), 170–75; G. Warshaver, "The Hardening of 'Pharaoh's Heart' in the Bible and Qumranic Literature," *Bulletin of the Institute of Jewish Studies* 1 (1973), 1ff.

then takes two forms. Some find in the hardening references a literary device around which an editor organized and gave coherence to the plague and crossing narratives.[18] Others, with a form-critical or traditio-historical approach, find in the hardening themes a convenient link for the existing narratives of the plagues.[19] B. S. Childs, using a form-critical method, denied that this motif linked independent plague narratives. The hardening motif, in his analysis, explained for the biblical writers why some of the divine miracles or signs failed to achieve their purpose—Pharaoh's hard heart thwarted their purpose.[20]

Robert S. Wilson agrees with most scholars in making the hardening theme a "secondary addition to the plague traditions."[21] But he cannot totally agree with Childs's suggestion of a theological or apologetic function for this motif. Wilson finds the standard three literary sources of J, E, and P represented here. J, the Yahwist, always uses the verb כָּבֵד either in the *hiphil* (Exod. 8:15[11], 32[28]; 9:34–35) or the *qal* stems (Exod. 7:14; 9:7). Except for the redacted Exodus 10:1, none of the other sources are alleged to use this verb for hardening. The Elohist (E) uses חָזַק, usually in the *piel* stem (Exod. 4:21; 10:20, 27). Only in Exodus 9:35 does E use the *qal* to describe Pharaoh's heart. The Priestly (P) writer(s) normally use the *piel* of חָזַק (Exod. 9:12; 11:10; 14:4, 8, 17), but, it is also alleged that they use the *qal* stem of this verb (Exod. 7:13; 22; 8:19[15]). In Exodus 7:3 the *hiphil* of קָשָׁה is also used by P.

Wilson concludes on the basis of this chronological rearrangement that "two trends emerge. First, the word כָּבֵד virtually disappears in the later sources and is replaced by חָזַק or rarely, by קָשָׁה. Second, the later sources tend to see Yahweh as the agent of hardening."[22] The three functions of our motifs, according to Wilson are these: (1) In J it has "literary functions but no discernible theological functions," (2) in E "For the first time the hardening is seen as directly responsible for the plague . . . and thus helps to unify the whole plague cycle," and (3) in P it "has theological function . . . portraying the plagues and the crossing as part of Yahweh's holy war to bring about his divine plan for Israel."[23]

Yet we cannot agree with the documentary divisions or the assigned functions. While some may argue that Psalm 78:43–51 preserves a "J" list of the plagues (plagues three [gnats] and four [boils], both in P, and nine [darkness, in E] are missing), certainly Psalm 105:28–36 preserves another

---

[18]Cassuto, *Exodus*, 92–135.
[19]Wilson, "Pharaoh's Heart," 20, cites Georg Fohrer as an example of this view.
[20]Childs, *Book of Exodus*, 174.
[21]Wilson, "Pharaoh's Heart," 21.
[22]Wilson, "Pharaoh's Heart," 23–24.
[23]Wilson, "Pharaoh's Heart," 35–36.

listing in which only plague five (cattle plague) (but see Ps. 78:49) and plague six (boils) do not appear. Scholars have failed, chides Cassuto,[24] to observe that the nine plagues are arranged in three cycles, each following a routine literary presentation so as to increase the effect of the monotony and the horror of Pharaoh's intransigence. Wilson correctly points out that the concept of hardening of the heart is fairly uncommon in the Semitic world, but it is indeed at home in the Egyptian realm. ". . . Ancient Egyptian does contain several expressions meaning 'to be hard of heart'! *mn ib*, literally 'firm of heart,' means 'constant, persevering, obstinate, headstrong, defiant'; *rwd ib*, literally 'hard of heart', means 'persistant, stout-hearted, unyielding', *nht ib*, literally 'strong of heart', means 'to be courageous, confident'; and *dns (dnś) ib*, literally 'heavy of heart,' means 'reticent.'"[25] This should be all the more reason why the text in its present form should be trusted in its claim to be a unity and to come from an Egyptian province.

How then should we describe the function and meaning of this hardening—especially Yahweh's making Pharaoh's heart obstinate? Pharaoh's hardening is a work of God and thus is but a sample of all those who neglect the numerous opportunities put before them.

It was not until the sixth plague that Yahweh made Pharaoh's heart hard. In the first five plagues it was always and only Pharaoh who steeled his own heart against any softening work that the plagues or their release could have had upon him. Even his own magicians confessed, "This is the finger [work] of God" (Exod. 8:19). Finally, the freedom of the will which Pharaoh enjoyed reached its fixed limits and Yahweh confirmed the notions of the monarch's heart which, by now, had become calloused and impervious to any of the further opportunities to reflect and recant.

Keil finds a twofold manner in which God produces hardness: permissive hardness and effective hardness.[26] He may withdraw and leave a person alone and allow him to go on his own way. God may also order those things in his providence, which through man's abuse, can become

---

[24]Cassuto, *Exodus*, 92–93; C. F. Keil and Franz Delitzsch, *Biblical Commentary on the Old Testament* (Grand Rapids: Eerdmans, 1956), 1:472–75 also agree. See Dewey Beegle, *Moses, The Servant of Yahweh* (Grand Rapids: Eerdmans, 1972), 93, complaint about "nit-picking" that makes "mincemeat of the text." Except for Exodus 9:30 (where "Yahweh Elohim" occurs), Yahweh is the consistent name used throughout the plague narratives.

[25]Wilson, "Pharaoh's Heart," 24, n. 22; See A. Erman and H. Grapow, *Wörterbuch der aegyptischen Sprache* (Leipzig: Hinrichs, 1926–63) 2:60–61; 410–11; 314–15; 5:468. Wilson acknowledges that Herrmann and A. S. Yahuda, *The Language of the Pentateuch in Its Relation to Egyptian* (London: Oxford University, 1933), 1:69 give Egypt as the source of the hardening motif.

[26]Keil and Delitzsch, *Biblical Commentary*, 456.

the occasion for a man's hardening. Thus the voice of morality and the multiplicity of divine mercies become weaker and muted until finally the heart of man becomes altogether calloused.

God is not the author of evil. There is no suggestion in Exodus 4–14 that he secretly influenced Pharaoh's will or forced a stubborn resolution, which otherwise was incompatible with Pharaoh's basic nature and disposition. Oftentimes, the very divine works that are meant to soften the heart have the opposite effect, depending on the condition of a person's heart, just as the same sun will produce opposite effects depending whether it falls on wax or clay. Repeatedly, the text stressed the fact that Yahweh's controlling purpose in sending the plagues was evangelistic: "so that you may know that I am the LORD. . ." (Exod. 7:5, 17; 8:10[6], 22[18]; 9:14, 16, 29, 10:2; 14:4, 18). But the divine gift of mercy had no permanent effect on Pharaoh, even though he almost recanted on several occasions.

Yahweh is Deceptive

In 1 Kings 22:2–23, Jeremiah 4:10, and Ezekiel 14:9, it would appear that the Old Testament presents the God of truth as being the sponsor of falsehood by inspiring prophets with false messages. Is the God of the Old Testament capable of deception?

It is a known characteristic of popular conceptions to express in an imperatival and active form things which we understand only to be permitted. Certainly when the devils begged Christ that they be allowed to go into the swine and he commanded them "go" (Matt. 8:31), he did no more than permit them. And when John records that our Lord commanded Judas, "What you are about to do, do quickly" (John 13:27), he does not intend to say that Christ authored his own betrayal. So here in 1 Kings 22:22, "Go and do it" (i.e., deceive Ahab's false prophets) signifies only permission, not a command or sponsorship.

What really took place then was that God allowed a lying spirit to speak through the false prophets to deceive Ahab, for that is what he had made up his mind he wanted to hear. The efficient cause of the deception was not God, but the lying spirit. Rushdoony, in a misplaced effort to rescue the lying of Rahab and the midwives, argues against absolute truth telling and vindicates it by declaring that 1 Kings 22:22–23 teaches that God placed a lying spirit in the mouths of Ahab's false prophets.[27] Rushdoony would absolve men and women from speaking the truth in unusual circumstances just as, he feels, God did in this case. What will Rushdoony say on Judas's behalf or even the demons who went hogwild into the sea? But the situation is as Greene states it:

---

[27]R. J. Rushdoony, *The Institutes of Biblical Law* (Nutley, N.J.: Craig Press, 1973), 548.

> God is represented as having deceived Ahab . . . only because the
> popular mind does not discriminate between what one does and
> what he only permits and also because it overlooks the great dif-
> ference between the sovereign God's relation to the permission of
> evil and ours. It is true that in I Kgs xxii God seems to do more
> than simply permit the deception. . . . What else, however, does
> this mean than that, as God's eternal plan contemplates both the
> existence and the development of evil, so it provides for its accom-
> plishment by the foreordained permission of evil on the occasions
> when and in the ways in which evil can by its own working serve
> the divine purpose? . . . This is not saying that God does evil that
> good may come. It is saying that He takes evil *already* here, evil
> actually in manifestation, evil that, if left uncontrolled by Him,
> would of itself hinder the good; and then so overrules the tendency
> of this evil that of itself, though contrary to its own intention, it
> advances truth. . . .[28]

Since Ahab had abandoned Yahweh his God, hardened his own
heart, and determined to use prophecy for his own purposes, God allowed
him to be ruined by the very instrument he sought to prostitute. Instead of
using the heathen nations as his rod of chastisement (Isa. 10:5), he uses
Ahab's false prophets. "The LORD has poured into them a spirit of dizzi-
ness" (Isa. 19:14).

Karl C. W. F. Bähr and W. G. Sumner[29] do not like the idea of
permission here (which has been used by ancient expositors since The-
odoret's day). It is rather an executive and judicial act of God wherein he
brings punishment on a person through the evil that person does and thus
punishes evil with evil.

C. F. Keil commented that "the words of Jehovah, 'Persuade Ahab,
thou wilt be able,' and 'Jehovah put a lying Spirit', etc. are not to be
understood as merely expressing the permission of God. . . . According to
the Scriptures, God does work evil, but without therefore willing it or
bringing forth sin."[30]

A brief comment should also be made on the charges of divine
deception in Ezekiel 14:9. Had the deception originated in God, it could
not be the object of punishment, as it indeed was in verses 12–16. Likewise, the strong assertions of Jeremiah in 4:10 and 20:7 are but nothing
else than complaints of the prophet who had mistaken the promise of God's
presence for insurance that no evil or derision would come on him, but in

---

[28]Greene, *Classical Evangelical Essays*, 210–11.

[29]Karl Christian W. F. Bähr, *The Books of the Kings* in *Lange's Commentary*, trans.,
enl., and ed. W. G. Sumner (New York: Scribner Armstrong & Co., 1872), 6:252–53, 257.

[30]C. F. Keil, *The Books of the Kings* (Grand Rapids: Eerdmans, 1950), 277.

no way can they be cited as giving foundation or credence to the charge that the Lord is deceptive.

Yahweh is Wrathful

There can be little doubt that the wrath of God figures largely in the Old Testament. Johannes Fichtner dramatizes such a claim by noting that of the nouns used for wrath in the Old Testament, 375 times they refer to the wrath of God and only 80 times for the wrath of men.[31] But how can this emphasis on the wrath of God be harmonized with the canonical depiction of God's love and grace?

So serious is this dilemma that many have tried to extricate God from it in one way or another. One way since the appearance of C. H. Dodd's commentary on Romans, in 1932, has been the idea of "impersonal wrath."[32] Dodd found that in thirteen of Paul's sixteen occurrences of wrath, he did not link it with God. But as K. N. E. Newell asked, what about the other three that did? (Rom. 1:18ff.; Eph. 5:6; Col. 3:6).[33] It is doubtful that Dodd's view can be successfully defended, even though it has gained much support recently.[34]

When the question turns to the source for Paul's special way of referring to the wrath of God, usually the chronicler's examples are raised.[35] It is true that he uses "wrath" in an absolute manner, for example, "wrath was on him" (2 Chron. 32:25; cf. also 19:10; 24:18; 28:13 and 1 Chron. 27:24). But there are fourteen occasions when wrath is personally associated with God, for example, "the LORD's anger burned against Uzzah" (1 Chron. 13:10; 2 Chron. 6:36; 12:7, 12; 19:2; etc.). Even the so-called absolute wrath is explained in personal terms: "the wrath of the LORD is upon you" (2 Chron. 19:2) often with "wrath" and "wrath of the LORD" being interchangeable as in "therefore the LORD's wrath was on him . . . therefore the LORD's wrath did not come upon them" (2 Chron. 32:25–26).

> Perhaps it could be suggested that the Chronicler reveals the "origin" of Paul's *terminology* for wrath, and this because the tendency to speak of God in Judaism by the use of surrogates included

---

[31]Johannes Fichtner, "ὀργή," *Theological Dictionary of the New Testament*, 5:392–409, especially p. 395, n. 92.

[32]C. H. Dodd, *The Epistle of Paul to the Romans* (London, 1963), 49, assures us that ὀργὴ του θεου is not "a certain feeling or attitude of God toward us, but some process or effect in the realm of objective facts."

[33]K. N. E. Newall, "St. Paul and the Anger of God," *Irish Biblical Studies* 1 (1979): 99–114.

[34]See four other arguments by Newall, "Anger of God," 106–7, using Rom. 9:22; 9:23; 12:19; and Col. 3:6.

[35]I am indebted to Newall, "Anger of God," 107–8, for the points in this argument from Chronicles.

aspects of God's nature spoken of in abstract terms; thus "wrath" may be the result of the process illustrated in the rise of absolute terms like "The Word," "the glory," "Wisdom," i.e. avoiding the use of the divine name.[36]

The whole question of divine anger (*ira Dei*) has had a long history of sharp debate even in the Christian church. There it became a question of divine passibility (i.e., whether God had the capacity to feel, suffer, or be angry) or impassibility (i.e., the denial of these qualities). Gnosticism took strong exception to any and every claim that God could experience anger, feelings, or suffering of any kind.

In the second century of the Christian era these arguments for impassibility and Gnosticism reached their zenith under a man named Marcion. Marcion's God was entirely apathetic, free from all affections, and incapable of being angry. Therefore he was forced to dismiss the God of the Old Testament as a "Demiurge" (a subordinate deity who was responsible for the creation of evil). Eventually, Marcion was expelled from the church in A.D. 144, and Tertullian wrote his *Against Marcion* in which he undertook to answer all the objectionable passages Marcion had raised.

But it is Lactantius's *De Ira Dei*, "The Anger of God" (last half of the third century) that began to address this question of defining and understanding the anger of God. God must, he reasoned, be moved to anger by the presence of sin and wickedness of those who are in a covenant relationship to him, just as he is moved to love those who please him. In Lactantius's own words the argument went like this:

> He who loves the good by this very fact hates the evil; and he who does not hate the evil, does not love the good; because the love of goodness issues directly out of the hatred of evil, and the hatred of evil issues directly out of the love of goodness. No one can love life without abhoring death; and no one can have an appetency for light, without an antipathy to darkness.[37]

But the problem is also one of definition. Too frequently we define anger as Aristotle did, "the desire for retaliation"[38] or the burning need to get revenge and to get even for some slight or actual harm done to us. With anger, some saw a "brief madness,"[39] but Lactantius defined anger as "a motion of the soul rousing itself to curb sin."[40]

---

[36]Newall, "Anger of God," 108.

[37]Lactantius, *De Ira Dei*, p. 51.

[38]Aristotle, *De Anima* 1,1. See the excellent discussion of this whole topic in Abraham Heschel, *The Prophets* (New York: Harper and Row, 1962), 2:1–86, especially p. 60, n. 4.

[39]Horace, *Epistolae* 1:2:62; see also J. C. Hardwick, "The Wrath of God and The Wrath of Man," *The Hibbert Journal* 39 (1940–41): 251–561.

[40]Cited by Heshel, *Prophets*, 2:82.

The problem with anger and wrath is that it can and does become an evil when it is left unchecked and uncontrolled. That, indeed, is what is wrong with most definitions of anger or wrath; they imply a loss of self-control, an impulsiveness, or a temporary derangement. It is no wonder that few want to link God with *that* definition.

On the contrary, God's anger is never explosive, unreasonable, or unexplainable. It is, instead, his firm displeasure with our wickedness and sin. It never controls him, it is merely an instrument of his will. Therefore, his anger has not shut off his mercies or compassions to us (Ps. 77:9). His anger marks the end of indifference, for he cannot remain neutral or impartial in the presence of sin (Isa. 26:20; 54:7–8; 57:16–19) but his love remains (Jer. 31:3; Hos. 2:19).

The wrath of God, like the zeal (קִנְאָה) of the Lord (a term sometimes linked with terms for wrath[41]), is an expression of the holiness (קֹדֶשׁ) of Yahweh: "I will be zealous for my holy name" (Ezek. 39:25). But the often proffered description of Yahweh's wrath as something that is fundamentally irrational and an inexplicable thing that breaks out now and again with enigmatic and mysterious, if not primal, force[42] is a figment of overactive scholarly and lay imaginations. Fichtner offers these examples for the irrational outbreak of the wrath of God: Jacob's wrestling at Jabbok (Gen. 32:23–32), Yahweh's dealings with Moses in his failure to circumcise his son (Exod. 4:24–26), or when he comes face to face with God in the golden calf incident (Exod. 33:20; cf. also Judg. 13:22; Isa. 6:5). The wrath of God, Fichtner affirms, will break out, presumably in an uncontrolled or irrational way, when his holiness has been violated as at Mount Sinai (Exod. 19:9–25; 20:18–21) in the requirement that only the Levites encamp closest to the tabernacle (Num. 1:52–53), or when the men of Bethshemesh peered into the ark of the covenant (1 Sam. 6:19), or when Uzzah instinctively reached out to steady the illegally carried ark on an ox cart (2 Sam. 6:7). Even Fichtner's appeal to David's census being prompted by Yahweh in 2 Samuel 24:1, rather than authored by Satan as 1 Chronicles 21:1 judges, is in poor taste.

The wrath of God never "borders closely on caprice,"[43] nor is it a "demonic element . . . bound up with his innermost being. . . ."[44] This is nothing else but the spirit of Marcion still hovering over the towers of learning and the steeples in the land. Abraham Heschel explained how

---

[41]E.g., Deut. 29:20; Ezek. 16:38; 36:6 or in parallelism to these terms: Deut. 6:15; Ps. 79:5; Ezek. 5:13; 16:42; Nah. 1:2; Zeph. 3:8. See my discussion of vengeance in chapter 4.

[42]P. Volz, as cited by Fichtner, "ὀργή," 401–2.

[43]Fichtner, "ὀργή," 402.

[44]Fichtner, "ὀργή," 402.

embarrassment over these emotional aspects of God in the biblical materials induced the historico-critical school to assume an evolutionary development in the character of God from a terrible, mysterious force to a good and loving Lord. They transferred all the sinister forms of the demonic over to the essential nature of God in order to deal with the power of magic. A God of such monstrous and awesome powers, they reasoned, would make all other demons, magic, and charms of no avail. Mused Heschel:

> This view, which is neither true to fact nor in line with the fundamental biblical outlook, arises from the failure to understand the meaning of the God of pathos and particularly the meaning of anger as a mode of pathos. "Pathos" like its Latin equivalent *passio*, from *pati* (to suffer), means a state or condition in which something happens to man, something of which it is a passive victim . . . emotions of pain or pleasure.
>
> We must not forget that the God of Israel is sublime rather than sentimental, nor should we associate the kind with the apathetic, the intense with the sinister, the dynamic with the demonic.[45]

The point is this: God's anger and wrath are indeed a terrible reality for both testaments,[46] a reality that will reduce to nothing every human attempt to erect one's life or the community's experience on the false bases of sin, evil, or injustice. The faithful who cry out for relief will have to wait only so long, and then with unexpected suddenness the holiness of God will manifest itself—but without shutting off his compassions to humanity (Ps. 77:9).

CHARGES AGAINST THE ACTS REQUIRED BY GOD

In addition to charging God with blemishes on his character, some are offended by the way the Old Testament represents God as explicitly requiring acts that, in some instances, our moral senses would disapprove or find repugnant. It is the divine command in each case that proves to be troublesome and raises the moral difficulty. We shall raise four of the problems most frequently cited as illustrations of some deficiency in the Old Testament view of God, namely, the divine order to Abraham to sacrifice Isaac, the plan to deceive or trick Pharaoh into letting Israel go, the tactic of borrowing Egyptian jewelry just before everyone suddenly and permanently left town, and the order "do not seek peace or good

---

[45]Heschel, *Prophets*, 27–28, 84.
[46]Remember the wrath of God is raised in the NT in Matt. 3:7; Luke 3:7; Rom. 1:18ff.; 3:5; 5:9; 12:19; Eph. 2:3; 5:6; Col. 3:6; 1 Thess. 2:16; 5:9; Rev. 14:10; 15:1.

relations with them [the Canaanites] as long as you live" (Deut. 23:6) and the related command to drive the Canaanites out summarily and destroy them totally. Each of these situations must be dealt with at some length.

Yahweh Orders Human Sacrifice

Genesis 22 has been represented as a divine command to commit murder in its most horrible form and, therefore, is totally out of character with the holiness of God. This incident is not to be classified with that of Achan's children (Josh. 7:24–25); Jepthah's daughter (Judg. 11:30–40); Rizbah's demands (2 Sam. 21:8, 9, 14); or Ahaz's, Manassah's, or Hezekiah's practice (2 Kings 16:3; 21:6; 2 Chron. 33:6) that Josiah abolished (2 Kings 23:10) and the prophets condemned (Jer. 19:5; Ezek. 20:30–31; 23:36–39).

The law clearly prohibited human sacrifice and spoke scornfully of those who ordered their sons to be offered to Molech (Lev. 18:21; 20:2). But then, neither did Genesis 22:2 encourage such, for the narrator is exceedingly careful to introduce his account as a "test" (נִסָּה; 22:1).[47] True, this notation was meant to help the reader, and not Abraham, for in his case it had to be a genuine trial and so he was not informed about it. But an event must be judged by its wholeness and not just by its introductory command.

Several have pointed out how Genesis 22:1, "some time later," makes a conscious effort to establish a relationship with the events of Genesis 12–21.[48] Especially significant is the comparison between Abraham's initial command in Genesis 12:1–3 and this one in chapter 22. In both he is commanded to "go" and to go to an undesignated place. In both cases there was sacrifice on the part of the whole family involved. But the initial command had a promise attached to it whereas the climactic challenge of chapter 22 did not.

The purpose of this "test" was well stated by J. L. Crenshaw:

> In a sense the story bears the character of a qualifying test. The fulfillment of the promise articulated in Genesis 12 and reaffirmed at crucial stages during Abraham's journey through alien territory actualizes the divine intention to bless all nations by means of one man. Abraham's excessive love for the son of promise comes dangerously close to idolatry and frustrates the larger mission. Thus is set the stage for the qualifying test.[49]

---

[47]See John I. Lawlor, "The Test of Abraham, Genesis 22:1–19," *Grace Theological Journal* 1 (1980): 19–35.

[48]Lawlor, "Test of Abraham," 32; Nahum M. Sarna, *Understanding Genesis: The Heritage of Biblical Israel* (New York: Schocken, 1974), 163.

[49]J. L. Crenshaw, "Journey into Oblivion: A Structural Analysis of Genesis 22:1–19," *Sounding* 58 (1975): 249.

The text actually does not say that his love for his son was threatening or was, indeed, excessive. In fact, we are not told why a test was necessary; only that God tested him.

It is at this point where Lawlor makes a most valuable contribution. The term, נִסָּה, "test", may hold the key to understanding exactly why God arranged this qualifying test for him. In addition to Genesis 22, נִסָּה is used eight other times in contexts where Elohim/Yahweh is called the "tester." In six of these cases, Israel was the one tested (Exod. 15:22–26; 16:4; 20:18–20; Deut. 8:2, 16; Judg. 2:21–22; 3:1–4), but in 2 Chronicles 32:31 Hezekiah was tested and David was the object of testing in Psalm 26:2. In all eight of these cases (though in Exod. 20:18–20, it is by implication), the "testing" is in relationship to obedience to God's commandments, statutes, laws, or ways. Thus Lawlor concludes:

> If the pattern seen in the use of the term *nissah,* when Yahweh/Elohim is said to be the "tester," can serve as a legitimate key for understanding its use in Gen. 22:1, then one may conclude that the reason Yahweh deemed it necessary to test Abraham was to know what was in his heart, to test his obedience to and fear of Yahweh when his promised and beloved son was at stake.[50]

But if it be objected, "What kind of God would subject man to this type of ordeal?" the answer will depend on which part of the narrative is emphasized. If the initial command to sacrifice Isaac is stressed, then the resulting image of God will be one of deception. But if the intervention of Yahweh to stay his raised hand and his subsequent blessing of Abraham is stressed, then one's conclusion will agree with Roland de Vaux's: "Any Israelite who heard this story would take it to mean that his race owed its existence to the mercy of God and its prosperity to the obedience of their ancestor."[51]

Geerhardus Vos surprises us with the estimate that the divine command to sacrifice Isaac "distinctly implies in the abstract the sacrifice of a human being cannot be condemned on principle. It is well to be cautious in committing one's self to that critical opinion, for it strikes at the very root of the atonement."[52] Vos's point is that Abraham is asked by God to offer life, the life dearest to him—his only son. But with the last minute intervention of the angel, a substitute of one life (in this case, a ram's life) for another is announced as acceptable to God. Therefore, Vos concludes,

---

[50]Lawlor, "Test of Abraham," 28.

[51]Roland de Vaux, *Ancient Israel* (New York: McGraw-Hill, 1965), 443 as cited by Lawlor, "Test of Abraham," 29.

[52]Geerhardus Vos, *Biblical Theology, Old and New Testaments* (Grand Rapids: Eerdmans, 1954), 106.

"Not sacrifice of human life as such, but the sacrifice of average sinful human life is deprecated by the O.T."[53]

I hardly know what to make of Vos's line of reasoning. How could any human life known to man after the Fall function as a gift, much less a substitute, to God? I have no biblical qualms about the principle of substitution, for that is germane to the text itself, but I cannot agree that Isaac as human life functions here to point theoretically or even principally to a blood atonement. The emphasis of the passage falls on the "test" aspect and the grace and mercy of God in maintaining his promise unaided by any conniving assistance of some of the promise's first recipients.

Yahweh Approves of Deceiving

In Exodus 3:18–20, Moses and the elders are divinely instructed to go meet with Pharaoh and at first to make only a moderate and limited request for a temporary leave of absence for three days in order to offer sacrifice to the LORD their God (see also Exod. 5:1–3; 8:25–26; 10:9–10).

This request was not a ruse to deceive Pharaoh or an example of telling a partial truth, namely, once Israel had cleared Egypt's borders they would suddenly announce, "Last one to make it safely into Canaan is the loser"—and everyone would run for freedom with abandon. Nor was this a case of illustrating Psalm 18:26, "to the crooked [Rashi glosses, "with Pharaoh"] you [God] show yourself shrewd."

Instead, the matter is as Augustine and the fifteenth-century Spanish exegete Abarbanel suggest: God deliberately graded his requests of Pharaoh from easier (a three-day journey with an agreed obligation to return) to a more difficult request (the total release of the enslaved people) in order to give Pharaoh every possible aid in making an admittedly difficult political and economic decision. The argument is that had Pharaoh complied, Israel could not have exceeded the bounds of this permission, but would have had to follow up this initial request with a more difficult one. However, God also knew the recalcitrance of the king of Egypt and so he, who reveals his secret (סוֹד) to his servants (Amos 3:7), warned Moses not to be discouraged when this moderate request was turned down, for God wanted Moses, Israel, and all who later read of this account to know what was in the heart of the man they were dealing with. Thus, it is impossible to show that God or Moses intended to deceive Pharaoh if they could sneak one by him. This explanation is just as adequate in meeting all the particulars in addition to being in harmony with what is known about the principals from other canonical sources.

This same view is advocated by Greene:

---

[53]Vos, *Biblical Theology*, 106.

. . . So far from God's course being the tricky one that many have tried to make it out to be, it was prompted by both justice and mercy. Mercy disposed Him to cause the favor asked of Pharaoh in the first instance to be moderate, that he could easily have granted it, had he chosen to do so and thus have disciplined himself to accede to the request for the release of the whole nation, a request which, if made at first, would have been too much for him.[54]

Greene continued, "the favor asked of Pharaoh [was deliberately designed by God] to be so reasonable that his obduracy might appear so much the more glaring, and might have no excuse."[55]

Yahweh Orders Borrowing Unreturnable Jewelry

Three separate passages in Exodus record the incident of the so-called spoiling of the Egyptians, namely, Exodus 3:21–22; 11:2–3; and 12:35–36.[56] But this moral difficulty is a modern translation problem more than it is real to the Hebrew text. The issue is this: Was Israel guilty of deception in asking for the objects of gold and silver? If so, how shall we explain God's explicit command for them to do so?

In all three texts the same verb appears that describes the way that the Israelite women acquired the jewelry. It is the verb שָׁאַל, which means "to ask" for something with no thought of return (e.g., Judg. 8:24; 1 Sam. 1:28). Thus the Septuagint rendered it αἰτέω and the Vulgate *postulo*. However, שָׁאַל also means "to borrow" in texts like Exodus 22:14[13], 2 Kings 4:3 and 6:5.

Since the issue cannot be settled definitively on the basis of the verb שָׁאַל, attention is turned to the verb נִצַּלְתֶּם, the *piel* form of נָצַל, in Exodus 3:22 and 12:36, meaning "You shall plunder the Egyptians." As in 2 Chronicles 20:25, it means "to plunder," but not by fraud, deceit, or cunning devices. נָצַל is a military metaphor that could involve taking away by force, but never by fraud.

Actually, the background on this incident begins with God promising Abraham, some six hundred years before this event, that after Israel had served four hundred years, ". . . they will come out with great possessions," בִּרְכֻשׁ גָּדוֹל (Gen. 15:14). Then at Sinai, Moses was promised when

[54]Greene, *Classical Evangelical Essays*, 218–19.

[55]Greene, *Classical Evangelical Essays*, 218–19.

[56]On this question, see G. W. Coats, "Despoiling the Egyptians," *Vetus Testamentum* 18 (1968): 450–57; Julian Morgenstern, "The Despoiling of the Egyptians," *Journal of Biblical Literature* 68 (1949): 1–28; E. W. Hengstenberg, "The Alleged Purloining of Vessels of the Egyptians by the Israelites," in *The Genuineness of the Pentateuch*, trans. J. E. Ryland (Edinburgh: T. & T. Clark, 1847), 417–32; Brevard S. Childs, "The Despoiling of the Egyptians," in *The Book of Exodus*, 175–77.

God called him that Israel would "not go empty" (Exod. 3:20–21). Psalm 105:37 drops the prefix word for "articles" or "vessels," כֵּלִים, and simply has "silver and gold." God brought them out of Egypt with silver and gold, for the silver and gold and the cattle on a thousand hills are his. He then has the right to dispose of them as he will.

How could the same God who ordered, "Be holy because I, the LORD your God am holy," sometimes command an unholy act? What a glaring contradiction the rendering of שָׁאַל as "to borrow, or loan" would bring on the words shortly to be sounded forth from Sinai, namely, "You shall not steal" and "you shall not covet"!

The text nowhere indicates that the request was for a temporary period of time or that the Egyptians were unwilling contributors. In fact, there is evidence to the contrary. God had promised that *he* would "make the Egyptians favorably disposed toward this people, so that when you leave you will not go empty-handed" (Exod. 3:20–22). Thus one of the reasons why the Egyptians acceded to the bold requests of the Hebrews is that God had temporarily softened the Egyptian's hearts by a secret impulse. Exodus 10:7 seems to hint that God had aroused a respect, awe, and natural sympathy for Moses among the Egyptians. Thus the request is divinely inaugurated and the response is divinely engineered. This fact is so pointedly a sign of God's intervention that the episode is raised three times in the text. It may also well be as Hengstenberg argues that the form of the punishment matches by analogy the transgression of the Egyptians. (Note how the staff or rod of the Egyptian task masters is matched by the staff or rod in Moses's hand as Isaiah 10:24 and 26 confirm.)[57] We conclude, then, that Israel merely "asked" and God strangely moved the hearts of the populace to respond lavishly. The result was as if they had "despoiled" or "plundered" the Egyptians when in fact they had only been given favor in their eyes.

Yahweh Orders the Extermination of Pagans

The divine command to exterminate from the face of the earth all men, women, and children belonging to the seven or eight nations of Canaan is one of the most frequently raised objections to seeing God as just and loving in the Old Testament. How can God's fairness and mercy be seen in such blanket and wholesale condemnation of entire nations?

All attempts to mitigate or tone down this command to totally wipe out the population are ruined on the clear instructions of texts like Exodus 23:32–33; 34:12–16; Deuteronomy 7:1–5; and 20:15–18. The presence of

---

[57]Hengstenberg, "Alleged Purloining," 429.

the term חֵרֶם,[58] in the sense of a "forced dedication," constantly was applied to the Canaanites and thus marked them for extermination.

Once again we are back to the question, "Will not the Judge of all the earth do right?" (Gen. 18:25) and "Does God pervert justice? Does the Almighty pervert what is right?" (Job 8:3). I believe the Old Testament does uphold the justice and righteousness of God even in this command to eradicate the Canaanites.

To place the whole question in perspective, let the principle of Deuteronomy 9:5 be cited:

> It is not because of your righteousness or your integrity that you are going in to take possession of their land; but on account of the wickedness of these nations, the LORD your God will drive them out before you, to accomplish what he swore to your fathers, to Abraham, Isaac and Jacob.

Therefore, there is no attempt to establish a tacit or real moral superiority of Israel, for the text informs us to the contrary in its explicit statements and narratives. The call of Yahweh cannot be traced to Israel's superiority in righteousness or numbers, "but it was because the LORD loved you and kept the oath which he swore to your forefathers" (Deut. 7:6–8).

Ronald Goetz, with some justification, wonders why it is, then, that ". . . Israel is helped *in spite* of her sins, while the Canaanites are destroyed *because* of theirs?"[59] The answer does not lie, as Goetz himself observes in the fact that Israel is vastly more righteous than the Canaanites, for that is indeed a semi-Pelagian Pharisaism; but it does lie in the increasing degrees of guilt that Canaan had accrued. Even Jesus appealed to this principle in dealing with a comparison of cities in his day as judged over against Sodom and Gomorrah (e.g., Matt. 10:15). There had been a patient waiting from Abraham's time "for the sin of the Amorites . . . [to reach] its full measure" (Gen. 15:16).

This is not to say that Israel was permitted or even ordered to treat all other nations the same way, for Deuteronomy 20:10–15 orders them to offer conditions of peace rather than extermination to all others. However, the verses that follow, namely verses 16–18, disallowed the same offer to be given to Canaan.[60] In fact, the Hebrew wars with other nations (except Canaan) were designed to be only in self-defense.

Why then were the Canaanites singled out for such severe treatment? They were cut off to prevent Israel and the rest of the world from

---

[58]See chapter 4 and our discussion of חֵרֶם there.

[59]Ronald Goetz, "Joshua, Calvin and Genocide," *Theology Today* 32 (1975): 266.

[60]See also Josephus, *Antiquities of the Jews* 4: 8:41.

being corrupted (Deut. 20:16–18). When a people starts to burn their children in honor of their gods (Lev. 18:21), practice sodomy, bestiality, and all sorts of loathsome vices (Lev. 18:23, 24; 20:3), the land itself begins to "vomit" them out as the body heaves under the load of internal poisons (Lev. 18:25, 27–30). Thus, "objection to the fate of these nations . . . is really an objection to the highest manifestation of the grace of God."[61] Greene likens this action on God's part, not to doing evil that good may come, but doing good in spite of certain evil consequences, just as a surgeon does not refrain from amputating a gangrenous limb even though in so doing he cannot help cutting off much healthy flesh.[62]

But there is more. Greene wisely observes that ". . . We may not object to God's doing immediately and personally what we do not object to His doing mediately, through providence. Now nothing is more certain than that providence is administered on the principle that individuals share in the life of the family and of the nation to which they belong; and that, consequently it is right that they should participate in its punishments as in its rewards. . . . Though many innocent persons could not but suffer, it was *right*, because of the relation in which they stood to the guilty, that this should be so."[63]

One more observation must be made here. Every forecast or prophecy of doom, like any prophetic word about the future except those few promises connected with the Noachic, Abrahamic, Davidic, and new covenants (which were unconditional and dependant solely on God's work of fulfillment), had a suppressed "unless" attached to them. At what moment that nation turns from its evil way and repents then at that time the Lord would relent and cease to bring the threatened harm (Jer. 18:7–10). Thus Canaan had, as it were, a final forty-year countdown as they heard of the events in Egypt, at the crossing of the Reed Sea, and what happened to the kings who opposed Israel along the way. We know they were aware of such events, for Rahab confessed that these same events had terrorized her city of Jericho and that she, as a result, had placed her faith in the God of the Hebrews (Josh. 2:10–14). Thus God waited for the "cup of iniquity" to fill up—and fill up it did without any signs of change in spite of the marvelous signs given so that the nations, along with Pharaoh and the Egyptians, "might know that He was the Lord."

The destruction of the Canaanites was on the same principle as the whole world was judged (except for eight persons) in the Deluge or the five cities of the plain (including Sodom and Gomorrah), or Pharaoh's army.

---

[61]Greene, *Classical Evangelical Essays*, 221.

[62]Greene, *Classical Evangelical Essays*, 221.

[63]Greene, *Classical Evangelical Essays*, 221–22. See also my discussion of "Corporate Solidarity" in chapter 4.

Usually those who object to these events are those who deny any compatibility of the doctrine of eternal destruction of the unrepentant wicked with the mercy and love of God. It is best to return to the above discussion of *pathos* and wrath in God to test our definitions.

SUMMARY

God's character and the acts he requires are fully consistent with everything that both testaments would lead us to expect in our God. The problem usually centers in a deficiency in our view of things and our ability to properly define terms or grasp the whole of the subject.

Chapter 17

The Morally Offensive Character
and Acts of Men and Women
in the Old Testament

Why does the Bible seem to hold up for emulation such heroes as Moses, David, and Solomon when it also frankly admits that each of their lives was anything but exemplary in at least one or more notable instances? It would appear that the Old Testament gives a divine endorsement to character and conduct that "our morally enlightened New Testament sensitivities" (isn't that the way we like to tell it?) could not approve. If David was a "man after God's own heart," why did he commit adultery? If Abraham is such a paragon of faith, why did he lie? The men and women God chose to represent him in the areas of politics and religion seem to be singularly poor choices. It is to such charges as these that we now turn in this chapter.

CHARGES AGAINST THE CHARACTER
OF OLD TESTAMENT MEN AND WOMEN

Perhaps no principle of moral hermeneutics is more important in placing a proper estimate on the normativeness of the character of Old Testament worthies than this: God's approbation of an individual must be strictly limited to *certain textually* specified characteristics. Or to put it in another way: divine approval of an individual in one aspect or area of his life does not entail and must not be extended to mean that there is a divine approval of that individual in all aspects of his character or conduct. Several examples of this extremely important principle may now be observed along with eight specific charges brought against these men and women.

They Were Liars

Various attempts have been made to extricate Abraham from the sin and guilt of lying. On two separate occasions he resorted to falsehood as a human expedient to save his beautiful wife from the clutches of lustful monarchs (Gen. 12:10–20; 20:2–18). Twice Abraham lied to Pharaoh and "Abimelech" (probably a title like "Pharaoh" for Philistine rulers) saying, "She [i.e., his wife, Sarah] is my sister" (Gen. 12:13; 20:2).

Now it is true that Sarah was his half-sister, and it is also true that in that culture it was sometimes possible to issue a "sistership contract" along with a marriage contract that then gave the wife greater protection.[1] But it is also obvious that neither of these two nuances were caught by either monarch, if that is what it had intended to produce. Both monarchs complained that they had not been adequately apprised that Sarah was indeed his wife. Thus, while Abraham mightily trusted God in leaving Ur (Gen. 12:1), in looking up at the stars and receiving the promise about a line of descendants as numerous as the heavenly bodies (Gen. 15:5–6), and in being willing to offer Isaac his son (Gen. 22), he certainly was not to be commended in his anxiety over his wife and the ruse he devised to protect her. The tragedy is that Abraham taught his son the same sin, which Isaac then used in Genesis 26:6–11. Again, we repeat with Greene, "Commendation of a character need not imply commendation of every element of the character."[2]

In chapter 14, we have already discussed the problem of defining truth or truth telling over against the "concealment" practiced by Samuel (1 Sam. 16:1–3). But we do not agree that the Hebrew midwives in Egypt (Exod. 1:17–21) or Rahab the harlot (Josh. 2:1–14; 6:25) qualify for this same exemption as we defended in that chapter.

The issue at stake in the case of the midwives and Rahab is whether God recognizes and approves of otherwise dubious methods that are alien to the integrity of his character in fulfilling the purpose of his will. Can strong faith coexist and be actuated by the infirmities of unbelief? It is true that Hebrews 11:31 includes Rahab as a woman of faith: "By faith the

---

[1]See Ephraim A. Speiser, "The Wife-Sister Motif in the Patriarchal Narratives," in *Biblical and Other Studies*, ed. A. Altmann. (Garden City, N.Y.: Doubleday, 1963); 15–28 and *idem, Genesis*, vol. 1 of *The Anchor Bible Commentary* (Garden City, N.Y.: Doubleday, 1964), 91–94.

[2]William Brenton Greene, Jr., "The Ethics of the OT" in *Classical Evangelical Essays in Old Testament Interpretation*, ed. W. C. Kaiser, Jr. (Grand Rapids: Baker, 1972), 213.

prostitute Rahab, because she welcomed the spies, was not killed with those who were disobedient." Likewise James 2:25: "Was not even Rahab the prostitute considered righteous for what she did when she gave lodging to the spies and sent them off in a different direction?"

But the areas of Rahab's faith must be strictly observed. It was not her lying that won her this divine recognition; rather it was her faith—she "believed in" the Lord God of the Hebrews and God's action in Israel's exodus more than she was "frightened" by the king of Jericho (Josh. 2:10–12). The evidence of her faith was seen in the works of receiving the spies and sending them out another way. Thus, she was well within the proprieties of biblical ethics, such as mirroring the holiness and character of God, when she hid the spies and took the legitimate precaution of sending them out another way. But her lying was an unnecessary accoutrement to both of the above approved responses. Her case is but another dramatic witness to the principle that divine approval of an individual in one situation is no guarantee of divine approval in any or all other areas. John Murray commented:

> It is strange theology that will insist that the approval of her faith and works in receiving the spies and helping them to escape must embrace the approval of *all* the actions associated with her praiseworthy conduct. And if it be objected that the preservation of the spies and the sequel of sending them out another way could not be accomplished apart from the untruth uttered and that the untruth is integral to the successful outcome of her action, there are three things to be borne in mind.
> (1) We are presuming too much in reference to the providence of God when we say that the untruth was indispensable to the successful outcome of her believing action.
> (2) Granting that, in the *de facto* providence of God, the untruth was one of the means through which the spies escaped, it does not follow that Rahab was morally justified in using this method. God can fulfill his holy, decretive will through our unholy acts.
> (3) . . . To justify the untruth because it is so closely bound up with the total result . . . is poor theology and worse theodicy.[3]

Doing evil that good may come may be good pragmatism, but cannot be squared with deontological ethics. Calvin, commenting on Joshua 2:4–6, is even more explicit:

> As to the falsehood, we must admit that though it was done for a good purpose, it was not free from fault. For those who hold what is called a dutiful lie (*mendacium officiosum*) to be altogether ex-

---

[3]John Murray, *Principles of Conduct* (Grand Rapids: Eerdmans, 1957), 138–39, 137.

cusable, do not sufficiently consider how precious truth is in the sight of God. Therefore, although our purpose be to assist our brethren, to consult for their safety and relieve them, it never can be lawful to lie, because that cannot be right which is contrary to the nature of God. And God is truth. And still the act of Rahab is not devoid of the praise of virtue, although it was not spotlessly pure. For it often happens that while the saints study to hold the right path, they deviate into circuitous courses.[4]

The case is not different with the midwives in Exodus 1:17–21. They too "feared God" and not the king of Egypt. They are praised for outright refusal to snuff out male infant lives. Their reverence for life reflected a reverence for God and so he built them into "houses" (בָּתִּים), permanent families in Israel. All of this is good and well.

But does the text give us warrant to speak an untruth under the proper conditions? The juxtaposition of the account of their lie to Pharaoh in Exodus 1:19 with the statement that God dealt well with them in verse 20 might appear to imply an endorsement of their lie. But this suspicion cannot be sustained in the text, for twice it attributes the reason for God's blessing them to the fact that they feared ("believed") God (vv. 17 and 21).

Others will suppose that we have here a case of partial truth, for "this assertion of the midwives was doubtless true in itself, although not the whole truth. . . . [It was a] withholding a part of the truth from those who would take advantage of the whole to injure or destroy the innocent [which George Bush argues] . . . is not only lawful but laudable."[5]

While we agree that Pharaoh has given up his right to know all the facts and that this could be a case of legitimate concealment of facts, just as in the case of Saul and Samuel (1 Sam. 16:1–3), we cannot agree that the midwives had any right to lie. Pharaoh does not deserve to know *all* the truth, but the midwives owe it to God to speak only the truth. If they truly had not made even one Hebrew male delivery during the months of Pharaoh's new program then their response was laudable and justified by Old Testament ethics. However, if they were partially true and partially telling a lie, they were just as blameworthy as Rahab, Abraham, Isaac, or Jacob were when they lied.

The requirement to tell the truth is no different with Elisha when he met the Syrian army outside of Dothan and, in response to a prayer addressed to God, they were all smitten with blindness. Elisha then approached them and said, "This is not the city. Follow me, and I will lead

---

[4]As cited by John Murray, *Principles of Conduct*, 139, n. 9.

[5]George Bush, *Notes on Exodus* (1852; reprint, Minneapolis: James and Klock, 1976), 20.

you to the man you are looking for" (2 Kings 6:19), and he led them to Samaria.[6]

Can this be an example of a legitimate so-called dutiful lie (*mendacium officiosum*)? I think not. Elisha was under no obligation to announce that he was the man they sought; he was under obligation to speak the truth. Apparently, he was outside the city of Dothan when he met them, so when he said, "this is not the city," he was no doubt correct. After all, how are we to know what he intended by that statement? A fair guess is that he meant it was not the city in which they would find the man they wanted. When he promised to lead them to the man they looked for, he carried through and was true to his word. Meaning or truth is not to be limited by the erroneous conceptions or temporary blindness of others—especially in times of war, but is to be dictated by all the facts and the verbal referents that are known by the one making the statement.

Some have, in this same vein of specious thinking, charged Joshua with *acting out* a lie or untruth when he feigned defeat a second time at Ai only to have some of his men rise up in ambush and set fire to the city in Joshua 8:3–29. But the LORD himself was party to this strategy (v. 18), as Murray points out. Then Murray makes this interesting comment, "The allegation that Joshua acted an untruth or a lie rests upon the fallacious assumption that to be truthful we must *under all circumstances* speak and act in terms of the data which came within the purview of others who may be concerned with or affected by our speaking or acting. This is not the criterion of truthfulness."[7] We, as speakers, cannot speak or act outside of a full consideration of all relevant facts and data known to us, but we are not held accountable or charged with falsehood if in an athletic contest or on a battlefield some cried "deception" because they failed in their responsibility to discover the real purpose of our actions.[8]

They Were Adulterers

In 1 Samuel 13:14, David is called a "man after his [God's] own heart." What, then, shall we say about his nefarious affair with Bathsheba? Are we somehow to legitimize his action?

The phrase, "a man after his [God's] own heart" is very similar to the one given on the eve of God's rejection of Eli and his family from being priests when Samuel was chosen: "I will raise up for myself a faithful priest, who will do according to what is in my heart" (1 Sam. 2:35). Thus, to do what is the will of God is to be a man after God's own heart.

---

[6]Murray, *Principles of Conduct*, 142–43.
[7]Murray, *Principles of Conduct*, 145.
[8]See chapter 14 and its discussion of deception.

However, this expression does not seem to be used with reference to a person's private or personal moral conduct; rather, it appears to be connected with the official duties of the office and the promotion of the worship and service of God from that office. In fact, only the numbering of the people in order to conduct an unauthorized conquest into foreign territory (2 Sam. 24) and his adulterous rendevous with Bathsheba (2 Sam. 11) are instances in which David appears to have neglected God. But after these experiences his conscience was extremely tender and his repentance was earnest and further evidence of a teachable spirit still warm towards God (Pss. 32 and 51).

They Were Murderers

The conduct of judge Ehud (Judg. 3:15–26), Jael (Judg. 4:17–20), and David's advice to Solomon concerning Joab and Shimei (1 Kings 2:5–8) would appear to indicate real character deficiencies, if not an outright Old Testament endorsement of assassinations.

But all of this assumes too much. Caution must always be exercised in moving from mere report or description to normative ethics. The fact of the matter in Ehud's case is that we must distinguish between Ehud's faith and Ehud's work. A. R. Fausset put it this way:

> Treacherous assassination is not a work emanating from the Spirit of God. Ehud's courage, patriotism and faith were accepted by God, but not what was defective in his action. . . . God employed Ehud to be Israel's deliverer and overruled his wrong act to carry out the divine purpose against Eglon. . . . In Ehud's instance, neither the principle nor the particular act was commanded by God. It was not said of Ehud, as it was of Othniel, that the "Spirit of Jehovah came upon him." Nor does Ehud appear among the examples of faith in Heb. xii.[9]

George Bush has an altogether different estimate of the moral character of this deed. Ehud's act, he argued, was to be vindicated on the grounds that God had raised him up as a deliverer for the country (v. 15). "How can we object to the way he did it so long as this task was accomplished? Have we not eulogized Brutus for stabbing Caesar and ridding the country of that tyrant?" asks Bush.[10]

But Bush too easily moves from authority for a task to legitimizing all the ways in which that job is accomplished. We cannot help but feel that Fausset presents much better evidence. Ehud is another case of the right

---

[9]A. R. Fausset, *A Critical and Expository Commentary on the Book of Judges* (1885; reprint, Minneapolis: James & Klock, 1977), 69.

[10]George Bush, *Notes on Judges* (1852; reprint, Minneapolis: James & Klock, 1976), 37–39.

man trying to do the right thing in the wrong way. The only possible way to view Ehud's act as ethical is to place it in a known state of war in which King Eglon would be susceptible to sneak attacks as were the people of Ai. But the text knows nothing about a state of war being declared between the two nations at this time—only an unbearable taxation system of tribute.

In the case of Jael, the nation was at war. Jael also was a relative by blood (the Kenites or Midianites were descended from Abraham) to the nation of Israel, now under attack by Jabin, king of the Canaanites in Hazor. Canaan was one of those nations that still lay under the divine indictment of extirpation.

Thus, almost in the sense of an avenger of the blood of a relative, Jael plans a stratagem that will vanquish the leader of the opposition. It is for this reason that she is eulogized as "most blessed of women" (Judg. 5:24).

> But from a moral standpoint, . . . at first glance it appears like the commendation of a base assassination, especially when one reads Judges 4:18–21 . . . [Shall we suppose] that in good faith she received Sisera and pledged him protection, but afterwards, while she saw him sleeping, God moved her to break her word and slay him? . . . The numerous manifestations of God, his frequent communications at that time with his agents, might suggest that Jael received a divine communication, but to consider her act otherwise morally wrong and to use this as a ground for its justification, is impossible. Right and wrong are as fixed and eternal as God, for they are of God, and for him to make moral wrong right is to deny himself.[11]

Jael's loyalty to Jehovah and to his people was her justification. It was part of the old command to exterminate the Canaanite (Deut. 20:16). The city of Meroz in Israel was cursed because it did not come to the assistance of Jehovah (Judg. 5:23), but Jael is blessed because she did.

The matter of Joab and Shimei is another issue (1 Kings 2:5–8). David found it often necessary to complain about the sons of Zeruiah being too strong for him and having too much military power to allow the punishment they (especially Joab) deserved on several occasions. To do so would endanger the peace of the kingdom and so for reasons of state it had to be deferred. Only when those reasons were removed was it propitious to proceed to punish the deliberate murderer Joab, as the law required. It should be noted that David does not require Solomon to put Joab to death, but only to deal wisely with this confirmed traitor and reckless autocrat.

David had granted Shimei a reprieve on his death sentence (com-

---

[11]Edward L. Curtis, "The Blessing of Jael," *The Old Testament Student* 4 (1884–85): 12–14.

pare 2 Sam. 19:23 with 1 Kings 2:8) but he warned Solomon to be careful, for Shimei would act to bring punishment on himself once again as events proved (1 Kings 2:40).

CHARGES AGAINST THE CONDUCT OF OLD TESTAMENT MEN AND WOMEN

The line of demarcation between character and conduct is not a hard and fast one, for the latter is but an expression of the former. Nevertheless, there are a number of acts that have attracted much criticism from those who see a lower ethical standard in the Old Testament than in the New Testament.

They Cursed Children

Few incidents in the Bible have called forth more criticism, consternation, and outright derision than the incident found in 2 Kings 2:23–25. As Robert Ingersoll loved to tell the story in his own style:

> . . . There was an old gentleman a little short of the article of hair. And as he was going through the town a number of little children cried out to him, "Go up, thou baldhead." And this man of God turned and cursed them. . . And two bears came out of the woods and tore in pieces forty-two children![12]

But there are several hermeneutical keys to unlocking the conundrums found in this text that has exasperated so many readers over the centuries.[13] The first is the identity of the persons involved: the so-called little children (נְעָרִים קְטַנִּים). That נַעַר (the singular form) has a wide range of usages is agreed by all; it includes everything from an "infant" (Exod. 2:6; 2 Sam. 12:16) to a mature Absalom in revolt against his father's kingdom (2 Sam. 14:21; 18:5) and a titulary for "servant, retainer" (2 Sam. 16:1), an "official" (2 Kings 19:6) or "soldier" (1 Kings 20:15–17; and Ugaritic texts). If the root is related to a South Arabic verb "to instigate rebellion," as Milton Fisher suggests, then "young toughs" or "teenage rowdies" may be as good a translation as any.[14] One point is clear: the possibility that these נְעָרִים קְטַנִּים were men in their twenties (as Isaac was in the story of his offering by Abraham in Gen. 22:12) or teens (as Joseph was in Gen. 37:2—"seventeen years old") is as good, if not a better translation, than "little children." The adjective, "little" (קְטַנִּים) appears to be

---

[12]Robert Ingersoll, *Ingersoll's 44 Lectures* (Chicago: J. Regan & Co., n.d.), 244.

[13]See the fine preliminary study of Richard G. Messner, "Elisha and the Bears," *Grace Journal* 3 (1962): 12–24.

[14]Milton Fisher, "נַעַר," *Theological Wordbook of the Old Testament* (Chicago: Moody, 1981), 2:585–86.

used here to indicate only a comparative degree of age rather than the size or tender years of the combatants. The same combination of words, קָטֹן נַעַר, is applied to Solomon after he began to reign when he was about twenty years old (1 Kings 3:7). The same words were applied to Hadad in 1 Kings 11:17, but he was old enough to flee the country and to marry Pharaoh's daughter! Therefore, it is fair to conclude that these were older boys or young men and not infants or toddlers.

The second surprise in this passage is that the prophet was not an old bald-headed, crotchety eccentric who had little or no patience for children because of his advanced age. If this incident at Bethel took place shortly after his ordination to the prophetic ministry by Elijah, Elisha could not have been more than twenty-five, for he lived almost sixty years after this event. As for his character, the woman at Shunem spoke highly of him to her husband saying, "I know that this man who often comes our way is a holy man of God" (2 Kings 4:9).

These rowdies hurled a word of insult at the prophet, "baldhead" (קֵרֵחַ). F. H. Wight remarked that "Baldness was scarce and suspicion of leprosy was often attached to it. Thus when the youths said of Elisha, 'Go up, thou bald head' (2 Kings 2:23); it [sic] was using an extreme curse, for the prophet being a young man, may not actually have been bald-headed."[15] But in addition to this epithet of bitter contempt, they jeered, "Go up, go up!" Could it not be, as Messner suggests, that these local toughs had decided to mock the translation of Elisha's companion in the fiery chariot by contemptuously urging him likewise to "blast off, blast off" (with my apologies for the anachronistic use of terms)? The verb contained in the taunt hurled at Elisha was precisely the same verb with which 2 Kings 2 began. It is more than likely that these young men reflected the low state of belief in Yahweh at this town renowned for its competing altar to the one in the temple in Jerusalem. Accordingly, the contempt and disbelief for anything and anyone connected with Yahweh was in keeping with the elevation of the concerns of the nation along with its own brand of civil religion over the claims of Yahwehism.

All this sets up the ethical problem. Did God's prophet really lose his temper? How did he "curse" these rowdies? "He cursed them (וַיְקַלְלֵם) in the name of the LORD (Yahweh)." While the term קֵלֵל can mean to "revile" and worse, it can also mean "to pronounce a judgment." Since "vengeance and recompense" belong to God alone (Deut. 32:35), Elisha did not utter a string of blue words, use profanity, or verbally assault these young men; instead he pronounced in the name of the LORD the threat-

---

[15]F. H. Wight, *Manners and Customs of Bible Lands* (Chicago: Moody, 1953), 96 as cited by Messner, "Elisha and Bears," 18.

ened judgment already known to all from Leviticus 26:21–22: "If you remain hostile toward me and refuse to listen to me, I will multiply your afflictions seven times over, as your sins deserve. I will send wild animals against you, and they will rob you of your children. . . ." Thus, Elisha only invoked God's judgment—and not out of regard for his own person or rights, but out of concern for the honor of God and his word!

It was not Elisha who brought the bears, nor even God, but the sins of this center of Baal worship and the worship of the calves of Jeroboam. As Richard Messner put it:

> This was a judgment designed to wake the people up, lest a worse disaster befall them. A loving God always warns, and pleads before his wrath descends. These blasphemous youths were the direct ancestors of a generation which was swept into captivity because of its abominable sins in the sight of the Lord, not withstanding the repeated admonitions of His prophets. [16]

It is also a serious matter to scoff at God's prophets, for to deride them is to mock God and the office and mission that he has ordained them to carry out. In 2 Chronicles 36:16 ". . . They mocked God's messengers, despised his words and scoffed at his prophets until the wrath of the LORD was aroused against his people and there was no remedy."

The two bears were not mentioned at all by Elisha in his pronouncement of judgment. He only called on the Lord's name. The mangling of the forty-two toughs was a reminder to the people who had tended to disbelieve the promises and positive ordinances of the law that the law was still true, even if they could only witness that fact in the judgments of the law.

They Married Harlots

Many readers of Scripture are shocked to read that the prophet Hosea was commanded by God to "take to yourself an adulterous wife" (Hos. 1:2). Hosea's marriage has been explained as everything from a vision or an allegory to an historical event.

In spite of some very prestigious names behind the view that portrays this command simply as an internal vision, such as C. F. Keil, E. W. Hengstenberg, and the Jewish interpreters—Maimonites, Eben Ezra, and Kimchi, it overlooks the fact that the object of the marriage was to beget children with significant names. This view also usually fails to see that the woman in Hosea 3 is the same Gomer mentioned in Hosea 1.

Neither is the allegorical interpretation of Calvin, Luther, Oslander, van Hoonacker, and Gressmann anymore helpful. The name

---

[16]Messner, "Elisha and Bears," 22.

"Gomer-bath-Diblaim" has no allegorical relevance and this view also overlooks the differences between chapter 2 and Hosea 1 and 3.

The depth of feeling and the whole point of the analogy drawn between God's adulterous bride, Israel and Hosea's wayward wife is best explained by a real rather than by a mental or symbolic experience. However, even for those who accept the historical view, there are wide differences of opinion on the meaning of "go, take to yourself an adulterous wife and children of unfaithfulness" (Hos. 1:2). For example, Thomas Aquinas thought Gomer was Hosea's concubine while Laetsch argued that Gomer was a harlot when Hosea married her. However, neither one of the views is compatible with previous divine directives. Concubinage was practiced by some Old Testament worthies, but it certainly was never condoned by God; this would be the only exception if it proved true. Furthermore, priests were forbidden by law to marry harlots (Lev. 21:1, 7, 13; and later in Ezek. 44:22). If it were immoral for priests to do so, it could not be any less wrong for Israel's prophets to do so as well.

Preference should probably be given to that historical view that argues that Gomer was *not* a harlot when Hosea was instructed to marry her. The telltale sign that signals to us that this is the case is the figure of speech known as zeugma, which occurs when one verb is joined to two objects while grammatically referring strictly only to one of them.[17] The verbs "go to and to take to yourself" are the Hebrew idiom for getting married (Gen. 4:19; 6:2; 19:14; Exod 21:10; 34:16; 1 Sam. 25:43) and strictly apply only to the wife and not to the children. There is an ellipsis of a third verb that must be supplied from the noun, namely, "and *beget* children of harlotry."[18] But the very fact that the text plainly says that "she bore to him a son" (Hos. 1:3) and that he named all three children (1:4, 6, 9—a right reserved for their real father), argues for the fact that the children gained the odious title, "children of unfaithfulness," subsequent to their births because of their mother's nefarious conduct. If this reasoning is correct (and we cannot see what other alternative exists in light of the clearest statements of the text, especially with the first of the three children), then is it not equally true that their mother is given the same designation by way of compressing and condensing into a single statement both God's original order and Gomer's subsequent character?

This type of construction where the result is put for what appears to be the purpose is not unknown in Israel. E. S. P. Heavenor pointed to Isaiah 6:9–12 where it looked as if Isaiah would preach *in order to* blind

---

[17]See E. W. Bullinger, *Figures of Speech Used in the Bible* (1898; reprint, Grand Rapids: Baker, 1968), 131–36 (cf. Gen. 4:20 and 1 Tim. 4:3).

[18]Bullinger, *Figures*, 57.

the people, but this was only to be the *result* rather than the purpose of his preaching.[19] The same phenomena exists in Jesus' use of parables (Mark 4:11–12) and the references to the hardening of Pharaoh's heart (Exod. 10:1; 11:10; 14:4).

Thus, we conclude that Gomer's children were not born out of wedlock or from adulterous unions. Nor is it possible that Hosea could have known that she even had a bent or predisposition towards such sexual promiscuity, for if he married with the full knowledge that she had previously been immoral what right had he to complain or issue a divorce? Rather, what was not known or evidenced before the marriage or during her childbearing years became visible as the marriage went on[20] and Hosea, reflecting on the total impact that this event had on his life and ministry as he wrote many years later on, combined God's original command with words that most adequately described what his bride became into one statement and wrote, "go, take to yourself an adulterous wife and children of unfaithfulness." But all of this came about as a result of his wife's sin, and it was *not* part of God's purpose that Hosea should marry a girl who had a known history of immorality.

It was this same woman that the Lord told him "Go, show your love to your wife again (Hebrew עוֹד goes with the verb "go" and not with "Yahweh said" as the Hebrew system of conjunctive and disjunctive accents, the LXX, Syriac, Vulgate, and numerous commentators correctly suggest), "though she is loved by another and is an adulteress." No wonder, then, Hosea exhibits the "heart and holiness of God." It is truly God's book of love for undeserving people in the Old Testament.

They Committed Incest

Not many will stumble at the immorality arranged by Lot's two daughters with their father in Genesis 19:30–38, but I will never forget the earnest, but grossly misled Bible reader who vigorously argued that his living carnally with his daughters was recommended by the Bible in Lot's example!

However, the solution is simply to distinguish between what the Bible records and what it teaches. Certainly the actions of Lot's two daughters is culpable and at the opposite end of the scale of holiness encouraged

---

[19]E. S. P. Heavenor, "Hosea, Book of," *The New Bible Dictionary*, ed. J. D. Douglas (London: Inter-Varsity, 1962), 540–41.

[20]Agreeing with this are the views of Francis I. Andersen and David Noel Freedman, *Hosea*, vol. 24 of *The Anchor Bible Commentary* (Garden City, N.Y.: Doubleday, 1980), 116. "The implication is that the illicit activity of the woman chosen by the prophet only commenced after the marriage was consummated. The injunction was proleptic in nature, its full content not realized until years later with the deterioration and effectual collapse of the marriage relationship."

in the Bible. While it is true, as my objector repeatedly pointed out, that neither the Old Testament nor the New Testament specifically said any-where, "Lot was wrong and he sinned" or "Dear reader, 'what do you think of this? Isn't this awful?'" contextual faithfulness requires such judg-ments. The Bible does not pause to moralize at every step along the way. It assumes that discernment without being pedantic and insulting to the reader's intelligence.

They Were Often Totally Lawless

So lawless were the times of the judges in Israel that the book itself explicitly drew attention to this fact, "In those days Israel had no king; everyone did as he saw fit" (Judg. 17:6; 18:1; 19:1; 21:25).

Especially obnoxious are the chapters in the so-called appendix to the Judges narratives, chapters 18, 19, 20, and 21. Everything is wrong in these chapters. To read these narratives with understanding, one must constantly shake his or her head in amazement at such horrible events. No one respects any law including the idol-making Micah (Judg. 18), the status-seeking Levite who stole the idols and moved on to a larger congregation (Judg. 18), the bigamous Levite (Judg. 19), or the lying tribes of Israel who grieved over the near demise of the tribe of Benjamin (Judg. 21). But in no way are the actions of the judges and their times recorded in the Scripture to serve as our example. The hallmark of that day, the book regretfully notes, is anarchy; holiness has been replaced by self-indulgence, except for the small glimmer of light seen in the Book of Ruth that probably takes place during the days of the Midianite invasions and the judge Gideon.

Gideon had tried to set the record straight by urging the people to adopt the stance that "the Lord will rule over us" (Judg. 8:23), but they opted instead for Gideon's son, Abimelech, and the consequences were tragic both for Abimelech and the men of Shechem and its villages (Judg. 9–10).

Here again is another excellent illustration of the need to dis-tinguish between what the Bible records and what it teaches.

They Sought Revenge

Samuel's action in hewing Agag, the king of the Amalekites, into pieces (1 Sam. 15:33) or David's delivering over seven of Saul's descend-ants to the Gibeonites (2 Sam. 21:2, 8) are often represented as examples of Old Testament saints unnecessarily seeking revenge on others.

Neither of these two situations had any reference whatever to sacri-fices. Agag was put to death as a criminal and not to placate anyone's emotions or personal hostilities.

The seven descendants of Saul, who were partly the children of a concubine and partly of a daughter of Saul were not aspirants or pretenders to the throne of David; therefore, David cannot be suspected in any way of trying to use the occasion to eliminate their candidacy. Neither must it be imagined that David delivered them up, the innocent for the guilty, in contradiction to the demands of the law (Deut. 24:16).

Of course, the phenomena of corporate solidarity (as discussed in chapter 3 above) must be seen as part of the explanation. But it may also be true that these seven men were punished with death not only because of their linkage with the life and action of their kinsman Saul, but also because they were involved with Saul as accomplices in the atrocities committed against the Gibeonites and had remained unpunished as yet.

One matter is clear, there is no vendetta or revenge in David's action. The Old Testament did not authorize men to strike back tit for tat or to take an eye for an eye or tooth for tooth. This *lex talionis*, or "law of the tooth" was a stereotype formula to guide the judges and not an excuse for settling private grudges (as we have explained in chapters 4 and 6).

In almost every one of the cases discussed in this chapter, the principle came down to this: commendation of a person or notable action need not imply commendation of every element of the men and women cited in the Old Testament. And along with that principle another must be noted: reporting or narrating an event in Scripture is not to be equated with approving, recommending, or making that action or characteristic normative for emulation by all subsequent readers. We must constantly distinguish, on the basis of explicit statements, and the immediate and larger contexts, between what the Bible teaches and what it merely, but sadly, must report in order to describe how far the people of God departed from the standard of the holiness of his person and the encouragements of his law.

Chapter 18

The Morally Offensive Precepts and Sanctions in the Law of God

Even when it would appear that God's character and actions can, on certain careful exegetical grounds already laid out, be extricated from charges of being unethical, there still remain two other areas requiring some further discussion than what has already been provided above: (1) the alleged deficient Old Testament views on women, slavery, and Hebrew favoritism; and (2) the alleged severity of such sanctions as Psalms of cursing, the death penalty, and the *talion*. Each of these can be successfully defended apart from any dogmatic or sectarian predispositions.

The charge on the first is that the Old Testament principle of brotherhood is at best very partial and given only an inconsistent treatment. In fact, some of these precepts are in direct conflict with the teachings and legitimate inferences that may be drawn from the New Testament. The charge against the second is that the sanctions or punishments demanded by the Old Testament are mercenary and, therefore, inferior if not immoral and repugnant to men and women of more noble thinking and generosity. However, both of these charges are lodged too facilely and are the result of grossly inadequate generalization, over-dependence on secondary sources and scholarship, or subjective reconstructions that are guilty of making the wish parent to the thought. In order to demonstrate that these two charges are improper, we will investigate seven of these areas that extend the exegetical groundwork already laid in the preceding chapters.

284

CHARGES OF OFFENSIVE PRECEPTS

There are three Old Testament areas that are usually singled out as deep violations of the high morality and Christian estimate of personhood: the Old Testament view of women, slaves, and the place and status of the Jewish nation as a "peculiar people" or "people for a possession," "a moveable treasure." Each is worthy of separate consideration.

Old Testament View of Women

Already in chapter 12 we have dealt extensively with some of the key texts that raised the question of the status of women as they were involved in marriage, but what of the testament's overall view of all women, single and married?[1]

If we may judge from the creation narrative, woman is an integral part of man; men and women belong to one whole with both being equally valued since both were declared to be in the image and likeness of God. The gallery of Old Testament women who achieved fame and distinction as prophetesses, judges, diplomats, or heroines include such names as Sarah, Rebekah, Miriam, Hannah, Abigail, the wise woman of Tekoa, the wise woman of Abel, Rizpah, the Shulammite, Huldah, and Anna. Their presence in the socio-economic life of the nation receives its fullest treatment in Proverbs 31 where the "good-wife" or "virtuous woman" independently enters into various real-estate ventures (Prov. 31:16) and maintains a cottage industry of the manufacture and sale of linen garments (v. 24)—all this with the evident approval of the text! While there are not many Old Testament examples of women in the economic world acting on their own, even though they are married, the New Testament notes that Ananias and Sapphira, his wife, both sold property (Acts 5:1); Lydia of Thyatira sold purple goods (Acts 16:14); and Aquila and his wife Priscilla were both tentmakers as was Paul (Acts 18:2–3). It is true that the second-century writer of Ecclesiasticus, Ben Sirach, only named men to his list of the nation's "distinguished men" (Ecclus. 44:1–50:29), but he could at least have included the judge and military strategist and leader, Deborah (Judg. 5); the king-maker, Bathsheba (1 Kings 1:11ff.); and the exceptional role played in politics by the mothers of the Judean and Israelite kings.

To women also belonged equal "rights" in worship and ritual. They participated fully in the religious activities centering first around the tabernacle and then around the temple. Undoubtedly they were included in the words "the whole community of Israel" (Exod. 12:3) who kept the three great festivals of Passover, Pentecost, and Feast of Tabernacles. In fact, in

---

[1]The literature on women in the OT is plentiful. See footnote 59 in chapter 12 for this bibliography.

the last named feast, Deuteronomy 16:14 specifically names a man's daughter, his maidservant, and widows as being among those who should participate.

Another religious right was the vow. The law on the Nazirite vow in Numbers 6:2–21 is introduced with specific reference to "a man or a woman" (v. 2). It is not unthinkable, then, that the legislation on the ordinary vow (Num. 15:1–16) should include women even though it is addressed in a general way to men without direct mention of women. This should also warn us about being overly restrictive when legislation fails to mention women; it may indeed only be a generic use of man and not a sexual limitation. That this is the case in this particular law is further confirmed by the fact that 1 Samuel 1:11 has Hannah making an ordinary vow that assumes that the legislation of Numbers 15 and 30:3–15 are regulating the same. These vows, according to Leviticus 27:1–25 could consist of offering service at the tabernacle of: (1) persons, (2) cattle, (3) houses, and (4) fields. The right of a husband or father to annul a vow made by his wife or daughter must not be viewed as another evidence of women being nonpersons or inferior to a male dominated society in the Old Testament, but as an evidence of a lack of any collateral to back the vow. Those women who had absolute control over their property, such as widows or divorced women, could vow it away as they wished (Num. 30:9). Only those who had no property under their own control would need their husband or father's backing (or refusal to stand behind the vow). But this in no wise obligated the woman to consult her husband or father before making the vow. Neither did it compel her to depend on the male intelligence for the formulation of these vows. As Katherine Bushnell observed, "The real object, then, of these statutes, is to *provide a proper time* when the one *who controlled* the family property might show reason why he objected to relinquishing that control to the extent that daughter or wife might make a suitable offering."[2]

Women might also participate in prayer as the example of Hannah praying in the sanctuary demonstrates (1 Sam. 1:10ff.; 2:1) or Rebekah who "went to inquire of the LORD" (Gen. 25:22). In fact, this free approach to God had the reverse pattern; there are more than a few illustrations of theophanies to women. The Angel of the Lord appeared to Sarah's maid, Hagar (Gen. 16:8–14), to Abraham and Sarah (Gen. 18:9–15), to Hagar again (Gen. 21:17–20), and to Samson's mother (Judg. 13:3–7).

It is the Book of Proverbs that sets forth women as persons of intelligence and will who are no mere chattel nor simply sexual objects.

---

[2]Katherine C. Bushnell, *God's Word to Women* (1923; reprint, Ray B. Munson, Jacksonville, Fla., n.d.), paragraph 185.

Only in one passage, Proverbs 5:15–19 is the wife described as a sexual partner. Elsewhere in the book she is portrayed as a teacher ranked alongside her husband, delighting together in the son they have taught to be wise. She is a manager of the household having the oversight of her own cottage industries, real-estate business ventures, and the servants. Her opposite is the "loose woman" who is the epitomy of "folly." The bad wife has one especially annoying trait: contentiousness. A contentious woman is likened to a "constant dripping on a rainy day" (Prov. 19:13; 27:15). But the antithesis to all of this is "wisdom," which interestingly enough, is depicted as a woman. Thus, instead of femaleness being the essence of lowliness and nothingness, it turns out that God has chosen womanhood to concretely represent the height of living: wisdom—God's antidote to folly and the wasted life!

Only three passages would appear to spread a derogatory note over the position and role of women in the Old Testament: the woman's part in the fall (Gen. 3), the law that assigned twice as long a period of uncleanness after the birth of a female as a male child (Lev. 12:2–5) and the Preacher's estimate that "I found one upright man among a thousand, but not one upright woman among them all" (Eccl. 7:28).

But in the first passage, surely the man turns out to be just as culpable as the woman, hence the only distinction that can be raised is that she was subjected to more pressure and trickery than he was (1 Tim. 2:14, "Adam was not the one deceived; it was the woman who was deceived"). The second objection we have already met in chapter 12 above. To this may be added the comments of Solomon Zucrow:

> The inference modern writers draw from the Biblical law, that the period of uncleanness after the birth of a female is twice as long as that after the birth of a male because of some innate impurity in the female has no basis at all. From this very law itself, as a matter of fact, the opposite can equally well be inferred, for it further enjoins that after the days of purification have passed the woman should be considered in a state of purity for a certain period and in the case of a female child this period is twice as long as that in the case of a male child. The fact is that we do not know the reasons for such laws and the reasons for this law may be, as the famous commentator and philosopher Iben Ezra said: "That the period of uncleanness and purity after the birth of a female and male child is to correspond with the time of the formation of the respective embryo, which, according to ancient belief, takes twice as long in the case of a female as in that of a male."[3]

---

[3]Solomon Zucrow, *Women, Slaves and the Ignorant in Rabbinic Literature* (Boston: Stratford, 1932), 25.

As for the allusion to Ecclesiastes 9:28, I must confess a certain amount of puzzlement. I doubt if it is possible to pass off this judgment as the ill-informed view of a misogynist. If Solomon is the author of this statement—and he may well be that—then we can hardly accuse him of being a woman hater. His problem seems to lay in another area. Nor does he seem to reflect any kind of chauvinism in Proverbs 12:4; 14:1; and 18:22. If wisdom was what he sought, then his point, in hyperbolic form ("not one in a thousand") is that few if any act as they ought (Eccl. 7:28) and not one woman (lady wisdom?) was among one of them?[4]

An Old Testament biblical theology of womanhood does not reflect all the fullness of a Pauline "there is neither . . . male nor female" (Gal. 3:28), but neither does it regard women in the same category as a man's donkey or his ox. Man and woman in the Old Testament exhibit both their equality, complementariness, and spheres of authority.

Old Testament View of Slavery

The law[5] recognized basically two types of slaves: the Hebrew bondsman and the foreign prisoner of war. In the postexilic historical books of Ezra and Nehemiah there is also a third type known as the נְתִינִים (*Nethinim*).

The origins and status of this third type cannot be traced, but Ezra 8:20 informs us that they were those whom "David and the officials had established to assist the Levites." The term נְתִינִים appears in the Pentateuch (Num. 3:9) referring to the Levites who were subordinate to the priests. It would appear then that "just as the Levites never became mere chattels to the priests, so these *Nethinim* never became real serfs. . . . Rather they were incorporated in the clerical order forming a part of the personnel attached to the temple. The difference between them and the Levites was only in degree: just as the Levites were inferior to the priests, so the *Nethinim* were inferior to the Levites."[6] They resided in Ophel (Neh. 3:26), a site close to the royal palace, and were immune from taxation like the priests and Levites (Neh. 7:73) and agreed "to walk in God's laws" (including refusing to intermarry with the gentiles in the land (Neh. 10:29–30).

The same kind treatment was accorded the Hebrew slave. No Israelite could be held against his or her will in a permanent state of servitude. Ordinarily a Hebrew could only be indentured for a maximum of six years. Since the land could not be sold but had to remain in the family perma-

---

[4]See Walter C. Kaiser, Jr., *Ecclesiastes: Total Life* (Chicago: Moody, 1979), 87–88.
[5]See chapter 6 for an exegetical discussion of these issues.
[6]Zucrow, *Women, Slaves*, 162.

nently, the only recourse that a Hebrew had for borrowing money was to sell his or her labor for up to six years.

Even when thousands of Judean prisoners fell into the hands of the Northern Israelite king, the prophet Oded warned that God's "fierce anger" would be upon them if they did not immediately release these prisoners whom they had proposed to retain for bondsmen and bondswomen. So the people "clothed all who were naked. They provided them with clothes and sandals, food and drink, and healing balm. All those who were weak they put on donkeys. So they took them back to their fellow countrymen at Jericho" (2 Chron. 28:8–16).

The result of Oded's appeal to a spirit of justice and equity was repeated during Nebuchadnezzar's seige of Jerusalem, when the people of God could think of no act of greater remorse and repentance than to release all Hebrew slaves. However, as soon as the threatened danger was removed, the people immediately pressed the burden back on those same slaves in spite of Jeremiah's censure. Therefore, he thundered: "You have not obeyed me; you have not proclaimed freedom for your fellow countrymen. So I now proclaim 'freedom' for you, declares the LORD—'freedom' to fall by the sword, plague and famine" (Jer. 34:8–18).

The last reference to any Jews being taken into slavery is the noble act of Jews redeeming those Hebrews who were carried off into Babylon and which Nehemiah held up as a great example to those who were causing economic slavery by high interest rates in Nehemiah 5:1–14. The slavery of Hebrews came to an end and there is no reference in postbiblical literature to any type of Hebrew slaves.

But what about the status of non-Hebrew slaves? Captives taken in a war had to be dealt with in some manner and so Israel chose permanent slavery (Lev. 25:46) rather than death as their way of punishing these captives. But this did not mean that their Hebrew masters had absolute power of life and death over the slaves. According to biblical law, a master could lose his life if he killed his slave. If he merely inflicted bodily injury on his slave, such as knocking out a tooth or injuring an eye, the slave immediately won his full emancipation (Exod. 21:20, 26). The foreign slave, along with the Hebrew household also had a day of rest each week (Exod. 20:10; Deut. 5:14).

A female captive who was married by her captor could not be sold again as a slave, and if her master, now her husband, grew to hate her, she too had to be liberated and was a free person (Deut. 21:14). Even marriage between slaves was recognized as sacred as that between free persons, and any violation of that covenant by another man, free or not, even while that slave was only engaged to another, was a sin requiring a guilt offering (Lev. 19:20–22).

Masters were urged to be lenient with their slaves and to restrain their anger even when they overheard them cursing them (Eccl. 7:22). Yet, for all its magnanimity, there was still an underlying repugnance for the evils associated with this institution. Deuteronomy 23:15–16 counselled: "If a slave has taken refuge with you, do not hand him over to his master. Let him live among you wherever he likes and in whatever town he chooses. Do not oppress him." Likewise Job asked, in that marvelous chapter of ethical insights that easily rivals many of the high standards of the New Testament:

> If I have denied justice to my menservants and maidservants
>   when they had a grievance against me,
> what will I do when God confronts me?
>   What will I answer when called to account?
> Did not he who made me in the womb make them?
>   Did not the same one form us both within our mothers?
>   (Job 31:13–15)

Philo Judaeus drew from this text the conclusion "That the very institution of slavery was the greatest of evils."[7] Philo observed that the Essenes, a Jewish religious sect from 150 B.C. that is often connected with the Dead Sea Scrolls and Qumran, detested slavery and prohibited any of its members from holding slaves.

Old Testament View of Particularismus (Hebrew Favoritism)

One of the most persistent charges brought against the morality and ethics of the Old Testament is its alleged partiality or particularism. Even though the English Deists brought this charge into prominence, it was Immanuel Kant who put it into its crudest form:

> So far from Judaism forming an epoch belonging to the universal Church, or being itself this universal Church, it rather excluded the whole human race from its fellowship, as a peculiar people chosen by Jehovah for himself, which bore ill-will to all other nations, and was regarded with ill-will by them in return.[8]

The best apology for the alleged particularism in the Old Testament lies in a straightforward presentation of God's relationship to Israel and the nations in the Old Testament. Two facts may be given to head the list: (1) the God of the Old Testament is the Creator, Lord, and Redeemer of the heavens and the earth, and (2) this God, made all peoples in his own

---

[7]The statement is Zucrow, *Women, Slaves*, 160.

[8]As cited by E. W. Hengstenberg, *Dissertations on the Genuineness of the Pentateuch*, trans. J. E. Ryland (Edinburgh: T. & T. Clark, 1847), 2:453.

image. Thus, one God must at all times and in all places be no less the God of the Gentiles than of the Jews even as Paul argued in Romans 3:29–30.

It is with the call of Abraham that particularism makes its first appearance, for Genesis 1–11 is certainly universal in its scope and outlook. But this charge is only to mistake the nature, ground, and aim of the call of Abraham. The universalism of Genesis 1–11 not only preceded Abraham's call, but is logically connected with it and accompanies the call. His blessing is for the purpose and the result of being the means by which "all peoples on earth" (the seventy nations just mentioned in Genesis 10) will be likewise blessed by God. Paul labelled this process and message nothing less than the "gospel" itself in Galatians 3:8.

Whatever is true about a temporary withdrawal of God from the nations at large when he called Abraham must be charged not to an action originating in God, but in the nations and their own falling away from the message given to their ancestors since Adam's day. Still there was a residual piety left, a "fear of God" (יִרְאַת אֱלֹהִים).

God is no less concerned about the heathen nations than he is for Israel. His work on their behalf is noted in driving out and dispossessing people whose wickedness merited it (e.g., the Rephaim and Horites in Deut. 2:21–22) in order to turn it over as an inheritance to the Ammonites and Edomites, just as he drove out the Canaanites for Israel. He also was active in leading other exoduses besides Israel's exodus from Egypt, for example, the Syrians from Kir, the Philistines from Caphtor, and the Ethiopians (Amos 9:7).

Then too, the high regard for all mankind was clearly taught in the Old Testament. Accordingly, Israelites were forbidden to oppress strangers (Exod. 23:9) and were ordered to treat them kindly (Lev. 19:33), for God himself loved these foreigners (Deut. 10:18). A curse is pronounced on the one who perverted justice for a stranger (Deut. 27:19; cf. Exod. 22:21; Deut. 24:17). Israel was told, "You and the alien shall be the same before the LORD" (Num. 15:15). The eschatological vision of the prophets was that all nations would say, "Come, and let us go up to the mountain of the LORD, to the house of the God of Jacob" (Mic. 4:2), for "[God's] house will be called a house of prayer for all nations" (Isa. 56:7). That had been Solomon's prayer request as he dedicated the temple (1 Kings 8:41–43). These, and many similar injunctions, show how false the accusation is that asserts that the God of Israel and his people conducted themselves towards the heathen in an exclusive and repulsive manner.

Instead of hate and indifference, there is an announcement of a call to the Gentiles to "Rejoice, O nations, with his people, for he will avenge the blood of his servants" (Deut. 32:43). The same call went out in many of the Psalms. Psalm 67 invited all the nations to sing and praise God for he had blessed them and Israel in his great plan of redemption.[9] No less joyful and universal in its outlook is Psalm 117. The apostle Paul perceived this same emphasis in Romans 15:1, 9–12 as he strung together these and other texts while demonstrating that the promise was given to the patriarchs *in order that* the nations at large might also become the recipients of the same grace of God. Anything less than this is reductionistic from a strict New Testament point of view.

Hengstenberg's concluding observation clinches the point:

> An infallible mark of absolute Particularism, is the externality of conditions with which the reception of the blessings of the Divine favor were connected. . . . But, who does not perceive that the exact opposite to this mark is found in the Pentateuch? Those who did not serve the Lord from the heart, were not merely excluded from his blessing, but a curse also blighted on them, the greatness of which corresponded exactly to that of the grace offered to them. Let any one only read Lev. xxvi., Deut. xxviii., xxxii., and judge whether on a soil which produced such threatenings against the mere carnal descendants of Abraham, a carnal Particularism could flourish.[10]

CHARGES OF OFFENSIVE SANCTIONS

Beside the offending precepts there were judgments, and in one case the opposite problem of rewards that caused difficulties for readers of the Old Testament. Each of these have been briefly presented in the preceding discussion, but we must now look at the whole issue involved in each.

Old Testament View of Imprecation

Included in the Psalter are prayers that appeal to God to pour out his wrath and judgment on the psalmist's enemies.[11] These psalms are

---

[9]For a more extensive treatment, see W. C. Kaiser, Jr., "Israel's Missionary Call," in *Perspectives on the World Christian Movement: A Reader*, eds. Ralph Winter and Steven C. Hawthorne (Pasadena: William Carey Library, 1981), 25–33, especially pp. 31–33.

[10]Hengstenberg, *Dissertations on Pentateuch*, 2:459–60.

[11]A few key bibliographic items include: Chalmers Martin, "The Imprecations in the Psalms," *Princeton Theological Review*, I (1903): 537–53; C. S. Lewis, "The Cursings" in *Reflections on the Psalms* (New York: Harcourt, Brace, 1958), 20–33; Johannes Vos, "The Ethical Problem of the Imprecatory Psalms," *Westminster Theological Journal*, 4 (1942): 23–38; J. Carl Laney, "A Fresh Look at the Imprecatory Psalms," *Bibliotheca Sacra* 138 (1981): 35–45; Roy B. Zuck, "The Problem of the Imprecatory Psalms" (Th.M. Thesis, Dallas Theological Seminary, 1957). B. B. Edwards, "The Imprecations in the Scriptures," *Bibliotheca Sacra* (1844): 97–110; Howard Osgood, "Dashing the Little Ones Against the

commonly classified as "imprecatory psalms" because of this element that is contained in the psalm, even if it is only a single verse. The difficulty this creates for some Old Testament readers is immense.

> Perhaps there is no part of the Bible that gives more perplexity and pain to its readers than this; perhaps nothing that constitutes a more plausible objection to the belief that the psalms are the productions of inspired men than the spirit of revenge which they sometimes seem to breathe and the spirit of cherished malice and implacableness which the writer's seem to manifest.[12]

The ethical issue at stake here is best posed by Johannes Vos: "How can it be right to wish or pray for the destruction or doom of others as is done in the Imprecatory Psalms? . . . Is it right for a Christian to use the Imprecatory Psalms in the worship of God, and if so, in what sense can he make the language of these Psalms his own?"[13]

Of the hundred and fifty Psalms in the Psalter, only three Psalms may be classified as mainly or totally imprecatory Psalms, namely, Psalms 35, 69, and 109. It must also be noted that except for the more frequently quoted Messianic Psalms (Pss. 1, 22, 110, and 118) these three Psalms of almost total imprecation are the next most frequently quoted Psalms in the New Testament. Using the figures of Chalmers Martin, there are only fifteen other Psalms that have any element of imprecation in them, and, in most of these, that element is often limited to a single line or a single verse. Together, all eighteen Psalms have three hundred and sixty-eight verses, of which only sixty-five include any element of imprecation. Even in the three main imprecatory Psalms, only twenty-three verses out of a total of ninety-five could be called verses with an element of imprecation in them.[14]

The real question, of course, is not the amount, but the substance and explanation of this material. As for some samples, we can quote the following:

> Break the arm of the wicked and evil man;
> call him to account for his wickedness (Ps. 10:15)

Rock," *Princeton Theological Review*, 1 (1903): 23–37; J. W. Beardslee, "The Imprecatory Element in the Psalms," *Presbyterian and Reformed Review* 8 (1897): 490–505.

   [12]Albert Barnes, *Notes, Critical, Explanatory and Practical on the Book of Psalms* (London: Blackie & Son, 1968) 1:xxv–xxvi as cited by J. Carl Laney, "Imprecatory Psalms," 35.

   [13]Vos, "Ethical Problems," 124.

   [14]Martin, "Imprecation," 537. Opinions vary as to the number and identity of the imprecatory Psalms. Laney, "Imprecatory Psalms" (p. 36) identifies "at least these nine": Psalms 7, 35, 58, 59, 69, 83, 109, 137, and 139. Chalmers Martin never identifies his eighteen candidates, but judging from his citations, they would include: Psalms 5, 10, 28, 31, 35, 40, 58, 69, 70, 71, 109, and 140. Vos, "Ethical Problems" (p. 123) singles out six Psalms: 55, 59, 69, 79, 109, and 137.

Break the teeth in their mouths, O God;
  tear out, O LORD, the fangs of the lions!
Let them vanish like water that flows away;
  when they draw the bow, let their arrows be blunted.
Like a slug melting away as it moves along,
  like a stillborn child, may they not see the sun. (Ps. 58:6–8)

Let the heads of those who surround me
  be covered with the trouble their lips have caused.
Let burning coals fall upon them;
  may they be thrown into the fire,
  into miry pits, never to rise. (Ps. 140:9–10)

How then shall we define "imprecation"? It is an invocation of judgment, calamity, or curse uttered against one's enemies who in these special cases are also simultaneously the enemies of God. Thus, the crucial features of imprecation are that (1) it is a prayer or cry to God, and (2) it contains a request that God judge, punish, or carry out what he has threatened to do to his enemies.[15]

Unsatisfactory attempts to solve this problem include: (1) non-transferable concepts of an earlier age of law that are no longer applicable in this age of grace, (2) a prediction of doom instead of seeing here a desire or wish for calamity on the head of the wicked, (3) an understanding that only spiritual and not real enemies are intended, or even (4) that these prayers are not inspired, but only glimpses of the personal vindictiveness of those uninspired (according to the views of some) parts of the Old Testament.[16]

What then do we make of such real expressions? The truth of the matter is that David was the author of most of these imprecatory Psalms, except for Psalms like 79 or 83, which are attributed to Asaph, or Psalm 137, which is exilic. However, the picture that we gain of David's action toward his enemies from the historical books of the Old Testament is one of consistently refusing to take matters in his own hands. He repeatedly refused to touch Saul's life even though he could have rationalized that he, not Saul, was now the declared king under God, and, that God had providentially delivered Saul into his hands several times in order to end Saul's life. But, no; David refused to think or to act this way. And when Saul died, David wrote the touching "Song of the Bow" in 2 Samuel 1 mourning Saul and Jonathan's death. David even executed the Amalekite for rejoicing over Saul's death and for claiming to have killed him.

Even in the imprecatory Psalms themselves, David still has kind thoughts for his enemies. Thus,

---

[15]Laney, "Imprecatory Psalms," 35–36.
[16]Vos, "Ethical Problems," for a discussion of these proposals on pp. 124–30.

> They repay me evil for good
>   and leave my soul forlorn.
> Yet when they were ill, I put on sackcloth
>   and humbled myself with fasting. . . .
> I went about mourning
>   as though for my friend or brother.
> I bowed my head in grief
>   as though weeping for my mother. (Ps. 35:12–14)

or

> In return for my friendship they accuse me,
>   but I am a man of prayer.
> They repay me evil for good,
>   and hatred for my friendship. (Ps. 109:4–5)

The point is that David had no spirit of vindictiveness or a desire to get even. In fact, in the Old Testament, love for an enemy was not optional, it was obligatory: "Do not seek revenge or bear a grudge" (Lev. 19:17–18); "Do not gloat when your enemy falls" (Prov. 24:17–18); and "If your enemy is hungry, give him food to eat" (Prov. 25:21–22). What is more, the so-called higher ethic of the New Testament found in Romans 12:20 ("If your enemy is hungry, feed him; if he is thirsty, give him something to drink. In doing this, you will heap burning coals on his head") is a quotation from Proverbs 25:21.

The New Testament likewise has its expressions of imprecation: "Alexander the metalworker did me a great deal of harm. The Lord will repay him for what he has done" (2 Tim. 4:14); "I wish they [those agitators] would go the whole way and emasculate themselves!" (Gal. 5:12); and "How long . . . until you judge the inhabitants of the earth and avenge our blood?" (Rev. 6:10). Thus, one cannot play the Old Testament off against the New Testament for an easy solution. Nor can one downgrade the Old Testament as if it gave a lesser standard for one's enemies and the love it required for them.

The solution to this problem can be found in the following principles of interpretation for imprecatory Psalms as set forth by Chalmers Martin.[17] These imprecations were:

(1) An expression of the longing of the Old Testament saint for the vindication of God's righteousness. If God did not triumph over wrong, the facts of experience would create an insoluable puzzle.

(2) Utterances of zeal for God and his kingdom. Attacks on David or the people of God because of their position or the part they played in the history of salvation was tantamount to an attack on God himself rather than these individuals. As God's representative in

---

[17]Martin, "Imprecation," 544–53.

the promised line of the "seed," David's enemies ceased to be private enemies and they became instead enemies of the God who had promised to send the man of promise.

(3) The harshness of these cries to God are indicative of the Old Testament saints' abhorrence of sin. These opponents to the psalmist are more than mere obstructionists or even public enemies; they are the embodiments of wickedness cast into the role of carrying out the program of all that is anti-God, anti-Messiah, and anti-promise. Doeg, Cush, and Ahithophel are not your average criminal or hostile types; they are the culmination and final fruit of all falsehood, greed, hate, cruelty, and treachery aimed against the very means of their own salvation.

(4) The humble requests that God would do what he had threatened all along would be the fate of the ungodly if they persisted in their opposition to his proffered goodness and mercy. C. Martin[18] places the positive teaching and prayers for cursing into the following pairs:

> (a) "Not so the wicked! They are like the chaff that the wind blows away" (Ps. 1:4);
> "May they be like chaff before the wind" (Ps. 35:5);
> (b) "you have broken the teeth of the wicked" (Ps. 3:7);
> "Break the teeth in their mouth, O God" (Ps. 58:6);
> (c) "their feet are caught in the net they have hidden" (Ps. 9:15);
> "may the net they hid entangle them" (Ps. 35:8);
> (d) "May all my enemies be ashamed and dismayed; may they turn back in sudden disgrace" (Ps. 6:10);
> "May all who gloat over my distress be put to shame and confusion;
> may all who exalt themselves over me be clothed with shame and disgrace" (Ps. 35:26).

It is easy to see how David could pass from the indicative to the optative, from stating facts to uttering prayers for the same matters.

But someone will still protest, but what about Psalm 137? The last two verses (8–9) are the most notorious of all the imprecations in the Bible:

> "O Daughter of Babylon, doomed to destruction, happy is he who repays you for what you have done to us—
> he who seizes your infants and dashes them against the rocks."

No one has dealt in a more definitive and satisfying way with this passage than Howard Osgood.[19] He urged us to keep in mind these problems:

---

[18]Martin, "Imprecation," 551.
[19]Osgood, "Against the Rock," 23–37.

(1) Jesus quotes Psalm 137:9 in Luke 19:44 in his lament over Jerusalem and uses the same verb, "*dash* you . . . and the children," used by the Septuagint to translate this verse. This is the only occurrence of this Greek word in the New Testament, so the allusion to this passage is certain.

(2) The word used for "your little ones" or "your children" (עֹלָלַיִךְ) does not specify age, but only the relationship that person bears to his parents. It may mean a very young infant as well as a grown up.

(3) The dashing against the rocks or down the cliff is a metaphorical, and not a literal, use of the phrase as can be noted from the fact that Babylonia is a perfectly flat alluvial country without hills, cliffs, or even rocks. They must go to Iraq or Arabia if they will be thrown down literal cliffs. Yet God says in Jeremiah 51:25, "I will stretch my hand against you [Babylon], roll you off the cliffs." This same metaphorical usage can be found in Psalm 141:6, "their rulers will be thrown down from the cliff, and the wicked will learn that my words were well spoken." How can they hear God's words after such an experience if indeed it is literal?

Thus, "blessed" of God are those who will be called by God to bring down Babylon to the dust in fulfilling Yahweh's promise to do so for the vengeance done against Zion.

We conclude then that neither Psalm 137 nor any of the other seventeen imprecatory psalms present a sub-Christian or an out-of-character ethic for the high standard of holiness set forth throughout the Old Testament.

Old Testament View of the Death Penalty

Three main types of penalty were prescribed in the Pentateuch for the most serious crimes against family, religion, and life. They were: (1) "cutting off" an offender from his people,[20] (2) restitution of the stolen property or goods, and (3) the death penalty.

It is the death penalty that concerns us here. This penalty was invoked for a wide range of crimes including the following:

---

[20]Gordon Wenham, "Law and the Legal System in the Old Testament," in *Law, Morality and the Bible*, eds. Bruce Kaye and Gordon Wenham (Downers Grove, Ill.: InterVarsity, 1978), 42–44, rejects the idea that "cutting off" might be an alternate way of describing capital punishment since "cutting off" is contrasted with judicial execution in Lev. 20:2ff. ("The man who escapes stoning must still face the possibility of being cut off"). He also rejects excommunication from the covenant community even though one case of incest parallel to the Hammurapi Code 154 demands expulsion and "cutting off" in Lev. 20:17ff. since this treatment is reserved for the unclean instead of criminals (Lev. 13:45f.; Num. 5:1–4). It is best then to interpret "cutting off" (נִכְרְתָה הַנֶּפֶשׁ) as the threat of direct punishment in the form of some type of premature death.

(1) Premeditated murder—Gen. 9:5–6; Exod. 21:12ff.; Lev. 24:17; Num. 35:16–21, 30–33; Deut. 17:6, 19.
(2) Adultery—Lev. 20:10; Deut. 22:21–24.
(3) Incest—Lev. 20:11, 12, 14.
(4) Bestiality—Exod. 22:19; Lev. 20:15–16.
(5) Sodomy—Lev. 18:22; 20:13.
(6) Homosexuality—Lev. 20:13.
(7) Rape of a betrothed virgin—Deut. 22:25.
(8) Kidnapping—Exod. 21:16; Deut. 24:7.
(9) False witness in a case involving a capital offense—Deut. 19:16–20.
(10) Priest's daughter committing fornication—Lev. 21:9.
(11) Witchcraft (divination and magic)—Exod. 22:18.
(12) Human sacrifice—Lev. 20:2–5.
(13) Striking or cursing parents—Exod. 21:15, 17; Lev. 20:19.
(14) Persistant disobedience to parents and authorities—Deut. 17:12; 21:18–21.
(15) Blasphemy—Lev. 24:11–14, 16, 23.
(16) Idolatry—Exod. 22:20; Lev. 20:2.
(17) False prophesying—Deut. 13:1–10.
(18) Anti-law, anti-court, and general lawlessness—Deut. 17:12.

It seems most likely that everyone of these cases could have a substitute penalty except that of premeditated murder. Composition was explicitly prohibited in the case of murder (Num. 35:31). Since this crime was singled out and this prohibition was sternly attached to it, we may assume that in all other capital cases, given the proper conditions, some substitution for one's own life was possible.

Accordingly, these penalties were the maximum penalties. But where the circumstances, conditions, or responses of the offenders provided additional grounds, a lesser penalty or even a commutation of this severe penalty apparently was in order. The only other offense that seems to be as major a matter as premeditated murder is the act of open, deliberate defiance and blasphemy of God. The Hebrew expression is בְּיָד רָמָה, sin with a "high hand" (Num. 15:27–36). This is deliberate rebellion against God and his word; "[he] blasphemes the LORD. . . . Because he has despised the LORD's word" (Num. 15:30–31). Such blasphemy is close to, if not exactly the same as, what the New Testament calls blasphemy against the Holy Spirit or the unpardonable sin (cf. Heb. 10:26–31). It is high treason against heaven and a revolt against all that God is or represents. The sign of this attitude is the "high hand" or the upraised clenched fist shook menacingly against God.

Now the importance of this sanction on the death penalty for ethical theory has almost been entirely lost in our day. It is because of our failure to see the legitimate connection between capital punishment and the altar in the tabernacle and temple. Of course the altar has a religious significance, but there is another significance that is missed or avoided, even by evangelical expositors. That aspect is: the altar is the place where the demands of the law and the justice of the law are fulfilled.

Patrick Fairbairn[21] calls attention to this second aspect of the law. For him, the death of Christ carried a legal aspect; Christ bore a judicial death. He was made a curse that he might redeem men from the curse of the law. Moreover, the death of Christ was a satisfaction, not just to God's honor (as most say today), but to God's justice; for, what is God's honor apart from his justice? His honor is nothing more than the reflex action or display of his moral attributes. His love was not unconditioned; rather in Fairbairn's words it was "conditioned by the demands of justice."[22]

The only way that justice could have satisfied the law was by death. There is no other way of meeting the demands of God's justice and his violated law if he were to redeem sinners; thus he endured the penalty due to us, which we as transgressors of the law had incurred, in order that we might be set free and be made through Christ the righteousness of God.

Old Testament View of the Talion

The so-called law of retaliation or *lex talionis*, "law of the tooth," is found in Exodus 21:23–25; Leviticus 24:19–20; and Deuteronomy 19:21.

We have already argued in chapter 4 that this law gave no comfort to a *private* spirit of retaliation. Its setting in the covenant code makes it crystal clear that these instructions were addressed to the "judges" (אֱלֹהִים, Exod. 21:22; 22:8, 9) who were to render the "judgments" (מִשְׁפָּטִים, Exod. 21:1). Accordingly, "an eye for an eye and a tooth for a tooth" was only a stereotyped formula that acted as a rule of thumb for the civil magistrates and urged them to make the punishment fit the crime, in other words, make the restitution match the losses—no more or no less.

J. B. Mozley's discussion is decidedly wrongheaded.[23] In his concept of progressive revelation both divine permission (involving the principle of accommodating an imperfect morality) and divine command (to keep these extravagant, rough, and irregular precepts) were necessary. Thus, the law of retaliation was:

---

[21]Patrick Fairbairn, *The Revelation of Law in Scripture* (1869; reprint, Grand Rapids: Zondervan, 1957), 247–52.

[22]Fairbairn, *Revelation of Law*, 251.

[23]J. B. Mozley, *Ruling Ideas in Early Ages and Their Relation to Old Testament Faith* (New York: Dutton, 1878), 180–200.

. . . simply legalising the right of private revenge [even though] it embodied a principle of public justice. . . . Therefore this rule of retaliation in the Mosaic Law is not to be interpreted as simply permissory; it has the nature of a precept and an injunction; a command to the persons to whom it was given to exert the right of punishing those who had wantonly harmed them, and making them smart for their insolence and brutality.[24]

Mozley compounds his error by extending it into his understanding of the Sermon on the Mount, as many modern interpreters also do. "The demand, however, of an eye for an eye, and a tooth for a tooth, was the fruit of a very imperfect moral standard, and our Lord passes sentence on it accordingly, as a rule made obsolete by the rise of a higher law."[25] Trapped by his own logic, Mozley now offers this incredible interpretation of Matthew 5:43 ("You have heard that it was said, You shall love your neighbor and hate your enemy"):

The latter part of this precept—Thou shalt hate thine enemy— nowhere occurs in so many words in the Mosaic Law; the whole precept, however, as it stands, undoubtedly represents, and is a summary of the sense of the Law. . . . All the other precepts which our Lord takes as instances of an inferior morality which the Gospel puts aside, are precepts out of the law, and there is no reason to distinguish this particular one from the rest with respect to its source.[26]

Mozley has not fully appreciated the significance of the sharp contrast that our Lord was making between what was being *said* in the oral law of the Jewish nation in the first century A.D. and what had been *written* in the Old Testament law. Mozley's specious reasoning about Israel's enemies—the Moabite, Ammonite, Edomite, and Philistine—with her need for inculcating a *esprit de corps* and a strong sense of separation in Israel during that early age of accommodating revelation will not stand. Even in the Old Testament, love for one's enemy was not an optional feature of the covenant community of faith. The so-called higher ethic of the New Testament (Rom. 12:17–21) could do no better than repeat the teaching of the Old Testament injunction found in Proverbs 20:22; 24:29; and 25:21. "Never repay evil for evil," for "it is mine to avenge; I will repay," says the Lord (Deut. 32:35; cf. Ps. 94:1). In fact, "If your enemy is hungry, give him food to eat; if he is thirsty, give him water to drink. In doing this, you

---

[24]Mozley, *Ruling Ideas*, 184–85. Mozley quotes Dean Alford from his *Greek Testament* in a note on Matthew 5: "But such was the public enactment of the Mosaic Law [that it] implied a private spirit of retaliation . . . as well as public retribution."

[25]Mozley, *Ruling Ideas*, 187.

[26]Mozley, *Ruling Ideas*, 188.

will heap burning coals on his head, and the LORD will reward you" (Prov. 25:21–22).

Should someone complain that the Mosaic law does not speak to this question of enemies, then they should refer to Exodus 23:4: An enemy's ox or donkey were to be treated with kindness when they were found helpless under their load (cf. Deut. 22:1–4). Indeed, the clearest passage in the law against hating all men is Leviticus 19:17–18:

> "Do not hate your brother in your heart. Rebuke your neighbor
> frankly so you will not share in his guilt. Do not seek revenge or
> bear a grudge against one of your people, but love your neighbor
> as yourself. I am the LORD."[27]

The enemy was also an individual to whom full dignity was owed as a creature made in the image of God. Job refused to indulge himself in a campaign to disregard his enemy: "If I have rejoiced at my enemy's misfortune or gloated over the trouble that came to him—I have not allowed my mouth to sin by invoking a curse against his life" (Job 31:29–30). If Job is from the same age as the patriarchs (Abraham, Isaac, and Jacob,—about 2000 to 1800 B.C.), as many contend, then we are given an Old Testament view of genuine regard for the individual, even though he belongs to an evil political or religious system that stood in total opposition to all that was revealed in Scripture.

We cannot agree that the Old Testament encouraged private vendetta or retaliation. It runs counter to the explicit directions of the text that place the talion in the hands of civil magistrates and in their hands alone. It also runs counter to the high worth and value the Old Testament gave to every man and woman made in the image of God.

Old Testament View of Eudaemonism

In contrast to deontologism, eudaemonism (literally, the state of being under the protection of a benign spirit) is that ethical position that stresses the goodness, happiness, and material rewards that come from satisfactory ethical action, whereas deontologism stresses instead the rightness of the action. Since we have argued more for a deontological Old Testament ethic of holiness, how does a eudaemonistic discussion play any part in the biblical text?

It has often been urged that the main motive for most ethical action in the Old Testament was a desire for material prosperity and success, or the anxiety to escape personal or national disaster. Such a charge, if true, would expose Old Testament ethics to the accusation that it was more

---

[27]Prov. 10:12; 16:32; 19:11.

pleasure minded and success oriented rather than being governed by principles and the standard of the person and being of God. This is commonly referred to as "Deuteronomic theology" or the "retributive motive." Deuteronomy 28 might lead some to conclude that those who follow Yahweh could anticipate blessing in the form of children, health, wealth, victory over one's enemies, and ideal weather for crops while the absence of these signs was a sure sign that disobedience to covenantal norms was the cause.[28] Therefore, the question is more than academic: was the ethical end, ultimate object, and final criterion of what ought to be said or done merely personal or national success, material prosperity and escape from disaster? If so, would this not be an inferior and less virtuous form of ethics than the more elevated New Testament ethic? Surely, Old Testament ethics could be reduced, in the main, to some form of hedonism or utilitarianism on these grounds.

However, neither hedonism nor a quest for a "this-worldly-success" is espoused in the Old Testament as a reward "caused" by piety. The success, reward, or escape from disaster is instead a "gift" accepted by the wise God-fearer from the hand of a gracious Lord. The basic view of material things takes form from God's pronouncements at Creation. God's repeated response to his own handiwork in creation was "it was good." Thus, both the Old and New Testaments endorse these pronouncements by their call to a thankful acceptance of all material things as coming from God and existing for God and man's use (Ps. 104:24; 1 Tim. 4:3–5). Material things are not an inferior creation nor are they to be opposed as illusory goals in life. The Fall brings a curse on the earth, but it does not make the good creation intrinsically or totally evil.

No book has been assailed more frequently for suggesting such profit, success, or escape motives for right behavior than the Book of Proverbs. R. N. Gordon[29] suggested seven categories of motives for Proverbs (number of references in Proverbs is in parenthesis):

(1) Material rewards or punishment (133).
(2) Non-material rewards (12).
(3) Obeying God for his own sake (16).
(4) Obeying God because he is Creator (23).
(5) Virtue as its own reward (9).
(6) Wisdom or knowledge sought for their own sake or for what they bring (17).

---

[28] J. G. Gammie, "The Theology of Retribution in the Book of Deuteronomy," *Catholic Biblical Quarterly* 32 (1970): 1–12; and W. S. Towner, "Retribution Theology in the Apocalyptic Setting," *Union Seminary Quarterly Review* 26 (1971): 203–14.

[29] R. N. Gordon, "Motivation in Proverbs," *Biblical Theology* 25 (1975): 49–56. See also J. K. Kuntz, "The Retributive Motive in Psalmic Wisdom," *Zeitschrift für alttestamentliche Wissenschaft* 89 (1977): 223–33.

(7) Life as an all encompassing motive (6).

The point is that the motives are numerous and often mixed. But even more to the point is the fact that all of life, and not just in its ethical decision-making time, is proclaimed as a gift. The so-called worldly emphasis of the Proverbs (along with the Wisdom Psalms) has its roots in creation and the law. Not only did the fifth commandment promise "long life in the land" (Exod. 20:12) and that it would "go well with you" (Deut. 5:16; cf. Deut. 4:40; 5:29, 33; and Eph. 6:3), but this same promise of life was repeated following the Red (or Reed) Sea incident (If you . . . do what is right . . . I will not bring on you . . . ," Exod. 15:26) and in Moses's last words to the people ("Take to heart all the words I have solemnly declared to you this day . . . they are not just idle words for you—they are your life" [Deut. 32:46–47]).

As Brueggemann observes, "In its worst form this sounds like works-righteousness, and no doubt the wise are sometimes tempted with that. But in its best form it is simply an affirmation and celebration of the peculiar and noble place of human persons in history."[30] Thus, it is not axiomatic to the Old Testament that there is a union of the ethical and the eudaemonistic; instead, there is a union of the good with life itself in the very creation and in God's plan for human wholeness.

But something else lies behind this charge that characterizes the Deuteronomic materials, wisdom Psalms, and wisdom literature as utilitarian or eudaemonistic. Philip Nel[31] questioned the accuracy of regarding wisdom admonitions as being eudaemonistic sayings, for it not only ignores their legitimate historical context in favor of the *assumption* that these sayings were originally profane and that they received a religious flavor only at a later date, but the charge also reflects a dualistic view of the world. However, Oriental man, much less the writers of the Proverbs, did not sharply segregate the profane from the sacred. Wisdom was religiously motivated with no conflict between faith and practice, belief and action.

---

[30]Walter Brueggemann, "Scripture and an Ecumenical Lifestyle: A Study in Wisdom Theology," *Interpretation* 24 (1970): 12. G. K. Chesterton stated the problem this way: "When once people have begun to believe that prosperity is the reward of virtue, their next calamity is obvious. If prosperity is regarded as the reward of virtue, it will be regarded as the symptom of virtue. Men will leave off the heavy duty of making good men successful. They will adopt the easier task of making out successful men good." Cited by Nahum N. Glatzer, *Job* (1969), pp. 236–37.

[31]Philip Nel, "A Proposed Method for Determining the Context of the Wisdom Admonitions," *Journal of Northwest Semitic Languages* 6 (1978): 33–39; idem, "Authority in Wisdom Admonitions," *Zeitschrift für die alttestamentliche Wissenschaft*, 93 (1981): 418–26. Nel cites W. Baumgartner, *Israelitische und Altorientalische Weisheit*, 1933, pp. 27–29; F. Baumgärtel, *Eigenart der alttestamentlichen Frommigkeit*, 1931, p. 38 and W. Zimmerli, *Zeitschrift für die alttestamentliche Wissenschaft*, 51 (1933), p. 194 as examples of eudaemonistic thinkers in *Zeitschrift für die alttestamentliche Wissenschaft*, 93 (1981), 418, n. 1.

The solution to these charges, and a search for the authority statutes of these sayings, is to be found not with G. Kuhn,[32] who links the "commandments" with God and the "admonitions" with guiding a person through the profane world. "The answer is to be found in the admonition itself and especially in the motivation clause connected to the admonition."[33] Motivational statements, observes Nel appear in seven forms; they come in: final clauses, subordinate clauses, result clauses or result-description statements, causal clauses, predication statements, promise statements, and conditional clauses.[34] Thus there is an intrinsic truth in all these admonitions, made explicit in their motivations that elucidate that truth in its reasonable, dissuasive, explanatory, and promissory character.

The motivational clauses also reveal the ethos for the admonitions in Proverbs. That ethos is Yahweh's created order and the knowledge of God that is directed by the יִרְאַת יְהוָה ("fear of the LORD") (Job 28:28; Prov. 1:7; 9:10; 15:33). The object of right living is to live in harmony with the created order and the knowledge of God. Only then will fullness, wholeness, success, and avoidance of tragedy be ours—both physically, materially, psychologically, and spiritually. For Proverbs to name one aspect, such as material success, is to invite success in every other area as well since life may not be fractured and neatly partitioned as it is currently fashionable to do in the West. The law promotes the same order that creation initiated and wisdom illuminated. Thus the ethos of the orders of creation is the ethos of the law and both form the ethos of wisdom. It is true that material success is much easier to witness by empirical means than say psychological wholeness or spiritual advances. Hence, one may appeal to it more readily, but in no case may we belittle such a motivation as being more carnal, worldly-minded, and less virtuous than other motives.

SUMMARY

Neither in its precepts nor its sanctions can Old Testament ethics be faulted with charges of favoritism, inconsistency, base motivations, gross severity, or worldly profit-mongering. A careful examination of each topic, given the present text of the canonical writer, will more than vindicate these writers and absolve them of these unwarranted charges.

---

[32]As discussed in Nel, "Authority," 421, n. 13.
[33]Nel, "Authority," 422.
[34]Nel, "Authority," 422–23.

PART V
CONCLUSION:
OLD TESTAMENT ETHICS AND
NEW TESTAMENT APPLICATIONS

Chapter 19

The Old Testament Law and New Testament Believers

Of what use, then, is the law to contemporary men and women? The classic theme of all truly evangelical theology is the problem of law and grace. Indeed the contrasts between the law that came by Moses and the grace and truth that came by Jesus Christ seem to be legion.

If one were to judge by one set of Pauline statements, it would appear that the law was no longer obligatory in any sense (2 Cor. 3:11; Eph. 2:15; Col. 2:14) now that it had served its usefulness and that the promise had come (Gal. 3:19–25; 4:1–5). The cry of the believer would seem to be: "we have been released from the law" (Rom. 7:6) and we "are not under the law" (Rom. 6:14); we "died to the law" (Rom. 7:4) now that Christ has fulfilled the righteousness of the law in us (Rom. 8:3–4; 10:4). The truth of the matter is that for many these statements are so definitive that no further investigation need detain us.

Nevertheless, this presentation of the law's relationship to grace is too absolute, antithetical, and incomplete for another set of Pauline passages, let alone much of the Old Testament itself. If we were to put the question bluntly to Paul: "Has faith [or grace] annulled the Law?" Paul would respond with all the vigor of his being, "Not at all!" "Rather," he would continue, "we uphold the law" (Rom. 3:31). "Annulled" (καταργέω) was the very same word, many have felt, Paul used in 2 Corinthians 3:11 to speak of the abolishing or rendering the law as inoperative.[1] What is more, the law itself cannot be made the scapegoat for my problem with sin, for the law is "holy," "just," "good," and "spiritual" (Rom. 7:12–14)! It certainly had a distinctive purpose: to bring us to Christ (Rom. 10:4; Gal. 3:24). But it had never been intended as an alternate, hypothetical, or even a main road to eternal life. For "if a law had been given that could impart life, then righteousness would certainly have come by the law" (Gal. 3:21). Alas, there never was such a law—all theories among evangelicals not withstanding! Thus we conclude that the law was never designed to offer anyone eternal life; it has never been intended to be set in opposition to the promises of God.

Had not the psalmists argued in this same line of thought? The law of the Lord, according to Psalm 19, was perfect, sure, right, pure, clear, true, righteous, and able to revive the soul, make the simple wise, rejoice the heart, enlighten the eyes, endure forever, and be much more desirable than gold, honey, or the honeycomb. Such praise for the law that frightens most believers is enough to boggle the mind!

Still the question remains: how shall we reconcile these two sets of Pauline attitudes towards the law? And how shall contemporary believers respond to Old Testament law?

THE RECONCILIATION OF PAUL'S STATEMENTS ON THE LAW

"Paul's attitude toward the law has been one of the most puzzling and seemingly insoluable in biblical study. . . . At the heart of the problem stands Rom. 10:4. . . ."[2] Heikki Räisänen in an essay entitled "Paul's Theological Difficulties With the Law" put it even more bluntly:

> Paul has two sets of statements concerning the validity of the law for Christians. According to one set the law has been abrogated once and for all. According to the other the law is still in force, and what it requires is charismatically fulfilled by Christians.[3]

---

[1]Walter C. Kaiser, Jr., "The Weightier and Lighter Matters of the Law: Moses, Jesus and Paul," in *Current Issues in Biblical and Patristic Interpretation: Studies in Honor of Merrill C. Tenny*, ed. Gerald F. Hawthorne (Grand Rapids: Eerdmans, 1975), 176–92.

[2]James A. Sanders, "Torah and Paul" in *God's Christ and His People: Studies in Honor of Nils Alstrup Dahl*, eds. Jacob Jerrell and Wayne A. Meeks (Oslo: Universitetsforlaget, 1977), 132.

[3]Heikki Räisänen, "Paul's Theological Difficulties with the Law," in *Studia Biblica 1978: in Papers on Paul and Other New Testament Authors*, Sixth International Congress on Biblical Studies, ed. E. A. Livingstone (Sheffield: University Press, 1980), 305.

The same affirmation and negation of the law in Paul is acknowledged in W. Gutbrod's essay in *The Theological Dictionary of the New Testament*.[4]

Now this is not the place to give a definitive answer—even if one were now available. But it would not be appropriate to conclude this seminal work on Old Testament ethics without facing this Pauline, and hence Christian, dilemma. Some clarifying statements may help to suggest possible lines of thought for resolving the tension observed here:

(1) For Paul, the law is explicitly "the law of God" (Rom. 7:22, 25; 8:7; cf. 1 Cor. 7:19). Therefore it continues to deserve our greatest respect, for it comes with divine authority.

(2) Often when Paul appears to be disparaging the law, he is instead debunking "legalism." We agree with C. E. B. Cranfield that Paul had no separate word-group to denote "legalism," "legalist," and "legalistic."[5] Consequently some of the passages translated as "law" are incorrect, for what he is opposing is the quest for a righteousness obtained as a result of one's own efforts and works. Paul mocks this fabricated do-it-yourself approach to salvation[6] and rebukes those Jews who "made a law out of righteousness" (νόμον δικαιοσύνης, Rom. 9:31; note the Greek word order—a fact that many English translations miss!), which they sought "as if it were possible" (ἀλλ' ὡς ἐξ, Rom. 9:32) to gain salvation by works. But the so-called righteousness that resulted from this legalistic attempt to earn one's salvation was "their own righteousness" (τὴν ἰδίαν, Rom. 10:3) in direct conflict with the righteousness proffered in the Old and New Testament! Having missed Christ, who was the goal and aim (τέλος, Rom. 10:4) of the law, they missed all. Such legalistic observances by Judaism of the law while rejecting Christ is to be left with the "letter" of the law (γράμμα, not the γραφή, "written word" Rom. 7:6; 2 Cor. 3:6) and not the "Spirit."

(3) Some Pauline phrases are abbreviated, as the context will usually show, and therefore wrong inferences may be made if one is not careful. For example, in Romans 3:21 the phrase "apart from the law" would appear to set the law aside except that the words, "has been made known" in the same verse and the full phrase in verse 28 "apart from *observing* of the law" show that it is not the law,

---

[4]W. Gutbrod, "The Law in the New Testament," *Theological Dictionary of the New Testament*, 4:1071.

[5]C. E. B. Cranfield, "St. Paul and the Law," *Scottish Journal of Theology*, 17 (1964): 43–68, especially p. 55.

[6]Walter C. Kaiser, Jr., "Leviticus 18:5 and Paul: 'Do This and You Shall Live (Eternally?),'" *Journal of the Evangelical Theological Society*, 14(1971): 25–27.

but the *works* (legalism) of the law that are the problem here. The same may be said of Romans 7:4 and 6, "You also died to the law" and "we have been released from the law." Verse 4 means that Christ's atoning death has released us from the bondage of offering up our own sacrifices while verse 6 discharges us in one sense so that (in the *same* verse) we may serve—not in the old "letterism" (γράμμα, not the γραφή!)—but in newness of the Spirit. And what is it that we serve? In Romans 7:25, Paul is "a slave to God's law!" Likewise, in 2 Corinthians 3:11 "what was fading away" is neither the law nor the religious system based on the law, but it is rather the *service* or *ministry* that Moses rendered is passing away while the *service* or *ministry* of the ministers of the gospel is unfading in comparison!

(4) Paul does regard the law as abolished when he means the ceremonial ordinances contained in the law. Such an explanation clearly fits Ephesians 2:15. Had the law in its entirety been intended in this "abolishment," Ephesians 6:2 would be somewhat of an embarrassment: "Honor your father and mother."

Paul loathed with a passion all distortions of the law of God established by faith (Rom. 3:31) into a tool for self-righteousness. Such legalism simply was not possible and Paul confronted it directly in his epistles. This explains the vast majority of texts that appear to be negative and contradictory to his positive statements on the law.

THE AMOUNT OF OBLIGATION A BELIEVER HAS TO THE LAW

Martin Luther dramatically contrasted two public sermons from heaven: the first in Exodus 19 and 20 with the second in Acts 2.[7] The first sermon is the law of God and the second is the gospel. Observed Luther: "There are two kingdoms: the temporal, which governs with the sword and is visible; and the spiritual, which governs solely with grace and with the forgiveness of sins."[8] Between these two kingdoms, Luther placed the Jews in the middle—half spiritual and half temporal. The law, Luther states emphatically:

---

[7]Martin Luther, "How Christians Should Regard Moses," in *Luther's Words*, ed. Helmut T. Lehmann (Philadelphia: Muhlenberg Press, 1960), 35:161–74. Also see Thomas N. Finger, "The Problem of Law During the Protestant Reformation," in *The Bible and Law*: Occasional Papers, No. 3 (Elkhart, Ind.: Institute of Mennonite Studies, 1982), pp. 65–94.

[8]Luther, "Regard Moses," 164.

is no longer binding on us because it was given only to the people of Israel. . . . Exodus 20[:1] . . . makes it clear that even the Ten Commandments do not pertain to us. . . . The sectarian spirits want to saddle us with Moses and all the commandments. We will skip that. We will regard Moses as a teacher, but we will not regard him as our lawgiver—unless he agrees with both the New Testament and the natural law.[9]

But the matter of the addresses on scriptural texts, if always pressed, would yield some very uncomfortable results for Luther and us. Was not Ephesians sent to the church at Ephesus? Are we not intruding and snooping on their mail when we make it ours as well? And was not the new covenant made explicitly with Israel—both in Jeremiah 31:31 and Hebrews 8:8 ("with the house of Israel and with the house of Judah")? Nevertheless, we believe that *we* now partake of the blood of the new covenant (1 Cor. 11:25) and the ministers of the Christian church are now ministers of the new covenant (2 Cor. 3:6).[10] The question of *claim* is indeed separate from the question of *authority,* but one must not conclude these matters too quickly without observing all factors involved.

In fact, our Lord warns: "Do not think [some apparently had and others will continue to do so] that I have come to abolish the Law" (Matt. 5:17). Jesus came not to denigrate or displace either the law (in its narrower sense) or the Old Testament (its wider sense); he came to fulfill the law and so to establish it. That law would stand "until heaven and earth disappear" or "until everything is accomplished" (Matt. 5:18).

So serious a matter is the law that Jesus warns that if we ignore that law (not Jesus' teachings replacing the law), or teach others to ignore parts of the law, except for those parts which have been accomplished such as the ceremonial aspects of the law, we will meet with disapproval in the kingdom of God (Matt. 5:19)!

If some had thought that Jesus was advocating a lax attitude toward the law and the Old Testament ("do not think"), then they had better be prepared for kingdom standards that exceed those of traditional Judaism (Matt. 5:20), but are in full accord with fulfilling the law so as to establish it.

There is no contrast between what the Old Testament law required and what the New Testament enjoined. James, in a similar style to the Old Testament names the law of brotherly love the "royal law" and urges

---

[9]Luther, "Regard Moses," 164–65.

[10]See my discussion on the persons addressed in the New Covenant, W. C. Kaiser, Jr., "The Old Promise and the New Covenant," *Journal of the Evangelical Theological Society,* 15 (1972): 15–16, reprinted in *The Bible in Its Literary Milieu,* eds. John Maier, Vincent Tollers (Grand Rapids: Eerdmans, 1979): 105–20.

Christians to fulfill it (James 2:8). Likewise, John refers to the law as if it were a well-known rule of righteousness and defines sin as a transgression of the law (1 John 2:7, 8; 3:7, 8, 23, 24; 5:2, 3; 2 John 5, 6). In fact, Peter's summary of a Christian lifestyle is the same as that of Old Testament law, "be holy in all you do; for it is written: 'Be holy, because I am holy'" (1 Peter 1:16).

The moral law, as revealed in the Old Testament, was the recognized standard of holiness that remained authoritative for Christ, the apostles, and the early church *because it was written*. It is proper to speak of the law as "being done away with" or of our having been "set free from" it only in the sense that now in Christ has the law reached its proper end and goal, for he perfectly fulfilled its commands in his life as well as his death. Since the law contained no power to enable men and women to perform what it commanded, this meant what was intended to be a means of joy and fulfillment actually turned out to be the death of all of us when we failed to keep its terms; for that same law required both perfection and justice. Only Christ could meet those terms.

Thus we believers are finished with the law in its ceremonial demands and ceremonial sanctions, but we will continue to find an abiding use for the law in these areas:

(1) The moral law continues to function as one of Scripture's formal teachers on what is right and wrong in conduct.

(2) The moral law continues to provide the standards by which men and women are convinced and convicted of their sin and guilt. We had not known sin, in some cases, except God's law had shown it for what it was.

(3) The moral law is a coercive force helping the redeemed to spot moral imperfections that still cling to their lives as they "are being changed from glory to glory."

There are distinctions within the law. We have argued above that Jesus weighted some commandments as being "weightier" than others (Matt. 23:23). But this does not allow the interpreter to set his or her own agenda. Only those laws from which Christ releases his church may be jettisoned; anything less than this leads to ethical latitudinarianism and forms of antinomianism. What is required in recognizing these greater and lesser commandments is notice of rank, significance, and primacy; not observance or nonobservance. Only the Lawgiver can set these latter terms.

One final passage must be considered here: 2 Corinthians 3:7–18. As Charles Ryrie has said:

> There is one other passage in the writings of Paul which, because it is more particular, is even more emphatic concerning the end of

the law. In II Corinthians 3:7–11 Paul makes the comparison between what is ministered through Moses and what is ministered through Christ. . . . Thus, this passage says that the Ten Commandments are a ministration of death; and furthermore, the same passage declares in no uncertain terms that they are done away (vs. 11). Language could not be clearer, and yet there are fewer truths of which it is harder to convince people.[11]

But we would wish to demur. Is not the contrast, rather, between the ministries of Moses and those who are preaching the gospel instead of *what* was ministered by Moses and *what* was ministered by Christ? The difference between those two views seems small until one realizes the huge gap that exists between revelation itself (what Christ ministers) and the preaching of ministers of the gospel. It is not the two covenants that are being contrasted, but instead the two ministries of two different sets of servants of God. In comparison to the service of present day gospel ministers, the service of Moses is pale and one of death and condemnation. But least the contrast be between the gospel itself and the law, let it be quickly remembered that the "gospel" likewise may be a "smell of death" to some (2 Cor. 2:16) just as Christ can be a "stone that causes men to stumble" and a "rock that makes them fall" (1 Peter 2:8). Thus it is not the Ten Commandments per se that are a ministration of death.

But it is just as clear that the Ten Commandments are not what have been done away with (2 Cor. 3:11). What faded in verse 11 is the same as in verse 7, the external glow on Moses's face that appeared each time he met with God (Exod. 34:29–35). Thus Moses's service and ministry with the people was a fading ministry. But observe with what "boldness" (παρρησία) Paul and the ministers of the New Covenant now minister!

Thus Moses' glory was truly from God, but it was only temporary and reflective. And even then his ministry was blocked since "the minds" of Israel "were made dull" (v. 14). Yes, even to this very day "the same veil remains" whenever the Old Covenant or Moses is read! This blindness can only be remedied and Moses' veil "lifted" and the glory (temporary and in need of renewal as it was) be revealed in its ultimate significance (and subsequent permanence in the contrasted ministry of Paul and the church's ministers) whenever men and women turn to the Lord. Only then is the veil "removed" (v. 14). Thus it is the "veil" that is to be "abrogated" or "removed" according to Paul and *not* as the New English Bible incorrectly adds: "because only in Christ is the *Old Covenant* abrogated" (italics

---

[11]Charles Ryrie, "The End of the Law," *Bibliotheca Sacra* 124 (1967): 243–44. The quote is essentially the same in *idem, The Grace of God* (Chicago: Moody, 1963), 102.

mine, since these words are not in the text, but are supplied by the translators). The subject of the verb surely is the same as that for "lifted up" in verse 14. It is the same *veil*.

SUMMARY

Believers are not finished with either the moral law or the Ten Commandments. It is so hard to dissuade some people of this principle because Scripture contains such strong arguments in Matthew 5:17–20 and 2 Corinthians 3:7–18.

But Christ is the "end [goal] of the law" (Rom. 10:4) just as Christ is the "end" or "goal" of our faith (1 Peter 1:9) and love is the "end" of the commandment (1 Tim. 1:5). In order to demonstrate to his Jewish audience that this is so, Paul establishes this thesis by quoting twice from Moses' law: Leviticus 18:5 and Deuteronomy 30:11–14. These two quotes are not antithetical in the Pentateuch, much less in Paul, for Paul uses the γὰϱ . . . δέ construction to introduce and join both of these quotes from Moses meaning "for . . . and", not "for . . . but" (notice Rom. 10:10, *"for* it is with your heart . . . *and* it is with your mouth," and again in Rom. 7:8 and 11:15).

The problem with most interpreter's use of the law is that it is B.C. in faith; not B.C. in time. That is, prior to faith there can be no genuine obedience to the law. Only the "obedience of faith" can show the real purposes of the law in the life of the believer and thus allow them to appreciate the gift of Old Testament ethics.

INDEXES

Index of Hebrew Words Discussed

Index of Scripture References

Index of Persons

Index of Subjects

Abomination, an: 118–19, 196, 199, 203, 213, 242
Abortion: 34, 35, 168–72
Adultery: 82, 83, 92, 124, 135, 201, 202, 270, 274–75, 298
  spiritual: 86
Affine(s) (by marriage): 94n, 189, 203
Affluence: 210–11
Alien (resident): 33, 35, 94, 108, 109, 110
Altar of God: 146–47, 148
Analogy
  of ethical action: 48
  of ideas: 128
Analogy of Antecedent Scripture: 28
Analogy of Faith: 28
Anger (of God): 258–61
Antinomianism: 145–46
Apodictic (law): 96, 97
Apostasy: 5, 131, 132–33
Application
  of ethical injunctions: 25, 26, 42
Asceticism: 210
Assassination: 275–76
Asylum (or place of refuge): 100, 104n
Atomism: 142–43
Authority: 47, 53, 54, 59

Ban (curse): 67, 74–75
Bestiality: 107, 114, 117, 119, 124, 125, 195–97, 268, 298
Biblical Theology: 33
Biblical Theology Movement: 51
Bigamy: 116, 187
Blasphemy: 92

Blessing(s)
  of the covenant: 77
  of individual or group: 69
  material and spiritual: 37, 150
Book of the Covenant. *See* Covenant Code
Boundary (lines): 135
Bribe(s): 110

Canon
  of NT: 61
  of OT: 43, 71
  within a canon: 53, 54
Capital punishment: 73, 91, 92, 96, 129, 148, 165–68, 175, 233, 297n
Casuistic (law): 96
Casuistry: 51, 61
Cartharists: 247
Center
  of OT ethics: 18, 29–31
Charges
  against God's acts,
    deception: 264–65
    extermination of pagans: 266–69
    human sacrifice: 262–64
    unreturnable borrowing: 265–66
  against God's character,
    deceptiveness: 256–58
    fickleness: 249–51
    hatefulness: 251–56
    repentence: 249–51
    wrathfulness: 258–61
  against OT human character,
    dishonesty: 271–75
    murder: 275–77

Charges (*cont.*)
  against OT human conduct,
    incest: 281–82
    cursed children: 277–79
    lawlessness: 282
    marriage to harlots: 279–81
    revengefulness: 282–83
Chastisement (of children): 156
Chattel: 123
Chauvinism: 34, 284, 290–92
Children: 155–58, 277–79
Civil strife: 162
Claims of the writers: 3–4
Collateral(s) (by marriage): 94n
Collectivism: 5n, 15, 69, 71
Command(s) of God: 33, 37
  grounds of: 32
  heavy: 45
  light: 45
  normative: 48
  particular: 25
  permanent: 89
  temporal: 89
  universal: 24–25, 48
Commandment
  The Great: 130
  First: 131, 152, 165
  Second: 131
  Third: 132
  Fourth: 133
  Fifth: 134, 152, 155–58, 303
  Sixth: 134, 164–80
  Seventh: 135, 181–208
  Eighth: 136, 209–21
  Ninth: 136, 222–34
  Tenth: 7, 136–37, 235–44
Communication: 50
Community: 17, 33, 37, 49, 52, 55, 56, 71
Composition (fixed): 104n
Concealment: 224–27, 271
Concubinage: 122–23, 280
Conjugal play: 194
Consanguine(s) (by marriage): 94n
Conscience: 51
  social: 109
Consistency (of commands): 26–28, 29, 30
Contextualization: 26, 43
Corporal punishment: 136
Corporate
  group: 5
  personality: 67–70
  solidarity: 67–70, 159, 283
Covenant(s): 77
  Abrahamic: 76, 78
  Davidic: 76, 78
  everlasting: 78
  marriage: 155
  Sinaitic: 76, 77

Covenant Code: 41, 46, 72, 96–111, 133, 170–72
Coveting: 82, 136–37, 235, 239
Creation: 21, 30, 89
  ordinances (orders or mandates of): 31, 35, 82, 122, 148, 153, 198, 205, 304
  theology: 31
Creativity
  in decision making: 55
Criminal law: 88
Cultural mandate: 154
Curse(s) (cursing): 78, 101, 150, 189, 233, 278

Death penalty: 91–92, 97n, 101, 118, 124, 166, 168, 297–99
Decalogue: 22, 33, 37, 41, 43, 46, 98, 127, 128, 129, 130, 131, 133, 137, 146, 152, 159, 164, 244
  analysis of: 84–95
  interpretation of: 83–84
  introduction to: 82–83
Deception. *See* concealment
Dedication (חֶרֶם)
  involuntary: 108
  voluntary: 108
Defilement: 202
Desire(s): 8, 161, 204
Deuteronomic Theology: 302
Difficulties
  moral: 21, 32
Discontinuity: 14
Disposition(s): 9, 17, 55
Dissimulation. *See* lying
Diversity
  in authorship: 27
  in ethic(s): 27, 31, 141
  in methodology: 13, 55
  in Scripture: 57–60
Divination (or magic): 92, 123, 232
Divorce: 94, 200–204
Donatist(s): 173
Duty(ies): 4, 5
  of life: 31
  to parents: 31
  of property: 31
  to superiors: 31
  of underlings: 31
  of work: 31

Ecology: 149
Embezzlement: 106
Embryo, human. *See* abortion
Employee: 98, 120, 216
Employer: 98, 136, 163, 216
Enemy: 301
Eshnunna Laws: 99, 104, 105, 106
Ethics
  central theme approach: 20–21